ORGANISE IDEAS

THINKING BY HAND, EXTENDING THE MIND

First published 2021

by John Catt Educational Ltd,
15 Riduna Park, Station Road,
Melton, Woodbridge IP12 1QT

Tel: +44 (0) 1394 389850
Email: enquiries@johncatt.com
Website: www.johncatt.com

ISBN: 978 1 913622 68 8

Typeset by John Catt Educational Limited

④ WHO?

⑤ WHEN?

Graphic organisers are word-diagrams and subject to a different scope of theories and studies than pictorial communication.

Chapters

FOREWORD

MARY MYATT

Organise Ideas is a gift to the profession. There is a drive to help our pupils know more and remember more, and if we are serious about this then we need to pay attention to the underlying structures of the material we teach. However, the written word is dense, and the spoken word is transient. If we want to tease out the concepts, structures, patterns and connections and capture these, then we need some smart tools to help us help our pupils.

Beautifully crafted by a master, Oliver Caviglioli, and his apprentice, David Goodwin, *Organise Ideas* lays out the power and the rationale for graphic organisers, or word-diagrams, as tools for thinking at the deepest level. Several important strands are developed in this book: one is that it is helpful to consider ideas as objects (Barbara Tversky). A second is that our brains were designed for "*having ideas, not holding them*" (David Allen). And a third is that grouping, ordering and sequencing ideas and facts into coherent structures is the route to building a powerful long-term memory.

Across five sections, Caviglioli and Goodwin summarise long-standing evidence that information is transient unless it is captured; that our brains need an external memory field to *park* all this interesting stuff so that it is available without overloading working memory; that visual representations of concepts both support understanding and help develop new insights and connections; and that we need to select the right organiser for the job in hand. I have used Mind Maps a lot in my own work, both in the classroom and personally. What I hadn't understood until I read this book was why they were so useful in helping me and my pupils identify key ideas, make connections and, most importantly, remember them. What I also hadn't appreciated was that there are 35 different types of organiser, and in this book we are shown how to consider the most appropriate for the task in hand.

To bring all this alive in the classroom, we have 50 colleagues sharing their work. How cool is that? In receiving this gift, we need to unwrap it carefully, pay attention to its insights and use it in our work. That's it.

OLIVER CAVIGLIOLI

Since watching his architect father create diagrams, Oliver has been fascinated by non-linear methods of creating and capturing ideas. Twenty years ago, he wrote a clutch of books on the topic. But with the adoption of cognitive science in UK schools, he felt the time was ripe for a renewal of the knowledge accumulated on graphic organisers. He was also keen to decouple it from dual coding theory and introduce some more relevant frames of reference. The main purpose, though, was to create a manual of graphic organisers, offer instruction on how to construct them, and show a range of applications via a staggering number of teacher contributors.

DAVID GOODWIN

As a geography teacher, David's early wanderings into the field of graphic organisers seem fitting. Cartography and graphic organisers have a lot in common: both convey meaning through their spatial arrangement of content. David's first encounter with graphic organisers was reading Oliver's books. *Thinking Skills & Eye Q*, in which Oliver demonstrates how graphic organisers can democratise expert thinking, captured David's interest. His fascination with non-linear word-diagrams (graphic organisers) grew as he discovered how they serve the learning process — as a tool for capturing and organising ideas and aiding reading and writing.

THE PARTNERSHIP

Passing the baton on to a younger generation is how Oliver sees the basis of this partnership. Of course, it is now also a firm friendship. After his *Dual Coding With Teachers* book, Oliver was somewhat reluctant to embark on a similarly intense project. But he also realised that his five decades of knowledge in this field would most likely disappear if he failed to pass it on. A young, talented and practising teacher was the perfect ally with whom to embark on this project. And with over 50 teacher contributors, Oliver is delighted with this generation's serious, practical and inventive use of these word-diagrams — aka graphic organisers — in their teaching practice.

DEDICATION

We dedicate this book to Art Fry, the inventor of a powerful cognitive tool — the Post-it note. With a word per note, it becomes Tversky's Idea Object, ready for manipulation into various configurations. Yes, thinking itself made manifest.

AYELLET MCDONNELL

BEN NORRIS

BEN RANSON

BRETT KINGSBURY

CATHERINE ACTON

CAROL HARIRAM

CHARLOTTE HAWTHORNE

CHRISTIAN MOORE ANDERSON

CLARE MADDEN

DAN RODRIGUEZ-CLARK

DAVID KING

DAVID MORGAN

DEEPU ASOK

ELLIOT MORGAN

EMMA SLADE

EVE CAIRNS VOLLANS

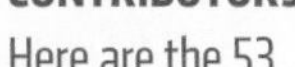

CONTRIBUTORS

Here are the 53 teachers who generously share their practices with word-diagrams across a range of ages and subjects. We salute you all.

FAHEEMAH VACHHIAT

FRAZER THORPE

GEORGE VLACHONIKOLIS

HELEN REYNOLDS

JAMIE CLARK

JANCKE DUNN

JJ WILSON

JOE BURKMAR

JOHN ETTY

JOHN HOUGH

JUSTIN WAKEFIELD

KAT HOWARD

KATE JONES

KELLY PEPPIN

LOUISE CASS

LUKE TAYLER

MADELEINE EVANS

MATT STONE

MEGAN BOWS

NICKY BLACKFORD

OLLY LEWIS

PETER RICHARDSON

PETER STOYKO

RACHEL WONG

SAM STEELE

SARAH JONES

SARAH LALLY

SARAH SANDEY

SELINA CHADWICK

SHAUN STEVENSON

SIMON BEALE

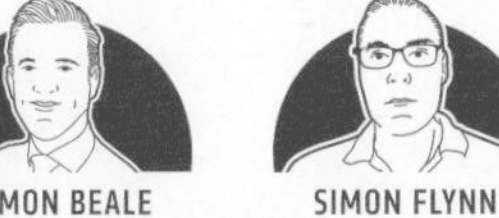
SIMON FLYNN

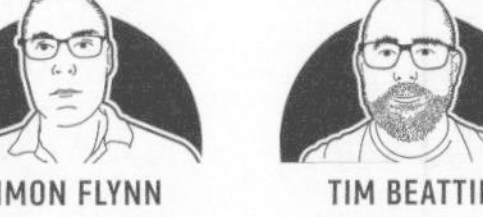
TIM BEATTIE

TOM HANSON

TOM ODDY

TOM SIMS

ZEPH BENNETT

EVIDENCE: ISSUES

EVIDENCE: FINDINGS

EVIDENCE: ONWARD

EVIDENCE: APPLIED

EMBODIED COGNITION — Our mind is not disembodied, working memory can be shared and tools shape our minds

GESTURE — Biological primary learning can help cheat memory constraints

DUAL CODING THEORY — The spatial component of the visuospatial channel is the key to understanding diagrams

COGNITIVE LOAD THEORY — Transient information is at the heart of cognitive load

EXTERNAL MEMORY FIELD — Making marks is key to overcoming the transience of verbal communication

SPATIAL METAPHORS — Our prelinguistic experiences form the basis of our later abstract thinking

LTM

WM

EXTERNAL MEMORY FIELD

SCHEMAS — Memory is a network of connections used to make meaningful predictions

COGNITIVE MAPS — We — like rats in a maze — orient ourselves with internal maps of our environment

NON-LINEAR THINKING — The way we store memories, spaces and ideas is non-linear

METACOGNITION — Examining our thinking is a lot easier when we can see it

ORGANISE IDEAS — At the heart of learning is the organisation of new ideas

IDEAS AS OBJECTS — We manipulate and arrange ideas as if they were objects

TEACHER EXAMPLES — Over 50 teachers show how all this theory works in action

THEORY: TAKE-AWAYS

GRAPHIC ORGANISER TAXONOMY

CONSTRUCTION INSTRUCTIONS

SERVANT STRATEGY

THEORY: CONCEPT STREAMS

INTRODUCTION

The aim of this book is to help teachers organise ideas with the use of graphic organisers. Or, as we more accurately define them, *word-diagrams.* While we use illustrations throughout, this is not a book about imagery, icons or pictorial communication.

But first, we have to clarify what these word-diagrams are. They are "*not linguistic in the way that speech and written text tend to be. Neither are they pictorial representations. This means that neither linguistic nor perceptual theories are sufficient to completely explain their advantages and applications*" (Blackwell, 2001).

For this reason, you will find some unfamiliar theories with which to understand why graphic organisers continue to achieve large effect sizes in studies across the decades.

The central theory is Merlin Donald's notion of the *external memory field.* This, he argues, is analogous to our working memory sketchpad. But it is very much larger and, as a consequence, helps develop what Darwin called "*longer trains of thought*".

Described by Keith Stenning and Oliver Lemon (2001) as "*data reductions*", these word-diagrams are ideas in the raw, devoid of linguistic style and flourishes. Syntax is temporarily bypassed in order to clarify thinking. And, as Frank and Andrew St George (1996) remind us, clear writing comes from clear thinking.

Such clarity doesn't come easily though. It takes concentration and persistence to create a coherent graphic organiser. The majority of this book is devoted to showing you how – step by step. Over 35 different types of organiser are explained and depicted, and over 50 teachers describe how they use them in their classrooms. We wish you many successes in manipulating your ideas!

① WHY?

② WHAT?

③ HOW?

DUAL CODING THEORY

Allan Paivio's theory, as it is commonly understood, inadequately explains the case of word-diagrams containing few or no visuals.

Dual coding theory in a nutshell

Probably for evolutionary survival reasons, we can hear in the dark. Our visual and auditory systems are separate and can function both simultaneously and on their own. They can even connect with each other, forming a paired unit of meaning. This means that if we learn a new word using its written form along with an image, we are encoding the meaning twice — thus, *dual coding*. So, when it comes to retrieving this twice-encoded meaning, we get two possible triggers: the word or the image, or both, doubling our chances of success.

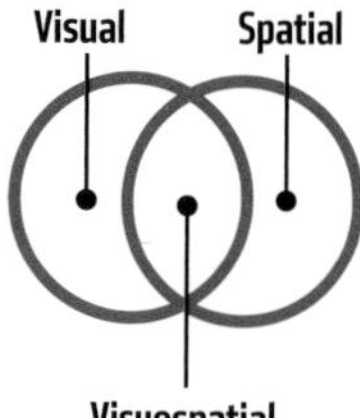

Dual coding story # 1

Paivio's theory, based on decades of research, is very sound. But the studies were based on the encoding and retrieval of lists of short, simple words. None of the complexities or concepts involved in word-diagrams were present. It focused on the verbal and the visual. Only a very small amount of research entailed the involvement of motor and touch perception.

Dual coding story # 2

Story # 2, by contrast, concentrates on the communication and understanding of concepts through use of the visuospatial component, not simple retrieval. Graphic organisers (i.e. word-diagrams) are both visual and spatial in nature. But, as you will discover on the opposite page, it's the space that really makes the difference.

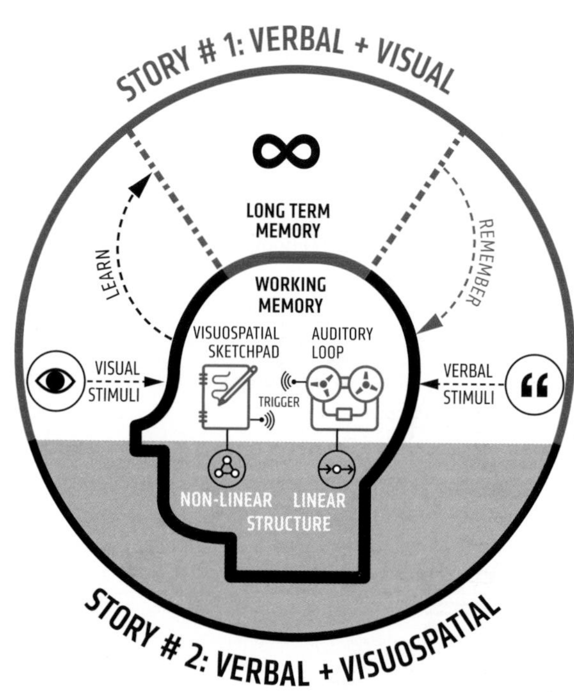

Reading maps with no sight

Every day, visually impaired people read embossed maps of towns. They access the raised marks through touch, sending messages from their fingers to their working memory and building up an internal cognitive map. The same principles apply when word-diagrams are read.

When visually impaired people explore the embossed signs and their linked spacing, meaning is collected and assembled. The visual factor is absent, showing that its role in the sighted user is to gain access to the spatial structure more easily than through touch alone.

Allan Paivio

…non-visual (eg motor or haptic) information … can be integrated in the memory trace.

Paivio, 1990

Structures, processes and understanding

Paivio noted in *Mental Representations* (1990) that text and visuals differed in their structure and the subsequent way they were processed. Text, unsurprisingly, is sequential in format. Syntax creates meaning within the horizontal line of words. But, as Paivio remarks, there are cognitive constraints to the reading process. Visuals are non-linear and processed, in Paivio's term, synchronously. This means that any part of the diagram is potentially available to scrutiny. Its spatial positioning in relation to other parts readily reveals its meaning as your eyes scan the diagram. This more rapid way of creating meaning was noted by Larkin and Simon in their 1987 study that concluded on the computational benefit of (well-formed) diagrams over (complex) text.

Atsushi Shimojima

The conceptual boundary between graphical and linguistic representations seems to be there, but we are not prepared to tell where.

Shimojima, 2001

NEXT | The extent to which the space in front of our eyes helps us think complex thoughts is explained by the external memory field

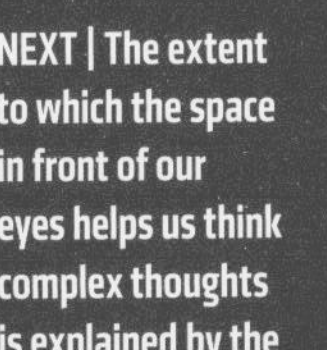

EXTERNAL MEMORY FIELD

Diagrams increase the capacity of working memory to organise ideas. To understand why and how, we take a wider and longer view than usual.

Merlin Donald's panoramic span

Merlin Donald is a neuroanthropologist, psychologist and cognitive neuroscientist. Such a background allows him to present an evolutionary perspective on the development of human cognition. Within this panorama, we learn that while the last stage in our evolution was the shortest, it also had the most profound impact on our brains (cognitive architecture, in psychology-speak). Externalising our thoughts helped us bypass the acute limitations of our biological working memory and, by so doing, extend the complexity of our thinking.

STAGES IN THE MAKING OF THE MODERN MIND

EPISODIC
- Ape
- Here & now thinking
- Specific, not general
- No representation

MIMETIC
- Early human
- Representational acts
- Conscious, self-initiated
- Public communication

MYTHIC
- Gestures
- Language
- Reconstruct the past
- Start of symbolism

THEORETIC
- External storage of info
- External memory field
- Iteration & reflection
- Public dialectic

Merlin Donald

External memory ... is the exact external analog of internal, or biological, memory.

Donald, 1991

Development through the eras

When considering the enormous changes in Donald's schema, we should remember that *"each cognitive adaptation in human evolutionary history has been retained as a fully functional vestige"*. Correspondingly, we see many instances of mimetic behaviour in some aspects of learning – think of how you learn by watching and imitating someone perform a skill. But among this range of incremental enhancements through the eras, the most significant, Donald concludes, is when ideas were captured in an external medium and made public. Now ideas could last beyond an individual lifespan and, consequently, be subject to ongoing iteration and refinement.

ESSS | External symbolic storage system

Below is part of a table devised by Donald that captures the unparalleled benefits of the external storage of information. For every positive attribute, the biological internal alternative is the opposite: limited and impermanent.

Media	Virtually unlimited
Format	Unconstrained, reformattable
Permanence	May be permanent
Capacity	Virtually unlimited
Size	Virtually unlimited
Refinement	Unlimited iterations
Retrieval	Unconstrained
Access	Unlimited

Transience hinders thinking

Working memory — call it consciousness — is very limited. Its content is transient. Thoughts come and go. These biological constraints curb the volume and complexity of our thoughts. In using only our unaided working memory, we're held back in producing what Charles Darwin called *"longer trains of thought"*.

Chunking is difficult in working memory

Cognitive scientists have shown us that chunking information helps greatly in its assimilation and retrieval. However, that strategy is available only in the externally held content. Aside from things like telephone numbers, we don't chunk well in our minds.

EXMF is your cognitive workspace

These, and other problems, are transcended when the internal contents of working memory are externalised and captured in the EXMF: the external memory field. Donald considers the area in front of our eyes to be our cognitive workspace — our sketchpad — where we can achieve what was virtually impossible within our biological working memory alone. Anyone engaged in a thought project always uses their EXMF as their true working memory.

The cognitive loop enables iteration

By establishing this cognitive workspace, we also enable a cognitive loop. Our captured thoughts, visible before us, are noted by our working memory. These, in turn, produce more, improved thoughts that are added to the workspace. It is this iterative and recursive dynamic that creates longer trains of thought.

The breakthrough of modern thought

Modern thought and the start of the theoretic era is attributed to the ancient Greeks. While previous civilisations had written accounts, they were pragmatic in nature. The Greeks, by contrast, used written language to theorise: they founded abstract geometry and formal mathematical proofs, a theory-based cosmology as well as the first systematic taxonomy of living species, not to mention advances in the arts and civic administration. By recording speculative ideas, they devised the process of incremental enhancements through the formation of debate — a public cognitive loop of iterative and recursive thinking. The invention of the ESSS and the application of the EXMF can be said to account for this step-change in cognitive activity.

NEXT | How Donald's idea of thinking beyond the boundary of the brain leads to the ideas of cognitive load theory

Merlin Donald

The true visuospatial sketchpad is the external working memory field.

Donald, 1991

COGNITIVE LOAD THEORY

If cognitive load theory is not to suffer from its own complexity, it needs its root to be identified – the transient nature of the spoken word.

One step at a time. A picture for every step.

Fred Jones

Fred Jones, once a teacher in a school for autism, in my favourite education video. Very highly recommended.

https://youtu.be/MlnPwzg6TiQ

82r3
6 | 495
-48
15
-12
3

The core of the problem

Sweller et al's 2019 summary of their theory added yet more effects to those of the original 2011 book. If you superimpose Merlin Donald's work on the development of the modern mind, you see that up until the last era (theoretic), all communication was verbal and, therefore, transient. Thereafter, when marks (writing and images) were used, the problems associated with the transience of verbal exchanges were solved but gave rise to a whole new type of problem: poorly designed and executed visual communication. Thus the surfeit of "*effects*".

Dual coding theory reframed

PROBLEM: TRANSIENCE → SOLUTION: MARKS → PROBLEM: POOR GRAPHICS → SOLUTION: GRAPHIC RULES

Explanation
If you accept Donald's theory of biological memory, you'll accept that transience is the major cause of our cognitive overload. Multiply the effect with volume, pace of delivery, abstraction and complexity.

Explanation
Again, as Donald has shown, transience can be addressed by capturing the content with marks on paper or screen. Without the pressure of time, we can scrutinise and deal with the content at our own pace.

Explanation
Yet when we read the long list of "*effects*" listed by Sweller et al (2011), all are related to the design of the very marks intended to thwart the load of transience. The solution has become the problem.

Explanation
Most, if not all, of these problems arise due to an ignorance of basic graphic rules, since validated by Mayer (2014). However, a grounding in these guides would have avoided such errors from the start.

Merlin Donald

Biological memory cannot lend itself easily to this type of organisation (chunking), and this undoubtedly imposed a serious limitation on human thinking.

Donald, 1991

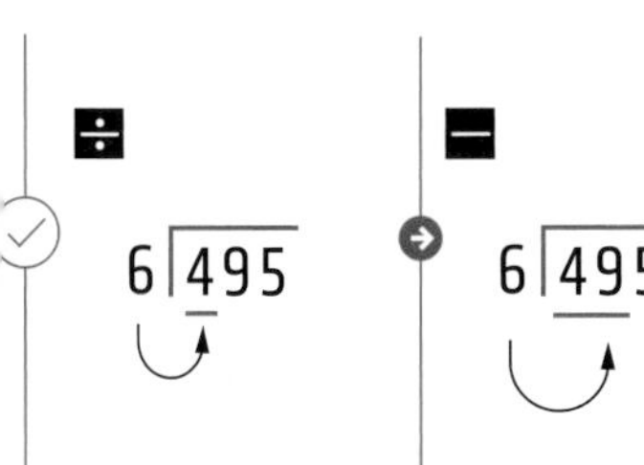
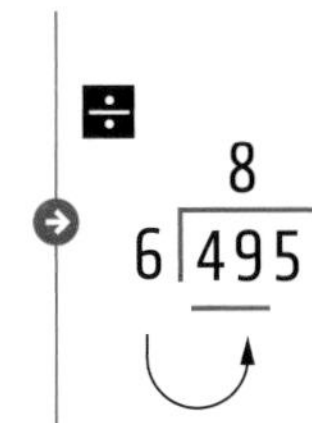
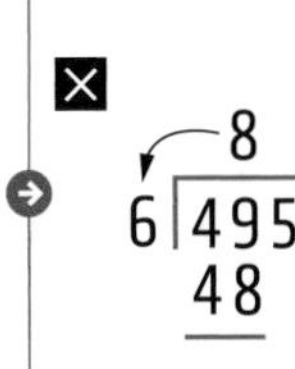
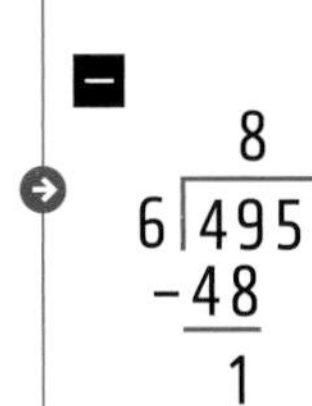

and so on, in similarly broken-down steps, until the completion of the process.

NEXT | Capturing ideas on screen and paper indicates how we regard them as objects

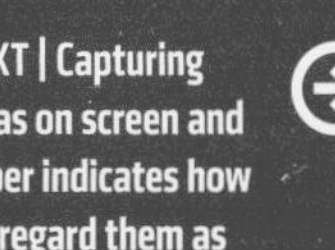

The task analysis quandary

Special education was founded on the strategy of task analysis. Breaking things down into their constituent parts is the way to access success. However, the very pupils who need this segmentation are the same ones who are easily overloaded with too many pieces of information. Once again, the solution becomes the problem. Chunking to the rescue.

Frederick Reif

It is easier to remember a few major steps than a long series of detailed steps.

Reif, 2008

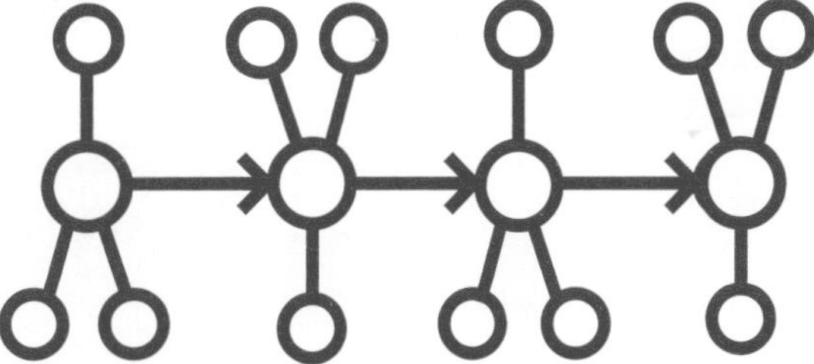

Flow Spray visual instruction plan

Donald says we can't chunk in our heads and Reif that detailed steps are too many to keep in mind. This is exactly the problem solved by the Flow Spray organiser. Here it is performing the function of a visual instruction plan, as recommended by Fred Jones (see above). We have all become familiar with the advantages of transforming multiple units of content into chunks, but are – we strongly guess – unaware of how this can work equally well with processes. A Flow Spray is no more than a chunked Flow Chart with attached elaborations.

Frederick Reif

Once a major step is recalled, it is then also fairly easy to elaborate it into the few detailed steps subsumed by it.

Reif, 2008

IDEAS AS OBJECTS

The metaphors we use to describe thinking give the game away. We *manipulate* and *arrange* ideas because we work on them as if they are objects.

Caviglioli et al, *Thinking Skills & Eye Q*, 2002

Pay attention to their metaphors

If you read carefully, you will see that these top educators frame ideas as objects...
Richard Mayer (2014) defines organisation as "*arranging the incoming information*".
Peps Mccrea (2017) writes of understanding being "*constructed, bit by bit*".
Kirschner and Hendrick (2020) explain what to do to "*get a grip*" on prior knowledge.
Frederick Reif (2008) describes the process of "*constructing a solution*" and "*decomposing*".
They are not alone. We all use this metaphor.

Barbara Tversky

The mind regards ideas as objects.

Tversky, 2019

THINKING SKILLS & EYE Q | 2002

The thoughts you have can be viewed as thought-objects. What we call reasoning is merely the manipulation of these thought-objects. When we put thought-objects into particular permutations, we are constructing concepts and schemas.

Oliver's revelation

Sometimes we work hard at discovering for ourselves what a book or paper could have told us in just a few minutes. This happened to Oliver when he struggled towards the realisation that we conceive of thoughts as if they were objects. Later, he learned that George Lakoff and Mark Johnson (1980) had thoroughly explored this fascinating area nearly two decades earlier. He wrote about his realisation in a book (*Thinking Skills and Eye Q*) and now revisits the notion, revitalised by the multidisciplinary interest in this topic.

TEACHER TALK – SCHEMA HIDDEN **TEACHER TALK WITH VISUAL – SCHEMA REVEALED**

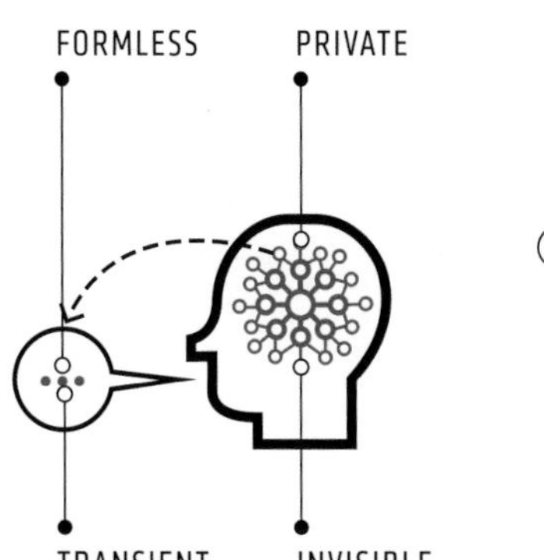

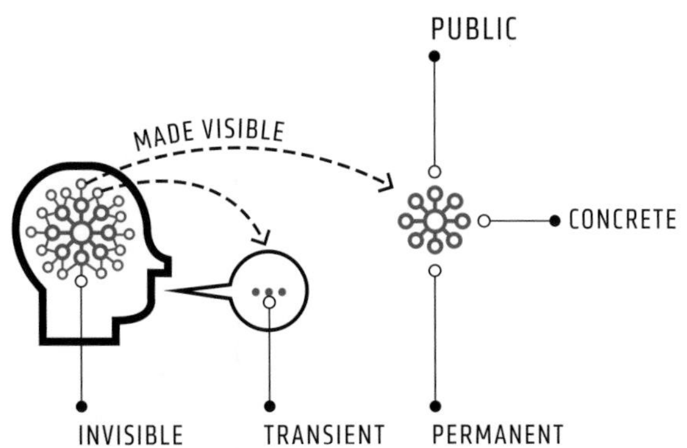

NEXT | How the manipulation of ideas as objects is a central concept in embodied cognition

Evidence that metaphors are powerful

Spatial metaphors are the foundation of abstract thought, argues Tversky (2019). So can there be a rationale for not making cognitive structures visible to students? It is inconceivable for architects to talk to engineers about a building in words alone. And as we have revealed in the few examples on the opposite page, framing schemas as constructions is ubiquitous. Everyone – and every teacher – does it, even if unaware of it. But once alive to this inescapable metaphor, shouldn't most explanations have a visible counterpart?

Barbara Tversky

They can provide a permanent, public record that can be pointed at or referred to. They externalise and clarify.

Tversky, 2019

Peeping behind the curtain

Providing a visual schema alongside a verbal explanation is more likely to meet the learning needs of all students than words alone (Mayer, 2004). It is an inclusive practice, ensuring everyone gets the gist from the start. But it does more than that. Showing what a theory or concept looks in its construction is akin to *peeping behind the curtain*. It invites students into the intellectual life, revealing the way ideas are built. Rather than diminishing the role of language, this insight gives students a new way to understand how language conveys meaning through its linear structure.

George Lakoff

Thinking is object manipulation; ideas are objects; communication is sending; understanding is grasping.

Lakoff, 2014

EMBODIED COGNITION

Understanding embodied cognition frees us from deeply held beliefs about where learning solely takes place. We are not merely computers-on-legs.

Resisting common sense

René Descartes, in the 1600s, gave significant philosophical weight to the everyday idea that our brains are very different from our bodies. But, as many disciplines have shown, he was wrong. That, though, won't shift beliefs that learning only happens in our *upper storey*. Embodied cognition confronts this assumption head on. While some of its most radical conclusions may jar, or seem irrational, the proposition that our bodies and brains are far more integrated than previously believed gives us an expanded perspective on learning.

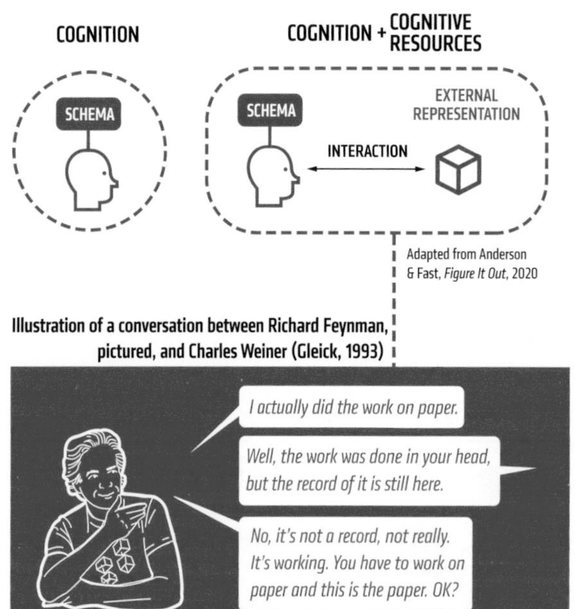

Adapted from Anderson & Fast, *Figure It Out*, 2020

Illustration of a conversation between Richard Feynman, pictured, and Charles Weiner (Gleick, 1993)

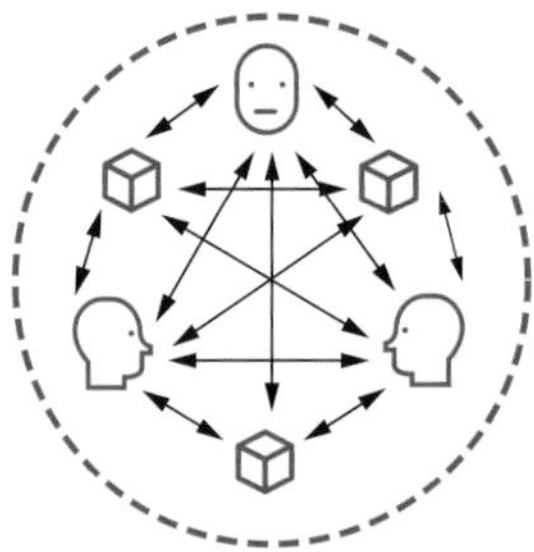

The impact of using tools

Without tools, wrote Thomas Carlyle, humans are nothing, but with them, they are all. So although we create our tools, their constant use ultimately results in them shaping us — changing our very nature. Now that our tools are more cognitive in nature, we shouldn't be surprised that they, too, affect our functioning.

Andy Clark

Cognition leaks out into the body and the world.

Clark, 2008

Tools R us

When learning to drive a car, there comes a time when it seems to become an extension of yourself. For game-players, this is even more so, as the joystick soon feels like a part of your body. With these examples in mind, the discussion about the precise boundaries of cognition suddenly seems more visceral and real than mere abstract conjecture. In this context, it's easier to grasp the meaning of what psychologists are calling epistemic actions — objects to support and extend your thinking. This use of space, within your EXMF (external memory field, see page 14), represents the case of your *extended mind* enabling you to distribute your thinking out on to paper — a cognitive loop between paper and brain.

EMBODIED COGNITION

BRAINBOUND	EXTENDED MIND	RADICAL

Cognition happens only within the brain	Cognition is distributed across brain, body & tools	Cognition can happen without internal mental representations

Adapted from Anderson & Fast, *Figure It Out*, 2020

The distributed cognition of word-diagrams

Word-diagrams – a more accurate and useful term than graphic organisers – are like projections of your schema. Their non-linear spatial arrangements of words, with explicit connections, reflect back to your current understanding. That, in turn, triggers in you an evaluation of the accuracy of the links before your eyes. In this cognitive loop, you react by automatically considering improvements. Only a few among us are able to achieve this level of thinking purely in the disembodied mind.

 Figure

 Similarity

 Closure

 Proximity

 Enclosure

 Connection

Principles of space

How we make sense of objects in space and the principles involved, some of which are shown on the left, are explained by gestalt psychology.

David Kirsh

How we manage the spatial arrangement of items around us is not an afterthought; it is an integral part of the way we think, plan and behave.

Kirsh, 1995

I gather all the vegetables I intend to use and place them beside the sink. As each vegetable is washed I place it aside, separating it from the unwashed vegetables. When all are washed I transfer them to beside the cutting board, where I keep my knives, and begin chopping each in the way I will need it.

From Kirsh, "The intelligent use of space", 1995

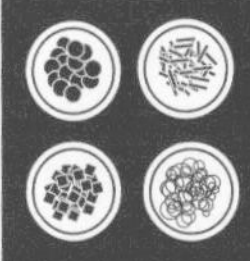

NEXT | The extended mind uses gestures as an aid for learning and communication

Space as a cognitive resource

Adult experts manage their use of space as a problem-solving resource, found researcher David Kirsh (1995). While working processes have been the focus of research, the spatial dimensions have been largely ignored. Through the careful planning of space, a considerable amount of *cognitive offloading* is achieved.

Three different types of space

In his studies, Kirsh categorised space into three types of spatial arrangements that: simplify choice, e.g. laying out cooking ingredients in the order you will need; simplify perception, e.g. putting single-colour jigsaw pieces into separate piles; and simplify internal computation, e.g. repeatedly reordering Scrabble word pieces.

Antonio Damasio

The body is not an innocent bystander in the mind business.

Damasio, 2007

GESTURE

Gesture is not mere hand-waving. It can help improve both explanation and understanding. Through tracing, it can also help reduce cognitive load.

Emblem

Different from gestures. Meanings well known. Standard formats. Not linked to speech.

Iconic [BOOK]

Represent movement or shapes of body, objects and people in space. Meaning is made concrete.

Metaphoric [LOVE]

Represent conceptual understanding of the issue discussed. Present an abstract idea, not concrete.

Deictic

Indicate objects, people and locations in the real world — whether visible or not — by pointing.

Beat

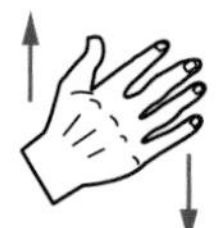

Beat to the rhythm of the speech. Unrelated to content of speech. Short, quick moves on the periphery.

Language is more than words

David McNeill's seminal 1992 *Hand and Mind* pointed out that gestures are an integral part of human discourse. Not only do gestures enable us to better communicate a variety of different types of meanings, but they also have an impact on thought itself. Although there are differences in the degree of animation while gesturing and variations in some of the metaphors expressed, gestures are universal. McNeill broke gestures into four main groups, each serving a specific function and with identifiable movements.

David McNeill

Gestures are an integral part of language as much as are words, phrases, and sentences — gesture and language are one system.

McNeill, 1992

Mapping gestures

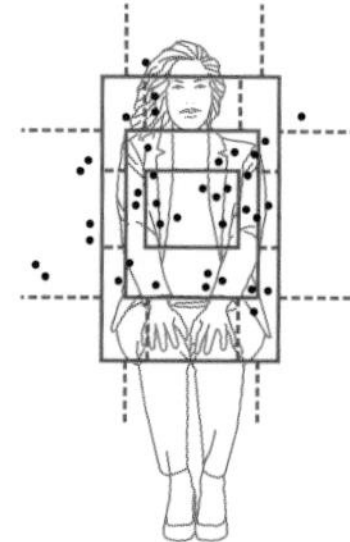

David McNeill mapped gestures & locations

Iconics: centre-centre
Metaphorics: lower centre
Deictics: periphery
Beats: bunches at several places

Gestures and thinking

The most revealing question for teachers is whether gestures merely express the speaker's thoughts or, in some way, contribute to the process of thinking. The timing of gestures is a giveaway: they happen fractionally before we speak, not afterwards. As such, gestures, not surprisingly, feed back to the speaker, in turn affecting her subsequent thinking. Additionally, we need to factor in the linear nature of language and, by definition, its constraints in expressing non-linear ideas and sensations. Gestures are multidimensional. Cognitive philosopher Andy Clark considers gestures to act as cognitive elements such that speech, gesture and neural activity unite to form an integrated cognitive system.

Susan Goldin-Meadow

The answer to the question *do gestures communicate?* is *yes, they do.*

Goldin-Meadow, 2014

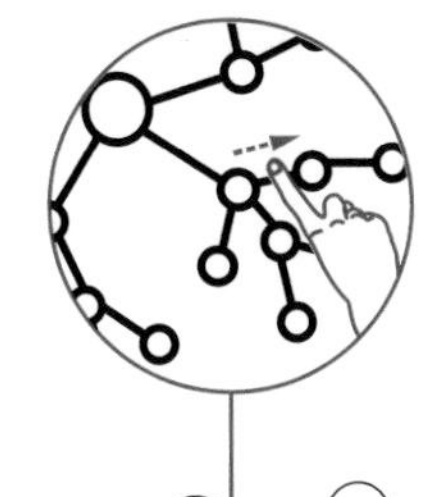

Part of the Recall & Recount WalkThru, from Oliver's book *Dual Coding With Teachers* (2019), which shows the benefits of tracing for stronger retrieval

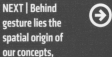

NEXT | Behind gesture lies the spatial origin of our concepts, expressed through linguistic metaphor

Gesturing strengthens your understanding

In *Mind In Motion* (2019), Barbara Tversky reports how subjects who gestured in their attempts to understand an online explanation of a mechanical system outperformed those directed not to gesture (they were told to sit on their hands!). Left to their own choice, over 70% gestured – a natural response.

Gesturing strengthens your explanation

The research on the impact of supporting your verbal explanations with gestures is also sound. Gesturing helps you emphasise aspects of the concept you are describing. Goldin-Meadow and Alibali are good sources of evidence.

Barbara Tversky

Gesturing while studying speeded up answering questions at test, indicating that the gesturing consolidated the information.

Tversky, 2019

Fred Paas

Gestures can support WM processing by temporarily off-loading WM resources normally devoted to internal maintenance of information, with the gesture physically maintaining the information ... and removing its demand from WM.

Paas et al, 2020

Tracing strengthens retrieval

For over 20 years, Oliver taught teachers to trace the branches of their maps as part of peer explanation. The impact of this extra sensory input was outstanding as the teachers later, from memory, redrew all aspects of their maps with an unprecedented level of fidelity. Only more recently has there been evidence to validate this approach – sometimes it pays not to wait for researchers to cotton on and validate what's been invented. Teachers were alerted to this phenomenon by John Sweller and colleagues' 2019 review of developments in cognitive load theory. It referred to Fang-Tsu Hu's PhD, revealing how tracing added to worked examples was more effective for comprehension and retrieval than worked examples alone.

Martha Alibali

Metaphoric gestures provide evidence about the psychological reality of the conceptual metaphors that underlie mathematical concepts.

Alibali & Nathan, 2012

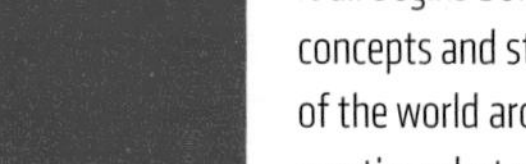

SPATIAL METAPHORS

Our prelinguistic encounters with the physical world determine how we think. We use these infant experiences later as metaphors to grasp abstract ideas.

Metaphors – but not as you know them

The metaphors that linguist George Lakoff and philosopher Mark Johnson studied in great detail for over 40 years are not the literary flourishes you might have learned about in your English lessons. Instead, we're dealing with something so fundamental to our thinking that we simply don't notice them. Yet without these metaphors, we would barely be able to think or communicate ideas. They're so embedded that they offer insights into cognition that can help us better understand why visual structures enable us to think clearly.

Infant image schemas

It all begins before we have language and concepts and start investigating the properties of the world around us. We notice regularities, creating what psychologists call image schemas. For example, when liquid is poured into a cup, we notice that the level rises. We conclude that More Is Up and we apply that prelinguistic mini-schema to increasingly abstract notions. It's all so natural that we're blind to the very phenomenon.

More Is Up

High morals

Low morals

The most important of the abstract notions expressed through physical metaphor are those of **Container** and **Path**, addressed opposite and in a later spread when organising the graphic organisers (i.e. word-diagrams).

Jean Mandler

Image schemas are the first conceptual structures.

Mandler & Cánovas, 2014

We all speak in spatial metaphors

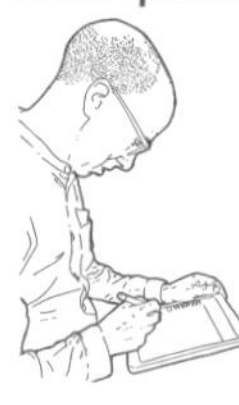

While waiting to make a presentation at a conference one day, Oliver decided to note all the spatial metaphors used by the keynote speaker in just a seven-minute period:

- early footholds
- overloaded
- widen your view
- leads us on
- demands on them
- find the space for
- had come out
- cover everything
- encounter
- we were very clear
- founding issues
- framework
- part of
- perspective
- precise area
- next step
- support
- massive question
- helping them see
- on the technical side
- on the advisory group
- a smaller involvement
- lay the challenge
- left out
- put in
- draw out
- core entitlement
- go far beyond
- had come out
- within the standard

The Container metaphor

When an infant plays, placing building blocks in and out of boxes, she is discovering the essential aspects of a container: inside, boundary, outside, centre, periphery.
And when the containers are her stacking cups, she moves on to discover the remarkable phenomenon of containers themselves being within larger containers. By experimenting in this way, she lays the foundation for her later work on Aristotelian logic.

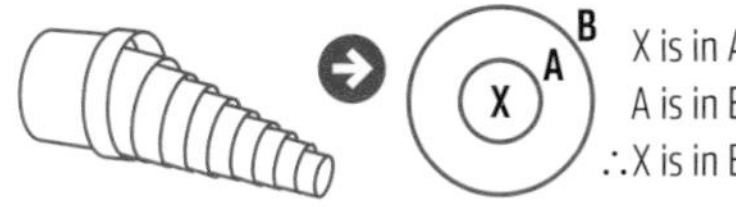

Certainly, in her later studies she will build on this foundation and express her thinking with related spatial metaphors. There is barely any other means of description. Knowing this helps teachers explain the use of categorisation in their subject. If children can stack cups and understand the notion of their being nested, they can understand subject hierarchies too.

George Lakoff & Mark Johnson

We typically conceptualize the nonphysical in terms of the physical.

Lakoff & Johnson, 1980

CONTAINER

When we conceptualise categories ... we often envision them ... using a spatial metaphor, as if they were Containers.

Lakoff & Johnson, 1999

PATH

The Path schema is one of the most common structures that emerge from our constant bodily functioning.

Johnson, 1987

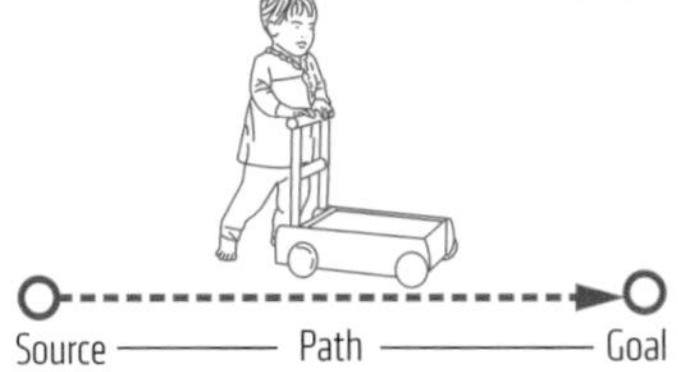

The Path metaphor

Infants soon learn that to make things happen takes force. That involves effort, getting from a starting position all the way to the intended destination. Psychologists investigating metaphors call this the Source-Path-Goal model. Like the Container metaphor, it is so engrained in us, so ubiquitous in our thinking, that its existence is seemingly invisible to us. Yet most, if not all, models of educational progress are based on it, as are managerial frameworks and associated language. All such models are based on the physical act of moving towards an intended goal. The language, once you spot it, is a giveaway:

- start out
- reach midpoint
- long way to go
- sidetracked
- on a journey
- change course
- bumps in the road
- end in sight
- delayed
- dangerous terrain
- next step
- a step at a time
- navigate

NEXT | A brief look at the neuroscience that validates the primacy of the spatial dimension of cognition

Barbara Tversky

The same neural foundation that serves spatial thought serves abstract thought.

Tversky, 2019

COGNITIVE MAPS

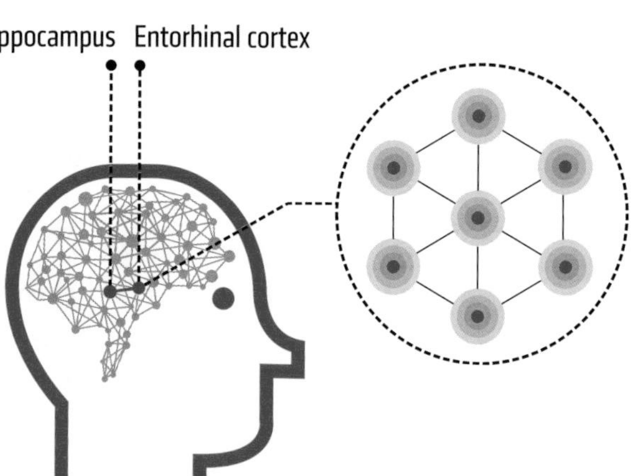

Neuroscience is revealing surprising aspects of how our cognitive maps mirror the mechanisms of how we navigate physical space.

The background of cognitive maps

Since the ancient Greeks and Romans, people have been fascinated by the link between our mind's internal spaces and our environment's terrains. Cicero, among others, wrote about the strategy of building memory palaces.

Cicero

Edward Tolman

In the 1940s, Tolman, a psychologist, argued that rats in his maze experiments created cognitive maps in order to remember routes to their food.

Jacob Bellmund

Cognitive maps built in service of episodic memory are tied to the external world by anchoring them to spatial and temporal reference frames.

Bellmund, 2020

Place cells

John O'Keefe's 1971 research revealed that rats had place cells near the hippocampus that helped them remember where they had been. The self-same cognitive maps, it turned out, that Tolman had proposed. It seems that we, too, have the same mechanism. Alas, the deterioration in Alzheimer's patients' locational memory is a sad but telling sign of its existence, or damage. Place cells are a sort of "*You're here*" signal. But unlike a paper map, these are stored and always available to you.

Grid cells

In the 2010s, the Norwegian neuroscientists May-Britt Moser and Edvard Moser explored the nearby entorhinal cortex, where they found something altogether more sophisticated – grid cells. Unlike place cells, these didn't rely on external cues. Now known as the brain's GPS, grid cells comprise of hexagons, seemingly projected on to the terrain in front of you. As you step forward, a signal from the precise position in the exact hexagon is sent to the brain, pinpointing where you are within this neural grid.

John O'Keefe	Edvard & May-Britt Moser
1971	2014
Place cells ⊕	Grid cells
NOBEL PRIZE	

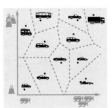

From: Bellmund et al, "Navigating cognition: spatial codes for human thinking", 2018

Mapping car purchase decisions

Spatially displaying information is a natural response to dealing with many factors – for example, when deciding what car to buy. When weight and engine power are the only factors (the axes), it's simple enough. Include variations of paint and it gets complex. Thus, the Veroni-calculated convex shapes that show dots representing prototypical choices.

NEXT | The research that space is the context of our ideas can help us to better organise them

Expanded concept of grid cells

Because place and grid cells carry information about space and time, capturing locations and memories, it's no surprise *Quanta* magazine opened its article on the topic with: "*Emerging evidence suggests that the brain encodes abstract knowledge in the same way that it represents positions in space, which hints at a more universal theory of cognition*" (Cepelewicz, 2019). Add to that neuroscientist Kim Stachenfeld's comments about spatial metaphors and we see many disciplines pointing to this embodied notion of cognition.

Kim Stachenfeld

Our language is riddled with spatial metaphors for reasoning, and for memory in general.

Stachenfeld, 2019

Implications for teachers

From Merlin Donald's anthropological insights into the making of the modern mind to these neuroscientific discoveries of place and grid cells, the central role of space in how we learn becomes ever more evident. As the diagram above indicates, space is the medium in which our thinking can be analysed. Consequently, it's no surprise that displaying the spatial configurations of our own thoughts creates a fruitful loop in which we reflect on and seek to improve them. The organisation of our ideas is made manifest.

Jeff Hawkins

I think we're on a cusp here, where all of a sudden we're going to have a new paradigm for understanding how the brain works.

Hawkins, 2021

Barbara Tversky

Ideas in conceptual spaces are like places in real spaces.

Tversky, 2019

ORGANISE IDEAS

CONTINUUM OF INFORMATION STRUCTURES

Random

List

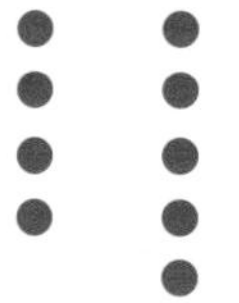

Network

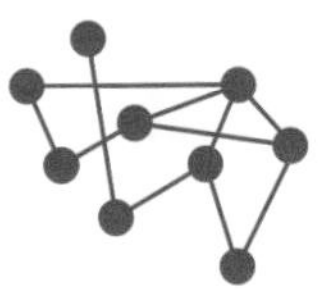

Hierarchy

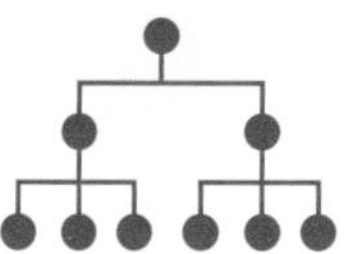

Without organisation, knowledge content is a mere list of discrete facts. But organising them through forging connections creates meaning.

The Cinderella status

Organisation is often considered to be no more than a secretarial skill, its core purpose to serve higher-order functions by tidying up. Cognitive science has adequately demolished this viewpoint. Indeed, Frederick Reif defines the ability to use knowledge effectively as dependent not only on the content itself but also on its organisation. However, students encountering new information – which is the predominant classroom situation – cannot organise unfamiliar content. So, it is critical, Reif argues, for teachers to show them how.

Frederick Reif

Poorly organised knowledge cannot be readily remembered or used. But students don't know how to organise their knowledge effectively.

Reif, 2008

Different knowledge structures

Reif (2008) says that knowledge organisation can be both internal and external, with effective learners using both because "*both forms of organisation are important and mutually affect each other*". But not all structures are equal in their benefits. Above is a continuum of information structures constructed by Reif to identify the differences.

Random | A random arrangement is disorganised and not helpful.

List | Familiar and useful for remembering steps of a sequence but not for identifying links between concepts or ideas.

Network | Perfect for connections but can also be so complex that navigation is difficult. Later, you will see how David avoids this pitfall.

Hierarchy | This is the most efficient for reading and retrieval due to its well-known structure that is consistent across different content.

Networks and hierarchies contrast in other ways. A network is created by associations and has no *top*, with each element equal and a potential entry point. A hierarchy differs by being a system of nested groups, as in the structure of folk taxonomies and family trees —thus its familiarity.

Michael Eysenck

Where the information being learned has a framework or structure that can be used to organise both the learning and the retrieval, then memory is often considerably improved.

Eysenck, 1994

Disorganised tools A

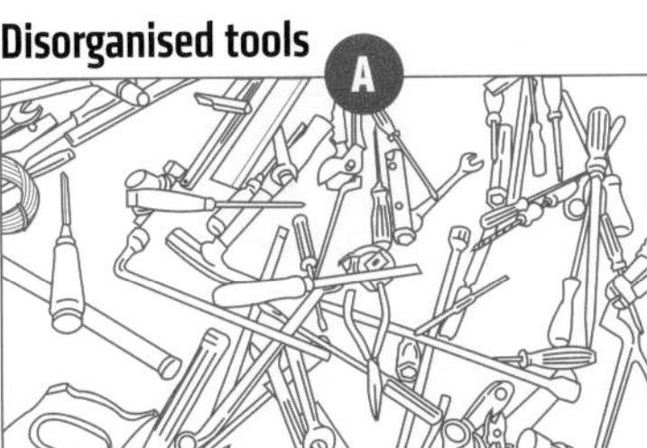

B **Organised tools**

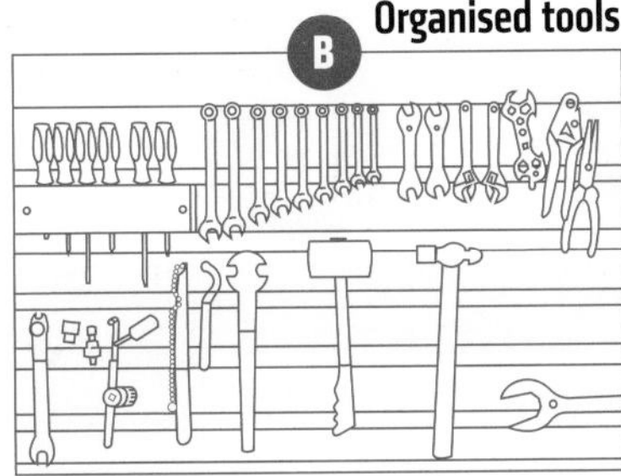

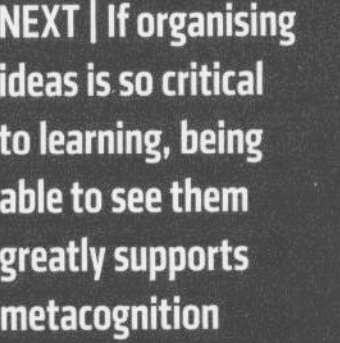

NEXT | If organising ideas is so critical to learning, being able to see them greatly supports metacognition

Henri Poincaré

Science is built of facts the way a house is built of bricks: but an accumulation of facts is no more science than a pile of bricks is a house.

Poincaré, 1902

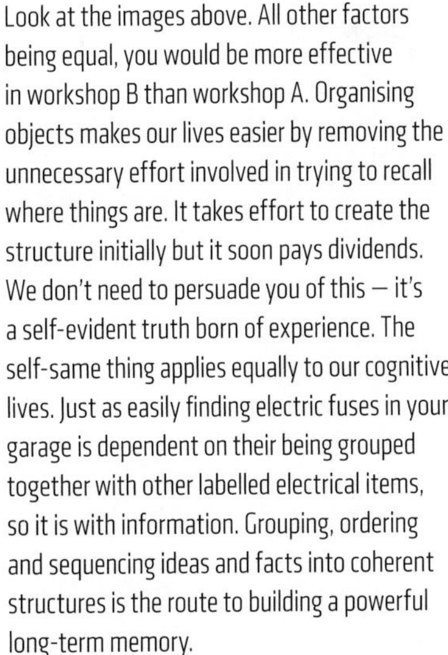

Organisation and efficiency

Look at the images above. All other factors being equal, you would be more effective in workshop B than workshop A. Organising objects makes our lives easier by removing the unnecessary effort involved in trying to recall where things are. It takes effort to create the structure initially but it soon pays dividends. We don't need to persuade you of this – it's a self-evident truth born of experience. The self-same thing applies equally to our cognitive lives. Just as easily finding electric fuses in your garage is dependent on their being grouped together with other labelled electrical items, so it is with information. Grouping, ordering and sequencing ideas and facts into coherent structures is the route to building a powerful long-term memory.

Logan Fiorella

To guide the cognitive process of organizing, students can engage in the learning strategy of mapping, which involves drawing a spatial arrangement of the key information.

Fiorella & Mayer, 2015

Organising: centre of the SOI model

Logan Fiorella and Richard Mayer's SOI model is an analysis of student learning. It includes: identifying and **selecting** the relevant parts of new content; and **organising** it into a cognitive structure in working memory in order to **integrate** it into long-term memory for later automatic retrieval and use.

Barbara Tversky

The mind regards ideas as objects.

Tversky, 2019

METACOGNITION

Given the agreed limitations of our working memories, reflecting on our thinking is a great challenge. But what if the thoughts are in front of you?

Getting meta about metacognition

A couple of years ago, Oliver worked with Alex Quigley and Eleanor Stringer of the Education Endowment Foundation on a visual to depict metacognitive conversations. Laying out the two domains (metacognitive knowledge and regulation) along with their three components, it became apparent that there could only be nine different topics of conversation. Such a rapid insight came about because of the visual capture of the constituent factors: they were projected and externalised. We also used this format to reflect on our group thinking.

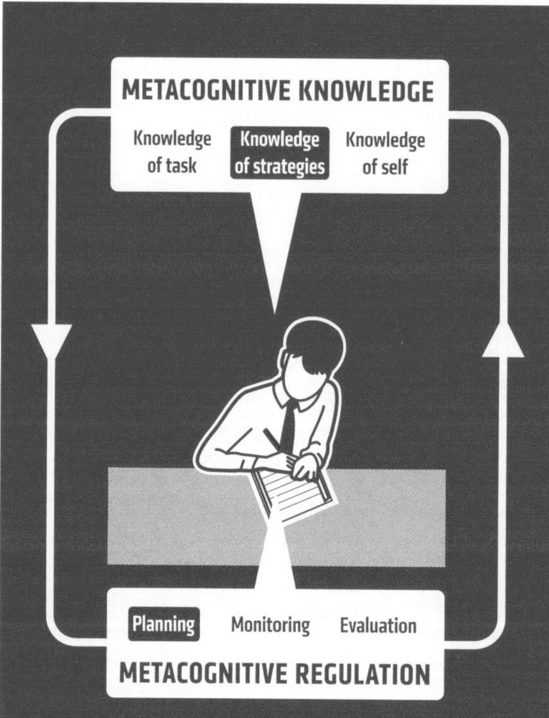

Nine metacognitive conversations

Over several decades, we've had a succession of enthusiastic but rather too abstract rediscoveries of the power of metacognition. Now, with the discovery of the nine possible conversations (see below), teachers at last have practical tools with which to support their students' metacognitive attention and action.

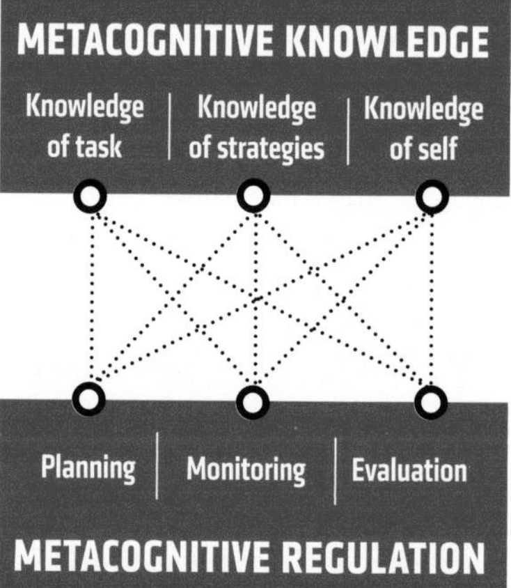

Three-point communication

Metacognition is greatly aided by a teacher. That involves conversations, with perhaps some probing questions. But receiving such questions can easily feel intrusive and, as a result, be counterproductive. That's where three-point communication can help. Instead of facing the student, sit or stand by their side. In this dynamic, your comments are directed towards their thinking – the third point (see above). Now, the comments become more objective. The message is separated from the messenger. Emotions no longer hinder reflection.

The external memory field

The above is one of Oliver's favourite jokes. Two philosophers walking and talking were overheard by a passer-by. One was saying to the other, *"And forty-secondly..."*. The joke is that mere mortals can't hold that amount of information in mind (i.e. in working memory). For the rest of us to have what Darwin called *"longer trains of thought"*, it is necessary for the ideas to be captured, on paper or screen, and to stay within sight. Back to Merlin Donald's external memory field. Seeing our thinking laid out in semi-permanent fashion within our sight greatly helps us to reflect on it.

The external memory field creates an external visuospatial sketchpad to rescue the internal one suffering from overload. Projected thoughts reflect back to the viewer in a cognitive loop that generates an inescapable metacognitive process and experience.

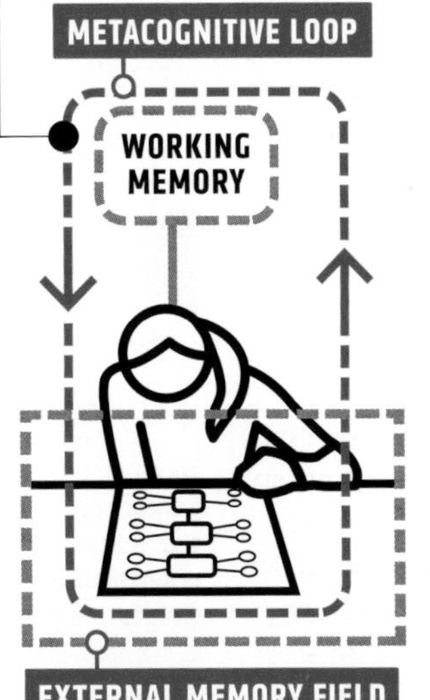

NEXT | Awareness of our thinking leads us to recognise its essential non-linear structure

Marie-Pierre Chevron

Organising knowledge in a concept map could constitute a useful metacognitive tool.

Chevron, 2014

NON-LINEAR FORMATS

Word-diagrams offer an alternative and supplementary way to depict concepts, helping increase every student's access to knowledge.

Non-linear is not non-verbal

Throughout the book, we also refer to graphic organisers as *word-diagrams* in order to avoid the misconception that this is a battle of words versus pictures. While graphic organisers are neither pictures nor sentences, they are filled entirely with words. It's their non-linear format that allows them to be what Stenning and Lemon (2001) call "*data reductions*". Larkin and Simon (1987) found this makes inferencing simpler. How words are grouped or sequenced in space can reveal their meaning with an ease and speed superior to some complex texts.

Peter Bradford

We do not think in a linear, sequential way, yet every body of information that is given to us is given to us in a linear manner.

Bradford, 1990

Satnav v maps?

Stephen Axon et al's 2012 study shows that when satnav is the invariable choice, traditional map skills deteriorate and we learn far less about the environment we traverse. As the strip map to the right shows (Smith, 1826), linear formats have been tried before. Every format has its advantages and disadvantages.

Strip map, 1826

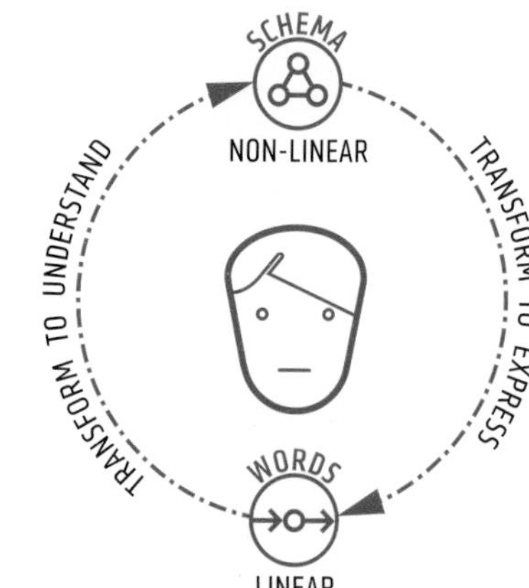

Joseph Novak

Moving from a linear structure to a hierarchical structure and back again is in some ways the fundamental educational problem.

Novak & Symington, 1982

Transforming loop

Concept map inventor Joseph Novak is the only person we know who has identified the transformational cognitive loop that takes place with the external linear world of classrooms and the internal world of non-linear schema formation.

Shakespeare can be considered central in the canon of English literature. By contrast, that irascible 1960s playwright, Joe Orton, is viewed by many as a peripheral figure – on the very edge, if not outside of, this established collection of great writers.

NEXT | A look into the non-linear nature of schemas

We teachers – perhaps all human beings – are in the grip of an astonishing delusion. We think that we can take a picture, a structure, a working model of something, constructed in our minds out of long experience and familiarity, and by turning that model into a string of words, transplant it whole into the mind of someone else.

Perhaps once in a thousand times, when the explanation is extraordinary good, and the listener extraordinarily experienced and skillful at turning word strings into non-verbal reality, and when explainer and listener share in common many of the experiences being talked about, the process may work; and some real meaning may be communicated.

John Holt, 1967

Concepts and language

On courses, Oliver shows teachers only the top left-hand image, with the text relating to Shakespeare and Orton, and asks if he could teach this concept to students in his former special school. When the concept is subjected to the top right-hand *data reduction*, the idea seems rather more feasible. In Kirsten Butcher's article "The multimedia principle" (2014), she writes that "*the spatial layout of verbal content can provide important conceptual information*". This verbal content she refers to includes semantic-spatial displays, aka our word-diagrams. In other words, using the principle of parsimony (better known as Occam's razor), word-diagrams ensure any unnecessary details are "*scrupulously removed*", in Novak's words (1998).

The linear/non-linear debate is not new

Allan Paivio (1990) writes of philosophers Berkeley and Mill's debate about how we process ideas: simultaneously or sequentially. Fellow philosopher Russell (1923) compared extracting meaning from texts and diagrams. In the 1940s, psychologist Tolman researched if rats in mazes had cognitive maps or sets of directions.

Bishop Berkeley

James Mill

Bertrand Russell

Edward Tolman

Susan Goldin-Meadow

Language is unidimensional but meanings are multidimensional.

Goldin-Meadow, 2014

SCHEMAS

Make no mistake: abstract models are not the same as reality. Schema theory is proving to be useful to teachers, but that doesn't make it true.

Getting clear on schema

Sometime in the 1980s, research on schema theory stopped. Its meaning had become so abstract and general that little sense remained. Then, through the advance of neuroscience, it regained academic utility and prominence. Meanwhile, the word *schema* has returned to teachers' lexicon, from which it disappeared for a couple of decades. In terms of the use and understanding of graphic organisers, schema theory is a useful point of reference. But, at all times, we need to recognise that it is only a model and reality is far less reasoned.

Rosch's classical example of birdness, with robin central and others at varying distances depending on their degree of similarity to the prototype.

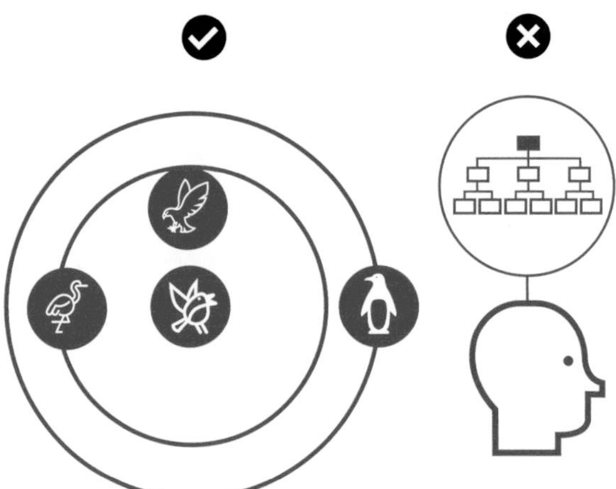

Eleanor Rosch

Prior to my work, categories and concepts were simply assumed, from philosophy, to be something explicit and formal.

Rosch, 1999

Prototype theory and categorisation

Eleanor Rosch, in her field studies in New Guinea (1974), began to doubt that humans categorised in the logical manner handed down from Aristotle through Locke and other philosophers. She found the idea to be fundamentally wrong. We do not go about defining detailed criteria for inclusion in or exclusion from clearly bounded categories. Instead, Rosch found that we place the best example of the category in a central position. All others are subsequently placed in radiant fashion according to their degree of similarity.

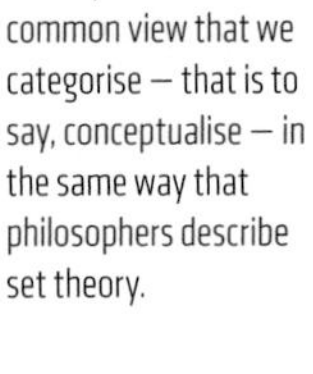

This represents the common view that we categorise – that is to say, conceptualise – in the same way that philosophers describe set theory.

Banishing Aristotle

The objective view of ideas created by the ancient Greeks is still with us. We don't categorise in the fashion that classical philosophy asserts. But that assumption might still be adopted by the psychologists we read and learn from.

George Lakoff

If the classical theory of categories falls, those philosophical views fall with it.

Lakoff, 1987

Douglas Hofstadter's own sketched "notion of a hub for airlines"

The **game** of: ring-a-roses

The **game** of: Greco-Roman wrestling

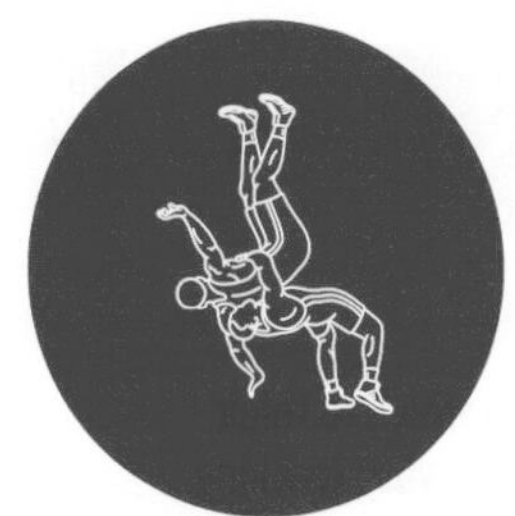

NEXT | A summary of the main points of the theories covered so far

Schemas: private and unique organisation

Douglas Hofstadter has written much on the centrality of analogies in thinking. His sketch above demonstrates his view that thinking is associative in nature. And, as his diagram to the right shows, also hierarchical. What we can take from his and others' views on this topic is that there is a difference between private and public schemas. The former are far messier and fuzzier than what is required for effective communication of knowledge. Students gain from the facility of creating formal public-domain schemas.

Douglas Hofstadter

Our minds have an unlimited quality for chunking.

Hofstadter, 2009

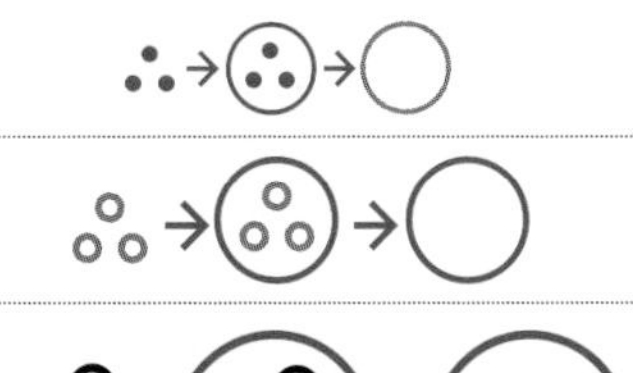

Language games

Ludwig Wittgenstein's investigation into language and its relationship to thinking included an analysis of the noun *game*.
He found: "*There is no characteristic that is common to everything that we call games.*"
The possible common attributes of rules, skill, competition and entertainment failed to unite such activities as Greco-Roman wrestling and children playing ring-a-roses. Even chess and draughts failed to find commonality. The only uniting concept was of family resemblances – far fuzzier than the rigours of categorisation.

Ludwig Wittgenstein

I can think of no better expression to characterize these similarities than *family resemblances*.

Wittgenstein, 1953

THEORY TAKE-AWAYS

Theories are tools with which to think of new ways to approach your teaching. They help organise your experiences and reflections.

Kurt Lewin

There's nothing so practical as a good theory.

Lewin, 1951

Malcolm Gladwell

People are experience-rich but theory-poor.

Gladwell, 2018

DUAL CODING STORY #2

Images are not critical – space is

Dual coding theory, as researched by Paivio, concerns the mix of words and images. As images are not needed in word-diagrams, the key is to understand their visuospatial structure. Words are arranged spatially in order to create links and meaning, unlike sequential texts.

WORD-DIAGRAM

Organise words in space

Relationships are depicted through their spatial links and positioning. Unlike syntax, spatial links are explicit and directly represented. Larkin and Simon's 1987 study showed that they can often be easier and quicker to understand than complex text, due to natural inferences.

EXTERNAL MEMORY FIELD

Externalise ideas to think better

Merlin Donald points out that biological memory is limited. Working memory is acutely constrained. But by projecting our thoughts out on to paper or screen, we create what Donald called an external memory field, in which much longer and more complex thinking can occur.

DISTRIBUTED COGNITION

Trace to strengthen memory

While working memory is limited, recent studies have shown that there are ways of augmenting its capacity. By using our bodies – in this case, tracing – we can collect information about a graphic organiser that adds to our working memory store and not at its expense.

EMBODIED COGNITION

Gesture to understand

Gesturing aids our understanding of mechanisms and structures. In studies, restraining this natural response resulted in lower learning scores than in a comparable group where there were no such constraints. Gestures help integrate spatial relationships.

SPATIAL METAPHORS

We mostly speak in diagrams

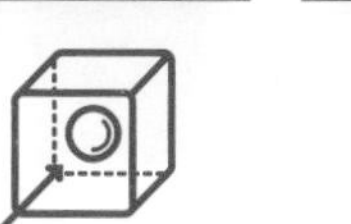

Most of our abstract thinking is based on our prelinguistic experiences with the physical world. What we learned about the spatial properties of the physical world is apparent in how we talk about concepts: central, peripheral, part of, overview, inside, boundary, platform, foundation.

PLACE & GRID CELLS

Places, memories and ideas

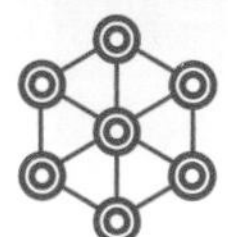

Nobel prize-winning studies have shown that the mechanism via which we remember where we've been is the same for the storage of memories. This grid cell maps them both out. And now there is growing consensus that this is also how ideas are stored and retrieved.

ORGANISING IDEAS

Organising is central, not peripheral

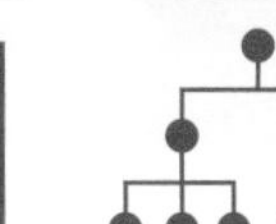

The skill of organising has often been relegated to a mere secretarial task. But Fiorella and Mayer put it at the centre of their learning model: select-organise-integrate (SOI). As in real life, so with ideas: when objects are organised clearly, we are far more likely to be able to find them.

ORGANISING FORMATS

Not all formats are equal

Frederick Reif has classified information structures from less to more useful. Lists are useful for a few tasks but little else. Tree diagrams are useful for grouping and do so with the same mechanisms across varied content. This familiarity and order makes them the best for memory.

DATA REDUCTIONS

Mind your language

If diagrams are often superior to verbal explanations (spoken or written), then we can conclude that their data reductions can be useful for teaching. Much like David Ausubel's advance organisers, they offer the main concepts of a topic before encountering the later detail.

LINEAR FORMATS

Try schema-friendly formats

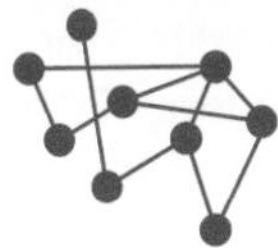

Students experience an overwhelming diet of linear explanations, yet schema are not linear in nature. In psychology books, they are invariably shown as networks. So, connecting new information to existing schema might be easier if the new information is itself non-linear.

NEXT | Concept streams capture the essential lines of reasoning behind the take-aways

Yogi Berra

In theory there is no difference between theory and practice. In practice there is.

THEORY: CONCEPT STREAMS

The ability to see our thoughts in our external memory field adds significance and coherence to a number of different theories.

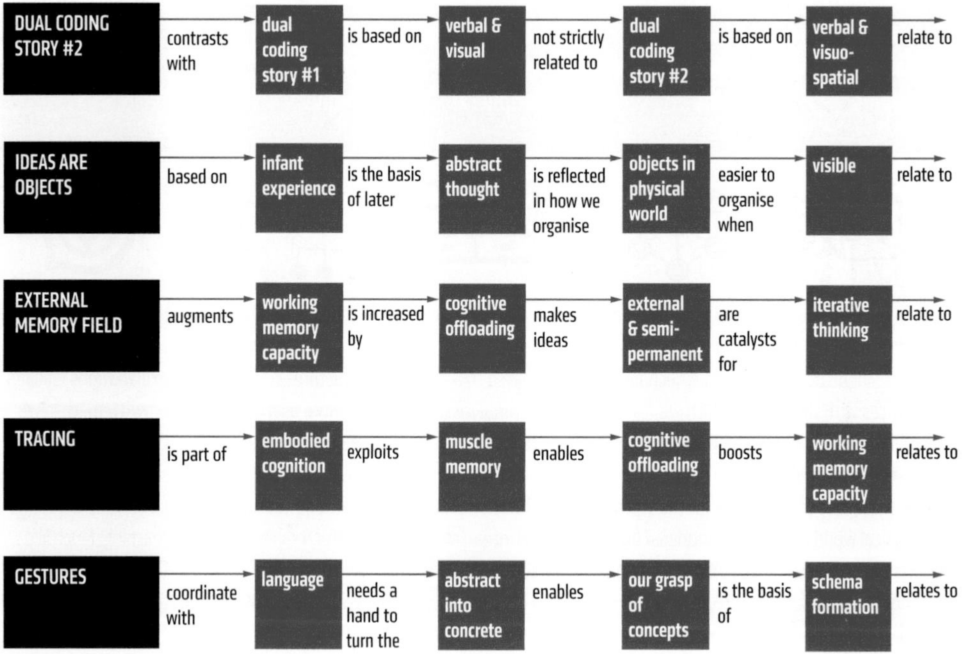

DUAL CODING STORY #2	contrasts with →	**dual coding story #1**	is based on →	**verbal & visual**	not strictly related to →	**dual coding story #2**	is based on →	**verbal & visuo-spatial**	relate to →
IDEAS ARE OBJECTS	based on →	**infant experience**	is the basis of later →	**abstract thought**	is reflected in how we organise →	**objects in physical world**	easier to organise when →	**visible**	relate to →
EXTERNAL MEMORY FIELD	augments →	**working memory capacity**	is increased by →	**cognitive offloading**	makes ideas →	**external & semi-permanent**	are catalysts for →	**iterative thinking**	relate to →
TRACING	is part of →	**embodied cognition**	exploits →	**muscle memory**	enables →	**cognitive offloading**	boosts →	**working memory capacity**	relates to →
GESTURES	coordinate with →	**language**	needs a hand to turn the →	**abstract into concrete**	enables →	**our grasp of concepts**	is the basis of →	**schema formation**	relates to →

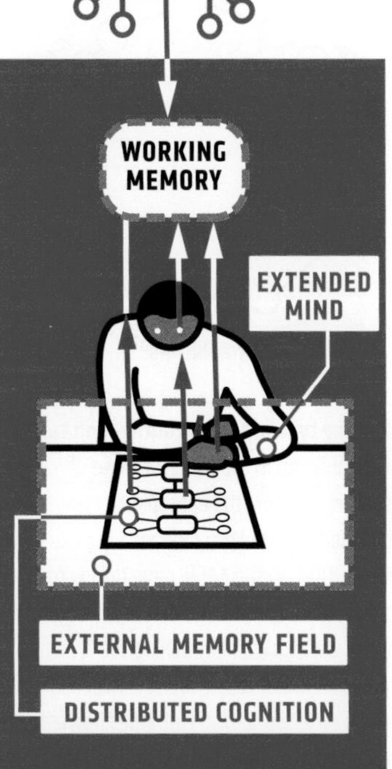

PLACE & GRID CELLS are found in the **entorhinal cortex** is seen to decline in most **Alzheimer's patients** lose sense and grasp of **location and memory** are considered evidence of **place and grid cell functions** relate to

ORGANISING IDEAS is identified in **Fiorella & Mayer's SOI model** involves the task of **linking to prior knowledge** is achieved by **grouping and ordering** enables new info to **integrate into schema** relates to

INFORMATION STRUCTURES have been analysed by **cognitive scientist Reif** ordered structures into a **hierarchy** is based on ease of **navigation** affects the efficiency of **memory** relates to

SCHEMAS have a **non-linear structure** differs from our **daily linear diet** needs changing in order to **connect to prior learning** involves a little known **invisible cognitive loop** relates to

SPATIAL METAPHORS evolve from when we are **toddlers** invent their own **primitive logic** is based on experiences with **objects in space** become the foundation of **abstract thought** relates to

EVIDENCE: ISSUES

Evidence is highly valued. But that doesn't mean it's easily found or understood – or even to be trusted and generalised beyond its boundaries.

Correct labelling – the first base

It's hard to find what you want when there's no common labelling. Kirsten Butcher (2014), reviewing studies on *semantic spatial displays* (her term), noted the following equivalents: knowledge maps | concept maps | graphical overviews | causal diagrams | argumentative diagrams | strand maps | mental model structure.
To which we can add: graphic organisers | semantic networks | visual tools | structured overview...the list goes on.

Replicability – repeating the findings

"Only 0.13 percent of education articles published in the field's top 100 journals are replications," wrote Charlie Tyson (2014). He had just read the paper by Matthew Makel and Jonathan Plucker (2014) on the topic. Educational research is similar to psychology research in its unimaginably low level of replication studies, nowhere near the level of, say, medical research. In addition, when replication studies do take place, there is a far lower level of successfully replicated results when there is no overlap with the original authors – i.e., in truly independent studies.

In the non-educational field of psychological priming, the esteemed psychologist Daniel Kahneman sent a now-famous email to colleagues warning of an imminent scandal regarding the lack of replicability (Kahneman, 2012). His solution was to have a *"daisy chain"* of repeated studies as a means of ensuring consistent conditions and checking results.

Daniel Kahneman

...to ensure that every detail of the method is documented and can be copied by others.

Kahneman, 2012

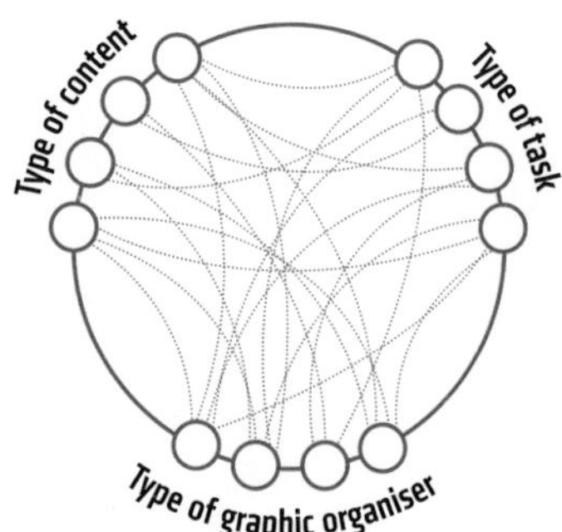

Matching type of tool to content and task

A critical factor in the successful use of visuals is selecting the appropriate type, concluded Ruth Colvin Clark and Chopeta Lyons (2004) in their 450-page review of studies. More specifically, that entails being precise and explicit in matching the type of graphic organiser (there are several, each doing a different job) to content (knowledge is structured in different ways) and to task (there are many different cognitive goals). Without this, any generalisation of a specific study is insecure and likely to be unsuccessful.

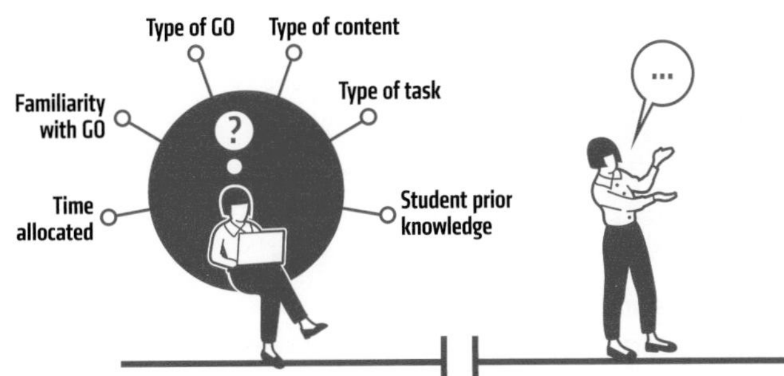

NEXT | Boundary conditions help focus our reading of research papers and identify how close the findings are to our own contexts

Meta-analyses – the lure of big numbers

John Hattie (2009) mesmerised the UK education world with his collection of huge numbers. Yet, a few years earlier, the first such popular meta-analysis from Robert Marzano and colleagues (2001) had been ignored. The considerably fewer studies than Hattie's work allowed Marzano et al to make more considered comparisons, as well as align the evidence with both theories and practice. Among Marzano et al's selected nine strategies, non-linguistic representations came in the mid-range, with an average effect size of 0.77.

Robert Slavin

Hattie is profoundly wrong. He is merely shoveling meta-analyses containing massive bias into meta-meta-analyses that reflect the same biases.

Slavin, 2018

Boundary conditions to the rescue

Fiorella and Mayer's *Learning as a Generative Activity* (2015) has been rightly heralded in the UK. Its breakthrough contribution, however, has not been widely recognised: the use of boundary conditions. With around 25-35 carefully curated studies, meaningful contrasts can be made. In addition, the visual strategies are divided into concept maps, knowledge maps and graphic organisers. In this way, we learn of the different effects of each among different age and ability groups of students. Such details are critical to teachers.

Christian Busse

Boundary condition exploration fosters theory development, strengthens research validity, and mitigates the research-practice gap.

Busse et al, 2016

EVIDENCE: FINDINGS

Word-diagrams offer an alternative and supplementary way to depict concepts, helping increase every student's access to knowledge.

Marzano's ranking by average effect sizes

Rank	Category	Average effect size
1	Identifying similarities & differences	1.61
2	Summarising & note-taking	1.00
3	Reinforcing effort & providing recognition	0.80
4	Homework & practice	0.77
5	**Nonlinguistic representations**	**0.75**
6	Cooperative learning	0.73
7	Setting objectives & providing feedback	0.61
8	Generating & testing hypotheses	0.61
9	Questions, cues & advance organisers	0.59

Hattie's findings

In *Visible Learning* (2009), Hattie identifies concept mapping as having an average effect size of 0.57. Perversely, he uses the established term *concept map* to mean all such *semantic spatial displays* (Butcher, 2014). Elsewhere, Hattie (2012) shows *organising and transforming* as having an effect size of 0.85. Given that this could serve as an accurate definition of the cognitive components of Hattie's concept maps, what's the difference? And if learning is better when visible, as he claims, why this confusing separation?

Marzano et al's findings

Marzano and his team (2001) use the term *nonlinguistic representations* to include word-diagrams as well as physical models, drawings and movement. This ties in with Paivio's explanation (1990) that the so-called visual channel is a conduit for all other non-verbal information. The interesting – yet unacknowledged – areas are where this strategy works in clusters with the other strategies of identifying similarities and differences (think Venn Diagrams) and advance organisers (in graphic form).

Robert Marzano

Probably the most underused instructional strategy of all – creating nonlinguistic representations – helps students understand content in a whole new way.

Marzano et al, 2001

Fiorella & Mayer's boundary conditions

Logan Fiorella and Richard Mayer's *Learning as a Generative Activity* (2015) examines eight effective learning strategies. Uniquely – we think – they filter the results through the lens of boundary conditions. By doing so, readers learn of some of the variables that modify the effectiveness of the techniques. This includes the differentiation of three types of mapping: concept mapping (used in both the specific sense and also as a general term), knowledge mapping (very loosely defined and not exemplified) and graphic organisers.

Mapping's boundary conditions

Concept map

EFFECT SIZE | 0.62

RANGE OF SIZES | -0.09 2.65

NUMBER OF STUDIES | 25

SUMMARY |

The best results for student-constructed concept maps were from poor readers or low-ability students.

Knowledge map

EFFECT SIZE | 0.43

RANGE OF SIZES | -0.35 0.91

NUMBER OF STUDIES | 6

SUMMARY |

The more pre-structured knowledge maps produced stronger effects for lower-ability students.

Graphic organiser

EFFECT SIZE | 1.07

RANGE OF SIZES | 0.46 1.82

NUMBER OF STUDIES | 8

SUMMARY |

All selected studies used matrices or compare and contrast structures. Measures were of recall, comprehension and transfer.

Peter Cheng

Claims in the literature about diagrams in general, which are derived from studies that examined just one single type of diagram, should be treated with caution.

Cheng et al, 2001

The warnings remain valid

Notwithstanding the welcome start of Fiorella and Mayer's work, there is still much to develop in terms of the necessary specificity of boundary conditions. In stark contrast to Fiorella and Mayer's findings that lower-ability students benefit most, Kirsten Butcher (2014) notes that "*students with higher prior knowledge did benefit significantly from the addition of diagrams to a text but that (unlike learners with lower prior knowledge) they learned equally well from simple or more detailed diagrams*". More clarity is still needed.

Kirsten Butcher

Discrepant findings in the research ... on learners with higher prior knowledge are somewhat difficult to reconcile.

Butcher, 2014

NEXT | Finding discrepancies in research is frustrating. Looking for themes can provide some welcome meaning

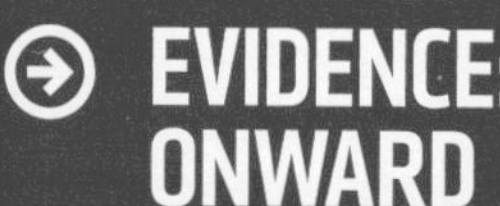

EVIDENCE: ONWARD

Research papers are more useful to teachers when they're grouped around themes that can directly influence how to change or validate practice.

Michelene Chi

Students who generated a large number of self-explanations ... learned with greater understanding than low explainers.

Chi et al, 1994

COMPUTATIONAL EFFICIENCY

A GO has an edge over text; it's easier to figure out. But can this ease have a detrimental effect on learning?

Larkin and Simon's 1987 paper shows that extracting meaning from a graphic organiser (GO) is simpler and faster than from text. This *computational efficiency* happens through the spatial positioning of words, making explicit what text reveals only through inference. But does this *visual argument* (Waller, 1981) come with a cost, ask Robinson and Schraw (1994). Yes, GOs can be too effective: they require less time and effort to understand, and if learning is the residue of thought (Willingham, 2009) then that can be a problem. But only if the teacher leaves it at that. When they create adjunct activities that demand effort – such as spoken or written elaborations, answering questions, filling in partially completed GOs – the problem can be avoided.

WHO BENEFITS MOST FROM GOs?

Lower-performing students, or those with less prior knowledge, are said to benefit most. Is this invariably true?

Hattie (2009) reports that Kim and colleagues (2004) show that GOs help students who have learning difficulties with their reading comprehension. Nesbit and Adesope (2006), among others, argue that students with lower verbal ability gain more from such exposure to higher-order notions. These findings are repeated by Fiorella and Mayer (2015), who identify that the impact of GOs, as measured by effect sizes, is significantly stronger for lower-performing students. This may lead teachers to invoke the redundancy principle for their more able students. This is a mistake, as Butcher (2014) explains: "*students with higher prior knowledge did benefit significantly from the addition of diagrams to a text.*" Seems it all depends on matching the complexity to the students.

GENERATING YOUR OWN GO

Novices can't organise new information. Yet generating a GO deepens learning. Is there a solution to this quandary?

Cognitive scientist Frederick Reif (2008) states the obvious when he says novices can't organise new, unfamiliar material. Yet Nesbit and Adesope (2006) find higher effects when students generate their own maps rather than just study a teacher's. Anderson (1990) explains that this is due to the effort involved in students' elaboration, though Horton et al's findings (1993) show that a collaborative venture works best with the teacher mapping to the students' terms. Meanwhile, Fiorella and Mayer (2015) explain that some learners need guidance in the mapping process. But Butcher (2014) warns that "*novice learners may not always benefit even from modest generative requirements*" and that "*students in the nongenerative condition learned more*".

NEXT | Boundary conditions help us focus our reading of research papers and identify how to our apply them to our own contexts

METACOGNITION – SEEING THOUGHTS

Metacognition sounds abstract. But when you can see your thoughts, they are easier both to amend and enhance.

Our *porous memory* (Sutton, 2003) is not adequately equipped to execute the challenges of metacognition. For that reason, the application of Merlin Donald's external memory field (1991) – projecting and displaying one's thoughts – is the solution to the problem of the "*fundamental generator*" of cognitive load (Sweller et al, 2011): transient information. We can extend the notion to include our thinking as well as external communication. It comes as no surprise, then, to see the Education Endowment Foundation (2018) highlight the use of GOs as an effective tool to support metacognition. In her paper on the metacognitive affordances of concept maps (2014), Marie-Pierre Chevron says they help us "*be aware of the evolution of one's own representation*".

Marie-Pierre Chevron

Organizing knowledge in a concept map could constitute a useful metacognitive tool to focus the teachers and learners' attention and efforts.

Chevron, 2014

EVIDENCE: APPLIED

The best choices are informed ones. Graphic organisers serve different purposes at various stages of the teaching and learning process.

This model is not a proposal

The model you see on the right is not intended to represent a set sequence to follow, nor is it something to be fitted into a single lesson. Don't consider the stages within it invariable, essential or confined to their place in the order. The model is an attempt to highlight moments in the interaction between teaching and learning where a graphic organiser might be useful. We are not evangelists for their use in any particular form, place or frequency. That, of course, is up to the teacher – now with more informed options.

GO OPTION

As GOs are known to trigger prior schema (Clark & Lyons, 2004), they are a good option for priming.

Prime prior knowledge

Reconnect to prior knowledge

TEACHER

As Shea (2021) blogs, priming schema before testing with retrieval gets better results. Like vaccines, "*The first jab makes the body receptive [and] ready for the booster.*"

STUDENT

Rather like a warm-up, priming prepares the mind for better retrieval. Students are then ready to retrieve more accurately and comprehensively.

GO OPTION

A graphic AO makes explicit the key relationships of the main ideas, critical for meaning-making.

Use advance organiser

Get the big picture

TEACHER

AOs can be expository, narrative, graphic or skimming. They start with the zoomed-out big picture, comprising the major principles that structure the nature of the content.

STUDENT

All students get the gist of the content, creating an inclusive classroom. The AO makes explicit the key ideas that help students absorb the details that follow.

GO OPTION

A GO, maybe as part of a MCQ, offers an alternative to other frequently used retrieval strategies.

Ask questions of prior knowledge

Retrieve prior knowledge

TEACHER

The testing effect strengthens memory and learning. It also reveals to teacher and students which gaps in knowledge are still present, ready to be addressed later.

STUDENT

Once primed, students *download* from long-term memory content, strengthening it in the process. Automatically, this starts to link to the main ideas of the just-presented AO.

GO OPTION

The visual structure of an AO triggers and houses students' predictions of its future elaboration.

Ask predictions of new content

Predict new content details

TEACHER

Revisit the main ideas of the AO and ask students to predict how they will play out, given the connections established with the retrieval of their prior knowledge.

STUDENT

Linking the ideas of the AO with their own retrieved knowledge, students will make hypotheses of what will follow. The impact on learning is large, say Marzano et al (2001).

GO OPTION

A carefully sequenced reveal of a GO helps support the transient nature of a teacher's explanation.

Explain new content & check

Listen, watch & answer questions

TEACHER

Avoiding overload with the segmented and sequenced content allows the teacher to check understanding as an integral – and accepted – part of the explanation.

STUDENT

With a controlled flow of information to deal with, semi-permanent in visual format and supported by teacher questions, students absorb and assimilate the new information.

GO OPTION

Seeing two GOs, side by side, enables a direct comparison between predictions and later discoveries.

Share intentions, check predictions

Refine predictions

TEACHER

Explain learning intentions that can now resonate with meaning, as they're based on the previous stages, helping reinforce connections to students' schema.

STUDENT

As Furst (2019) blogs, predictions greatly aid meaning-making – the engine of memory. Confronting their misconceptions assists students in their development of ideas.

GO OPTION

A GO can serve as a speaking & listening framework, securing focus and scaffolding expression of ideas.

Set up Think, Pair, Share

Rehearse explanation

TEACHER

Direct students to rehearse their answers for a forthcoming public Q&A session. Remind them to be prepared to explain the reasoning behind their answers.

STUDENT

In pairs or triads, the students practise the selection, organisation and articulation of their answers. They use the opportunity to rehearse their answers for the next stage.

GO OPTION

GOs can be used to pinpoint the exact source of students' misconceptions by explaining the links.

Check for understanding

Explain & learn from feedback

TEACHER

Probe students' understanding by questioning how they have organised their selected information: the links, comparisons, sequences and causal dependencies.

STUDENT

Students aim to persuade by explaining the accuracy and validity of their answers. They do this by making explicit the organisation of their reasoning.

GO OPTION

A Flow Spray GO aids independent work, as the sequence and success criteria are integrated visually.

Set up practice

Apply understanding

TEACHER

Modelling the thinking behind the execution, the actions themselves and any necessary scaffolds – along with the clarity of instructions – sets up successful practice.

STUDENT

Clarity on what a successful outcome looks like, along with step-by-step details of the process, help develop independent practice with growing metacognitive strands.

GO OPTION

The same Flow Spray GO can be used for post-practice checks on the steps and results of the process.

Check practice, give feedback

Explain, adjust, learn

TEACHER

Direct feedback, with constant reference to the set of instructions, helps students spot their own mistakes, enabling reflection and auto-correction: the fruits of metacognition.

STUDENT

When given a clear route map to success, students will refer to that rather than passively awaiting guidance from their teacher. Independence has to be designed.

GO OPTION

Returning to a GO in a pre and post fashion makes comparisons clear and explicit to their creators.

Set up review of predictions

Re-evaluate initial predictions

TEACHER

Organise a review of the predictions by contrasting with the developed knowledge, prompting students to examine the basis of their original thinking and assumptions.

STUDENT

Examining similarities and differences of the forecasts and what was learned forces students to make sense of discrepancies. New links are forged in establishing meaning.

GO OPTION

How and why a GO would be useful at this stage.

Ask questions of the content

Retrieve content knowledge

TEACHER

Retrieval questions.

STUDENT

This is where we say how a GO can assist the teacher and why. Maybe, too, the type of GO or its use.

The biggest pitfall when using graphic organisers is selecting the wrong type. Choice based on personal preference is not an appropriate approach. Instead, start with the information under question and your purpose, then select the type of organiser on that basis alone.

Chapters

INTRODUCTION

ORGANISING ORGANISERS

Putting graphic organisers in order

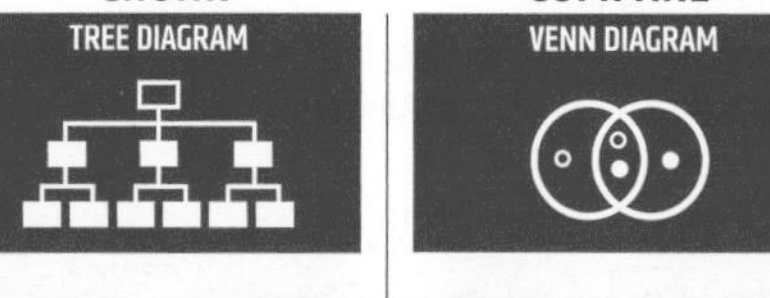
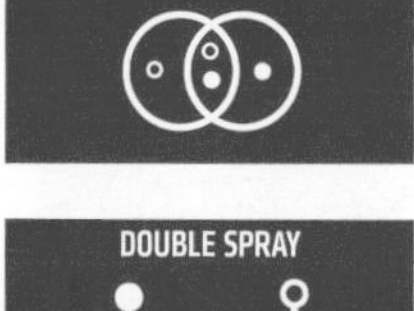
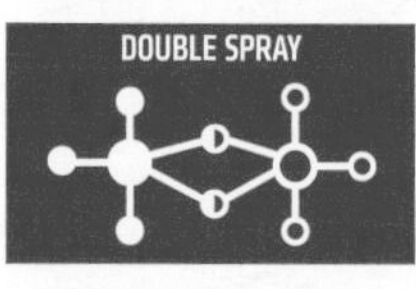
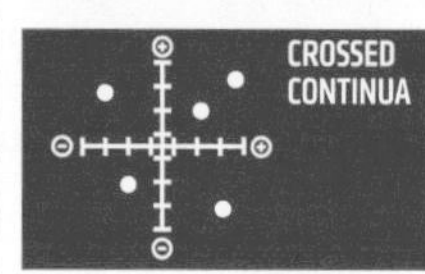

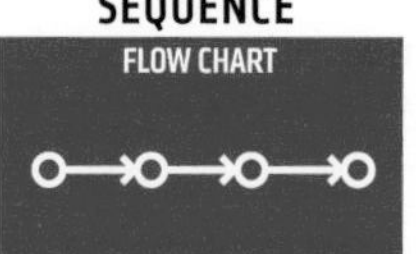

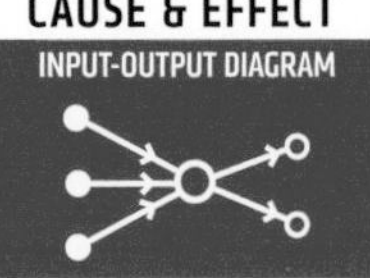
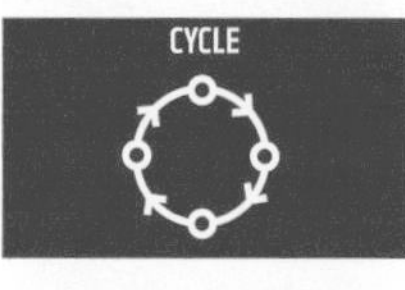
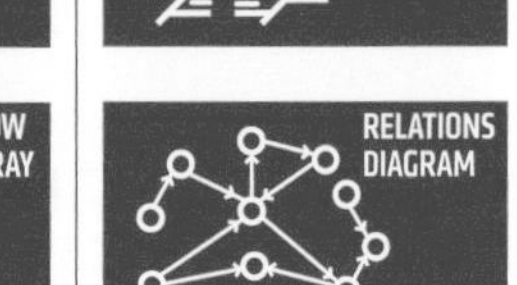
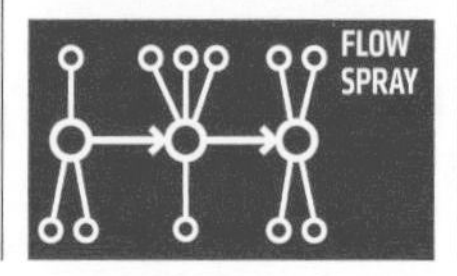

To understand the structure that holds knowledge together is to better understand the topic in question. This analysis supports the transfer of knowledge to new situations.

The importance of categories

It is very tempting to think of categorisation as little more than low-level secretarial work. The truth is very different. Very little intellectual, or indeed practical, accomplishment is achieved without the foundation of categorised information (Levitin, 2014)

Graphic organisers need categorising

Without meaningful categories, graphic organisers are merely a list of potentially useful tools, with no overarching purpose. With categories, GOs transform into devices to understand, assimilate and create meaning. They become knowledge tools, with a decided value in knowledge communication and metacognition.

Knowing about knowledge

Surface, rote learning is disconnected, lacks meaning and is consequently difficult to transfer into new situations (Fiorella & Mayer, 2015). There is a current focus on subject knowledge, and paying attention to its underlying structure can deliver big dividends in terms of better teacher explanations and student metacognition.

Boundaries

We should not be ignorant of the research on the fuzzy nature of category boundaries (Rosch, 1978) when considering the validity of this model. Of course, there will be instances of organisers that sit across the lines of demarcation. That's not invalidating – just obvious.

Oliver's challenge

Twenty years ago, Oliver created the model you see above (Caviglioli et al, 2002). He used to issue challenges to the teachers on his courses to identify one aspect of their subject teaching that could not be adequately analysed and taught through this model. From infant school to FE college, and from special school to private and grammar school, Oliver never encountered a single example.

Consider then, the metacognitive possibilities of signalling the nature of the topic to be taught by firstly announcing what type of knowledge it is. If knowledge is important, then how can its fundamental structure not equally be fascinating and helpful to know?

LAKOFF & JOHNSON Philosophy in the Flesh 1999	**THE CONTAINER MODEL**		**THE PATH MODEL**			
PEHRSSON & DENNER Semantic Organizers 1989	STASIS (CLUSTER)		CHANGE (ORDER)			
COOPER Think and Link 1979	CLASSIFICATION	COMPARISON & CONTRAST	SEQUENCING	CAUSE & EFFECT		
WALKER Sentences and the Web of Knowledge 2018	CATEGORIES	COMPARISON	SEQUENCE IN TIME	CAUSE & EFFECT	MAKING LINKS	
MARZANO et al Classroom Instruction that Works 2001	CONCEPT GENERALIZATION PRINCIPLE		TIME SEQUENCE	PROCESS CAUSE/EFFECT EPISODE	DESCRIPTIVE PATTERNS	
HYERLE Visual Tools for Constructing Knowledge 1996	CLASSIFYING PART-WHOLE	COMPARING & CONTRASTING	SEQUENCING	CAUSE & EFFECT	DEFINING IN CONTEXT	DESCRIBING ATTRIBUTES
WRAGG & BROWN Explaining 1993	CONCEPTS		PROCEDURES PROCESSES	CAUSE & EFFECT CONSEQUENCES	PURPOSES & OBJECTIVES	RELATIONSHIPS
MOHAN Language and Content 1986	CLASSIFICATION	EVALUATION DESCRIPTION	SEQUENCE	PRINCIPLES	CHOICE	
CAVIGLIOLI Dual Coding With Teachers 2019	**CHUNK**	**COMPARE**	**SEQUENCE**	**CAUSE & EFFECT**		

INTRODUCTION

SELECTING ORGANISERS

Tools do different things. It's essential to choose the correct tool for the job

A graphic organiser should not be selected based on its surface graphic features, or on whether it's a favourite. Start from the job in hand and then make an informed choice.

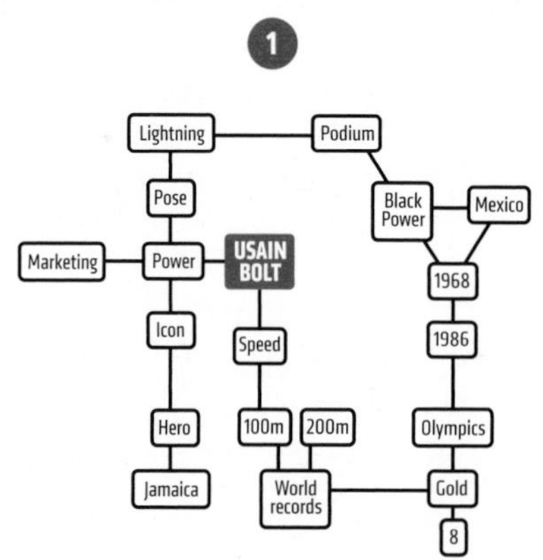

Ruth Colvin Clark

Chopeta Lyons

You will get the best results from visuals selected on the basis of their functionality rather than their surface features.

Clark & Lyons, 2004

Comparing three maps

Of the three maps shown on this page, which two do you think are the most similar? In providing your answer, give your reasons for your selection. As you read in the quote on the left, Ruth Colvin Clark and Chopeta Lyons report that the single most common mistake made by teachers in executing dual coding communication is choosing the incorrect type of visual for the job. The same applies to graphic organisers.

Numbers 2 and 3 are the most alike because they are hierarchies, whereas number 1 is based on associations. The graphic similarities of 1 and 3 are irrelevant.

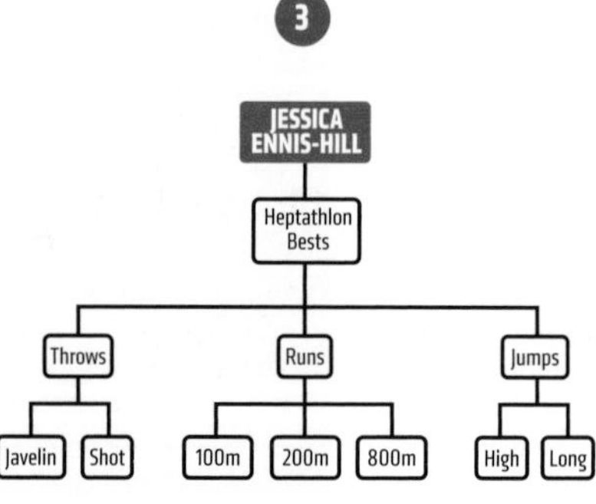

George Lakoff

Mark Johnson

We typically conceptualize the nonphysical in terms of the physical

Lakoff & Johnson, 1980

CONTAINER

When we conceptualise categories ... we often envision them ... using a spatial metaphor, as if they were Containers.

Lakoff & Johnson, 1999

PATH

The Path schema is one of the most common structures that emerge from our constant bodily functioning.

Johnson, 1987

THE CONTAINER MODEL		THE PATH MODEL	
CHUNK	COMPARE	SEQUENCE	CAUSE & EFFECT
		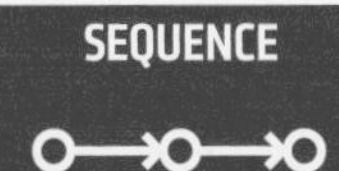	

Test yourself on selecting the correct type of graphic organiser

Answer the four questions below with three-part answers.

Part one | What are the keywords that determine the type of knowledge required?

Part two | What is the model (Container or Path) that these keywords point to?
Is it about content (Container) or processes (Path)?

Part three | Given the above, what type of graphic organiser should be selected?

Your questions:

1 | What exactly is the current coronavirus?

2 | How did the previous SARS virus play out?

3 | In what ways are the current coronavirus and SARS similar?

4 | What impact did the SARS virus have on the global economy?

---

1 | The keyword/s are **What** and/or **is**. The model is **Container**. The organiser is **Chunk**.

2 | The keyword is **play out**. The model is **Path**. The organiser is **Sequence**.

3 | The keyword is **similar**. The model is **Container**. The organiser is **Compare**.

4 | The keyword is **impact**. The model is **Path**. The organiser is **Cause and Effect**.

INTRODUCTION

TESTING THE MODEL

Theories and models need testing. This one has had 20 years of it

Twenty years ago, Oliver used to ask teachers on his courses to test the proposition that their subjects can be analysed entirely through this framework. Here's one story.

George Lakoff

Barbara Tversky

Ideas are not floating in air.

Lakoff, 2013

The mind regards ideas as objects.

Tversky, 2019

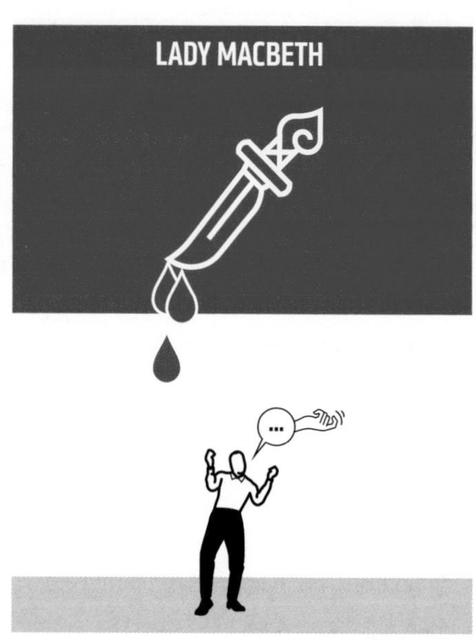

1 ISSUE THE CHALLENGE

On one occasion, a teacher asked Oliver how the framework of four types of information analysis would deal with the question of accounting for the changed psychological profile of Lady Macbeth from the opening to closing scenes of Shakespeare's play. On the right you can follow Oliver's response.

CHUNK

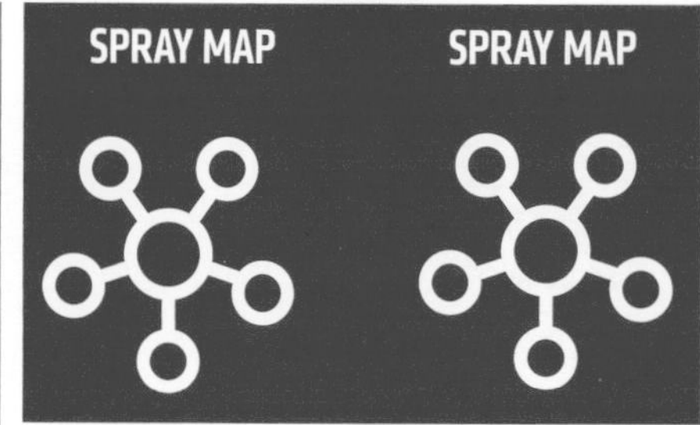

2 IDENTIFY BOTH PROFILES

Before any comparison could be made, Oliver needed first to establish the characteristics of two entities. So, in this case, he needed to diagnose the nature of Lady Macbeth's psychological make-up at the start and end of the play. To represent this passage of time, he walked to the two ends — building two separate Spray Maps — to indicate the temporal span.

COMPARE

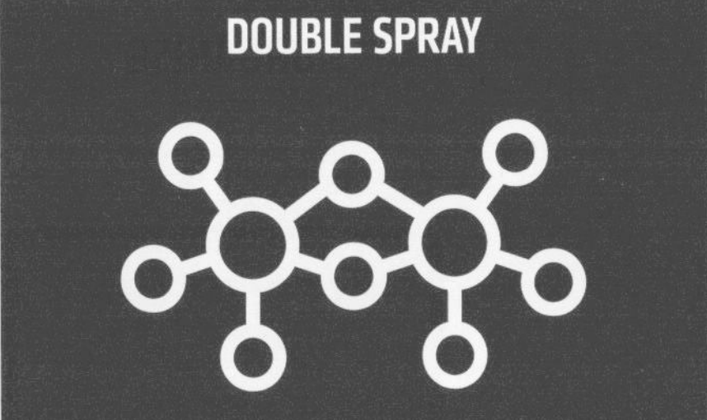

3 COMPARE THE PROFILES

Having established two separate profiles, it became possible for Oliver to make direct comparisons. Identifying similarities and differences – the highest-ranking strategy in Marzano's list (2001) – was accomplished with the construction of a Double Spray in the centre of the stage to represent, metaphorically, how the two ends of the play were brought together.

SEQUENCE

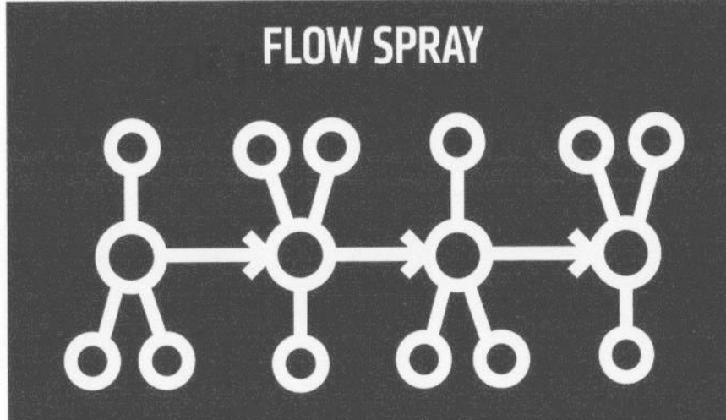

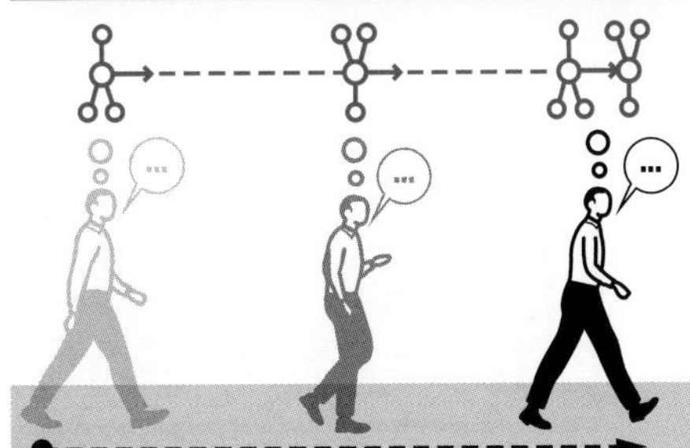

4 IDENTIFY WHAT HAPPENED

The establishment of the changes that occurred in Lady Macbeth's psychology over the course of the play prompted an examination of the major incidents of the plot. To symbolise this storyline, Oliver again walked from the audience's left to right, narrating the major events of the plot, explaining how a Flow Spray offered opportunities to elaborate each notable episode.

CAUSE & EFFECT

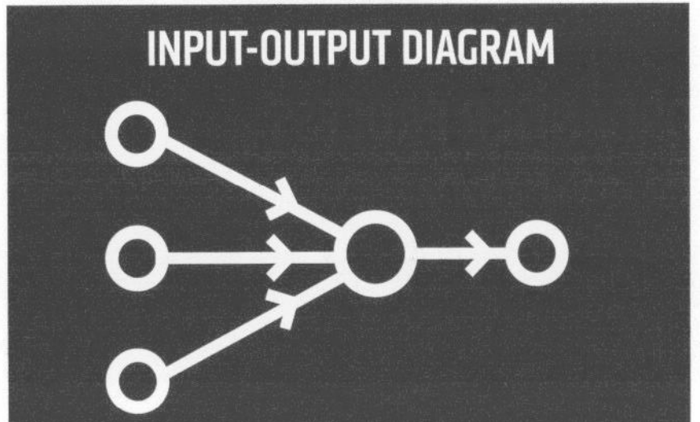

5 SELECT SIGNIFICANT EVENTS

Finally, Oliver was able to review the summary of the plot and relate its significant narrative turns by relating them to the presented changes in Lady Macbeth's profile. As causal influences rarely have a direct, linear impact, an Input-Output Diagram accommodated several routes of causality. Again, Oliver looked back from the denouement to the symbolic passage of time.

INTRODUCTION

ORGANISER PROCESS

The steps behind the successful execution of a graphic organiser

Psychologists agree that organising information is central to the learning process. But there are few who propose practical strategies for its execution.

The SOI model

The renowned cognitive scientists Fiorella and Mayer make their SOI model of cognition central to their 2015 book *Learning as a Generative Activity*. It is a deliberate move to emphasise the limitations of a rote-only approach to learning. Active cognitive processes are essential for meaningful learning, building the deeper understanding needed for students to be able to transfer "*what they have learned to new situations*". This advocacy for generative learning is not an attack on rote learning. Far from it. It is important, then, not to create a false dichotomy between the two and provoke an unproductive factional dispute.

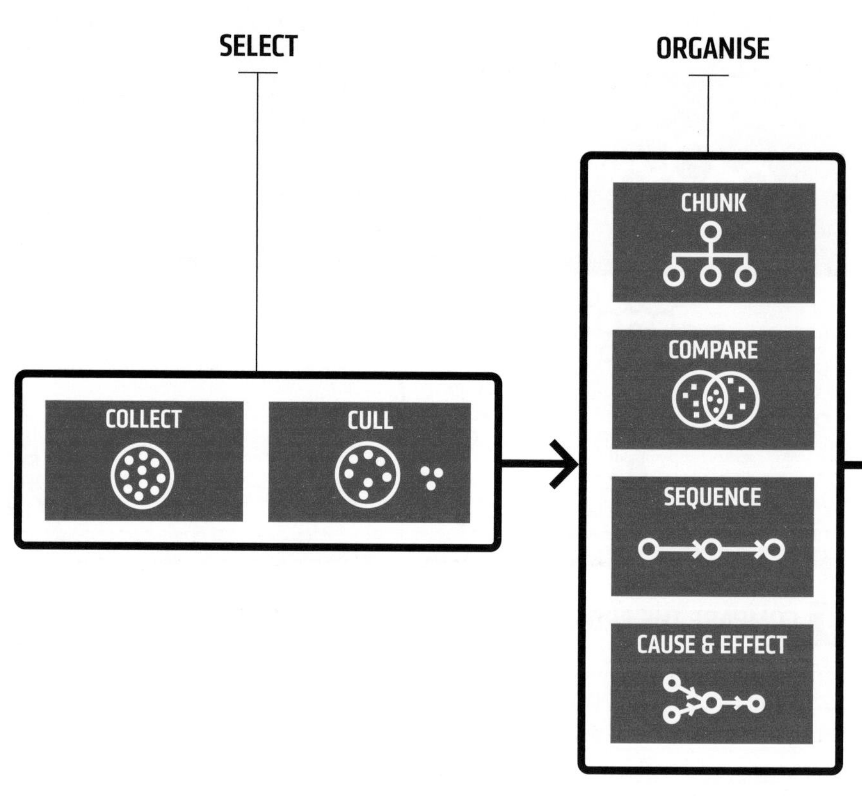

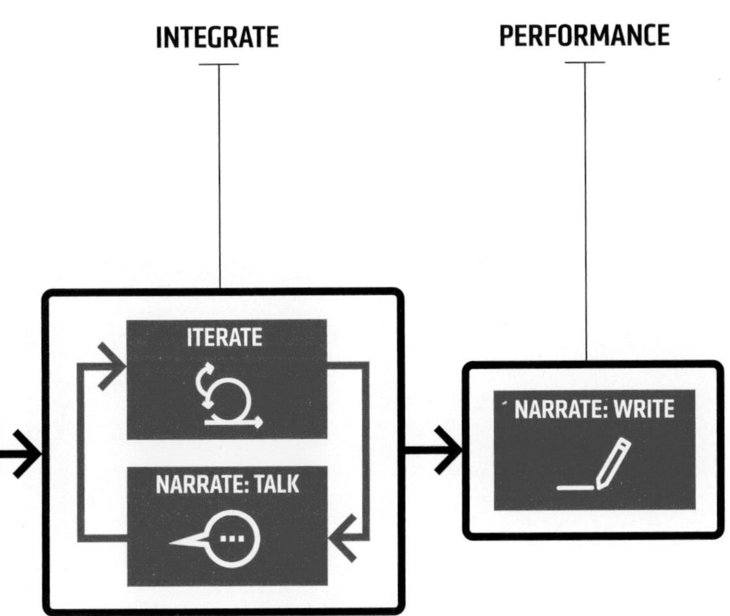

Logan Fiorella & Richard Mayer

An important instructional implication of the SOI model is that the instructor's job is not only to present information but also to make sure his or her students engage in appropriate processing during learning – including selecting, organizing and integrating.

Fiorella & Mayer, 2015

The pivotal role of organising

As enthusiastically as we learned of the SOI (select-organise-integrate) model and its promotion of meaning-making as the overarching principle to keep in mind (Furst, 2019), we also noted that there is little, if any, information about practical strategies to develop students' organisational powers. Graphic organisers make the organisational processes explicit by considering ideas to be objects, as wisely observed by Barbara Tversky (2019). And alongside this profound insight of hers, we should note that the execution of these internal cognitive processes is made manifest because it takes place within students' own external memory field (Donald, 1991).

2 WHAT? | CONTAINER: CHUNK

PURPOSE

In their various ways, these graphic organisers all look at whole-part relationships in defining the topics under question. Consequently, you will see hierarchical structures as well as connections and boundaries.

VOCABULARY

Each category of graphic organiser represents a type of reasoning. It is no surprise, then, that each has a list of associated words and phrases. It is useful to be aware of these words and provide them, when appropriate, to your students when discussing and explaining their organisers and transforming them into text.

---

connect | connection | link | within | part of | excluded from | big picture | zoom out | zoom in | detail | attribute | characteristic | association | category | classify | classification | the whole | pattern | concept | constituent | overview | theme | notion | superordinate | subordinate | hierarchy | hierarchical | define | definition | higher order | lower order | nested | network | web | matrix | inter-related | inherent | elaborate | exemplify | illustrate | in depth | level | absorbed within | contains | common attributes | component | clarify | superior | inferior | feature | trait | unit | criteria

SPRAY MAP
60

A tool with which to start off thinking. It allows a non-linear capture of ideas before organising them.

TARGET MAP
62

Identifying what is included in the topic and excluding what isn't is the function of this tool, setting in the larger context.

CLUSTER
64

A strategy invented to stimulate associations to fuel creative writing, this tool is in direct contrast to all the others here.

AFFINITY MAP
66

Mostly used with sticky notes, this aims at grouping together separate items, and then labelling the newly-formed pack.

SETS MAP
68

This is a pure container model where boundaries are formed around common attributes, also showing shared memberships.

TREE DIAGRAM
70

The classic method of depicting hierarchies through the grouping and layering of component parts in a nested structure.

MIND MAP
72

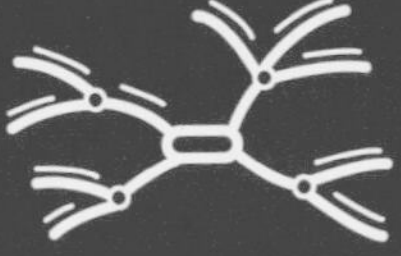

A radiant, space-efficient way of arranging what is, essentially, a Tree Diagram, based on different levels of hierarchies.

INDUCTIVE TOWER
74

A method of working from single units of information into layered hierarchies, rising until the final, overarching title is found.

CONCEPT MAP
76

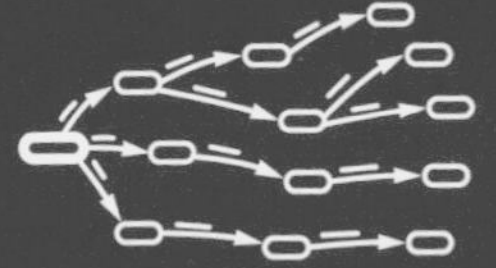

Comprising of mini, kernel sentences, a Concept Map links the component parts to form a coherent, connected narrative.

IDEA BOX
78

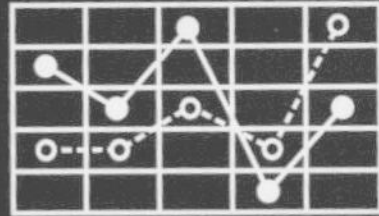

Based on da Vinci's method, this method of tabulating all possible variations stimulates exploration of innumerable combinations.

TYPE | **CHUNK**

SPRAY MAP

A pre-organisational format with which to capture ideas

Before thinking can happen, you need to have a bundle of thoughts to juggle around and organise. This simple tool is one for capturing ideas, facts, opinions and judgements.

The organiser process

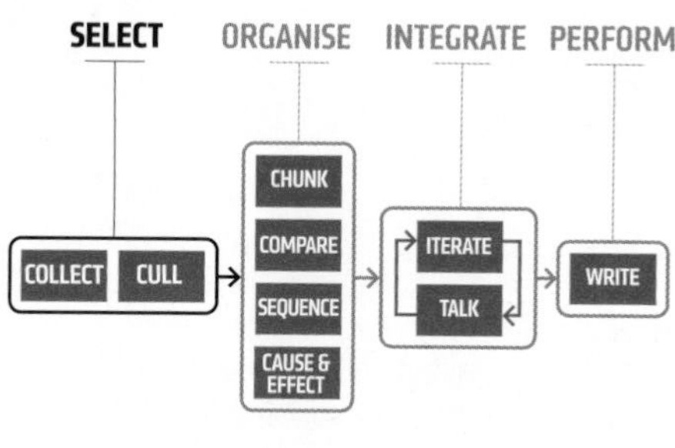

Content-free Spray Map

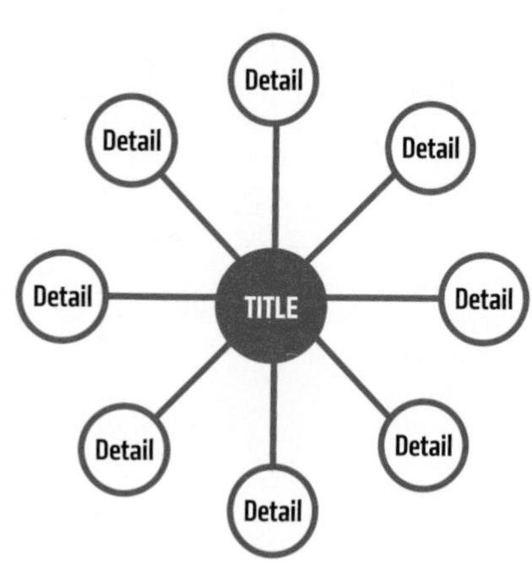

Name

We have adopted the term Spray Map because the word *spray* invokes a sense of being without organisation, or being *pre*-organisation. Other terms found elsewhere include: bubble map | single bubble.

Purpose

Before being able to arrange thoughts into different permutations, one needs to have thoughts at the ready. The purpose of this organiser is to collect thoughts as a prerequisite to thinking. In this sense, a Spray Map is not an organiser as such but a pre-organiser – a collector.

Spray Map for the Three Pigs story

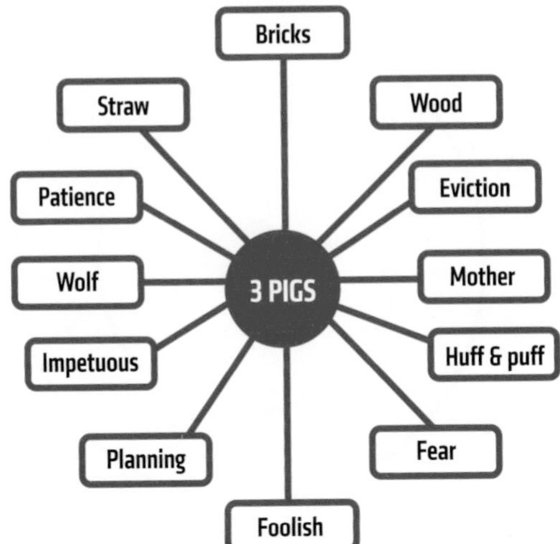

List

- Bricks
- Wood
- Eviction
- Mother
- Huff & puff
- Fear
- Foolish
- Planning
- Impetuous
- Wolf
- Patience
- Straw

David Allen

Your mind is for having ideas, not holding them.

Allen, 2015

Benefits

Writers note that it is very effective to divorce the roles of creation and editing. The latter constrains the former. This tool enables you to project and capture thoughts. As our working memory is subject to severe constraints, remembering and manipulating ideas is far more effective if they are projected on to paper or screen first.

Prompts

- Think back to anything you already know about...
- Let your mind wander and imagine all the things possibly linked to...
- Get 20 items related to...
- Work with a partner and, together, come up with at least 20 items about...

TYPE | **CHUNK**

TARGET MAP

A tool to cull, focus and contextualise the ideas collected with a Spray Map

Identifying non-inclusion of ideas in a topic helps clarify the nature of the topic itself. And also leads naturally to creating layers of relevance within the topic boundary.

Content-free Target Map

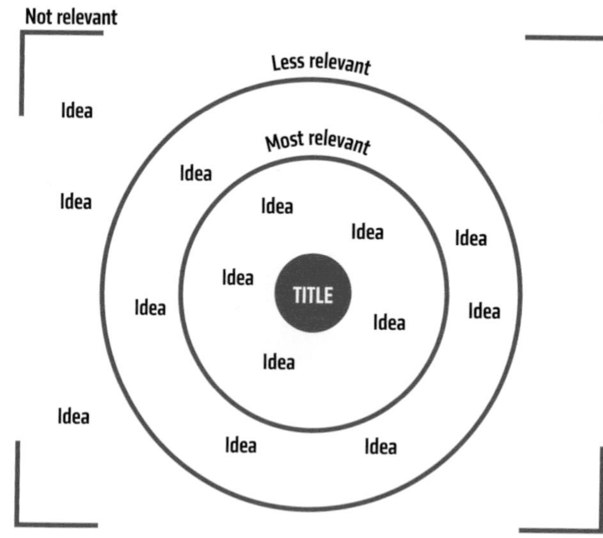

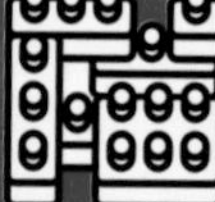

Construction instruction
Page 134

Name

This type of tool is sometimes called: circle map | single set diagram.

Purpose

The purpose is to establish the boundary of the topic under question by identifying the nature of the attributes such that you can distinguish inclusion and exclusion. Thereafter, finer graded differences about relevance can be achieved.

Snow White Target Map

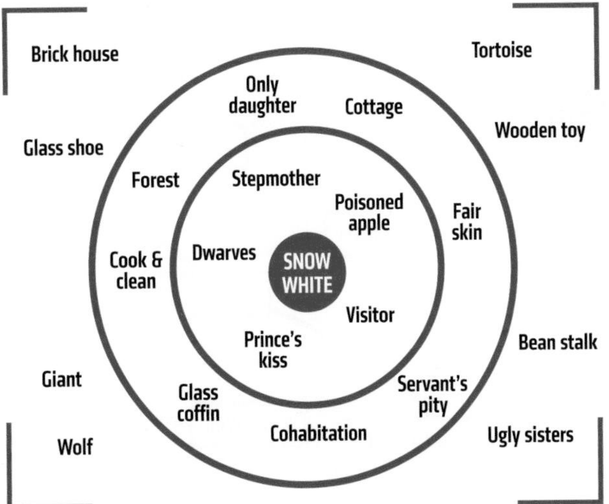

Mun Ling Lo

According to Variation Theory, meanings do not originate primarily from sameness, but from difference.

Lo, 2012

Benefits

In the same way that the principal task of problem-solving is to analyse the problem before engaging in finding solutions, so any topic under investigation needs to be satisfactorily defined.

Prompts

- Can you find some non-examples?
- Think of some things that look relevant but, in reality, are not.
- Where would you draw the line between what is more or less relevant and what is not?
- If you had to boil it down to just a few things, what would they be?

TYPE | **CHUNK**

CLUSTER

A creative-writing tool that can be used for idea generation

Our schemas are built more on association than we care to admit. Unearthing the associations allows us to organise them, later, into hierarchies.

Content-free Cluster

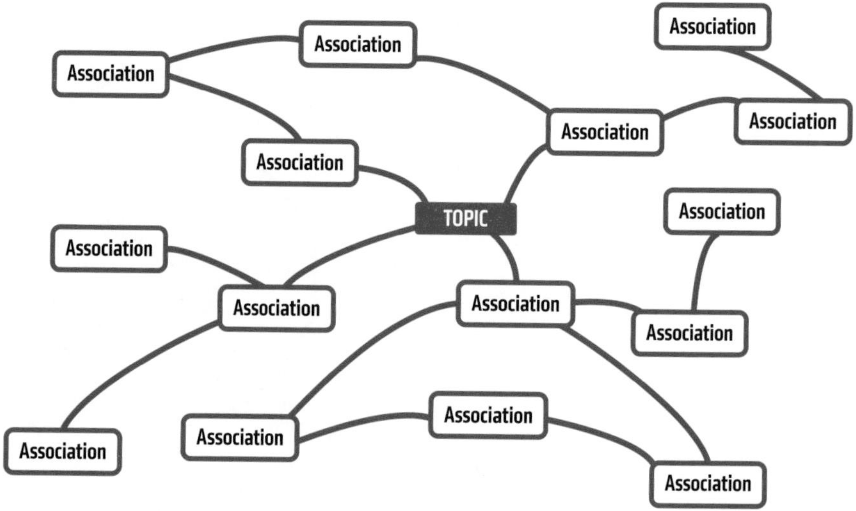

TOPIC

Association
Association
Association
Association
Association
Association
Association
Association
Association
Association
Association
Association
Association
Association
Association
Association

Name

This type of tool is elsewhere called: spider web | webbing | mubble | web diagram | central idea graph | concept web.

Purpose

This is a mechanism to allow deep-seated associations to emerge. Initially devised for a creative-writing class, this simple tool would be termed by many as a brainstorming one. Presenting information based on associations alone is ineffective, but the links conjured in this process generate content ripe for later organisation.

Cluster for the Three Pigs story

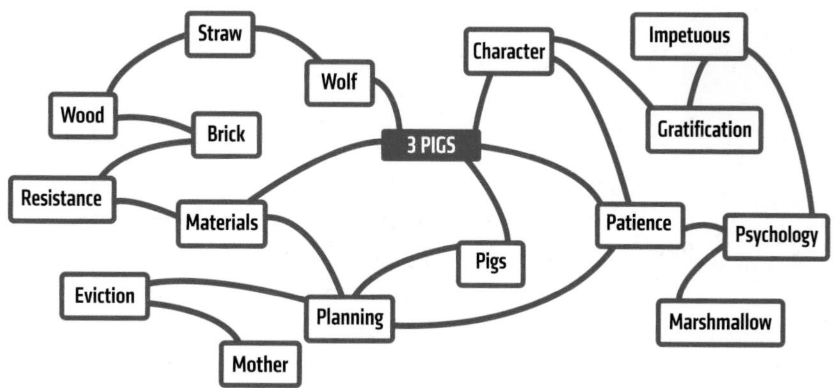

Gabriele Rico

In chaos, things are fluid enough to begin to take shapes and patterns that are constructive, that we can use.

Rico, 1991

Benefits

Students often think they know far less than they do. This tool and mechanism teases out all the related associations on to paper or screen. With no sense of judgement, at this initial stage, students feel freer to concentrate simply on generating ideas.

Prompts

- Let your mind loose, capturing whatever it brings up.
- What possible links or associations can you think of?
- When you think you've finished, create some more associations.
- What else can you dig up about...?

TYPE | **CHUNK**

AFFINITY MAP

A method to sort individual items into meaningful groups

The abstract-sounding *pattern making* is grounded in sorting – just as in the nursery, sorting items into groups involves identifying common attributes. Adults can be more explicit about these shared features and the possible alternative configurations.

Content-free Affinity Map

Group title	Group title	Group title	Group title
Item	Item	Item	Item
Item	Item	Item	Item
Item	Item	Item	Item
Item	Item		Item
Item			Item

Construction instruction
Page 136

Name
This type of tool is elsewhere called: Affinity Diagram | grouping | the JK method (after its supposed developer, Jiro Kawakita) | nominal group technique.

Purpose
The aim is to create order and meaning by grouping, establishing a smaller number of items with which to work. In a group situation, a shared understanding is created when members explain the reasoning behind their groupings.

Affinity Map for the Three Pigs story

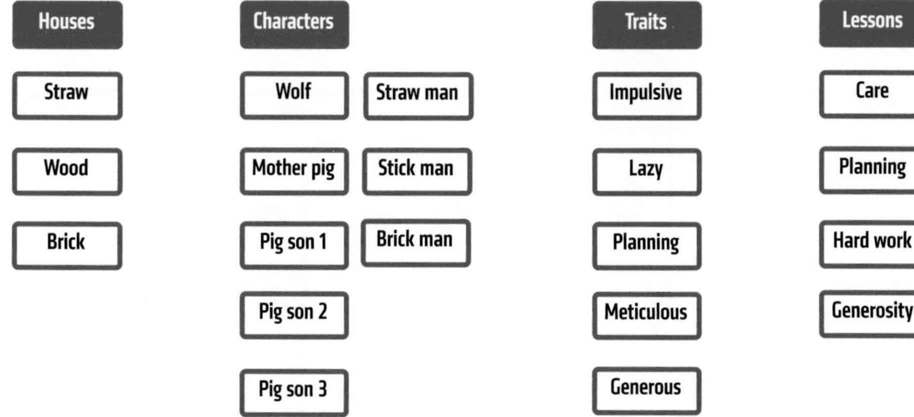

Dave Gray

Affinity mapping is a common method that uses meaningful space to sort a large set of nodes into a few common themes.

Gray et al, 2010

Benefits

Anything to delay detailed organisation by remaining focused on the line of reasoning is beneficial. Any misconceptions are readily exposed when students have to articulate their reasoning and the required attributes for inclusion in their groupings.

Prompts

- How do these things group together?
- Maybe start with creating pairs, then join those up.
- Think about why you have grouped these in this way.
- What title would you give to your separate groups?

TYPE | **CHUNK**

SETS MAP

A boundary-defining map that identifies overlapping constituencies

This, more strictly speaking, Euler diagram is used in non-mathematical contexts to clarify entities and shared membership. Sometimes used to analyse arguments, Sets Maps can be drawn with the youngest pupils – as was the case when early logic was part of the infant mathematics curriculum.

Content-free Sets Map

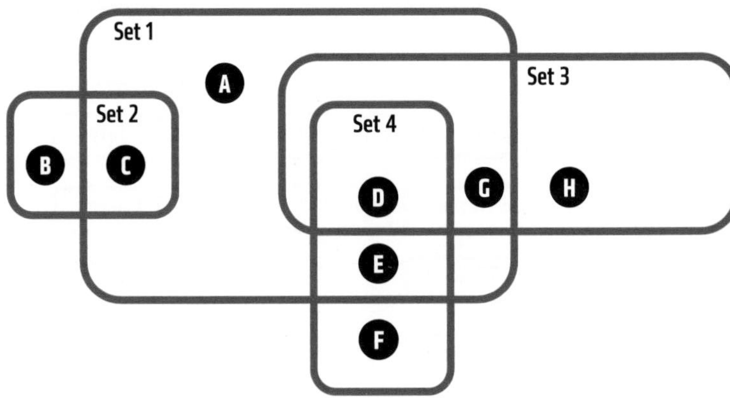

Name

This type of tool is elsewhere called:
Euler diagram | blobs.

Purpose

The purpose is to clarify and establish boundaries – what something consists of and if it has any shared membership with other entities.

Sets Map of the British Isles

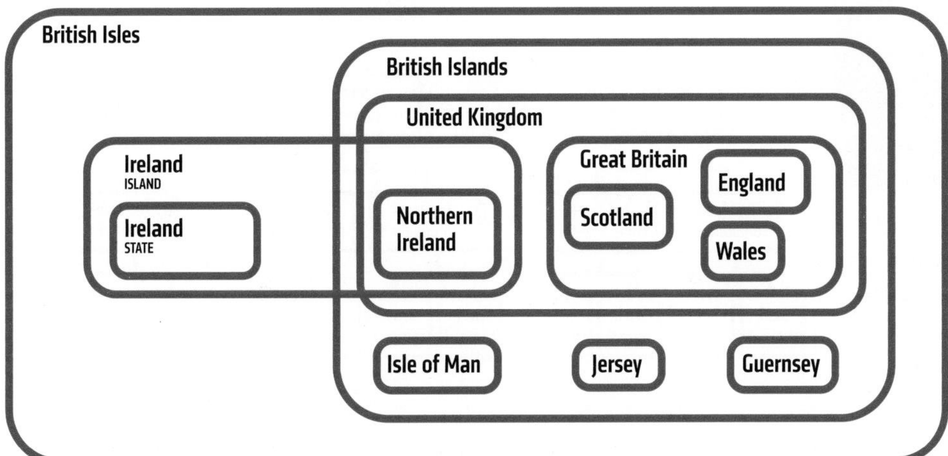

Don Moyer

Blobs do an excellent job of distinguishing boundaries and showing what's inside and out. Overlapping blobs are a simple way to show areas of coincidence.

Moyer, 2010

Benefits

As a means of explanation and a mechanism to test student understanding, this is an excellent strategy. Misconceptions arise naturally when confronted with the decisions that have to be made regarding membership of one or several entities.

Prompts

- Does this belong in this section and why?
- Look to see if it also belongs – at the same time – in another group.
- Check whether you have placed your item in only the group/s you think it belongs to.
- Explain your placement to your partner.

TYPE | **CHUNK**

TREE DIAGRAM

The classic hierarchy in top-down branching format

From folk taxonomies to Aristotle's formal categorisation and onwards, information has been organised, primarily, in hierarchical fashion. Identifying layers of hierarchies establishes the constitution of the topic under question.

Content-free Tree Diagram

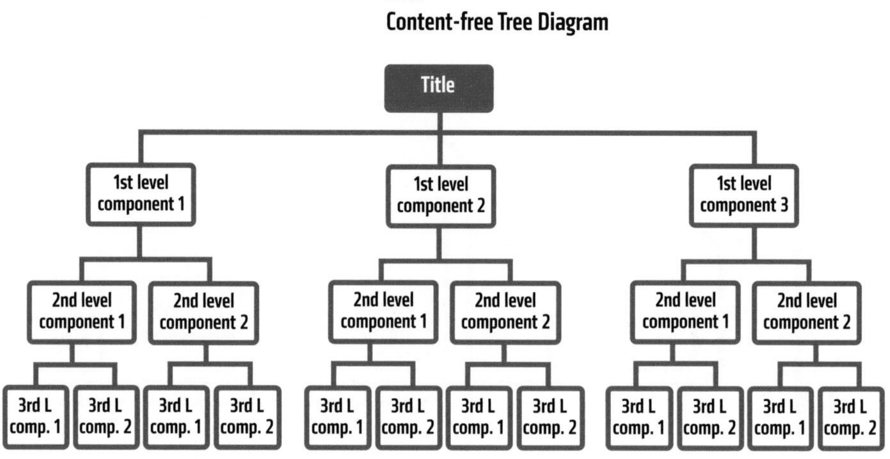

Construction instruction
Page 138

Name

This type of tool is also called: brace map | tree map | branching diagram | family tree.

Purpose

The key purpose is to identify the layers of content that comprise the topic, connecting the higher-order, superordinate generalisations at the top to the details of the subordinate layers below. To make explicit the whole-part relationships — nested knowledge.

Three Pigs Tree Diagram

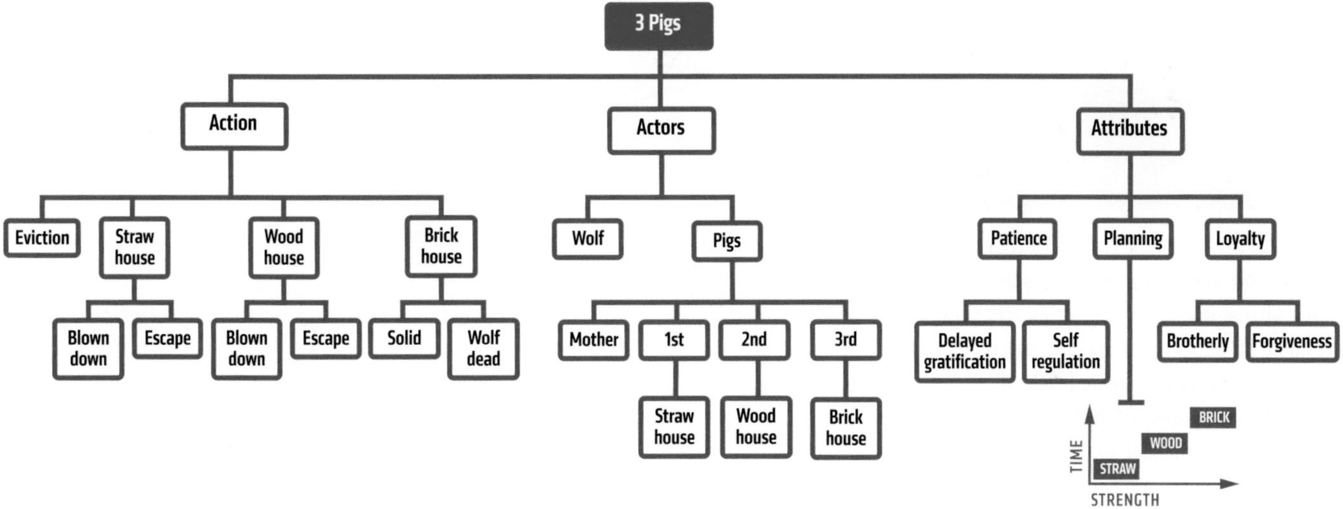

- **3 Pigs**
  - Action
    - Eviction
    - Straw house
      - Blown down
      - Escape
    - Wood house
      - Blown down
      - Escape
    - Brick house
      - Solid
      - Wolf dead
  - Actors
    - Wolf
    - Pigs
      - Mother
      - 1st
        - Straw house
      - 2nd
        - Wood house
      - 3rd
        - Brick house
  - Attributes
    - Patience
      - Delayed gratification
      - Self regulation
    - Planning
    - Loyalty
      - Brotherly
      - Forgiveness

TIME
STRAW
WOOD
BRICK
STRENGTH

Benefits

The first stage in thinking is to establish a definition and description of the topic under question. Knowing the links, from the lowest-order details to the highest-order abstractions, gives students a helicopter view of the knowledge that aids understanding and also, as Reif states, memory.

Prompts

- Is this item part of this group?
- Is this group part of that group, or above it?
- What could you call this group?

Frederick Reif

Specific information can be found by starting from the top knowledge (the root of the tree) and successively fanning out from there along the branches of the tree.

Reif, 2008

TYPE | **CHUNK**

MIND MAP

A much-misunderstood tool that is, in essence, the same as a Tree Diagram

Often confused with the creativity-triggering Clusters tool, mind mapping allows the rigour of Tree Diagrams to be more efficiently arranged on paper or screen. Through its radiant, spatial layout, lower levels of hierarchy can be adequately displayed. Compare this to the self-same content of the Tree Diagram on the previous spread.

Construction instruction
Page 140 | 142 | 144

Content-free Mind Map

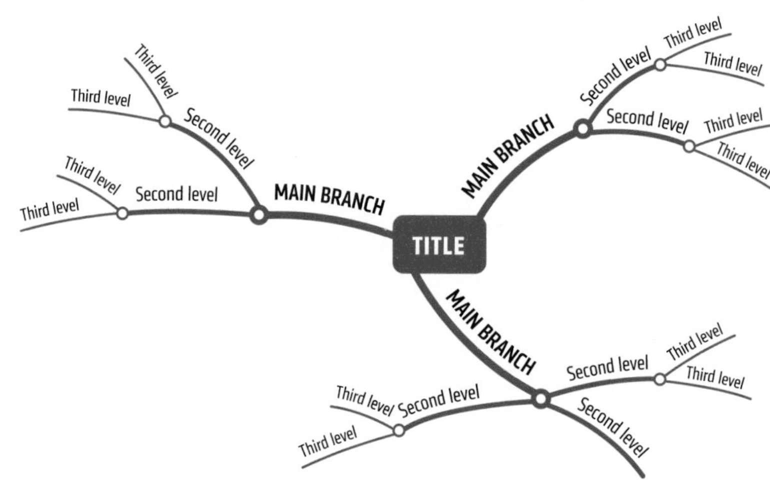

Name

This type of tool is elsewhere called: spider web | webbing | mubble | memory map | network nodes mapping.

Purpose

The core purpose of this tool is categorising information. Tony Buzan's original BOI (basic order ideas) map was his way of explaining hierarchies, headed by the superordinate abstraction (the branches nearer the centre).

Mind Map for the Three Pigs story

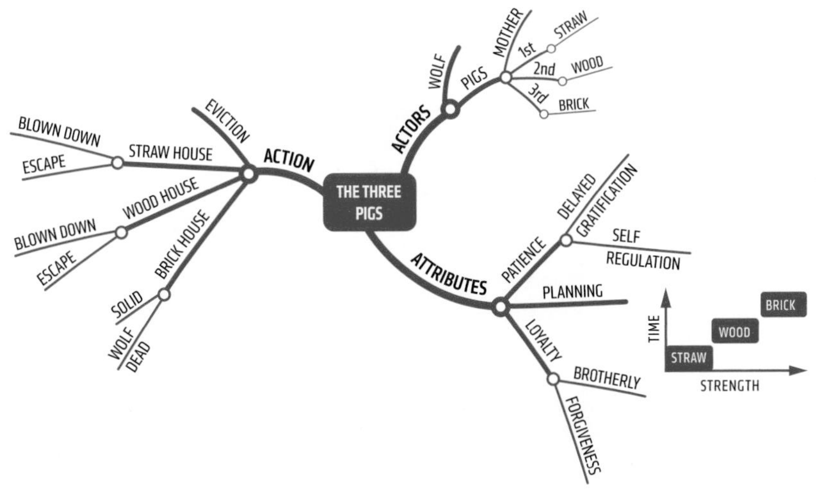

Tony Buzan

Mind mapping is a technique based on memory and creativity and comprehension and understanding.

Benefits

The radiant permutations allow for additions to be made incrementally, at the correct level and as part of iterative thinking. Hand-drawn Mind Maps are highly individual and, with the addition of images and colour, can further support memory and recall. However, despite Buzan's declarations, Mind Maps are not magical, unique configurations. Useful, yes.

Prompts

- Where does that word belong?
- Think of branches as Russian dolls, each containing a further branch within it.
- Decide whether to start from the centre, working from generalisation (BOI) to the details, or vice versa, building up meaning by identifying the more central branches.

TYPE | **CHUNK**

INDUCTIVE TOWER

A development of forging meaning through grouping in increasing levels of abstraction

While teacher-directed deductive thinking has proved to be the most effective, there is still room to develop students' ability in inductive reasoning. This involves moving from experience to concept, to abstraction and on to principles. An Inductive Tower, developed by John Clark of the University of Vermont, is a tool for this type of thinking.

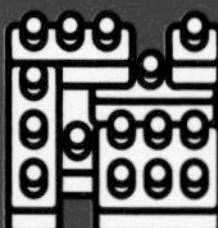

Construction instruction
Page 146

Name

We know of no other names for this organiser.

Content-free Inductive Tower

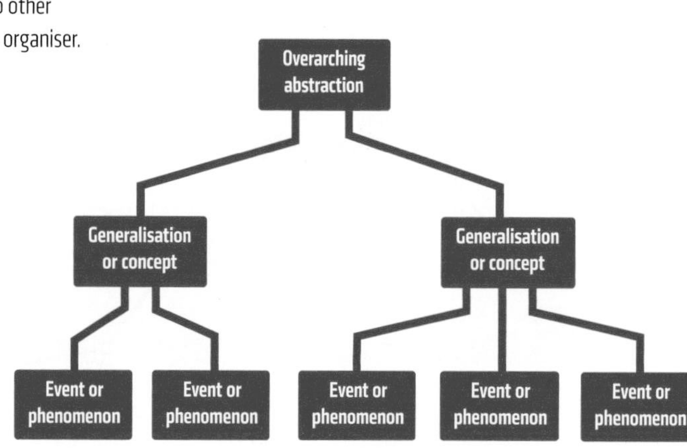

Purpose

The construction of this organiser forces students to identify commonalities in the formation of groupings. In order to name these collections, higher-order, abstract words are needed that deepen students' understanding and increase their facility with these words.

Benefits

The hierarchical connections between experiences and facts, and their abstract descriptions, are made explicit. The concrete is linked to the abstract – one of the six major strategies emanating from cognitive science that were identified by The Learning Scientists (Weinstein & Sumeracki, 2018).

Prompts

- What would you call these?
- Why have you grouped these together?
- What would you call these groups?
- Could an item belong to another group as well?
- Could you say something about these groups in a sentence or two?

Inductive Tower on global warming

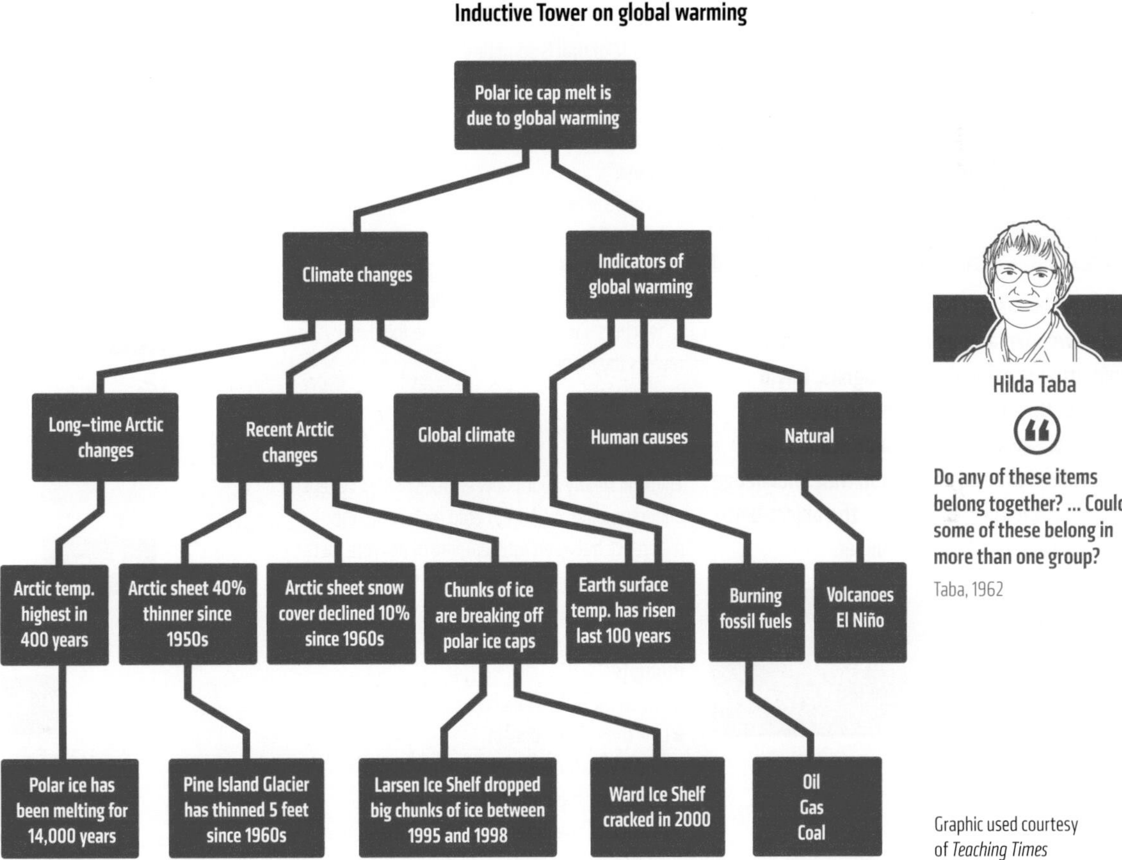

Hilda Taba

Do any of these items belong together? ... Could some of these belong in more than one group?

Taba, 1962

Graphic used courtesy of *Teaching Times*

TYPE | **CHUNK**

CONCEPT MAP

One of the oldest graphic organisers, the most research-based and probably the most difficult to make

Invented by Joseph Novak in the early 1960s and developed alongside one of the most eminent educational psychologists, David Ausubel, the Concept Map is the premier graphic organiser. Its design principle was constructed around the notion that knowledge is built around propositions – the object-verb-object structure of this organiser.

Construction instruction
Page 148 | 150

Name

This type of tool is sometimes known as:
semantic network | knowledge map | concept web.

Purpose

The construction of a Concept Map mirrors the network of propositionals that is a schema. It demystifies teacher explanations for students, and reveals students' proto-understanding to teachers. Like a projection of the mind, it reveals the hidden structure.

Benefits

Thinking clearly about how entities connect deepens understanding. A Concept Map represents the difference between rote learning of discrete facts and their meaningful integration.

Prompts

- List all the entities involved.
- Link those that connect.
- Find a verb for each linking arrow that best represents the nature of the connection.
- Arrange all the different linked entities into a single coherent map.

Content-free Concept Map

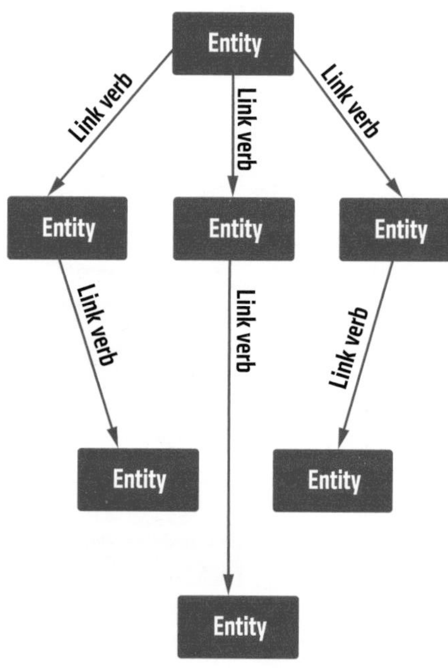

Concept Map for the Little Red Riding Hood story

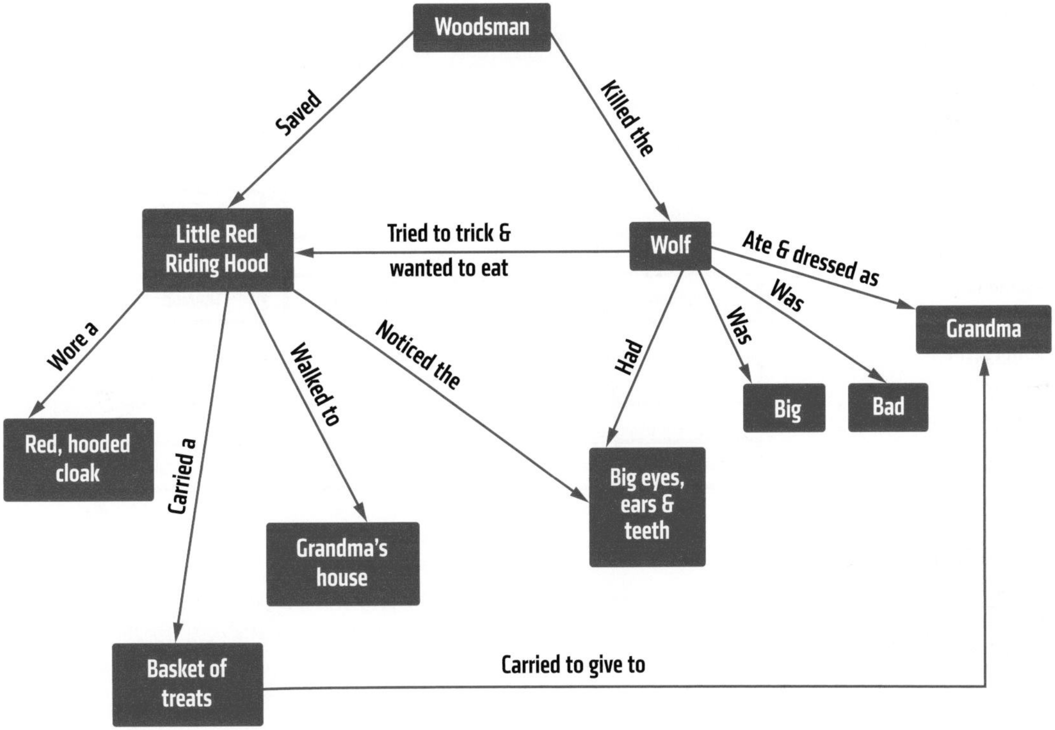

Woodsman
Saved
Killed the
Little Red Riding Hood
Tried to trick & wanted to eat
Wolf
Ate & dressed as
Grandma
Was
Was
Had
Big
Bad
Wore a
Walked to
Noticed the
Red, hooded cloak
Carried a
Big eyes, ears & teeth
Grandma's house
Basket of treats
Carried to give to

Joy Branlund, Southwestern Illinois College/CC BY-NC-SA 3.0 (https://serc.carleton.edu/details/images/40202.html)

Joseph Novak

In my view, concept maps are the most powerful evaluation tool available to educators, but they can only be used when they are also first used to facilitate learning.

Novak, 1998

TYPE | **CHUNK**

IDEA BOX

A brilliantly simple way to uncover the source of creativity — near unlimited permutation of different connections

In contrast to the mysteries of creativity, this strategy reveals its essential component — putting new things together in novel ways. Given our very limited working memory, the possibilities of doing this in our head will always be constrained. Projecting all possible variations on to our external memory field opens up untold innovation.

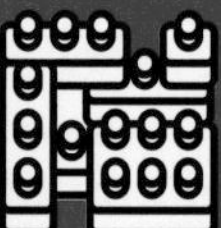

Construction instruction
Page 152

Application with the Idea Box for a lamp design, from think-speak.com

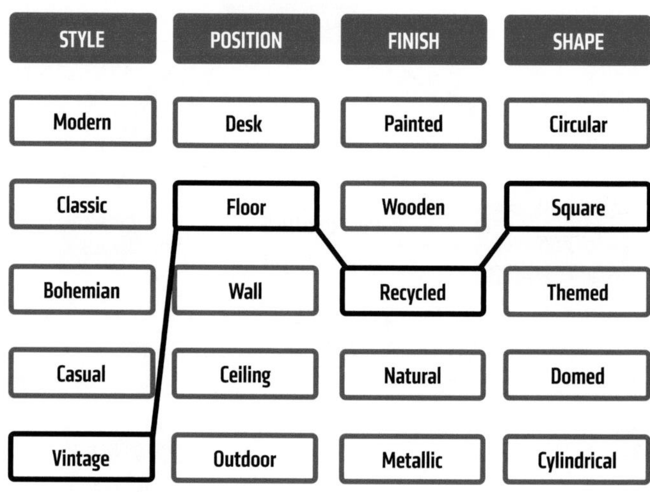

Name

This type of tool is elsewhere called: morphological analysis | da Vinci method | attribution matrix.

Purpose

The purpose is to allow almost unrestrained experimentation with the possibilities of connecting different variations, until a satisfactory permutation is arrived at.

Original morphological analysis for the Swiss bomb shelter, offering 2,304 possible solutions

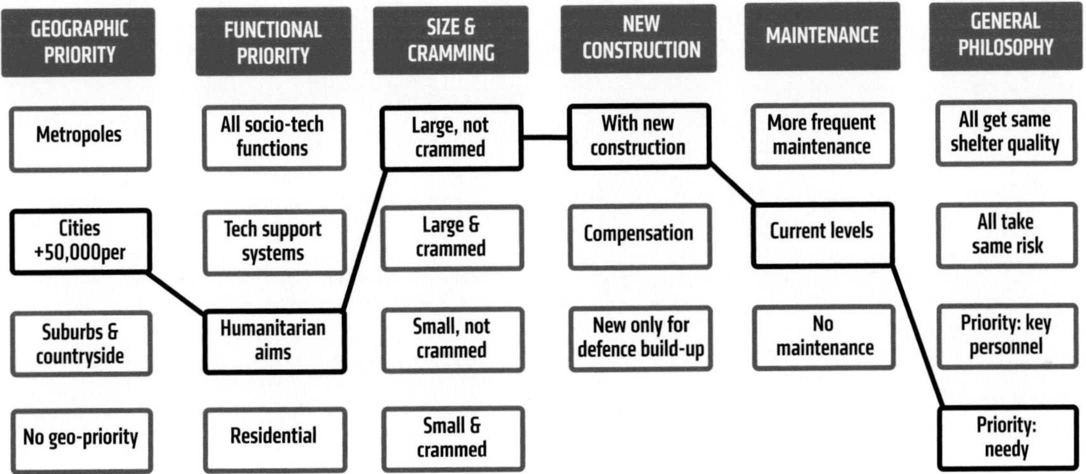

Fritz Zwicky

Morphological analysis is simply an ordered way of looking at things.

Zwicky, 1948

Michael Michalko

Creativity is paradoxical. To create, a person must have knowledge but forget the knowledge, must see unexpected connections in things but not have a mental disorder.

Michalko, 2011

Benefits

By displaying very many options in one's EXMF, working memory limitations are transcended. And any limiting beliefs about one's creativity are also demolished as new combinations are easily discovered.

Prompts

- What are the components that make up...?
- How many variations can you think of for each of these components?
- Force yourself to write down options you think are unwanted – at the moment.
- Have fun exploring all possible permutations.

2 WHAT? | CONTAINER: COMPARE

PURPOSE

Comparing and contrasting is the focus of these graphic organisers. They achieve this by identifying similarities and differences through a range of different spatial structures.

VOCABULARY

Each category of graphic organiser represents a type of reasoning. It is no surprise, then, that each has a list of associated words and phrases. It is useful to be aware of these words and provide them, when appropriate, to your students when discussing and explaining their organisers and transforming them into text.

---

unique | similar | similarity | different | differences | contrast | comparison | identical | shared | features | contrary | differences | in common | discrete | differing | whereas | same as | additionally | in parallel | likewise | however | nonetheless | just as | likewise | moreover | at the same time | despite that | meanwhile | nevertheless | unlike | conversely | even so | yet | alike | also | as opposed to | as well as | both | comparatively | different from | however | in comparison | in contrast | in the same way | just as | just like | less than | likewise | much as | on the other hand | opposite | similarity | on the contrary | despite this | apart from | conversely | whereas |

VENN DIAGRAM
82

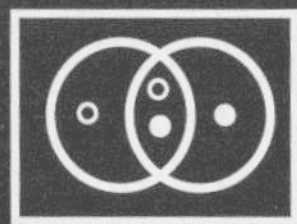

Set membership helps identify similarities and differences through shared and discrete boundary locations.

DOUBLE SPRAY
84

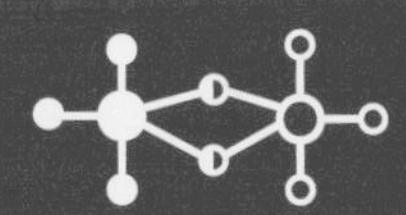

The meeting of two separate Spray Maps identifies similarities (joined in the middle) and differences (on the periphery).

MATRIX
86

Grouping characteristics in a matrix allows for identification of shared and dissimilar patterns across a number of topics.

FORCE FIELD ANALYSIS
88

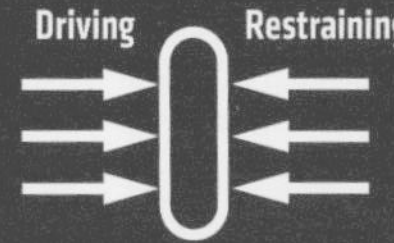

This helps separate influences that either support or restrain a plan for change, brought about by comparing each one.

SWOT ANALYSIS
90

A business tool that identifies and compares strengths, weaknesses, opportunities and threats (SWOT).

BRIDGE MAP
92

Used for analogies, this simple tool highlights a relationship pattern in order to provide the missing analogical pattern.

CONTINUUM
94

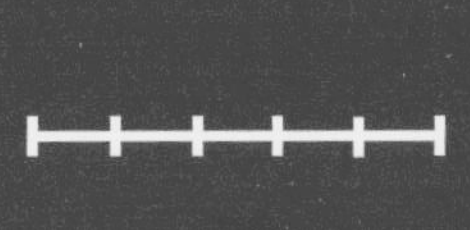

A simple graded line used to identify relative positions of different items, which involves their comparisons.

CROSSED CONTINUA
96

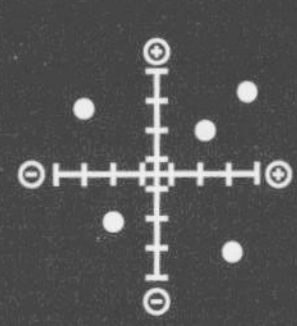

The same graded lines are used in a two-dimensional grid, allowing for more sophisticated comparisons of the subjects.

TYPE | **COMPARE**

VENN DIAGRAM

One of the oldest and most enduring of the organisers, the Venn Diagram is well known and used universally

The overlapping circles provide an instant sense of comparison, with shared and discrete attributes clearly delineated. In practice, however, students can make the process problematic by misconstruing the volume of the overlap as being representative of the degree or number of shared attributes.

Content-free Venn Diagram

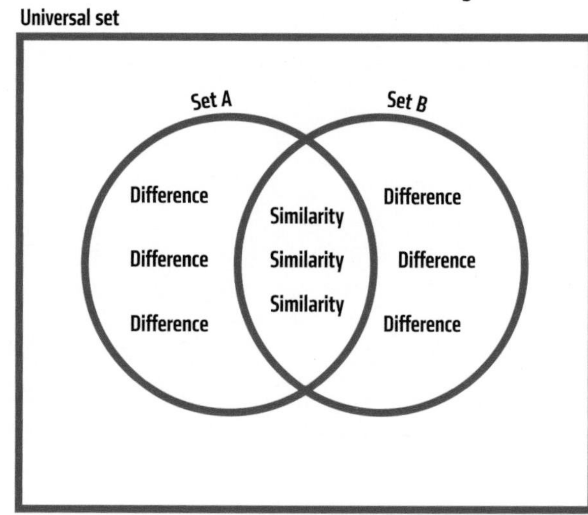

Name

While the term Venn Diagram seems to be universally adopted, there have since been several developments. One is the Edwards-Venn diagram, ingeniously designed to accommodate up to six overlapping sets.

Purpose

The purpose is to identify similarities and differences when comparing two items.

Venn Diagram of the Three Pigs story

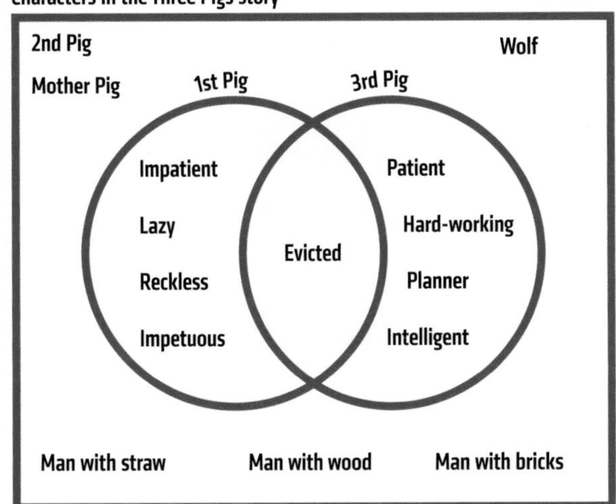

John Venn

We endeavour to employ only symmetrical figures, such as should not only be an aid to reasoning, through the sense of sight, but should also be to some extent elegant in themselves.

Venn, 1881

Benefits

Clarity on membership of a entity is paramount in establishing understanding. An awareness that concepts are framed by boundaries that determine the inclusion or exclusion of members is a firm foundation for more advanced thinking.

Prompts

- What do these two share in common?
- Which parts would you say are unique to each?
- What should in the middle sector, belonging to both?
- Could you argue for your choices, your placements?

TYPE | **COMPARE**

DOUBLE SPRAY

An alternative to the Venn Diagram for comparisons

By creating two separate Spray Maps first, comparison is greatly aided. Bringing them together results in explicit links to the central similarities and external differences. The equivalent process with a Venn Diagram can be problematic as students often misconstrue the degree of physical overlap as being representative of the degree of similarity.

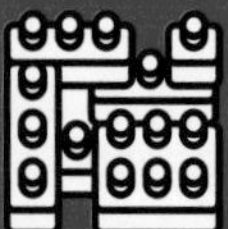

Construction instruction

Page 154

Content-free Double Spray

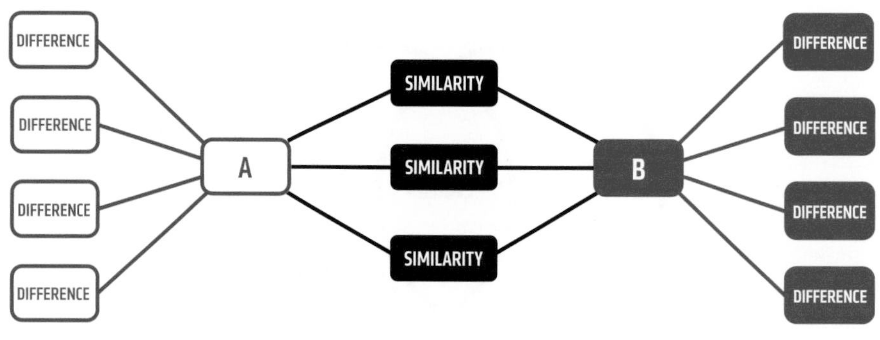

Name

This type of tool is elsewhere called: double bubble | double bubble map.

Purpose

The aim is to identify the similarities and differences between two separate entities. To avoid the overload of identifying the attributes of the two items and, at the same time, analysing their commonalities and variances, create separate Spray Maps to divide the task into more manageable chunks.

Double Spray of Jack & Pinocchio

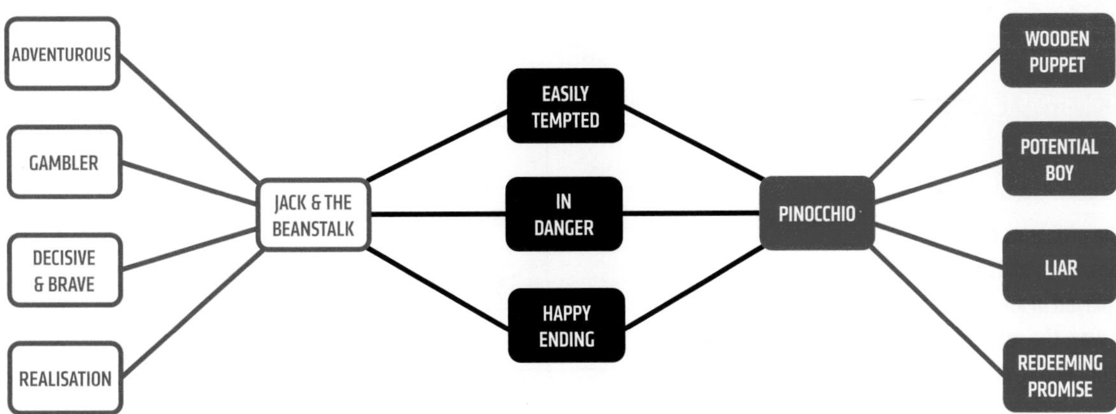

Benefits

Comparison is probably the most fundamental of all our learning strategies. It is often implicit in much of our explanations. Making it overt – and splitting it into two phases – gives students clarity and provides a stepping-stone to a greater grasp of abstract conceptions.

Prompts

- In what ways are these similar?
- What qualities do these two items share?
- How exactly are they different?
- In what specific ways do these two differ?

Bethany Rittle-Johnson

Comparison is a powerful learning process that has been leveraged to improve learning in a variety of domains.

Rittle-Johnson & Star, 2011

TYPE | **COMPARE**

MATRIX

The common table or matrix displays all the elements of your analysis for easy reading

A Matrix solves many of the problems of working memory limitations. With all the components of a topic displayed in an organised and methodical way, the reader can focus on reading and connecting various combinations.

Content-free Matrix

	Characteristic | **A**	Characteristic | **B**	Characteristic | **C**	Characteristic | **D**	Characteristic | **E**	Characteristic | **F**
Subject **1**	■			■	■	
Subject **2**		■	■		■	
Subject **3**	■		■			■
Subject **4**		■		■		■
Subject **5**	■		■		■	
Subject **6**			■	■	■	

Name

This type of tool is elsewhere called: table | gathering grid | decision chart | compare and contrast chart.

Purpose

The main purpose is to display multiple potential connections in order to make comparisons. This happens through either vertical or horizontal reading. The paper "How to study a matrix" (Jairam et al, 2012) shows that horizontal reading (rows) and a horizontal-and-vertical approach work best.

Matrix for the Three Pigs story

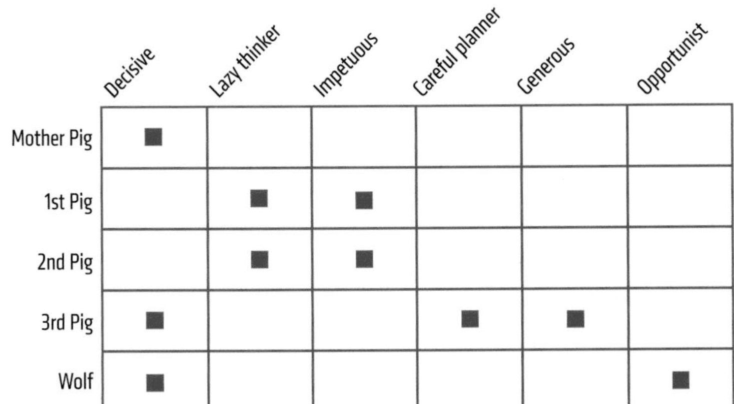

	Decisive	Lazy thinker	Impetuous	Careful planner	Generous	Opportunist
Mother Pig	■					
1st Pig		■	■			
2nd Pig		■	■			
3rd Pig	■			■	■	
Wolf	■					■

Dharmananda Jairam

This study investigated how best to study a matrix. Fifty-three participants studied a matrix topically (1 column at a time), categorically (1 row at a time), or in a unified way (all at once). Results revealed that categorical and unified study produced higher: (a) performance on relationship and fact tests, (b) study material satisfaction, and (c) associative strategy use than topical study.

Jairam et al, 2012

Benefits

Comparing a wide range of attributes across multiple elements could easily overwhelm working memory. The tabulation of this information avoids this danger. Direct comparisons are easily made and judgements formed because of this visual facility.

Prompts

- Looking across the rows, can you see where there are similarities and where there are differences?
- If you scan the matrix, can you spot any patterns?
- After reading across a row, look above and below to see if you can notice any similarities.
- Which rows stand out as being different? Why?

TYPE | **COMPARE**

FORCE FIELD ANALYSIS

A rational attempt to judge the potential of a proposed plan and avoid many unconscious biases

Invented in the 1940s by Kurt Lewin, the Force Field Analysis was used for his work as a social psychologist. Now it is used as a way for organisations and individuals to assess the viability of a proposed plan. Identifying the supportive and resistant forces – and maybe weighting them – allows for an objective analysis of the possibility of success.

Construction instruction
Page 156

Content-free Force Field Analysis

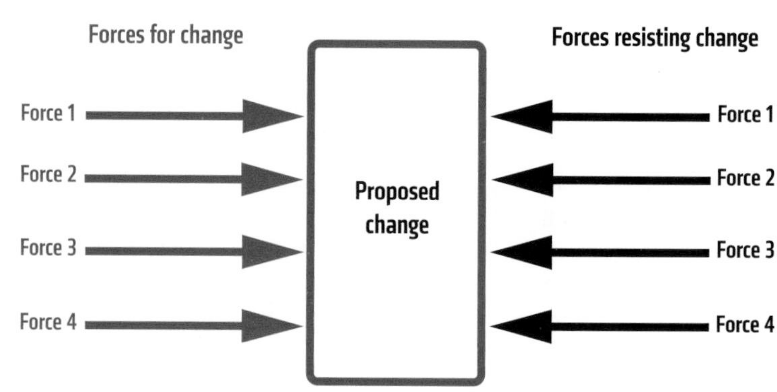

Name

This type of tool is not known by any other name.

Purpose

To investigate and weigh up the conflicting influences that aid or hinder a proposed plan for change. Weighting the influences – or forces – demands a justification of the judgement that further considers any heretofore unexamined biases.

Force Field Analysis of Pinocchio's character development

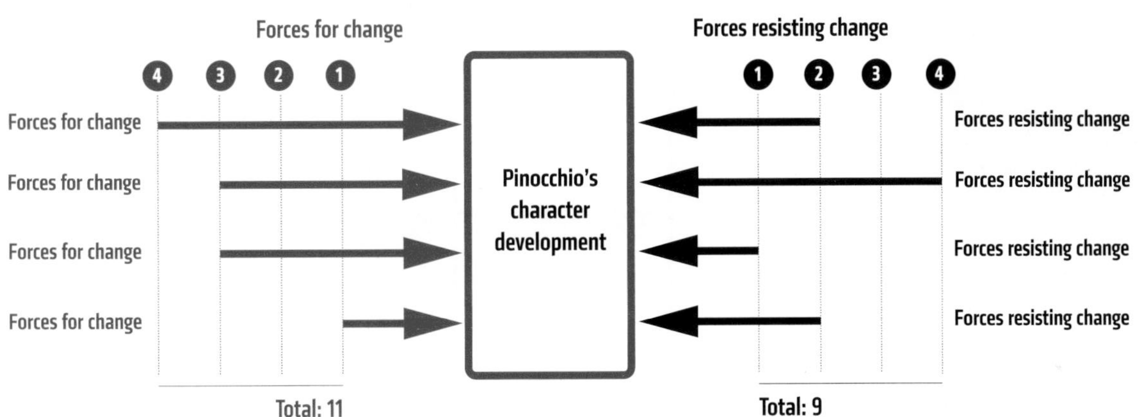

Kurt Lewin

Our behaviour is purposeful; we live in a psychological reality or life space that includes not only those parts of our physical and social environment to us but also imagined states that do not currently exist.

Lewin, 1948

Benefits

The format and its process give opportunities to be systematic in examining the balance of powers. Noting down the opposing forces to change favours a rational and less emotive response. At the same time, it tempers an overly optimistic – even naive – estimation of an easy accomplishment.

Prompts

- What might make this plan difficult to achieve?
- What aspect of the plan has the wind behind it?
- What makes the plan likely to succeed?
- If you were to say how powerful these forces are, could you rank them from 1 to 4?

TYPE | **COMPARE**

SWOT ANALYSIS

A corporate tool to analyse the dynamics – both positive and negative – that determine success

Invented and developed by Albert Humphrey in the corporate sector, this tool soon became familiar to all Fortune 500 companies. And then equally familiar in therapeutic and coaching contexts. The honesty demanded in compiling the four quadrants forced a level of reflection and candour often missing in self-deceiving optimism.

Content-free SWOT Analysis

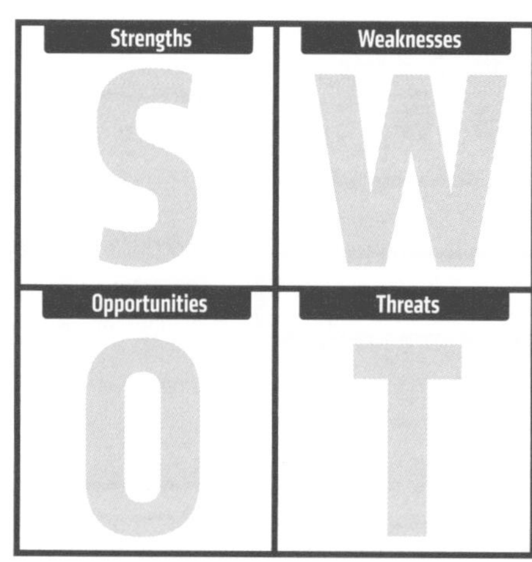

Name

This tool is associated with its cousin, SVOR (strengths, vulnerabilities, opportunities, risks). It is also known as WOTS-UP and TOWS.

Purpose

The aim is to peel back the layers of a company in order to arrive at better decision-making. Similarly so for individuals, the framework demands levels of honesty that are sometimes uncomfortable.

SWOT Analysis for Pinocchio

Strengths	Weaknesses
■ Promise	■ Liar ■ Easily tempted
Opportunities	**Threats**
■ Potential boy status	■ Manipulative ■ Offers

Albert Humphrey

By sorting the SWOT issues into the 6 planning categories one can delineate short and long-term priorities. This approach captures the collective agreement and commitment of those who will ultimately have to do the work of meeting the objectives.

Humphrey, 2005

Benefits

As with all attempts to achieve a rational, objective and comprehensive perspective, the benefits are better thinking and decision-making.

Prompts

- If another person were to sum up your strengths, what might they say?
- If a neutral observer were to list your weaknesses, what might they note down?
- What could possibly threaten your success?
- Do you see any opportunities in this picture?

TYPE | **COMPARE**

BRIDGE MAP

An approach to support analogies and analogical thinking

For some students, simply placing two related items near each other triggers an understanding of their relationship. This understanding can then be transferred to the following parallel structure.

Content-free Bridge Map

Name

We are not aware of alternative names for this map.

Purpose

The core purpose is to visually represent a relationship – and only the relationship – in order to foster an understanding that can be transferred into creating another example of the same relationship.

Bridge Map examples

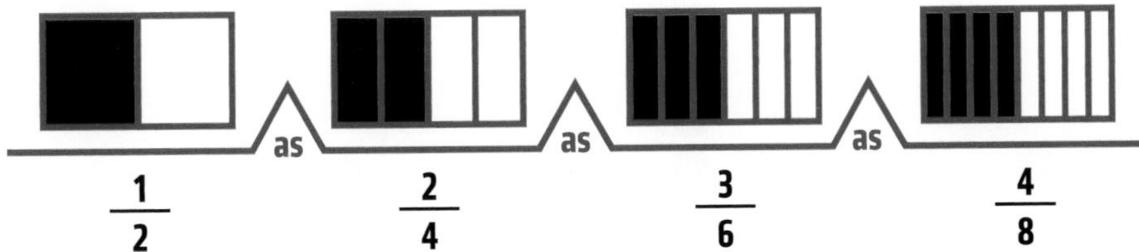

Benefits

Being able to identify relationships allows for nuanced comparisons. Bridge Maps enable a level of analysis that penetrates beneath the surface details.

Prompts

- How do these two items relate to each other?
- In what ways is this relationship shown elsewhere?
- How many examples of this relationship can you find?

David Hyerle

A bridge map for seeing analogies may be extended horizontally or vertically to bridge a concept analogically and extend to form a metaphor with multiple levels of relationships.

Hyerle, 1996

TYPE | **COMPARE**

CONTINUUM

A simple graphic to fill in and calibrate the gaps between two opposite ends of a spectrum

More nuanced judgements can be encouraged when students place items along a Continuum. The calibration of the line can be at different scales.

Content-free Continuum

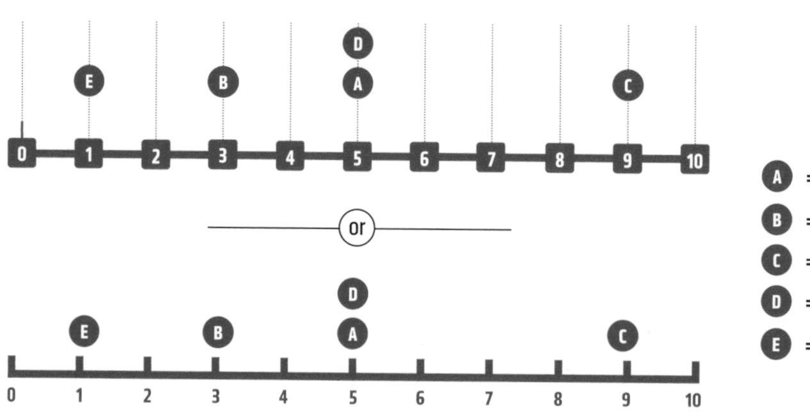

Name

We know of no alternative name for this tool.

Purpose

By having a graded, calibrated line between two opposites, choices by default become more considered than simply opting for either end of the continuum.

Continuum for the Three Pigs story

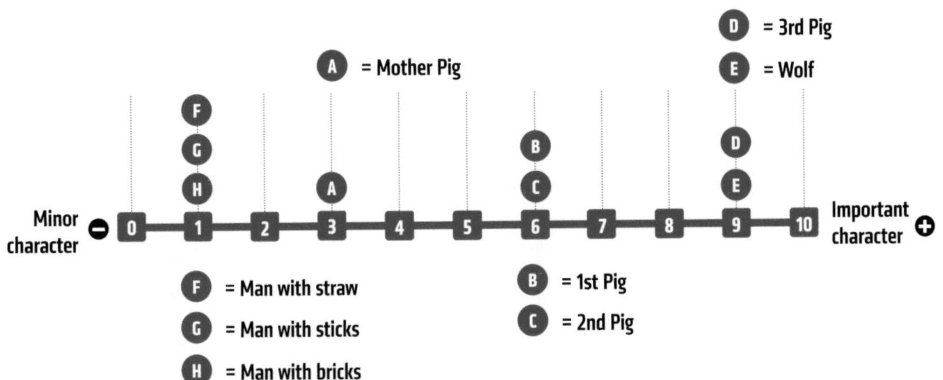

Benefits

Students are forced to think of evidence and examples with which to justify their judgements. This moves them away from either/or thinking.

Prompts

- What makes you think that is the correct place?
- With what are you comparing this placement?
- What would qualify as a position further along the line?

Stephen Jay Gould

We inhabit a complex world. Some boundaries are sharp and permit clean and definite distinctions. But nature also includes continua that cannot be neatly parceled into two piles of unambiguous yeses and noes.

Gould, 2006

TYPE | **COMPARE**

CROSSED CONTINUA

A mechanism with which to plot judgements on a 2D canvas

While a Continuum transcends the polarised views of two extremes, it can nonetheless sometimes be limited in depth. Crossing two continua, however, instantly demands finer judgements and produces a richer picture of the subjects under scrutiny.

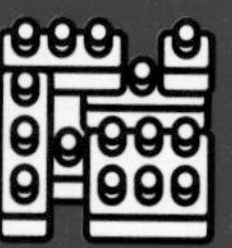

Construction instruction
Page 158

Content-free Crossed Continua

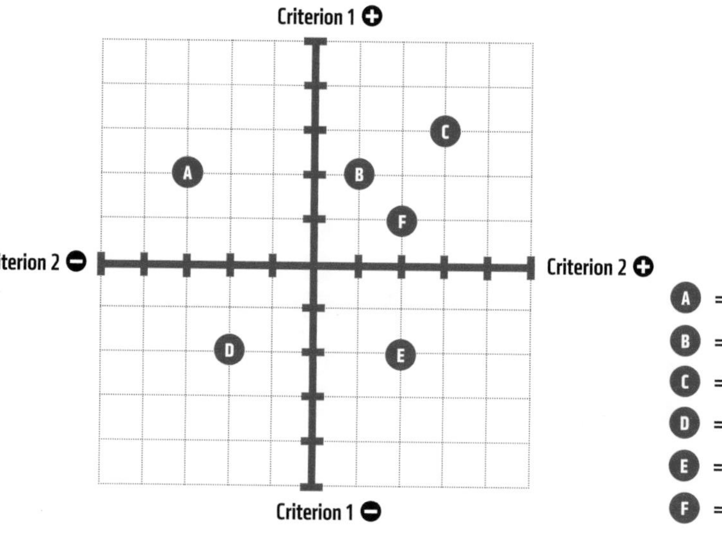

Name

This type of tool is elsewhere called: priorities grid (as it is often used in business time-management contexts).

Purpose

The aim is to produce a deeper evaluation of the topics under question. Crossing two continua triggers a more evaluative response.

Crossed Continua for the Three Pigs story

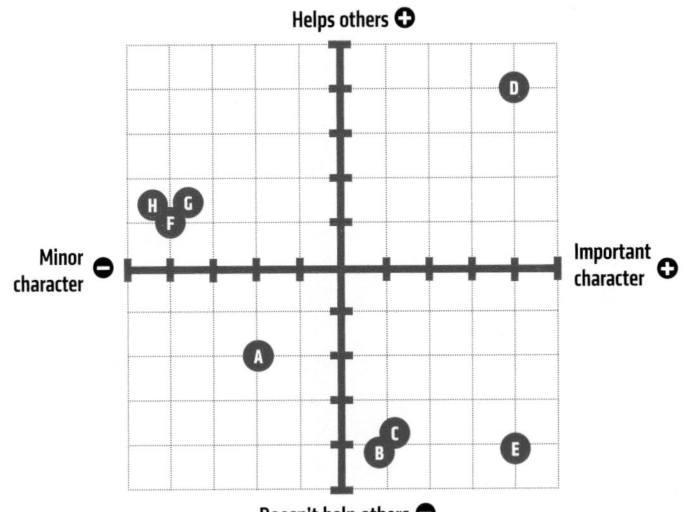

A = Mother Pig
B = 1st Pig
C = 2nd Pig
D = 3rd Pig
E = Wolf
F = Man with straw
G = Man with sticks
H = Man with bricks

Geoff Petty

Continua can be crossed to represent two independent criteria.

Petty, 2006

Benefits

By seeing the positions of the topics spread around the grid created by the Crossed Continua, viewers get an instant picture of their relative evaluations. They benefit from more than one perspective. By creating a Crossed Continua, students are encouraged to develop more nuanced, rounded judgements.

Prompts

- Take one continuum in turn.
- In the second continuum, try not to be influenced by the first one.
- Step back, so to speak, from the plotting and decide if the placements represent your opinion.
- Return and adjust if needed.

2 WHAT? | PATH: SEQUENCE

PURPOSE

Untangling the past into an objective sequence, or planning for a series of actions in order to accomplish a project, all require a set of tools. Sequence organisers do this in a variety of ways and for different purposes.

VOCABULARY

Each category of graphic organiser represents a type of reasoning. It is no surprise, then, that each has a list of associated words and phrases. It is useful to be aware of these words and provide them, when appropriate, to your students when discussing and explaining their organisers and transforming them into text.

---

before | earlier | previously | formerly | preceding | until that time | in advance | starting with | in the first place | at the onset | before all else | originally | initially | to begin | next | after | subsequently | later | henceforth | in turn | following | next step | phase | stage | cyclical | sometimes | every so often | on occasion | intermittently | concatenation | seldomly | rarely | periodically | at times | finally | to finish | penultimately | lastly | at last | to conclude | in conclusion | ultimately | in the end | at the same time as | concurrently | immediately | meanwhile | not long after | preceding | recently | whenever | eventually | to start | frequently | sporadically | to follow |

TIME LINE
100

Plotting past events – or future projects – into a chronological order needs just a simple line to represent the passage of time.

FLOW CHART
102

Used to establish a chain of events for either past or future processes, the Flow Chart is most people's favoured tool.

FLOW SPRAY
104

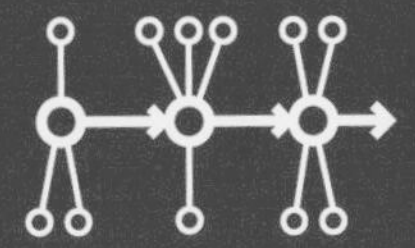

When the individual events of a process are numerous, a Flow Spray chunks them into coherent units that contain the details.

CYCLE
106

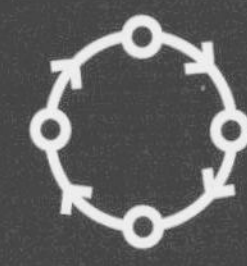

Some processes revolve into circular patterns, creating a cycle, best seen as a reoccurring Flow Chart.

CYCLE SPRAY
108

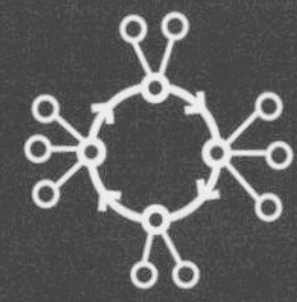

As with a Flow Spray, a Cycle Spray chunks up the steps into larger phases in order to better accommodate the details.

STORY BOARD
110

Mostly used for planning future narratives, a Story Board can be thought of as a purely pictorial Flow Chart.

GANTT CHART
112

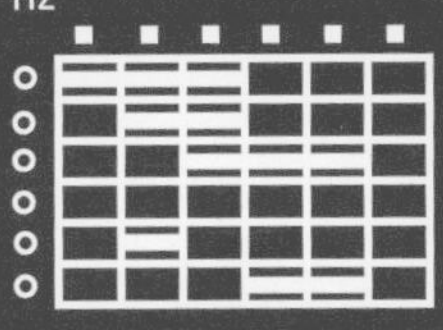

A planning tool that specifies tasks to be completed in which order, by whom, by when and if any dependencies are involved.

SWIM LANES
114

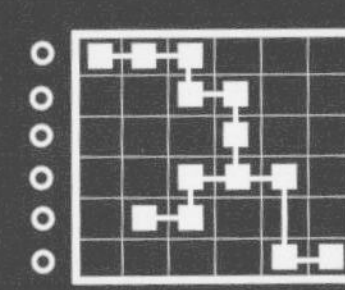

This is a type of Flow Chart that is organised around people with a focus on dependencies – how actions depend on prior ones.

TYPE | **SEQUENCE**

TIME LINE

A diagram to show the correct sequence of events calibrated along a Time Line

From historians to TV cops, the Time Line helps shape understanding of the past and aids its explanation. Arranging events in their order of occurrence in time is the science of chronology.

Content-free Time Line

Event A	Event B	Event C	Event D	Event E	Event F	Event G	Event H	Event I	Event J	Event K
Date | time | phase	Date | time | phase	Date | time | phase	Date | time | phase	Date | time | phase	Date | time | phase	Date | time | phase	Date | time | phase	Date | time | phase	Date | time | phase	Date | time | phase

Name

We are not aware that this diagram is known by any other name.

Purpose

Although similar to a Flow Chart, a Time Line attaches dates, or times, to the sequence of episodes. Establishing this accuracy becomes the platform from which later investigations into possible causal relationships can take place – the temporal before the causal.

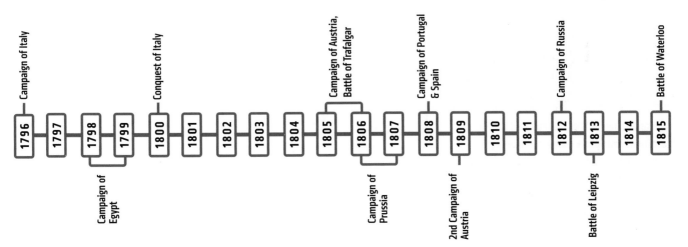

Time Line for Napoleon's military campaigns

1796 — Campaign of Italy
1797
1798–1799 — Campaign of Egypt
1800 — Conquest of Italy
1801
1802
1803
1804
1805–1806 — Campaign of Austria, Battle of Trafalgar
1806–1807 — Campaign of Prussia
1808 — Campaign of Portugal & Spain
1809 — 2nd Campaign of Austria
1810
1811
1812 — Campaign of Russia
1813 — Battle of Leipzig
1814
1815 — Battle of Waterloo

Benefits

Temporal relations — what happened, when — can be difficult to identify in some texts. Removing the syntax and complex language can help, if only temporarily, to establish a Time Line. Doing this moves the often abstract into a concrete, and visual, format.

Prompts

- Examine the topic under question and from that establish the scope of the Time Line.
- Next, decide on the time markers — the calibration.
- Study the topic and extract the events you want to be included.
- Plot the events in their correct sequence in alignment with their timing, in coordination with the Time Line.

Joseph Scaliger

In 1583, began the science of chronology.

Richards, 1998

TYPE | **SEQUENCE**

FLOW CHART

A diagram that identifies a sequence of actions joined together by arrows

Content-free Flow Chart

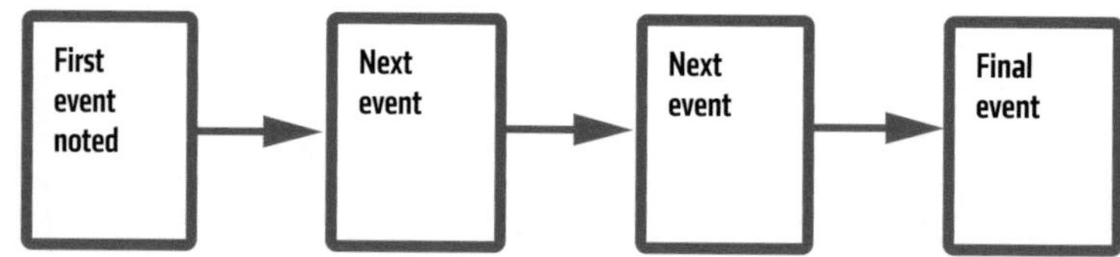

Frank and Lillian Gilbreth formulated the Flow Chart for industrial purposes of efficiency, as with many such diagrams. This organiser has since been used in a great many other contexts and for different purposes. There are few topics in which a series of actions can't be sequenced for better understanding.

Construction instruction
Page 160

Name

This type of tool is almost universally known as a Flow Chart, but you may also encounter these terms: event chains | plot diagrams | flow maps | sequence charts.

Purpose

The purpose is simple enough: to identify a sequence of events that has either taken place or will take place.

Flow Chart for Little Red Riding Hood story

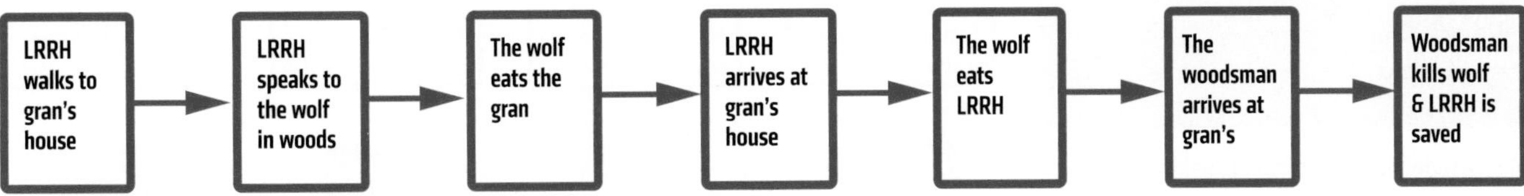
LRRH walks to gran's house
LRRH speaks to the wolf in woods
The wolf eats the gran
LRRH arrives at gran's house
The wolf eats LRRH
The woodsman arrives at gran's
Woodsman kills wolf & LRRH is saved

Benefits

Establishing the correct sequence of events greatly aids clarity of thinking and accuracy of conclusions in a number of different subjects. For future events, a Flow Chart focuses the mind on the preparation necessary to ensure all the events take place effectively.

Prompts

- What was the initial event?
- Are you going to order all the tiny events, or group them into larger units?
- Collect the events under question before putting them into a sequence.

Frank Gilbreth   Lillian Gilbreth

Motion Study is a means to permanent and practical waste elimination – hence a prerequisite to efficient preparedness that shall be adequate, constructive and accumulative.

Gilbreth & Gilbreth, 1917

TYPE | **SEQUENCE**

FLOW SPRAY

A chunked Flow Chart, reducing the number of episodes and connecting any component parts

Most students benefit from breaking down events into smaller segments. Yet that risks overloading them with too much unstructured information. Chunking events into larger episodes is a solution that also offers the opportunity to create clusters of subordinate details around each episode.

Construction instruction

Page 162

Content-free Flow Spray

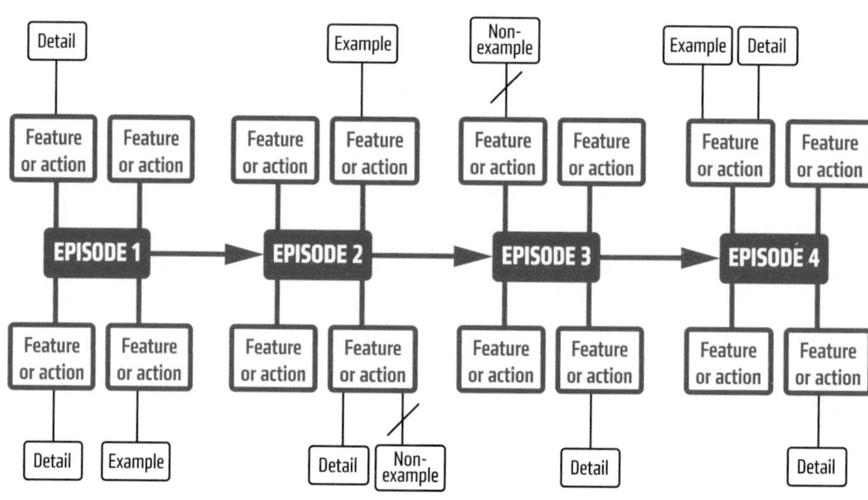

Name

This type of tool is elsewhere called: episodic cluster | flow bubble.

Purpose

As with all chunking, the aim is to reduce cognitive load and also, by the same mechanism, create meaning. Chunking isn't arbitrary: it imposes meaningful boundaries around key events or collections of smaller episodes. These mini maps are then the centre for the collection of smaller events, details and examples.

Flow Spray for Snow White story

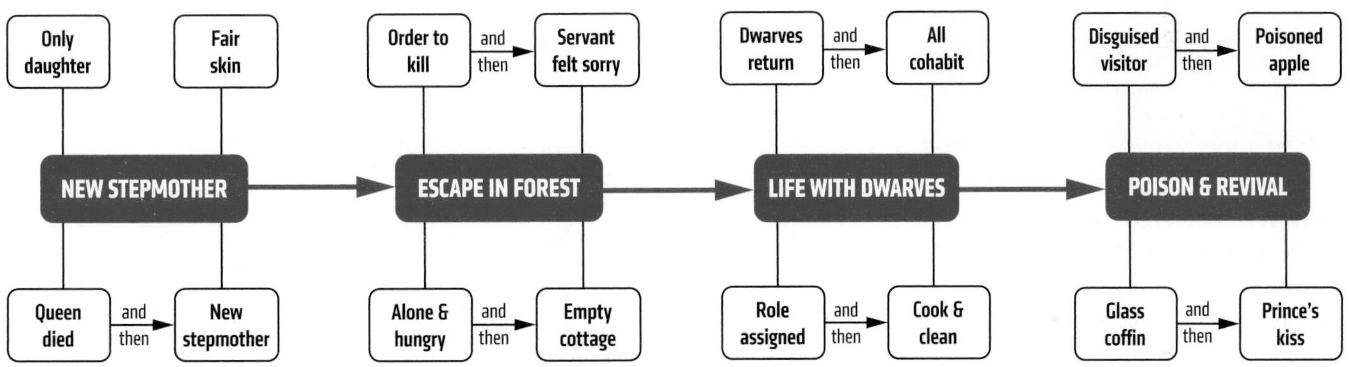

Benefits

Flow Sprays offer the cognitive benefits of both the big picture and the details – i.e. zooming out and zooming in, offering the experience of seeing both the wood and the trees. Students learn that time can be manipulated in order to better understand what happened. Or, in reverse, to better plan for what they want to happen.

Prompts

- How could you group these actions into, say, four major episodes?
- What details do you think link naturally to these episodes, so they become meaningful to a reader?
- What examples could you attach to add meaning?
- What non-examples are there that could consolidate understanding and avoid any misunderstandings?

Robert Pehrsson

Clusters often form part of episodic organizers. In most cases each episode ordinarily becomes an action cluster describing the episode, sometimes involving both static descriptions and time sequences.

Pehrsson & Denner, 1989

TYPE | **SEQUENCE**

CYCLE

The linear structure for time or processes invariably leads to the Cycle diagram

A Cycle is a model that, in effect, distorts reality, as nothing reverses time in the way that this diagram suggests. Nonetheless, a pattern of returning to a similar stage in a process can be depicted effectively with a Cycle diagram.

Content-free Cycle

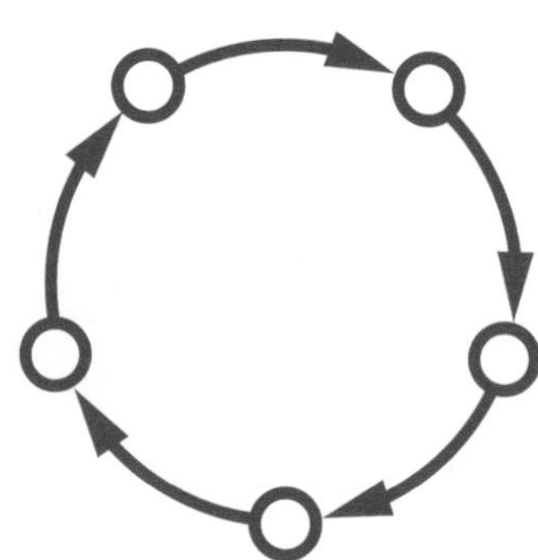

Name

This type of tool is nearly always known as a Cycle, but is sometimes also called: cycle chart | cycle map.

Purpose

As the title explains, the purpose is to depict a cyclical pattern that repeats itself. While the West views time as a linear phenomenon, it also recognises the presence of repeating patterns of actions or stages. The Cycle clearly shows this and its details.

Cycle for the Buddhist Wheel of Life

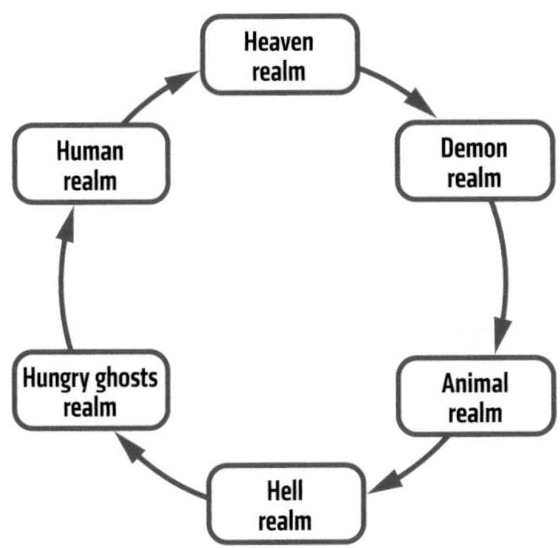

Mark Johnson

Most fundamentally, a cycle is a temporal circle. This circular representation of a cycle is inadequate insofar as it fails to include a salient dimension in our experience of cycles, namely their climactic structure.

Johnson, 1987

Benefits

A Cycle can be used by teachers to help students recognise that a cyclical pattern, while not visible, can be identified, captured and communicated. A Cycle is a perfect – and simple – way to achieve this.

Prompts

- Capture all the actions or stages of the Cycle in a list or a simple collection of sticky notes first.
- Once captured, place the notes in a circular pattern, checking on the sequence as you progress.
- Finally, ensure the repetitive nature of the Cycle is apparent, makes sense and accords with reality.

TYPE | **SEQUENCE**

CYCLE SPRAY

A Cycle diagram that accommodates either smaller, chunked-down actions or attributes of them – or both

While the idea of chunking *things* is now well known and applied, less so is the practice of chunking time, or events. A Cycle Spray does this in the same manner as a Flow Spray. Grouping actions into larger events, and attaching their details, gives a clearer picture, allowing for zooming out and zooming in.

Content-free Cycle Spray

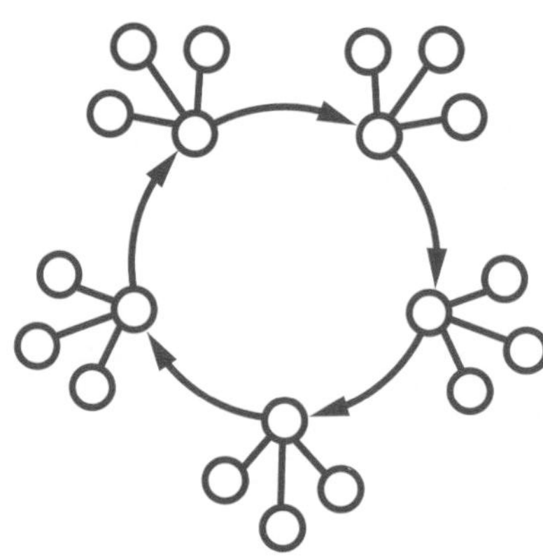

Name

This type of tool is rarely used elsewhere and, consequently, has no other names.

Purpose

The Cycle Spray allows teachers to zoom out on a big-picture view of a cycle. After establishing the notion in students' minds, teachers can then zoom in on the details while avoiding an overload.

Cycle Spray for the Buddhist Wheel of Life

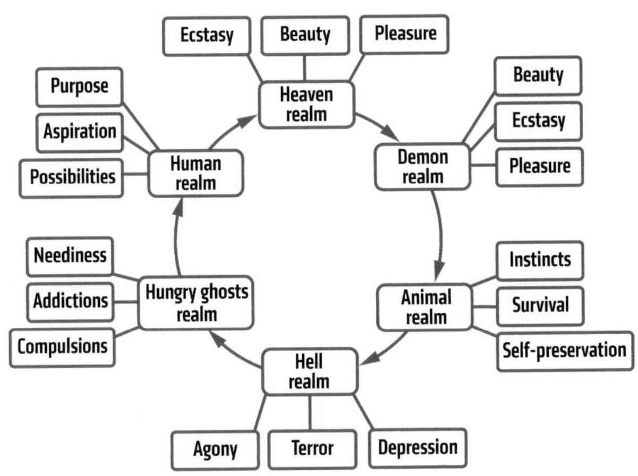

Benefits

Using a Cycle Spray helps teachers avoid the dilemma of either giving students a confusing and overwhelming amount of detail, or limiting how much is taught. With a Cycle Spray, teachers can transcend this problem and show the main cycle dynamic as a structural framework with which to attach the details.

Prompts

- How could you group all the actions into fewer numbers of large stages or phases?
- Attach the smaller actions to their respective stages.
- Discover the attributes or features of these stages and link them accordingly.

Jordi Fonollosa

By segmenting a sequence of elements into blocks, or chunks, information becomes easier to retain and recall in the correct order.

Fonollosa et al, 2015

TYPE | **SEQUENCE**

STORY BOARD

The film and animation key tool is also used in classrooms to clarify the development of plot

When young pupils are shown a Story Board, they get a navigational device to help them better assimilate the details within the topic. Whether teacher- or pupil-created, a Story Board is inclusive, ensuring everyone gets the gist.

Content-free Story Board

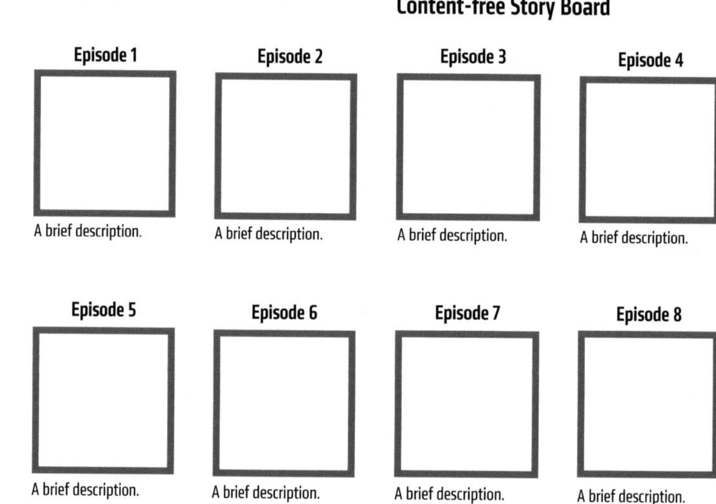

Name

This diagram is universally known as a Story Board.

Purpose

A Story Board can help pupils navigate and remember a story. Or indeed any narrative, whether fiction or non-fiction. If created by the pupils, a Story Board can support them to experiment with the development of an idea.

Story Board for Little Red Riding Hood story

Episode 1

LRRH lived in a cottage with her mother

Episode 2

Mother asked her to deliver food to Grandma

Episode 3

LRRH walked through a forest to the cottage

Episode 4

In the forest lived a woodcutter & wolf

Episode 5

The wolf followed LRRH & ran to Grandma's

Episode 6

The wolf ate Grandma & disguised as her in bed

Episode 7

LRRH arrived and went straight in

Episode 8

The woodcutter killed the wolf

Benefits

A Story Board marries creativity with organisation. It demands that attention is given to the audience's intended responses by focusing on the plot. Above all, it translates imagination into a concrete, visual story.

Prompts

- Don't focus on the artwork, more on the ideas.
- Sketch on sticky notes and experiment, moving them around until you arrive at the most satisfactory order.
- What are the main scenes?
- Think about creating some cliffhanger moments.
- Read out the story to a friend, to see if it makes sense to them and grabs their interest.

Pie Corbett

Each story has a story map or board as a visual reminder.

Corbett, 2008

TYPE | **SEQUENCE**

GANTT CHART

Identifying dependencies – based on who is doing what and when – is the major focus of a Gantt Chart

Invented in the early 20th century by Henry Gantt, this diagram for planning was part of that era's focus on industrial efficiency. Since, it has been adopted by a wide variety of different professions in pursuit of different goals – but with the idea of more efficiently *getting things done*.

Content-free Gantt Chart

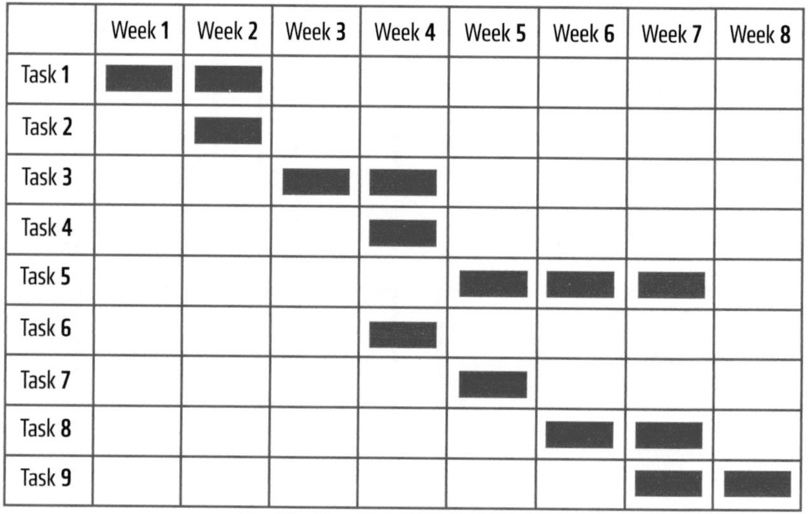

	Week **1**	Week **2**	Week **3**	Week **4**	Week **5**	Week **6**	Week **7**	Week **8**
Task **1**	■	■						
Task **2**		■						
Task **3**			■	■				
Task **4**				■				
Task **5**					■	■	■	
Task **6**				■				
Task **7**					■			
Task **8**						■	■	
Task **9**							■	■

Name

This type of tool is sometimes elsewhere called: planning table | task schedule.

Purpose

Gantt Charts are designed to align and coordinate effort and resources in the most economical way. Essentially, that entails identifying what are called *dependencies*. These are relationships in which one task cannot start without the completion of a prior one. Of course, equally, some tasks can start independently of another's completion.

Gantt Chart for a cooking a fried breakfast

Tasks | Minutes	1	2	3	4	5	6	7	8	9	10	11	12	13	14	15
Prepare ingredients	■	■													
Prepare equipment		■													
Get crockery, utensils			■	■											
Warm plates				■	■	■	■	■	■	■	■	■	■	■	
Grill bacon					■	■	■	■	■	■	■	■	■	■	
Grill tomatoes						■	■	■	■	■	■	■	■	■	
Lay table							■								
Fry sausages							■	■	■	■	■	■	■		
Toast bread												■	■	■	
Fry eggs													■	■	
Serve															■

Benefits

Identifying and communicating such a level of detail is difficult in text alone. The parsing of tasks via a Gantt Chart is very practical and makes achievement very possible. The diagram can also be used to re-engineer projects and analyse where inefficiencies, even breakdowns, took place and how they might have been avoided.

Prompts

- Put all your tasks on sticky notes first.
- Arrange the matrix with calendar, people and tasks so that the notes can be temporarily placed on it.
- Re-order the task notes until you, and your team, are confident the most efficient sequence has been achieved.

Henry Gantt

The greatest problem before engineers and managers today is the economical utilization of labor.

Gantt, 1919

TYPE | **SEQUENCE**

SWIM LANES

A method of plotting a plan of action for who does what and in what order

First developed in the 1940s as multi-channel Flow Charts, the term *swim lane* was coined by Geary Rummler and Alan Brache in the 1990s. As with other industrial planning tools, Swim Lanes can used, when appropriate, to analyse a sequence of events in the past, in fiction or indeed non-fiction.

Content-free Swim Lanes

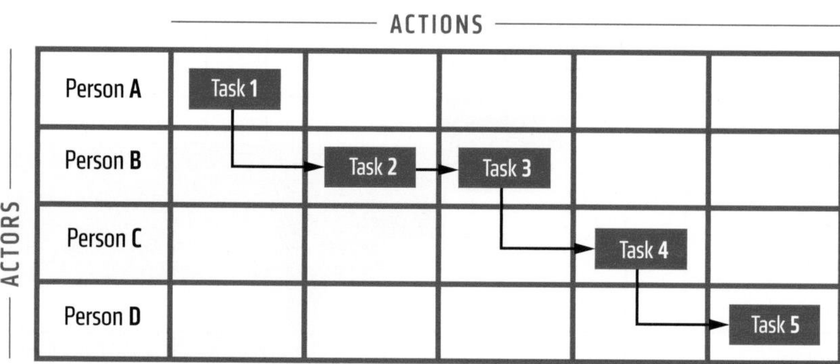

Name

This type of organiser is also called, on occasion: swim lane diagram | functional band | Rummler-Brache diagram | swimming lanes process mapping.

Purpose

The aim is to add what is missing from a Flow Chart – the details of the operation. Of particular importance are the tracking and accountability of each actor, whose responsibilities feature in their lane. Actions are ordered in terms of dependencies and parallel timings.

Swim Lanes for the Three Pigs story

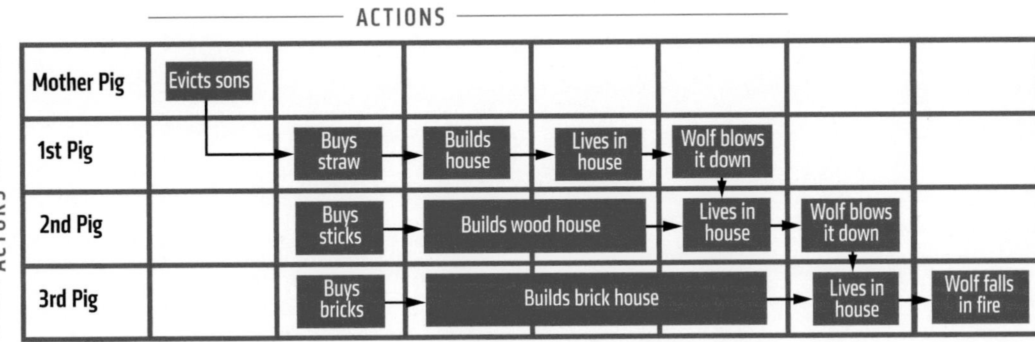

ACTIONS
ACTORS
Mother Pig
Evicts sons
1st Pig
Buys straw
Builds house
Lives in house
Wolf blows it down
2nd Pig
Buys sticks
Builds wood house
Lives in house
Wolf blows it down
3rd Pig
Buys bricks
Builds brick house
Lives in house
Wolf falls in fire

Gary Rummler

Design for 80 percent and build separate paths for exceptions. Eliminate or reduce the impact of low-value steps. Simplify complex steps. Combine simple steps ... Use parallel paths wherever possible

Rummler & Brache, 1990

Benefits

Personal responsibilities and their dependencies are visually apparent. This clarity of plotting develops a shared understanding.

Prompts

- Who are the actors in the plan?
- What are the actions needed for success?
- Assign each actor a lane and start to plot the actions for the most efficient execution.
- Identify the dependencies and try to exploit any potential parallel actions.

② WHAT? | PATH: CAUSE & EFFECT

PURPOSE

Probably the most challenging of the four types of organiser, these tools demand a clear link from condition to consequence. Causal thinking can often be built upon the knowledge developed by the use of other types of organisers.

VOCABULARY

Each category of graphic organiser represents a type of reasoning. It is no surprise, then, that each has a list of associated words and phrases. It is useful to be aware of these words and provide them, when appropriate, to your students when discussing and explaining their organisers and transforming them into text.

---

because | due to | reasons | fault | catalyst | causes | inevitable | influence | repercussions | consequences | effects | contributing factors | implications | preconditions | provoke | prompt | as a consequence | therefore | accordingly | due to the fact | on account of | therefore | whereas | since | so | determines | hence | stems from | bring about | leads to | in conclusion | as a result of | is caused by | thus | owing to | as a consequence of | leads to | contributes to | which caused | brings about | comes from | due to the fact that | owing to | thereby | provokes | originates | so that | resultingly | prompted by | contributing factor of |

FISHBONE DIAGRAM
118

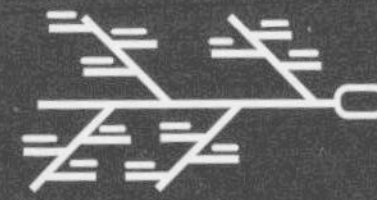

A structure that shows a pattern of causes; rather than a straight line of causation. Can be used to show weighted judgements too.

INPUT-OUTPUT DIAGRAM
120

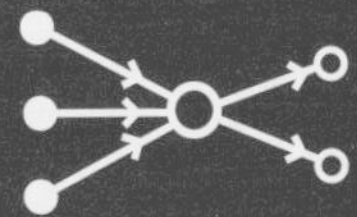

A simple and useful tool to start pupils thinking about cause and effect with a clear input-output dynamic.

RELATIONS DIAGRAM
122

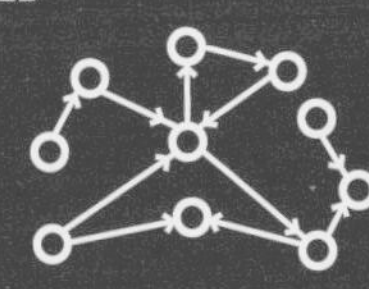

A more complex arrangement of causal links and associations, resulting in a pattern that shows the major lines of influence.

CRITICAL PATH ANALYSIS
124

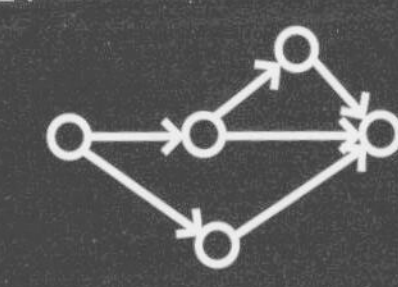

A planning tool in which dependencies are made explicit, informing the possible and quickest route to completion.

ALGORITHM
126

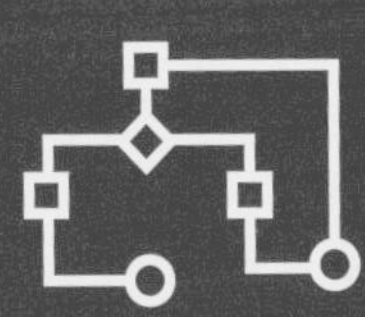

A decision-making tool that makes explicit the choices and their subsequent routes. Can be used for planning or analysis.

FLOWSCAPE
128

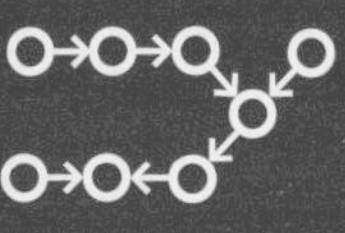

A specific process designed to reveal the lines of influence in softer, values-driven perceptions of particular situations.

CONSEQUENCES MAP
130

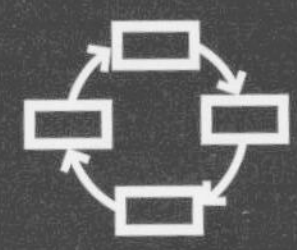

A systems thinking tool that reveals the differences between a reinforcing and a balancing loop.

TYPE | **CAUSE & EFFECT**

FISHBONE DIAGRAM

Also known as the Ishikawa industrial tool, this diagram analyses the causal factors behind a given situation

Created by Kaoru Ishikawa as part of the Japanese *total quality* movement, this organiser is used in education to analyse situations in subjects ranging from history to literature. It displays the categories of causal factors very clearly. In its advanced formats, it can also depict grades of influence.

Construction instruction
Page 164

Content-free Fishbone Diagram

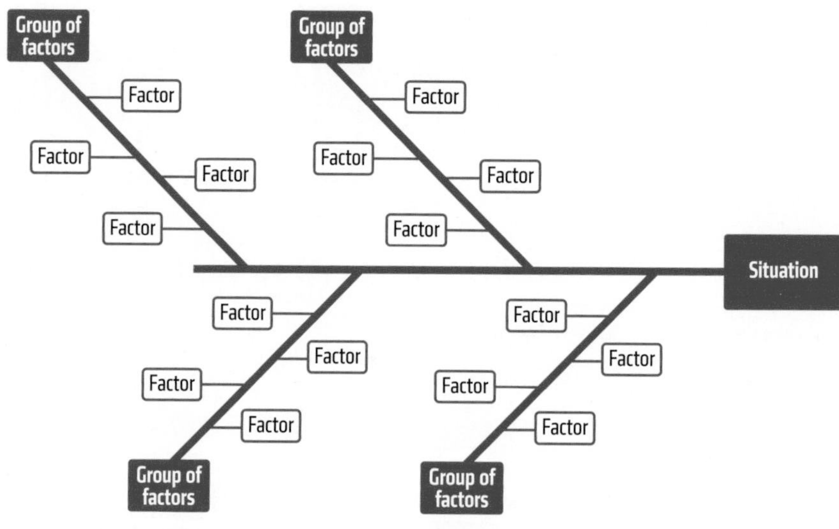

Name

In industry, this type of tool is called the Ishikawa diagram.

Purpose

The intention of this diagram is to analyse the causes – or at least the forces of influence – behind a particular situation. Instead of merely listing them, grouping them and placing them in this format provides a clarity of perception, helping to foster a deeper understanding and insight.

Fishbone Diagram for the Cinderella story

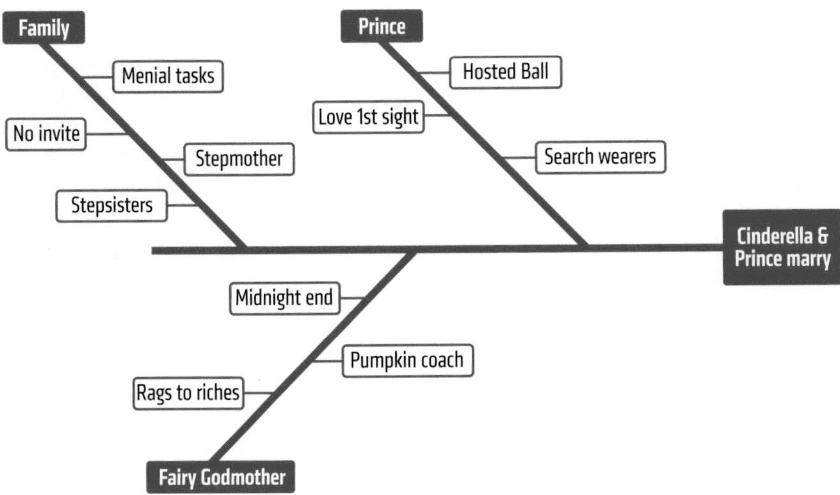

Benefits

Analysis can often appear rather abstract for some students. Manipulating the collection of causes into meaningful patterns develops mirror schemas in students' minds. Causal relationships seem to come alive, triggering conjecture and discussion on the causal relationships proposed.

Prompts

- Collect all the possible causes first.
- See if you notice any common features and group them together.
- Find an appropriate title for these four-or-so groups.
- Place the groups and their titles in the fashion you see in a Fishbone Diagram.

Kaoru Ishikawa

Think of at least four factors which influence your problem. See if a shift on one of these causes can give you a different effect to explore.

TYPE | **CAUSE & EFFECT**

INPUT-OUTPUT DIAGRAM

A tool to plot the dynamics of causal factors and their effects, pivoting around a hinge event

Introduced to the world by Wassily Leontief in his 1966 book *Input-Output Economics*, this tool has since been used in a vast array of contexts. The simplicity of its diagrammatic format is its great strength, allowing for clarity of perception of the relationship between causes and effects.

Content-free Input-Output Diagram

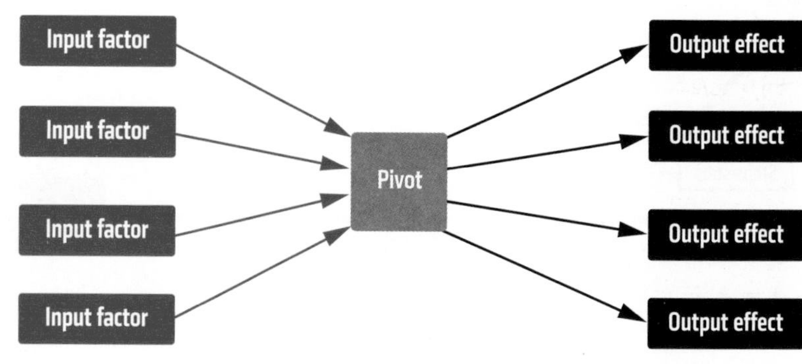

Construction instruction
Page 166

Name

This type of tool is elsewhere called:
SIPOC (suppliers, inputs, process, outputs and customers) | IPO (input, process, output).

Purpose

The purpose – as is plainly depicted – is to identify the causal link between a range of different causes (or influences) and their consequences. This relationship pivots around a significant event.

Input-Output Diagram for environmental management

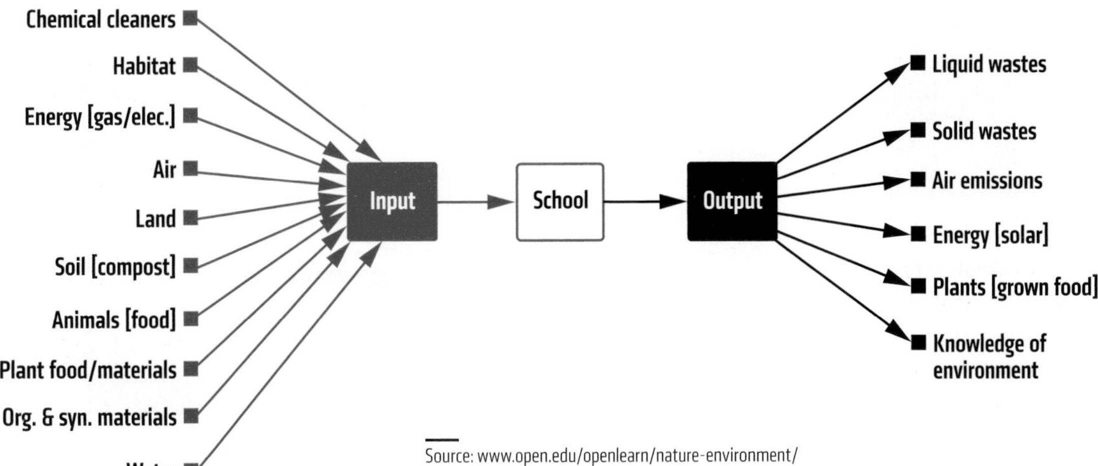

Source: www.open.edu/openlearn/nature-environment/environmental-management-and-organisations/content-section-11.1

Benefits

Developing students' thinking beyond a simple billiard ball metaphor can be difficult. Instead of designating a single event most close in time to an event as the cause, and its single subsequent reaction the effect, an Input-Output Diagram presents a more complex picture, yet retains a simplicity of depiction.

Prompts

- Identify the pivotal event under question.
- Capture all the possible causal (input) factors.
- Evaluate this collection and retain the valid factors.
- Capture all the possible effect (output) factors.
- Evaluate this collection and retain the valid factors.
- Construct the diagram based on the above.

Wassily Leontief

The most elaborate statistical investigation furnishes nothing but shapeless heaps of raw material, utterly useless unless fitted into a firm theoretical framework.

Leontief, 1937

TYPE | **CAUSE & EFFECT**

RELATIONS DIAGRAM

An interrelationship diagram that aims to reveal the complex nature of relationships beneath a situation

Developed by Peter Chen for data analysis, this diagram helps us avoid our inclination to search for a single source behind a situation. This tool is designed to make evident the nature of these complex causal relationships. Depicting this network of influences can help identify the best points of action.

Content-free Relations Diagram

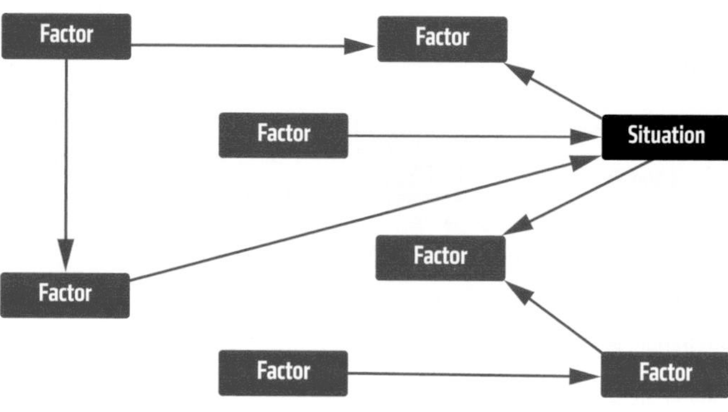

Construction instruction
Page 168

Name

This type of tool is elsewhere called: interrelationships diagram | network diagram | relations digraph | entity relationship model | spaghetti diagram.

Purpose

The intention behind constructing such a diagram is to make evident the multi-layered network of influences that lead to a particular situation. By recognising this, effective analysis and subsequent action is more likely to take place.

Relations Diagram for the Third Pig's safe home

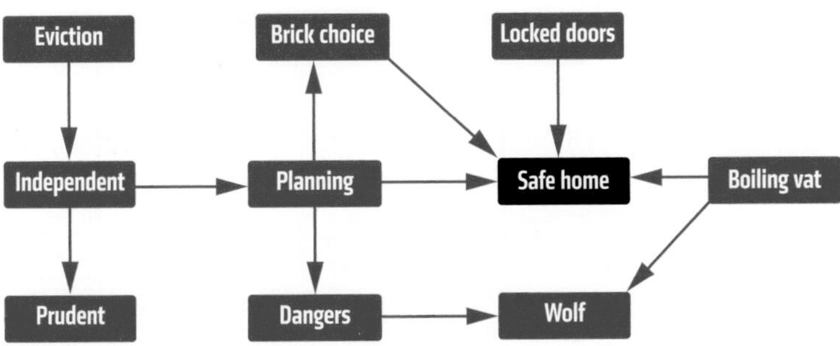

Peter Chen

Entities and relationships are a natural way to organize physical things as well as information ... The ER concept is the basic fundamental principle for conceptual modeling. It has been with us since thousands of years ago and will be with us for many years to come.

Chen, 2004

Benefits

As ever with this category of graphic organisers, the aim is to develop students' thinking beyond a simplistic billiard ball metaphor of causality. By requiring them to construct such a diagram —and discuss the links — students soon realise the complexity behind the seemingly simple surface features of situations.

Prompts

- Collect all possible factors in the establishment of the given situation.
- Organise them (sticky notes work very well) in arrangements where you can avoid crossed arrows.
- Link up the factors when they have a relationship of some sort or another.

TYPE | **CAUSE & EFFECT**

CRITICAL PATH ANALYSIS

A pre-organisational format with which to capture ideas

This tool is similar to Eliyahu Goldratt's theory of constraints, explained in his 1984 book *The Goal*. It focuses on identifying the constraints that will be the determining factors in the success of a project. Often that entails calculating the length of time a component takes to be completed. The organiser helps map the best route through this complexity.

A simple Critical Path Analysis

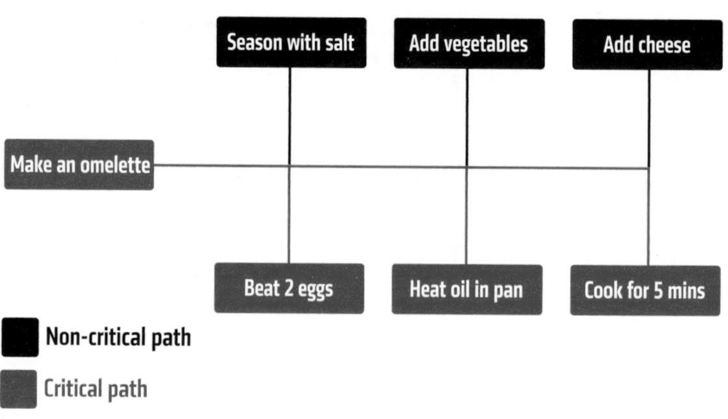

Source: www.workamajig.com/blog/critical-path-method

Name

This type of tool is elsewhere called: critical path method.

Purpose

The aim is to identify the most efficient route through the various components that combine to make a project. This *critical path* entails knowing, and avoiding, any unnecessary delays while certain tasks are completed. Arranging tasks in a sequence that avoids non-essential dependencies speeds up the process.

Critical Path Analysis for the Three Pigs story

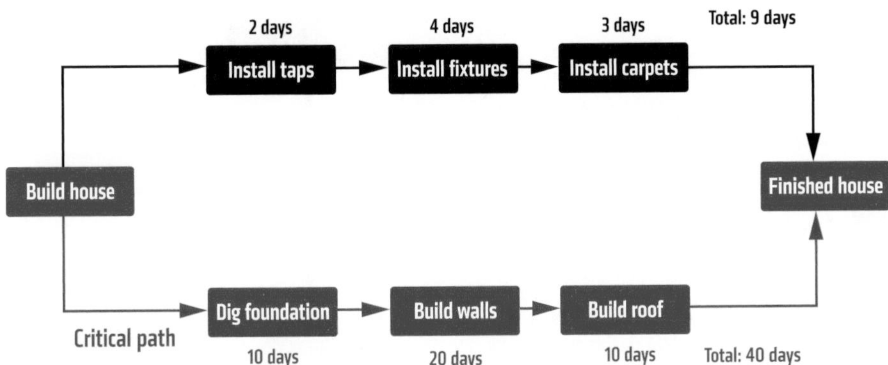

Management must be able to collect pertinent information to accomplish the following tasks:

1. **To form a basis for prediction and planning**
2. **To evaluate alternative plans for accomplishing the objective**
3. **To check progress against current plans and objectives, and**
4. **To form a basis for obtaining the facts so that decisions can be made and the job can be done.**

Kelley & Walker, 1959

Benefits

Using this diagram teaches students how to analyse the parts of a process. It gives them a tool with which they can investigate the clearest and quickest path to success.

Prompts

- What are all the tasks to be completed?
- How long will each one take?
- Which tasks can start only once another has finished (dependencies)?
- Arrange the tasks in the sequence that totals the least amount of time.

TYPE | **CAUSE & EFFECT**

ALGORITHM

Life can be viewed as a series of decisions. These decisions and actions can be called algorithms

The term *algorithm* is a corruption of the name of the Persian mathematician Muhammad ibn Mūsā al-Khwārizmī (c.780-850). While usually associated with mathematics, an Algorithm can be applied to any decision-making process, whether it involves creating something or solving a problem. A recipe is an Algorithm.

Name

This type of tool is elsewhere called:
decision tree | programme | recipe.

Purpose

The purpose of an Algorithm is to capture and communicate the steps and decisions involved in a successfully executed process, so that it is instructive and can be repeated.

Benefits

Teachers can capture their explanations and instructions in an Algorithm in order to demystify the execution of a process. Making this process clear and non-transient (that is to say, not just spoken) gives students independence. The Algorithm can be a constantly available reference. Some have called it a virtual teacher because of this constant support.

Prompts

- What are all the actions in this process?
- Can you put them in the most effective sequence?
- What decisions have to be made, and at what points, in order to travel through the process most smoothly?

Simple Algorithm

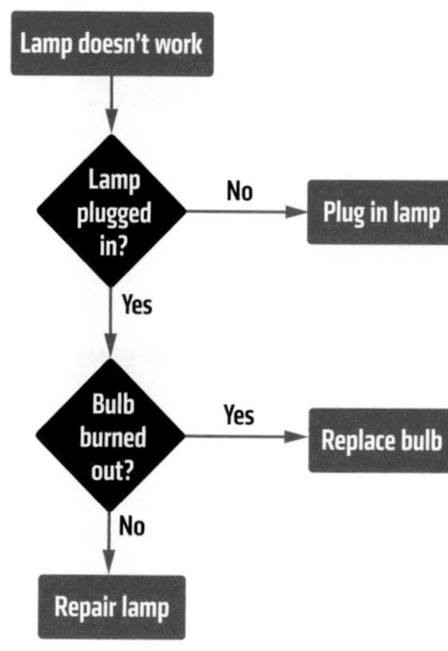

Algorithm for the Three Pigs story

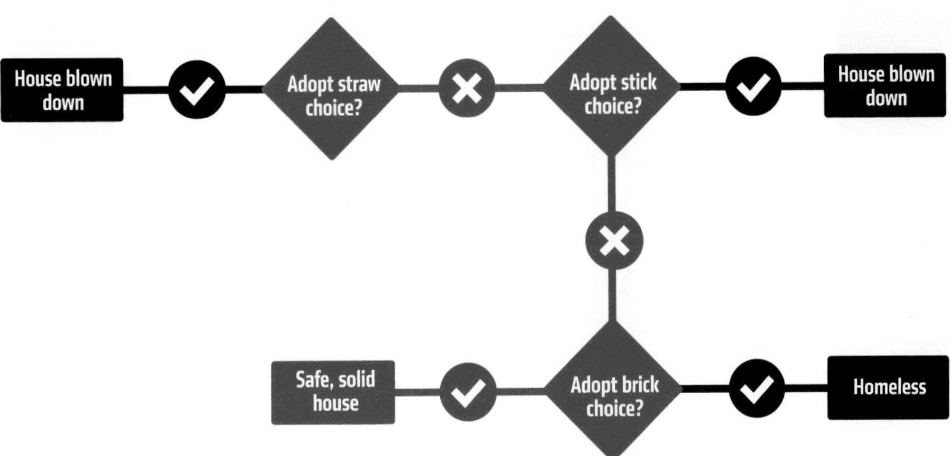

Muhammad ibn Mūsā al-Khwārizmī

That fondness for science, ... that affability and condescension which God shows to the learned, that promptitude with which he protects and supports them in the elucidation of obscurities and in the removal of difficulties, has encouraged me to compose a short work on calculating by al-jabr and al-muqābala, confining it to what is easiest and most useful in arithmetic.

Al-Khwārizmī, 2009

TYPE | **CAUSE & EFFECT**

FLOWSCAPE

An ingenious way to figure out how our perceptions knit together to form a point of view – an opinion

This tool is designed to help people recognise their network of perceptions in order to better address problems. It is included here as an additional strategy to analyse various streams of influence in any given situation. For history or literature, it may offer an alternative method to frame interpretations.

Construction instruction
Page 170

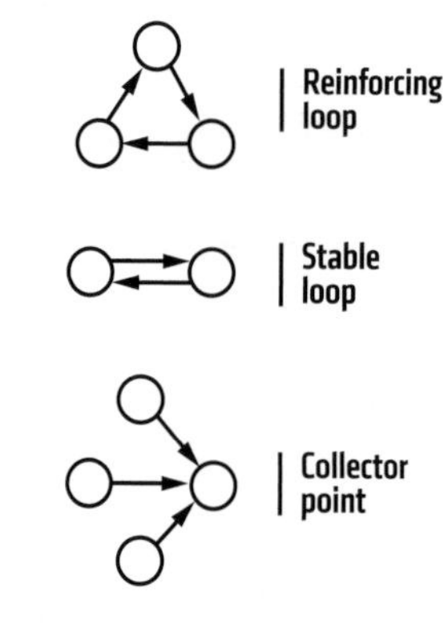

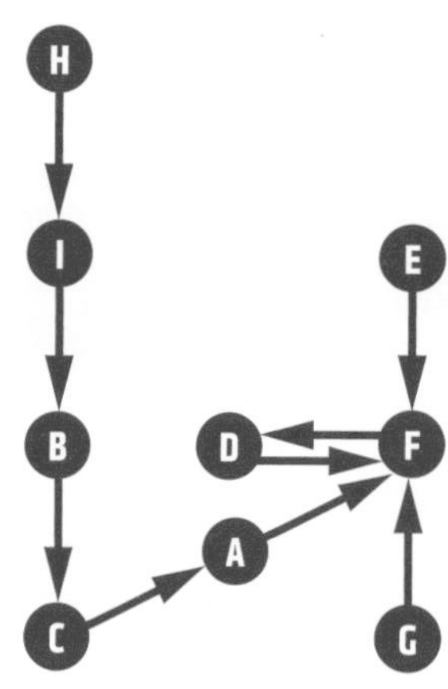

Name

While this tool may graphically resemble the Relations Diagram, its very specific method of construction makes it significantly different.

Purpose

The Flowscape is designed to uncover our usually subconscious responses and their interrelated lines of influence. Its graphic format reveals these major points of leverage.

Flowscape of the Third Pig's success

- **A** | **Eviction**
- **B** | **Self-regulation**
- **C** | **Planning**
- **D** | **Patience**
- **E** | **Courage**
- **F** | **Building skills**
- **G** | **Knowledge of danger**
- **H** | **Independent thinking**
- **I** | **Hunger**

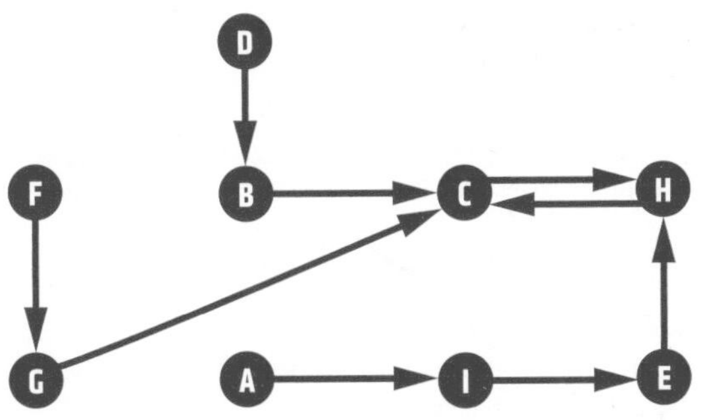

Edward de Bono

Can we get to look at our perceptions regarding any particular matter? Can we change perceptions – and if so, where do we start?

De Bono, 1993

Benefits

As analysis is such an important skill, any tool that aids its process is highly valuable and adds to students' repertoire of cognitive skills.

Prompts

- Think of the flow, or direction, from one item to another.
- Don't spend too much time deciding, as this tool is designed to uncover your *unconscious* perceptions.
- There is no correct configuration – it's meant to stimulate reflection on your triggers.

TYPE | **CAUSE & EFFECT**

CONSEQUENCES MAP

An organisational structure that maps the chain of consequences – often unforeseen – of design decisions

This design organiser forces the user to look ahead in order to imagine any possible negative consequences of seemingly objective or neutral decisions. Applied to behaviour management, it allows three-point communication to help the student anticipate the far-reaching effects of negative behaviour on their wellbeing.

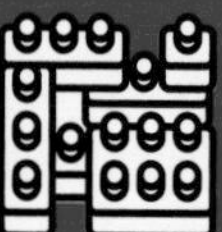

Construction instruction
Page 172

Name

We are not aware of an alternative name for this tool.

Purpose

As grand as this might sound, the Consequences Map helps the user be wiser than otherwise they would be. Its sole purpose is to look into the future in order to map out the chain of consequences that invariably accompanies both design decisions and behaviours.

Benefits

Using this tool regularly promises opportunities for students to consider a more thoughtful approach to their decision-making. It is a counter to impetuous, impulsive behaviour. It is also a mechanism for more thoughtful design.

Prompts

- What might your strategies be in order to attain your goal?
- What might happen as a result of your implementing your strategies?
- What might the problems be later on?

Content-free Consequences Map

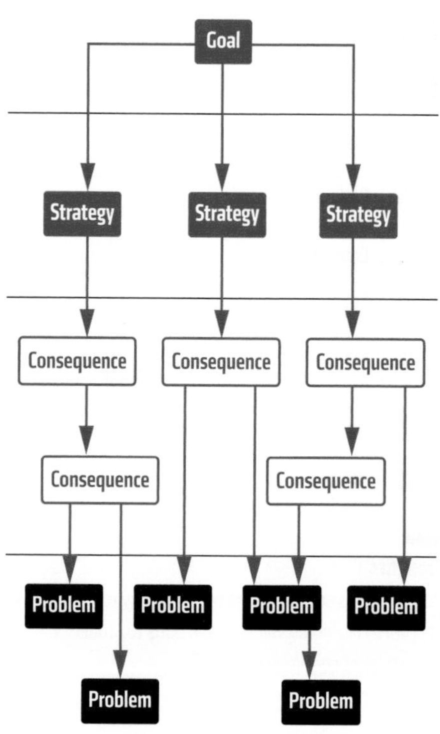

Consequences Map for a designing an urban railway

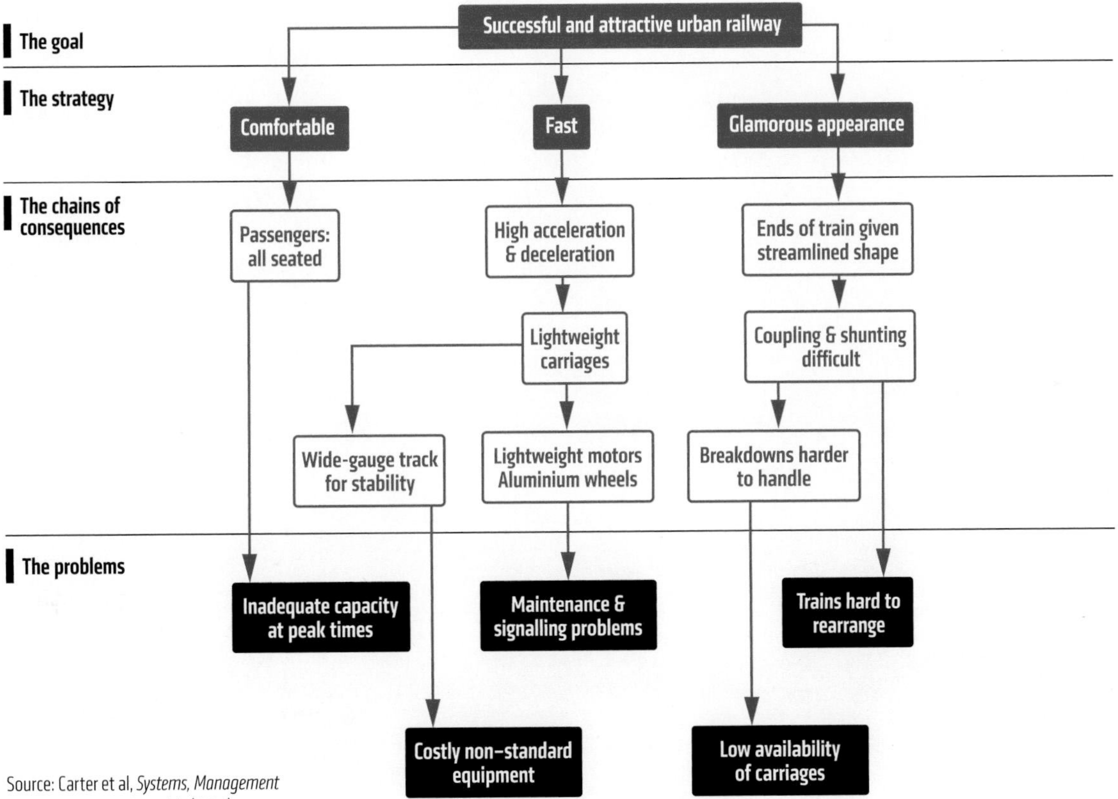

Source: Carter et al, *Systems, Management and Change: a graphic guide* (1984)

Pat Mirenda

Results indicated that the verbal contingency had no effect, whereas contingency mapping was related to immediate, dramatic, and sustained reductions in problem behavior and increases in alternative behavior.

Brown & Mirenda, 2006

Construction instructions for a selection of the graphic organisers in the previous chapter.

Chapters

CONTAINER: **CHUNK** 134	Spray Map 60 **Tree Diagram** 138	**Target Map** 134 **Mind Map** 140	Cluster 64 **Inductive Tower** 146	**Affinity Map** 136 **Concept Map** 148	Sets Map 68 **Idea Box** 152
CONTAINER: **COMPARE** 154	Venn Diagram 82 Bridge Map 92	**Double Spray** 154 Continuum 94	Matrix 86 **Crossed Continua** 158	**Force Field Analysis** 156	SWOT Analysis 90
PATH: **SEQUENCE** 160	Time Line 100 Story Board 110	**Flow Chart** 160 Gantt Chart 112	**Flow Spray** 162 Swim Lanes 114	Cycle 106	Cycle Spray 108
PATH: **CAUSE & EFFECT** 164	**Fishbone Diagram** 164 **Flowscape** 170	**Input-Output Diagram** 166 **Consequences Map** 172	**Relations Diagram** 168	Critical Path Analysis 124	Algorithm 126

TYPE | **CHUNK**

TARGET MAP

Clarifying the nature and boundary of the topic under question is time well spent for later development work

Establishing boundaries is essential. With no clarity on this, students can be working on misconceived notions. Setting out what is and is not included in the definition helps cement understanding. For that reason, in contrast to regular Target Maps, the external area is devoted to non-examples. Identifying what is not included helps define what is.

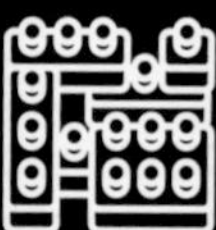

Construction instruction

1 | Capture the content

Purpose

Before any analytic thinking can take place, there has to be content. So this stage is all about creating material to work on. This is best achieved prior to any editing or analysis. Dividing these quite different modes of thinking is useful.

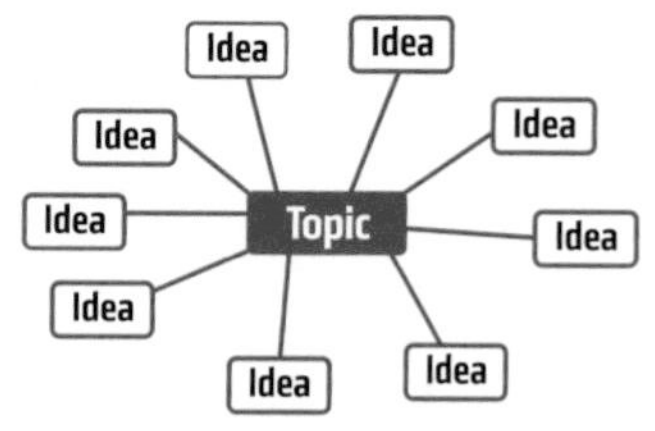

Action

Any method of idea capture will do. A list or a Spray Map can be used. The only issue with a list is that some sort of hierarchy is inevitably inferred by the students, if not implied by the teacher. The spatial nature of a Spray Map allows for the inclusion of new material as the words trigger more thoughts.

2 | Identify the non-relevant

Purpose

The objective here is to divide the relevant from the non-relevant. Or, in terms of direct instruction or variation theory, to divide the examples from the non-examples.

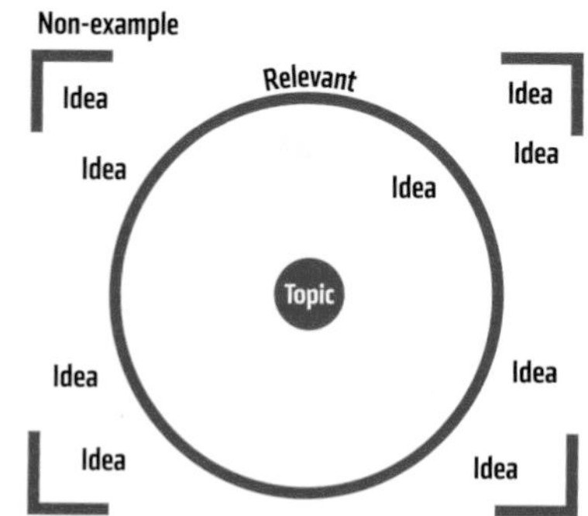

Action

Think of non-examples that are perhaps incorrectly thought of as examples – those near the boundary. The more you do this and question your students on why they are non-examples, the stronger their growing understanding of the topic under question will be.

3 | Add the relevant ideas

Purpose

Having established what is not relevant or accurate, students are now ready to add what they think is relevant content.

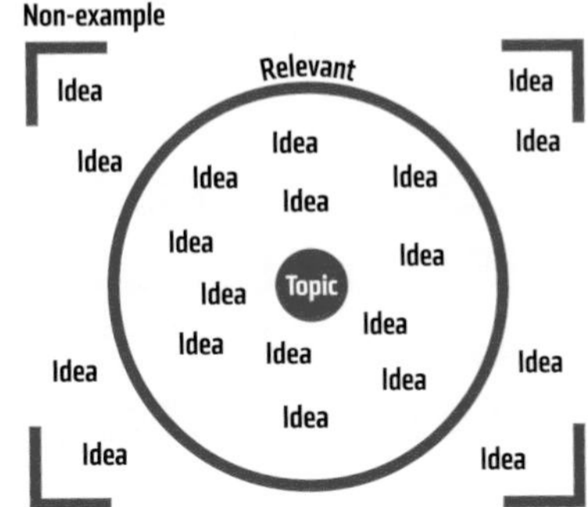

Action

Now, add the content that is relevant within the inner *relevant* circle. Continual contrast with the external non-examples will prove to be a constant source of clarification.

4 | Distinguish levels of relevancy

Purpose

If required, the next stage can be a refinement of the qualification *relevance*. An inner circle helps identify which are the most relevant ideas or facts of the topic.

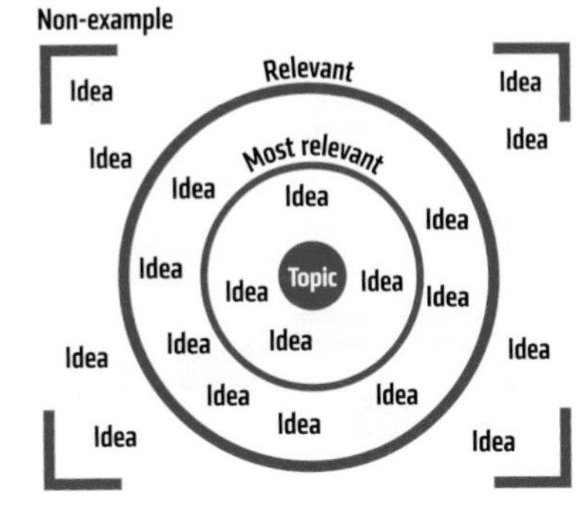

Action

Draw an inner circle and start to divide the content into two circles of relevance: relevant and most relevant.

5 | A completed Target Map

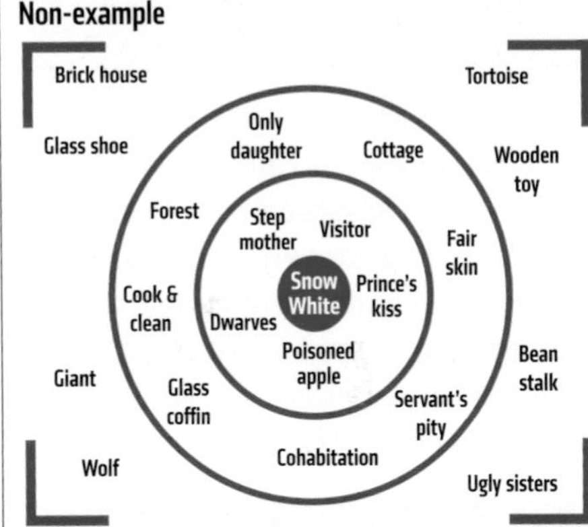

TYPE | **CHUNK**

AFFINITY MAP

Grouping — or generalising — is how we create meaning. This organiser offers a simple way to do this

Generalising is a natural process, but it is also often unconscious. From this lack of awareness, stereotypes are born. An Affinity Map makes the process explicit, as well as breaking it down into several discrete steps. Creating one with a partner, a group or a class establishes shared understanding. It is the mainstay of many professional workshops.

Construction instruction

1 | Collect the content

Purpose

The first job is to collect all the ideas you, your colleagues or your students have about the topic at hand. Contribute each item as a separate entity — there is no grouping at this stage.

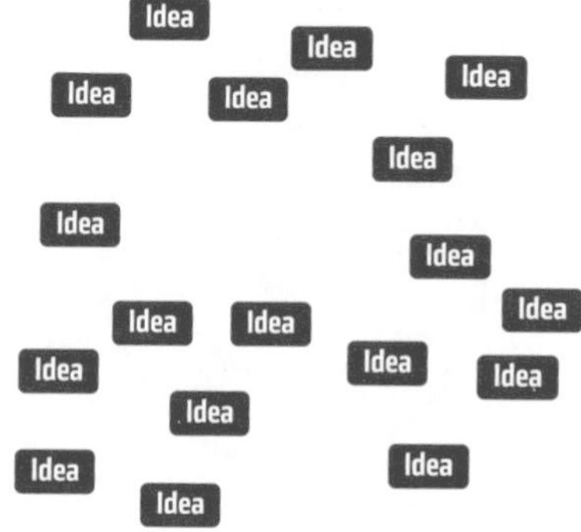

Action

As the construction of an Affinity Map involves repeated reconfiguration, it's best to use sticky notes or their digital equivalent. In a workshop context, let each person place their sticky notes, one at a time, as they read out the words to the group. At this stage, there is no discussion — just the collection of ideas.

2 | Create pairs

Purpose

Although all students generalise, for most of them, most of the time, it's unconscious. Familiarising them with this process and gently identifying pairs is the best strategy, and is most likely to demonstrate what is meant by identifying shared attributes.

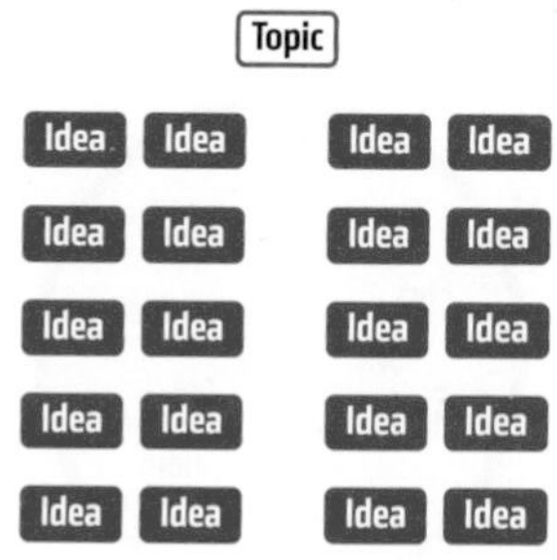

Action

Either model or ask your students to work in pairs to identify pairs of words on sticky notes. You might like to give some examples, explaining how they share characteristics. The pairing is done simply by moving the words close to each other. New ideas often arise from this activity. Include these later stickies.

3 | Create groups

Purpose

The search for similarities is now extended to the formation of groups. No specific number is needed, but often there are around three to six groups. More than this and it can start to get complicated.

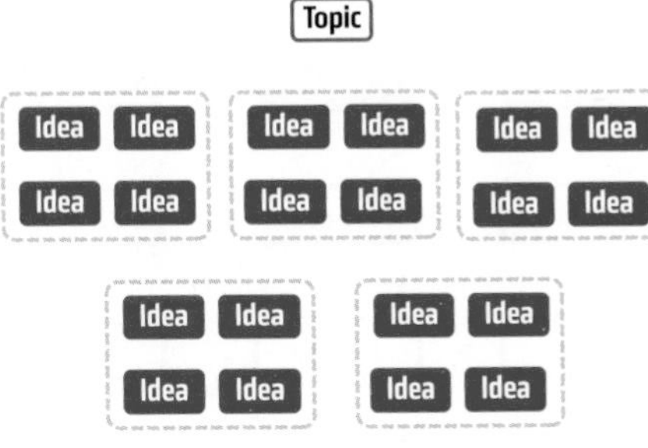

Action

Select one pair and look for another pair that is most similar. Similarity will, again, be based on shared attributes. Continue this until larger groups are formed. The groups don't have to be of equal size.

4 | Title the groups

Purpose

Summarising the groups of assembled words – searching for the nature of their shared attributes – leads to their naming. This might involve the use of more generalised, abstract words.

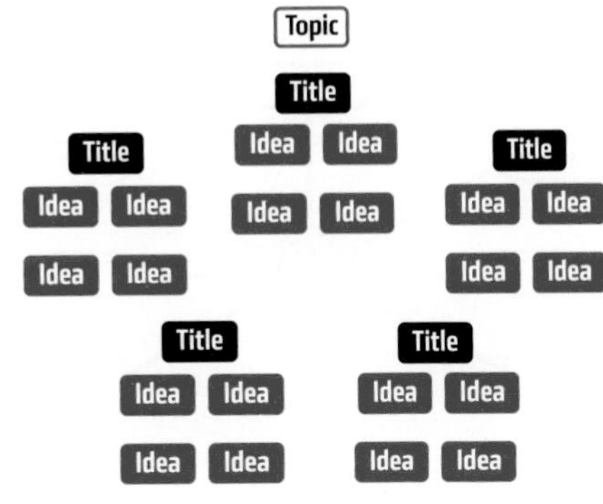

Action

New sticky notes are introduced at the head of the grouped words, on which the titles are written.

5 | Review the arrangement

Purpose

It's always useful to remind students to review their work – especially their thinking. Here, the groupings of sticky notes directly represent their thoughts and decisions.

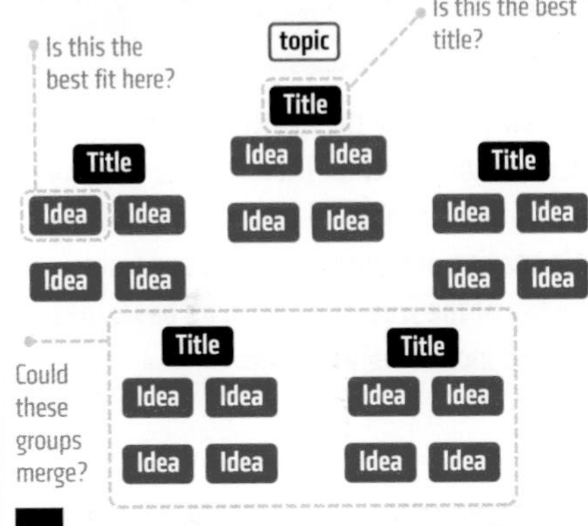

Action

If you use paper sticky notes, make sure you take a photo to capture an early configuration before you or your students rearrange it. Remember to capture digital configurations too. Ask your students to explain and justify their moves and decisions.

TYPE | **CHUNK**

TREE DIAGRAM

Reveal the hierarchical structure of a topic by constructing a Tree Diagram

Tree Diagrams are the quintessential hierarchical structure. Their familiar structure makes them a concrete tool for categorising information and ideas. As you move from the top of the Tree Diagram to its base, ideas become increasingly specific.

Construction instruction

1 | Collect ideas

Purpose

A Spray Map separates the collection and organisation of ideas. The result is you are likely to capture more ideas in the early stages and construct a more coherent organisational structure in the latter stages. A Spray Map helps you extend your working memory.

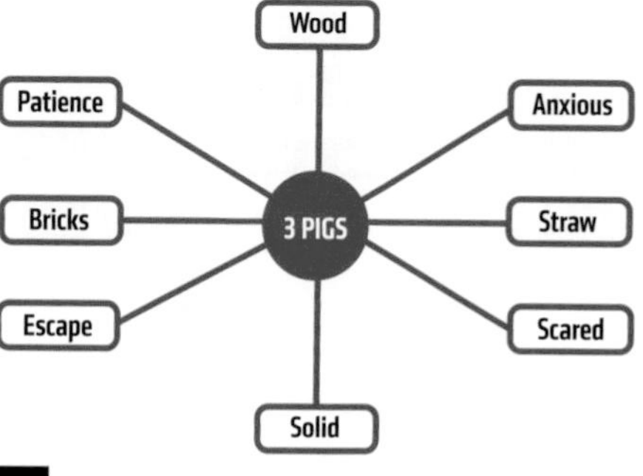

Action

List all the ideas and facts of the topic under study. Use a Spray Map to capture ideas, or use sticky notes or text boxes on a screen. Emphasise that the first step is to capture ideas in your external memory field. Explain how this first step will allow you to be more successful at organising in the subsequent steps.

2 | Divide up ideas into groups

Purpose

Using an Affinity Map helps establish the topic's hierarchical structure. When using sticky notes, it's as if the ideas are objects – easy to arrange and reconfigure if you change your mind.

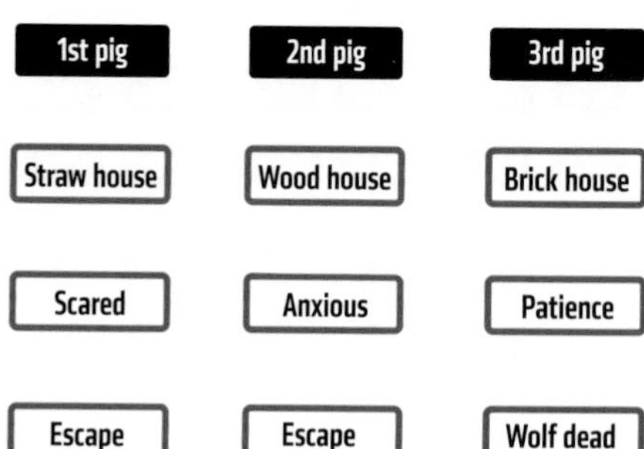

Action

Arrange the sticky notes, or text boxes on the screen, into different groups, while narrating your thinking. Give each group a title. Include your students by asking for groupings and the reasons for them. If needed, begin by pairing ideas and then joining different pairs into groups containing common attributes.

3 | Divide up into smaller groups

Purpose

Using an Affinity Map helps you divide groups into subgroups. By doing so, you reveal the different layers of the topic's hierarchy. Such a task can help you identify more ideas and potential misconceptions. Additionally, it serves as good preparation for the assembly of your Tree Diagram.

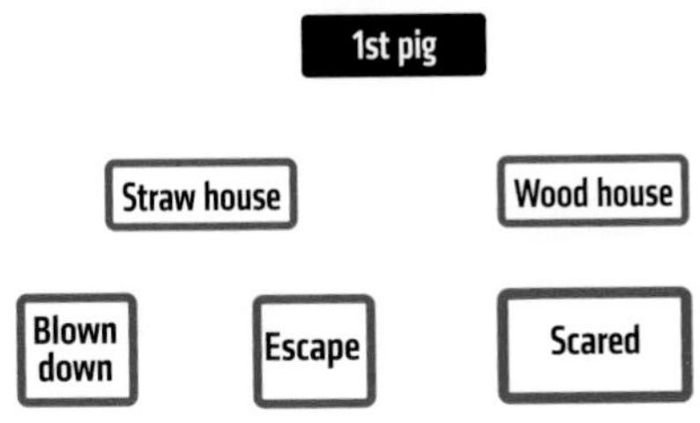

Action

Explore by finding smaller groups within larger groups. Arrange them underneath and give them a title. Include your students by asking for their groupings. Check their reasoning by asking them to articulate the required attributes for inclusion.

4 | Draw the Tree Diagram

Purpose

Tree Diagrams are a familiar graphic organiser. Used for family trees, animal taxonomy and management, their structure is consistent across different uses. The branching system allows you to see how ideas are categorised, from the more specific, lowest-order ideas at the bottom, to the more abstract, higher-order titles at the top.

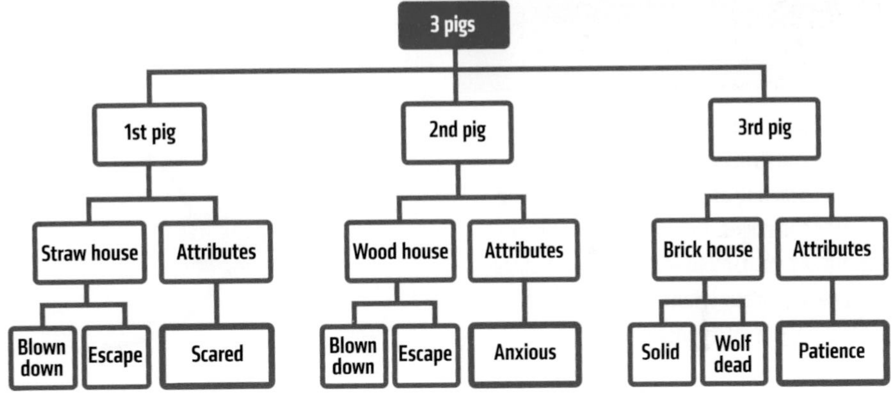

Action

When assembling your Tree Diagram, try to ensure each rung of hierarchy is physically level. You can construct your Tree Diagram digitally or via hand-drawing. A word of caution: your Tree Diagram will broaden at its base. If drawing by hand, be aware of this and plan accordingly. While constructing your Tree Diagram, don't forget to narrate your thinking. Also, make any refinements or enhancements if the opportunity arises.

TYPE | **CHUNK**

MIND MAP: DEDUCTIVE METHOD

Working deductively, construct a mind map from top to bottom

The deductive method of mind mapping involves constructing the map from top to bottom. Starting at the centre and working towards the edges, the ideas become more specific. As such, Mind Maps are hierarchical, capitalising on our infant experiences of placing objects into containers.

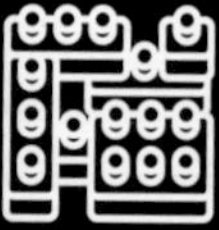

Construction instruction

1 | Identify the first-level branches

Purpose

Mind Maps, like cartographic maps, give you the *lie of the land*. But, like their counterpart, completed Mind Maps can overly exert your limited working memory. By teaching students step by step how to construct a Mind Map, you reveal the topic's underlying structure and ensure no energy is lost in the confusion of trying to read it.

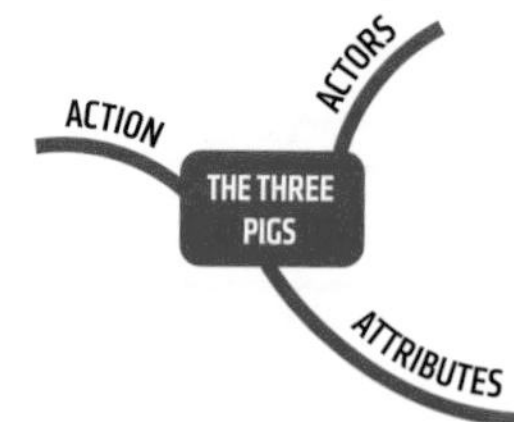

Action

Write the topic in the centre of a landscape page. Radiating outwards, capture each of the first-level titles (superordinate categories) that provide the topic's organisational structure. To take advantage of the Mind Map's economy of space, write each first-level title along or either side of its own branch.

2 | Add second-level branches

Purpose

Hierarchies are ubiquitous. As infants, we began developing an Aristotelian logic for categorisation. Why should knowledge be any different? By adding second-level branches to a Mind Map, you unearth the whole-part relationships of a topic – the nested knowledge.

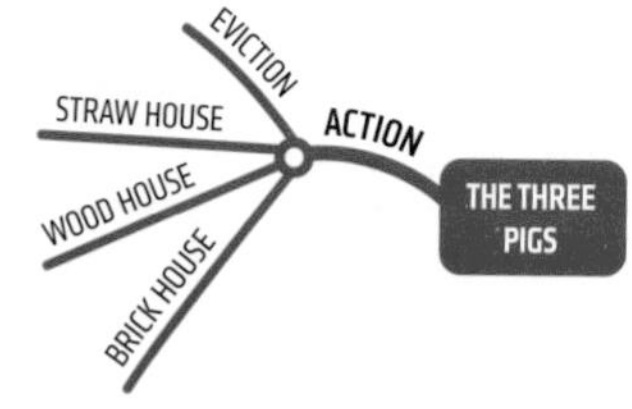

Action

Break each first-level branch down into second-level branches by grouping ideas that appear to have shared attributes. Capture ideas on sticky notes or text boxes on the screen, so that they can be visibly arranged. Include your students by negotiating with them the best groupings.

3 | Divide up into smaller groups

Purpose

By the time you reach the third-level branches, space becomes a cognitive resource. By grouping ideas based on their shared attributes, you create nested knowledge – categorised information that is more likely to be retrievable. The ideas on the Mind Map become more specific as it fans out.

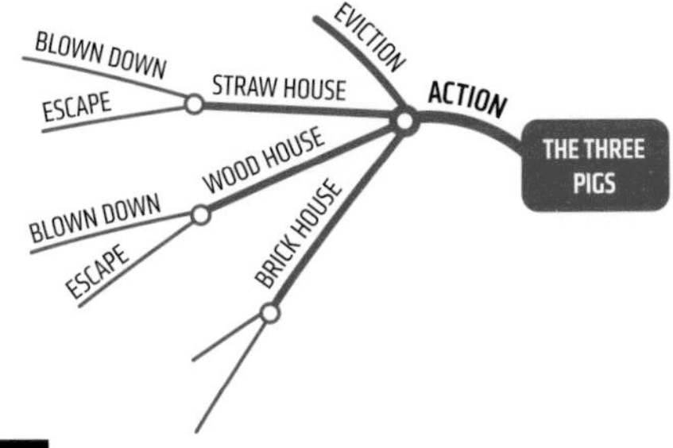

Action

Explore finding smaller groups. If required, include fourth-level branches and beyond. Remember to maintain the hierarchies and carefully talk through your thinking. By doing so, you might find that ideas become cumulative – further associative ideas emerge.

4 | Complete the map

Purpose

With all of the ideas categorised and laid out, your thinking is made visible. In your students' and your own external memory field, making iterations to how ideas are organised is likely to be more successful than trying to do so internally. A completed Mind Map provides a system of nested groups. As such, it is easier to find things. This applies cognitively, too.

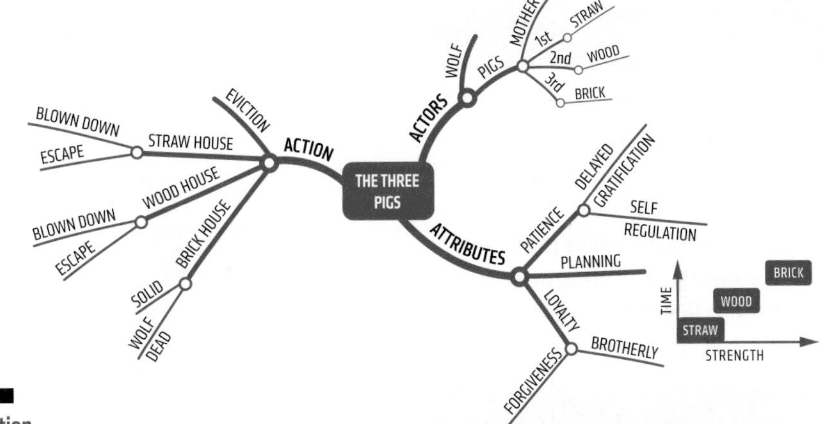

Action

As you complete the Mind Map, seek to add or correct ideas, or reconfigure branches that don't stand up to common sense. Induct your students into the process by having them complete their own map and collaborate with you. While narrating your Mind Map, model to your students how you trace each branch with your index finger. Point out that this extra sensory input helps strengthen your memory of the topic's content.

TYPE | **CHUNK**

MIND MAP: DEDUCTIVE TO INDUCTIVE METHOD

Transition from deductive to inductive construction

The inductive method of mind mapping involves constructing the map from bottom to top. It requires students to collect and examine information, grouping it into concepts. As such, it can be more challenging than the deductive method. Here, we show you how to transition from the deductive to the inductive method of mind mapping.

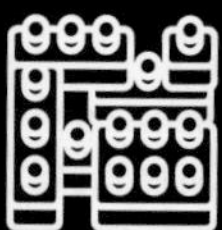

Construction instruction

1 | Identify the first-level branches

Purpose

You know that organised knowledge is exploitable and retrievable. But without clear instructional coaching and guided practice, students will falter when organising knowledge. By modelling to your students the process of grouping ideas into coherent structures, they are more likely to develop a powerful long-term memory.

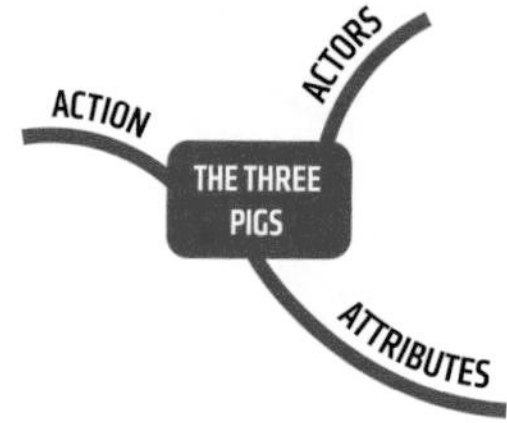

Action

Mind Maps aren't special. They are merely Tree Diagrams with ideas arranged radiantly. But they come into their own when they capture the lower levels of a hierarchy. By writing along, or either side, of their branches and orientating your page landscape, you gain more workspace.

2 | Collect ideas

Purpose

The first-level branch provides a prompt as to the ideas we want to organise. If asked to list items stored in a garage, you would likely be able to list many objects. While garage items are familiar and possibly easy to organise into groups internally, to-be-learnt ideas are likely to be less familiar. As such, this stage is only about listing ideas for each first-level branch.

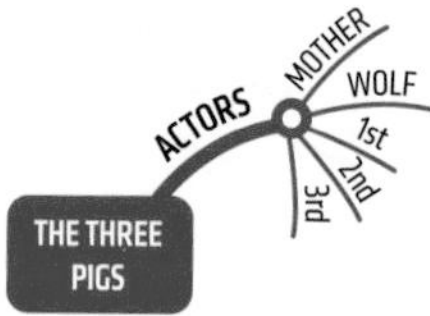

Action

For each first-level branch, record the subsidiary ideas and facts that have shared attributes. Include your students by asking them for ideas and facts to add. Check their reasoning by asking them to justify the inclusion and categorisation of their ideas.

3 | Tidy up the branches

Purpose

As we begin to *tidy up the garage*, grouping items based on common attributes, we induct our students into a metacognitive process. With your initial ideas reflecting back to you in your external memory field, it becomes easier to enhance and amend them – you can break up each first-level branch into second-level branches and beyond.

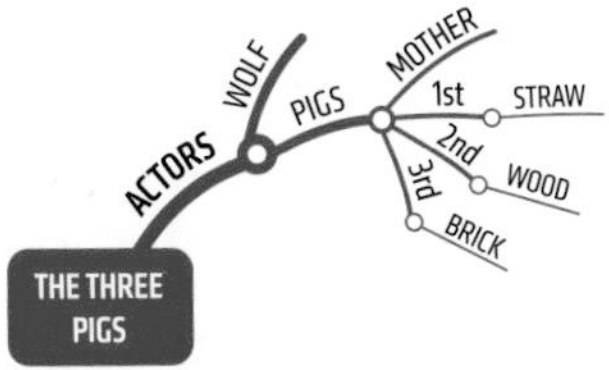

Action

Point out that in its current configuration, your Mind Map is nothing more than a radiant list. Using sticky notes or text boxes on a screen, explore arranging ideas into groups. Include your students in the process. To encourage metacognitive dialogue, praise their involvement in this iterative process.

4 | Continue to map the groups and sub-groups

Purpose

Much like your internal schema, a Mind Map should not be considered complete. You can always look to assimilate and reconfigure your ideas based on new information. But, unlike your internal schema, your public schema – in this case, a Mind Map – offers a more effective method for communicating knowledge.

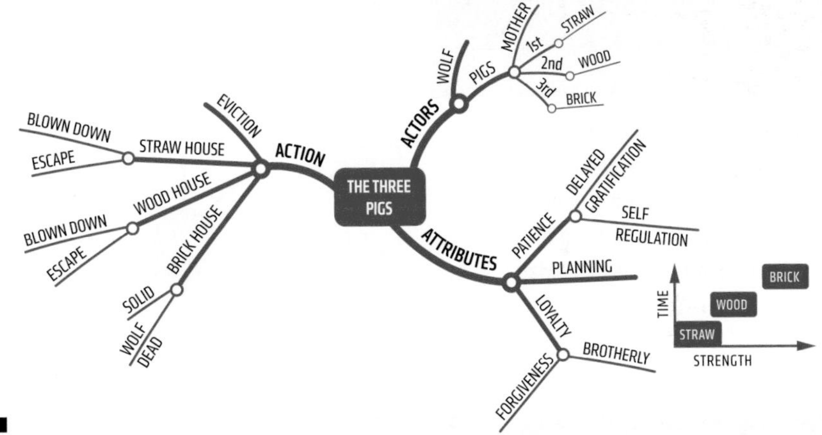

Action

With the help of your students, continue to tidy up each branch of the Mind Map. Acknowledge when new iterations culminate in the discovery of new or novel ideas. Point out that the more coherent their Mind Maps, the more likely those maps will enhance their memory, boost their confidence during discussions, and improve their writing proficiency.

TYPE | **CHUNK**

MIND MAP: INDUCTIVE METHOD

Working inductively, construct a mind map from the bottom to the top

The inductive method of mind mapping is the direct opposite of the deductive method. Specific ideas and facts are grouped and given titles. These titles will later form the branches closest to the centre of the Mind Map.

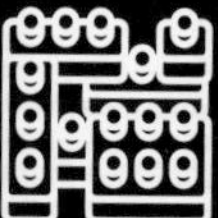

Construction instruction

1 | Collect ideas

Purpose

The first step is to remove the effort of simultaneously trying to collect ideas and organise them. Such a mental task is likely to overwhelm even those who are experts. Using a Spray Map, or sticky notes, or text boxes on a screen, allows you to capture your initial ideas in your external memory field.

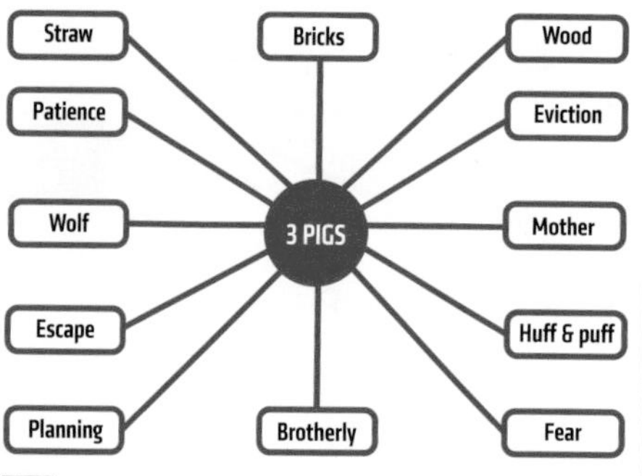

Action

Identify the focus of the to-be-constructed Mind Map. Use a Spray Map to capture ideas, or use sticky notes or text boxes on a screen. Point out that the first step is to capture ideas in your external memory field, where they can be categorised more freely.

2 | Divide ideas into groups

Purpose

By using an Affinity Map, you create order and meaning – you identify patterns. Items that are close together are automatically perceived as being similar. Capitalise on this phenomenon by physically grouping ideas that seem to belong together.

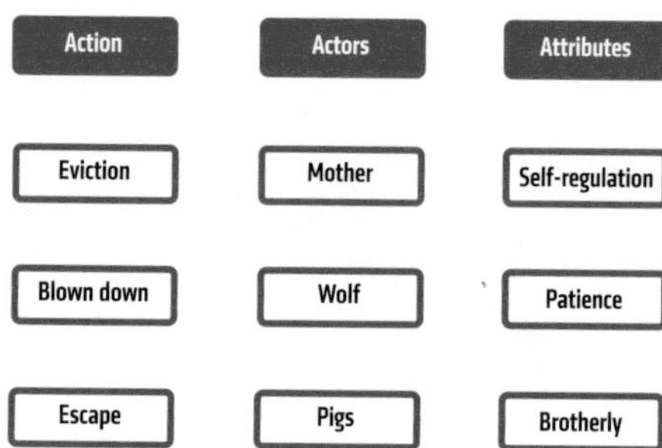

Action

Create an Affinity Map either by using sticky notes or text boxes on a screen. Physically group ideas that seem to belong together because of shared attributes. Involve your students by asking for their groupings. Explore any misconceptions by asking students to articulate their decisions.

3 | Divide into smaller groups

Purpose

When ideas are made visible, like Scrabble tiles, they are ripe for organising. As you begin to organise ideas into group and subgroups, you may discover more ideas. The discovery of new ideas is possible because you are not overexerting your working memory by trying to organise ideas internally.

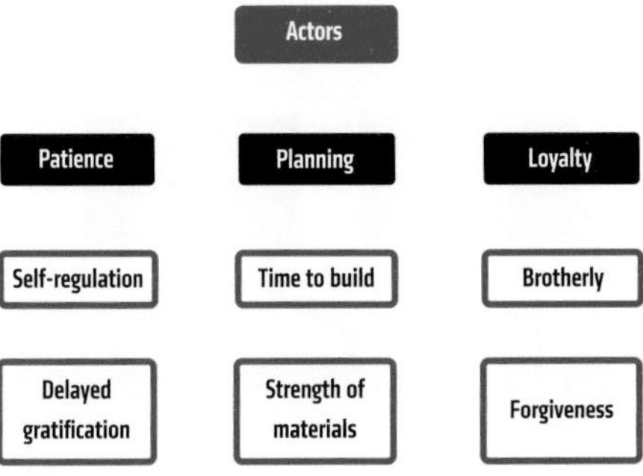

Action

Explore finding smaller groups within larger groups. Arrange them underneath. Narrate your decision-making when categorising ideas and point out to students how organising ideas potentially helps you discover more ideas.

4 | Map the groups and sub-groups

Purpose

Arriving at a coherent structure takes effort. This effort pays dividends in the form of a tool that supports reading, writing and discussions. The process of constructing a Mind Map presents many opportunities to check for understanding.

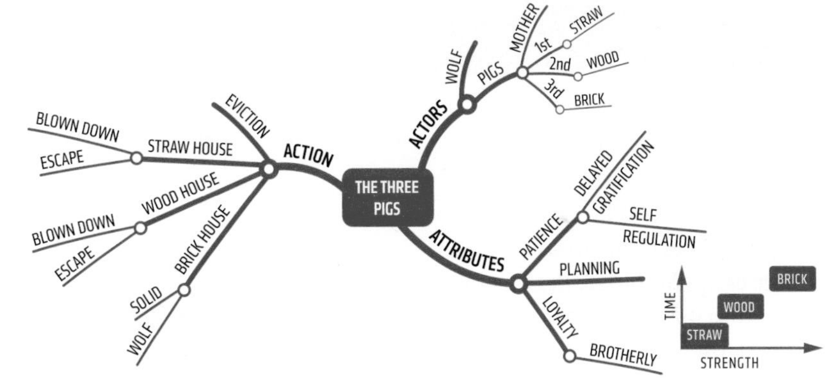

Action

While mind mapping, maintain the hierarchies you and your students have identified. Follow the steps we have outlined: orientate the page landscape, write along or either side of each branch, and make refinements. Demonstrate how the Mind Map's structure can be transformed for speaking and writing. Explain how the process is a valuable rehearsal for future endeavours.

TYPE | **CHUNK**

INDUCTIVE TOWER

A method of categorising, from the details up to increasing levels of abstraction

Most teaching involves teachers telling students the principles of their subjects. Rightly so. There are, however, also opportunities for students to construct knowledge structures themselves, or at least to see them being constructed. This happens from the bottom (the details) to the top (the abstractions). Teachers can model and scaffold this process visually in this way.

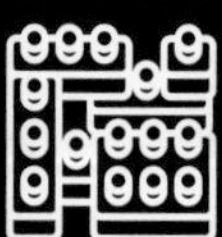

Construction instruction

1 | Start from the bottom facts

Action

In order to group items together in an inductive fashion, the foundation of the most detailed, concrete elements needs to be spread out at the bottom of the tower. Below, because of the constraints of space, only the left-hand content is shown. The process we are explaining is to be applied to all the remaining content. Below, you can see how the two facts (concerning polar ice melt and Pine Island Glacier) are both described at a more abstract level – a temporal perspective is given.

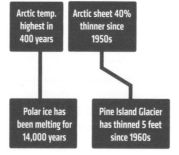

Arctic temp. highest in 400 years

Arctic sheet 40% thinner since 1950s

Polar ice has been melting for 14,000 years

Pine Island Glacier has thinned 5 feet since 1960s

2 | Continue at a higher level

Action

After having established higher-order descriptions across the whole foundation row, continue upwards, making links across similar descriptions.

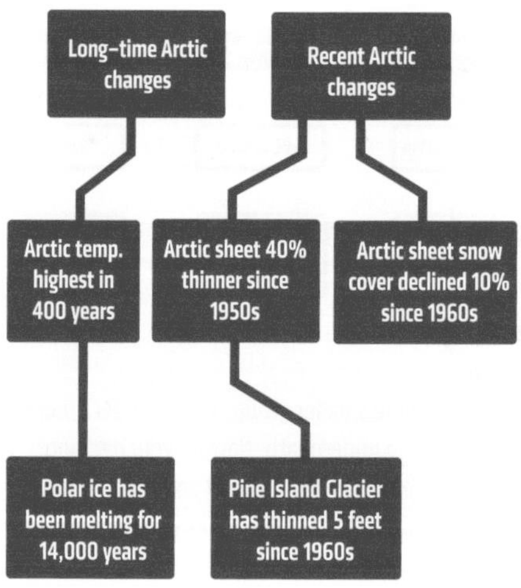

3 | Continue the process

Action

The process continues up to the next level. Notice how much more abstract and generalised this level of description needs to be.

Climate changes
Long-time Arctic changes
Recent Arctic changes
Arctic temp. highest in 400 years
Arctic sheet 40% thinner since 1950s
Arctic sheet snow cover declined 10% since 1960s
Polar ice has been melting for 14,000 years
Pine Island Glacier has thinned 5 feet since 1960s

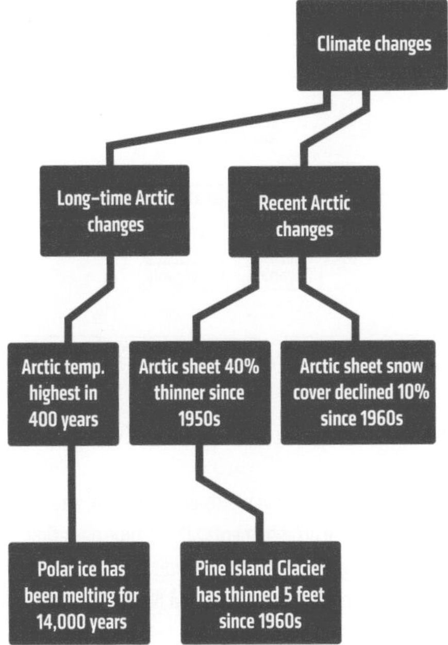

4 | Complete the tower

Action

Reach across to the other side of the tower and find the concept for the highest level of abstraction.

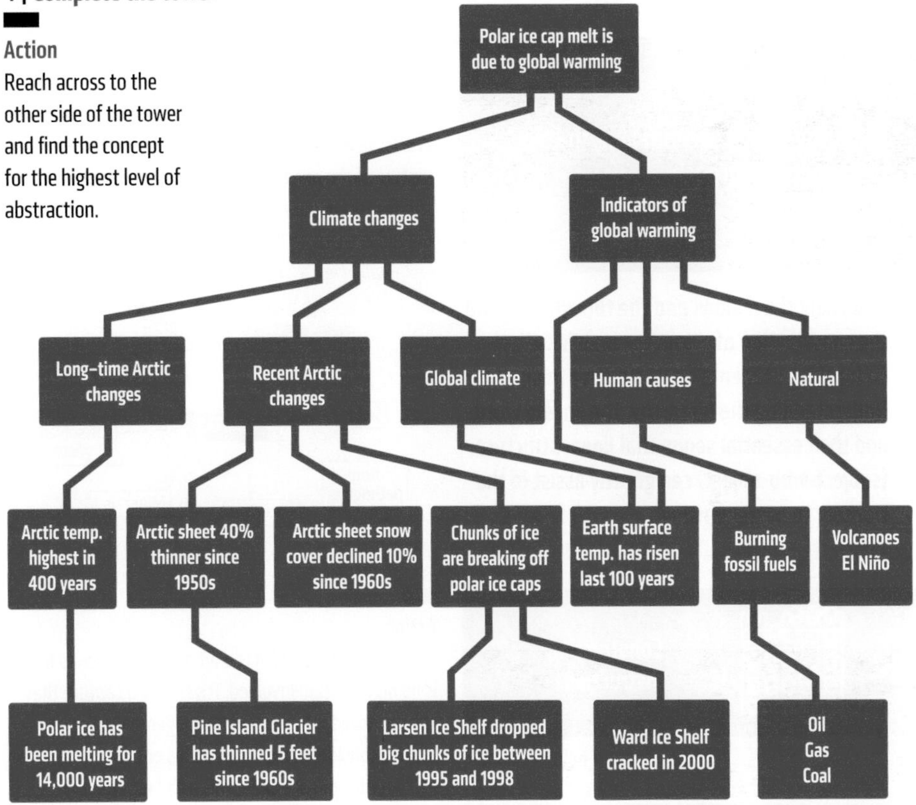

Polar ice cap melt is due to global warming
Climate changes
Indicators of global warming
Long-time Arctic changes
Recent Arctic changes
Global climate
Human causes
Natural
Arctic temp. highest in 400 years
Arctic sheet 40% thinner since 1950s
Arctic sheet snow cover declined 10% since 1960s
Chunks of ice are breaking off polar ice caps
Earth surface temp. has risen last 100 years
Burning fossil fuels
Volcanoes El Niño
Polar ice has been melting for 14,000 years
Pine Island Glacier has thinned 5 feet since 1960s
Larsen Ice Shelf dropped big chunks of ice between 1995 and 1998
Ward Ice Shelf cracked in 2000
Oil
Gas
Coal

TYPE | **CHUNK**

CONCEPT MAP

An introduction to modelling the Novak hierarchical approach

Modelling the actions and the thoughts behind the construction of a concept map is critical to teaching students how to create their own. Understanding the hierarchy, the linking words and their essential sequential linear structure (subject-verb-object) can greatly assist in the transfer to better writing.

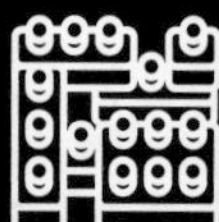

Construction instruction

1 | Identify the concepts

Purpose

The major aim is to break up the construction of the Concept Map into different stages. This first stage avoids cognitive load by concentrating solely on the capture of the relevant concepts. By placing them on sticky notes in our external memory field, no effort is wasted in trying to keep them in mind.

Action

Use a Spray Map, which is a bit of a misnomer as there is no organisation involved. It's simply a capture that can be moved into different arrangements. For this reason, consider using sticky notes or a digital version. Explain why you are doing this as a first step before organising.

2 | Rank the concepts

Purpose

The objective is to establish a hierarchy of the ideas captured in the Spray Map. Why bother with the hierarchical structure? Because Joseph Novak – the originator of the Concept Map – considers it critical to knowledge structure. Sticky notes are easy to move, and move again, into different arrangements.

Action

Move the sticky notes, or words on the screen, into different vertical arrangements, all the time narrating your reasoning. You may want to include your students in this by asking for placements and the reasons for them. Explain and exemplify other, better known hierarchies.

3 | Start the map

Purpose

The key part of the modelling starts with the creation of the kernel sentences that characterise Concept Maps. Explain how the linking words are verbs, joining the *subject* to the *object* – a mini-sentence. And then point out how the *object* then becomes the *subject* of the subsequent sentence lower down.

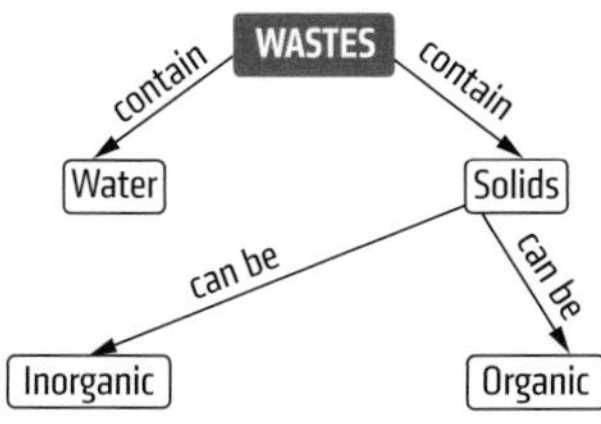

Action

Carefully talk through your thinking – however obvious it may seem – as you create the kernel sentences on the board. You may want to give other examples of these mini-sentences. Continually check for understanding and get students to explain the process to those who might not understand initially.

4 | Complete the map

Purpose

Repeating the self-same thinking process for the construction of each subsequent kernel sentence strongly establishes the pattern in students' minds.

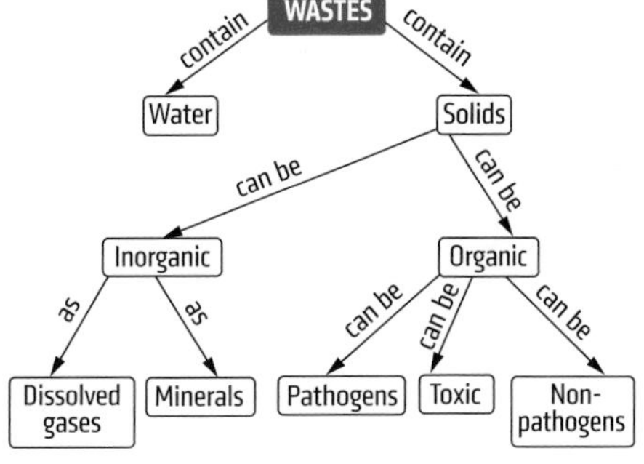

Action

Continue with the same process until the map is complete. Point out that there should be an arrow head on each joining line. The arrow has to point in the direction of the subject-verb-object kernel sentence.

5 | Narrate the map

Purpose

Point out that the value of a map is measured by the degree to which students' understanding is translated into narratives, spoken or written. So, throughout the mapping process, students should be very clear about the map's utilitarian and subservient role to the formation of effective narratives.

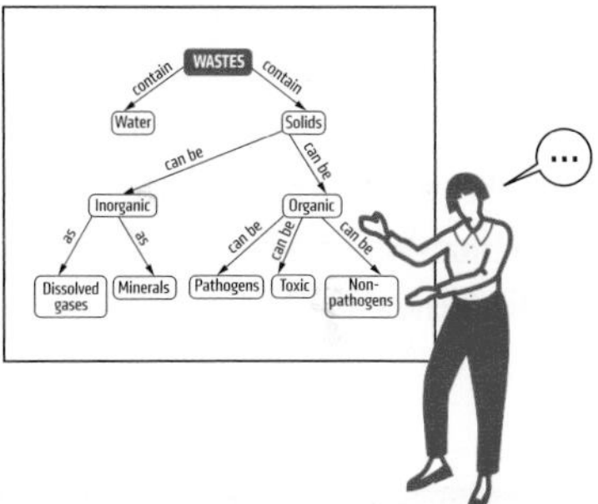

Action

Demonstrate how to verbally elaborate the short kernel sentences into longer and more complex forms. Make evident, too, how the structure of the map helps direct the flow of your narrative. Emphasise that such efforts to turn maps into narratives can be seen as excellent rehearsal for subsequent writing.

TYPE | **CHUNK**

CONCEPT MAP: NON-HIERARCHICAL

Reveal the constituent concepts and the relationships between them

Teach students your thinking and decision-making step by step when constructing a Concept Map. The less rigid non-hierarchical method of concept mapping provides an access point for those who are less familiar with the Novak hierarchical method.

Construction instruction

1 | Identify the concepts

Purpose

Concept Maps are probably the most difficult graphic organiser to construct. But do not let that deter you. With careful planning, you will reap the rewards of your efforts. Like anything you construct in life, you first need to gather some components – in this case, concepts.

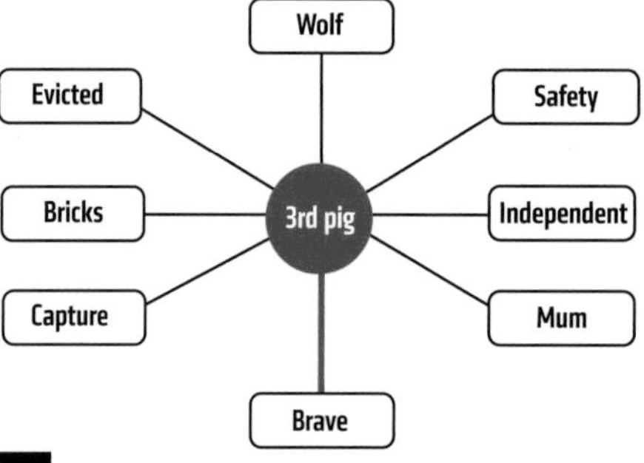

Action

Capture all the concepts that you intend to map. You can use a Spray Map, or sticky notes, or text boxes on a screen. Whichever tool you decide to use, capture each concept separately to make it easier when arranging them.

2 | Pair concepts

Purpose

Concept Maps are made up of kernel sentences (this is our term). Two concepts are linked by an arrow and a verb to form a simple subject-verb-object sentence. Ideas on sticky notes are easy to arrange and rearrange when creating kernel sentences.

Action

Model the pairing of concepts that connect in meaning. Explore how individual pairs might link with other pairs, all the time narrating your reasoning. Explain how concepts link and involve your students by asking them to articulate their understanding of connected concepts.

3 | Create kernel sentences

Purpose

It is the kernel sentence that illuminates the relationships between concepts. These mini-sentences are characterised by a verb joining a subject to an object. The verb captures the relationship between concepts.

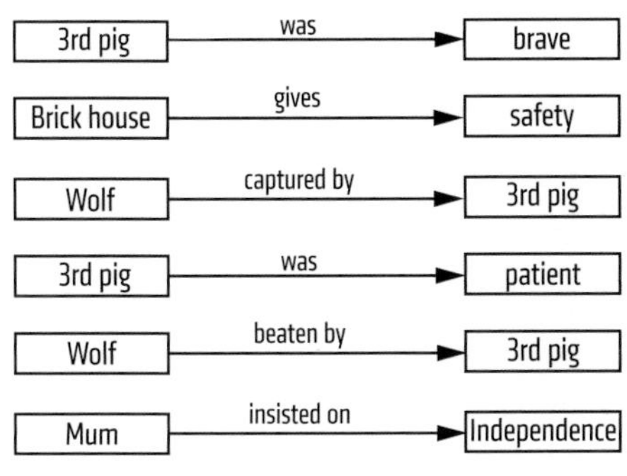

Action

As you create each kernel sentence, narrate your thinking. Draw an arrow – with the arrowhead indicating the direction of influence – between linked concepts. Check your students' understanding by cold-calling: ask them to elaborate on the nature of identified connections.

4 | Begin constructing your map

Purpose

Having an understanding of how concepts connect deepens our understanding. Concept Maps allow you to demystify your thinking, providing students with an explicit representation of your schema. The rewards for your effort include a better grasp of a topic, clearer writing, more confident and meaningful discussions, and a powerful long-term memory.

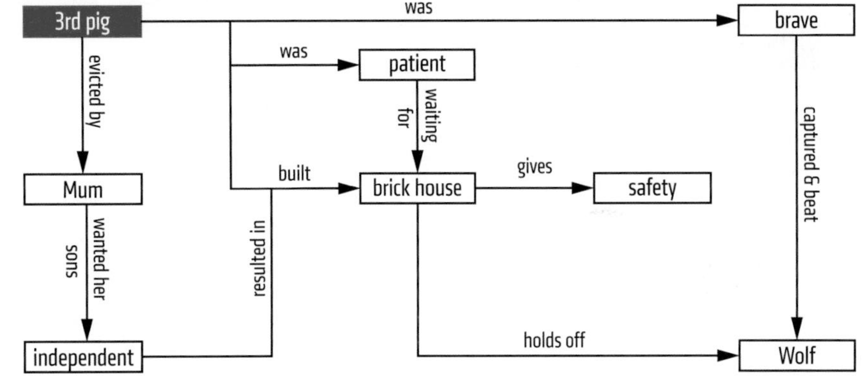

Action

Traditionally, Concept Maps are arranged from the top to the bottom. But both hierarchical or non-hierarchical Concept Maps can be arranged from left to right. The orientation of your page, and the arrangement of concepts, is governed by the volume of content and links. Working collaboratively with your students, map the connections between separate kernel sentences. Praise your students if they identify how the Concept Map can be refined or enhanced. Throughout the process, use the Concept Map as a prompt to check for understanding. Think-Pair-Share and concept mapping unite to rigorously check how well your students have grasped a topic.

TYPE | **CHUNK**

IDEA BOX

Sometimes also called the da Vinci method, this combination tool will hurl you into the creative process

Rather than waiting until you have the feeling of creativity – some wait forever – make a start with this method. Lay the foundations of innovation by following these steps that will, invariably, lead you to far more creative choices than your imagination would have ever conjured up for you. Beat the limitations of your working memory and use your external memory field for more creativity.

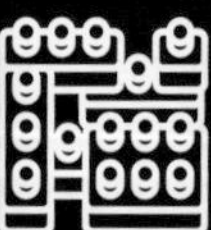

Construction instruction

1 | Identify and select the parameters

Purpose

The parameters of the project are the categories of all the elements that make up the project. Below are the chosen parameters (there are others) for the design of a lamp. The empty boxes represent the as-yet undefined *elements*.

STYLE	POSITION	FINISH	SHAPE

Action

List the parameters along the top axis. Don't use too many, though, as the possibilities soon escalate: 10 parameters with 10 elements each produce a possible 10 billion combinations.

2 | List the variations for each parameter

Purpose

It is the kernel sentence that illuminates the relationships between concepts. These mini-sentences are characterised by a verb joining a subject to an object. The verb captures the relationship between concepts.

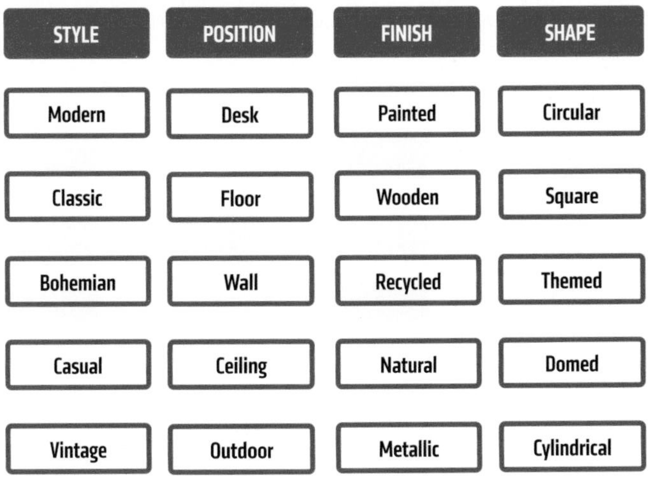

Action

Fill the boxes with the different types of elements for the chosen parameters. How many styles of lamp are there? And what type of finish could there be? Think along these lines to stimulate ideas.

3 | Try out different combinations

Purpose

Now is the fun of discovering – again and again and again – the vast number of variations possible in the design of a lamp. When, at a later date, you are faced with another creative project, you will profitably remember this exercise.

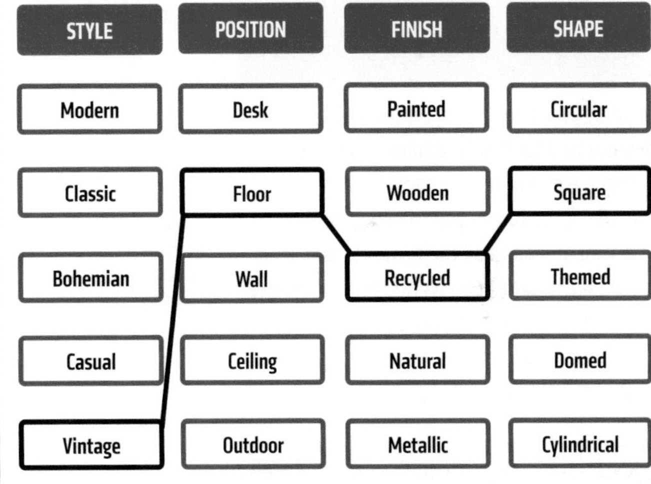

Action

Select one element per parameter, mark them in some way and join them up. It might be a good idea to take a photo of this single combination. Then start afresh on a new combination. And continue until you can evaluate your favourite mix.

TYPE | **COMPARE**

DOUBLE SPRAY

The union of two Spray Maps makes explicit the similarities and differences between two topics

The merging of two Spray Maps creates a concrete tool for the fundamental learning strategy: comparing. The construction of a Double Spray forces you to separate the collection of ideas and their comparison, thus lessening the burden on working memory. The spatial arrangement of similarities and the use of connecting branches emphasise the shared attributes between two topics.

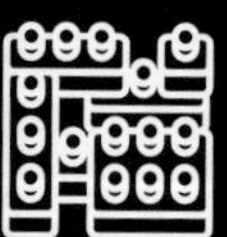

Construction instruction

1 | Create a Spray Map of topic A

Purpose

For any comparison to take place, you first need content to compare. A Double Spray is the merging of two Spray Maps. Therefore, it seems self-evident that the first two steps when constructing a Double Spray are to produce two individual Spray Maps. The Spray Map should be your go-to tool when collecting ideas, as its radiant structure makes it easy to make additions and there can be no mistaken inference of a hierarchy. The Spray Map divides the collection and organisation of content – useful, given that working memory is subject to severe constraints.

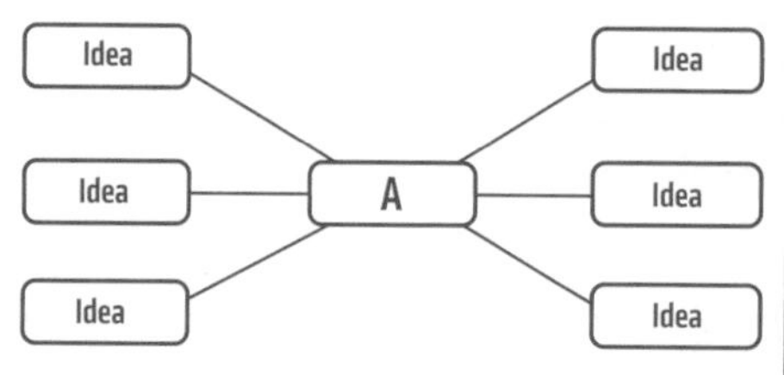

Action

Collect the ideas for topic A and radiantly arrange them on a Spray Map. You might choose to collect ideas from previously learnt material. If so, the Spray Map serves as a useful retrieval practice tool. Alternatively, you could select content to compare from a piece of text.

2 | Create a Spray Map of topic B

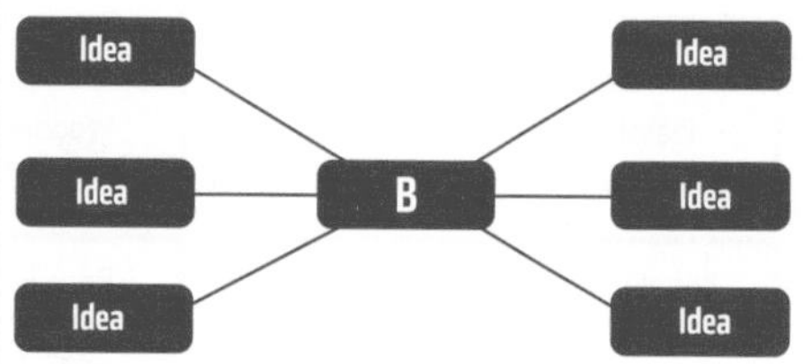

Action

Repeat step 1 for topic B.

3 | Join the two Spray Maps

Purpose

The Double Spray forces you to separate the collection and comparison of ideas. Remember, we automatically recognise items and ideas that are close together as being similar. In a Double Spray, the ideas are arranged vertically in the centre and linked with branches to both topics. The linked branches visually emphasise the connections. The use of colour can enhance this further.

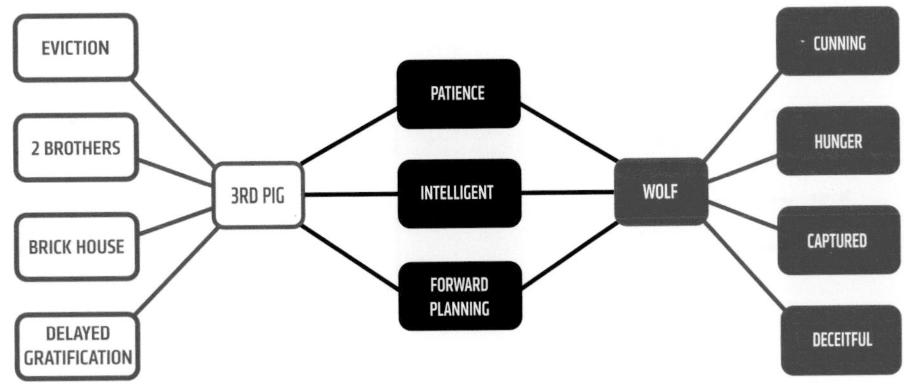

Action

With the construction of two Spray Maps, the jump to completing a Double Spray is small. Identify the ideas from topic A and B that have shared characteristics. Arrange all the similar ideas centrally between the two topics. For each similar idea, connect it to both topics using a branch. Try to leave sufficient space, vertically and horizontally, between the ideas and their member topics, for annotations (see step 4). Arrange all the ideas that are different around the outside of their topic. Horizontally align ideas from topic A and B that are the polar opposite. Explore the use of two to three colours to emphasise the similarities and differences, as we have above.

4 | Identify differences in sameness

Purpose

By annotating the connecting branches of the centrally similar ideas, you will achieve more nuance. The central ideas are similar and, in their evidence or application, different. Such annotations force you to analyse the extent to which the shared attributes are similar.

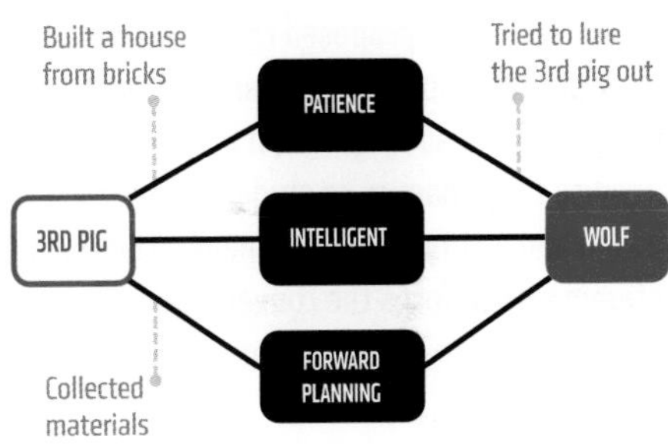

Action

Analyse the extent to which the central commonalities are similar – add evidence along the branches. Involve your students by asking: In what specific ways are these ideas similar? What evidence supports your thinking? Use cold-calling and Think-Pair-Share to check your students have got the gist.

TYPE | **COMPARE**

FORCE FIELD ANALYSIS

A diagram to systematically evaluate perceptions of the chances of success of a proposed change

Usually applied to proposed changes, this organiser can also be used to analyse past events. As with all diagrams, it is better to organise the dynamics so students have to reason and justify their judgements. The visual reference helps focus the conversation and sustain attention. Conversations become, as a result, more objective.

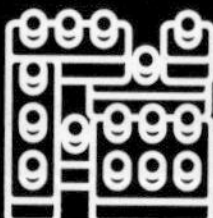

Construction instruction

1 | List the forces for change

Purpose

Proposed changes have forces for and against their realisation. Start with the positive ones.

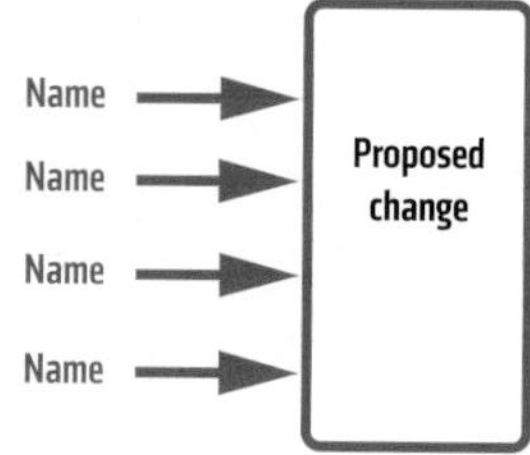

Action

Line up the forces for change on the left-hand side of the block that represents the proposed – or indeed actual – change. This diagram can be used to evaluate future changes or analyse past events.

2 | List the forces resisting change

Purpose

Similarly, line up the identified forces that resist the proposed change.

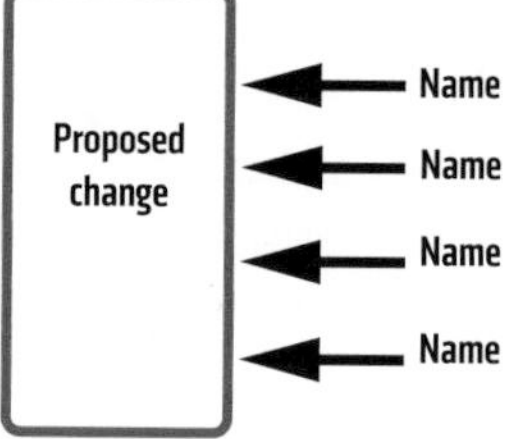

Action

On the other side of the proposed change, add the forces that resist its realisation. Line these up in a way that relates to the opposite, positive forces. This alignment aids in the analysis as you compare their relative impact.

3 | Add weighting lines

Purpose

Add some finer judgements to the two lists through the use of weighted lines.

Forces for change

4 3 2 1

Name

Name

Name

Name

Proposed change

Forces resisting change

1 2 3 4

Name

Name

Name

Name

Action

Now consider the relative force or potential for impact of the positive and negative forces. Using whatever calibration you decide (we have used four grades), draw the lengths of the arrows to represent the perceived strength of the forces.

4 | Evaluate the total strength of both forces

Purpose

Assign value to the forces and total them for a summary evaluation.

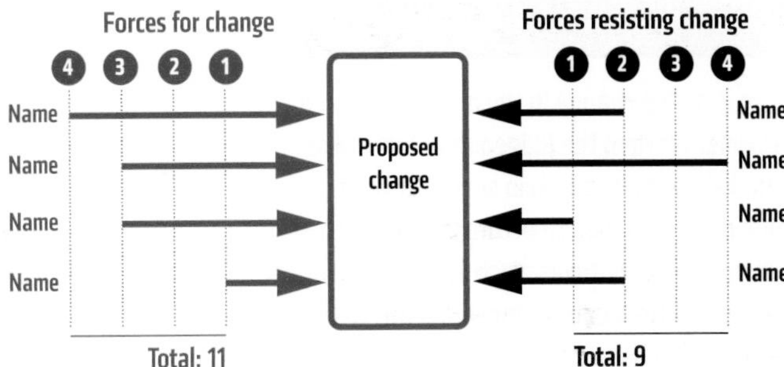

Action

After having drawn the lengths of the arrows to align with the weighted lines, now total the scores to arrive at a summary evaluation.

TYPE | **COMPARE**

CROSSED CONTINUA

This diagram helps students make judgements from two perspectives, adding depth to comparisons

There is a step change in the demands placed on students when the judgements they have to make are related to two sets of criteria. Thinking is stretched to accommodate both. Without a visual canvas, such judgements might seem too abstract for some. But when placed within the external memory field, this two-dimensional thinking is straightforward.

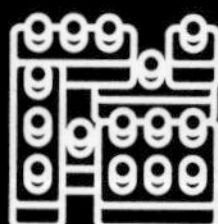

Construction instruction

1 | Create one Continuum

Purpose

Start the Crossed Continua with a single Continuum that allows differentiation of status/attainment.

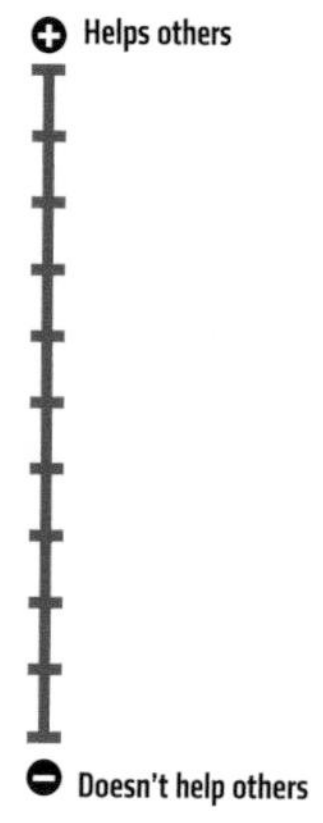

Action

With the subjects to be compared in mind (here, the Three Pigs), select and create a single Continuum against which you can make judgements. Here we have the concept of *helping others*. If you think it helpful, add calibration marks to aid the plotting.

2 | Add the second Continuum

Purpose

Adding the second Continuum creates a 2D canvas against which evaluations can be made.

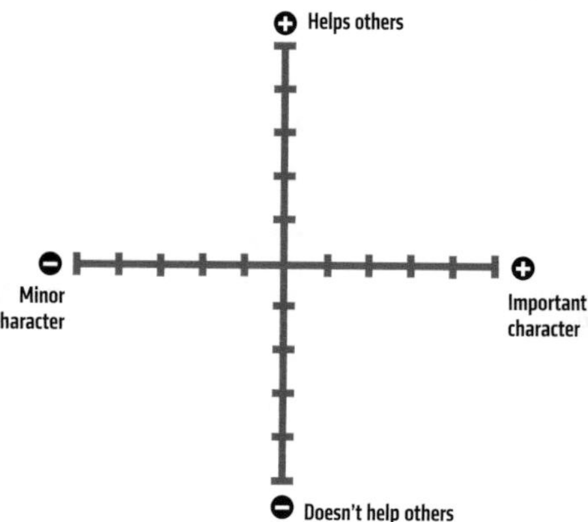

Action

Add the second (calibrated) Continuum perpendicular to the first. At the end of each Continuum are the values against which you will make your judgements. Most configurations have the positive statuses at the right and top.

3 | Add a background grid

Purpose

For some, the blank canvas is insufficiently structured, so a grid of the projected calibration marks is added.

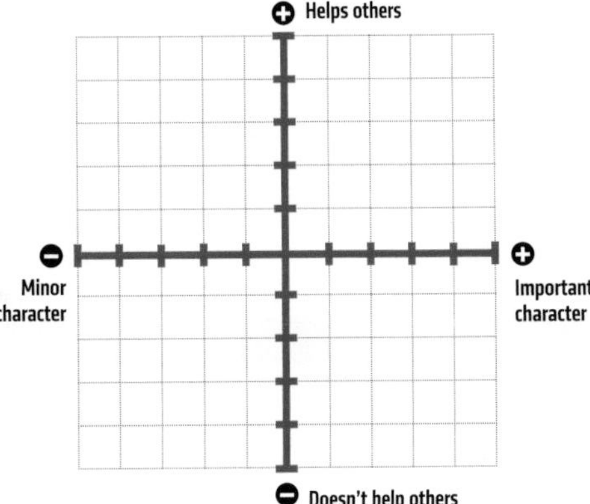

Action

Using lighter lines than the Crossed Continua, create the grid based on the marked calibrations. This aids the user to trace, from the two Continua lines, the exact position they want to specify in their plotting.

4 | Plot the subjects

Purpose

The diagram is now ready for the positions of the characters to be plotted.

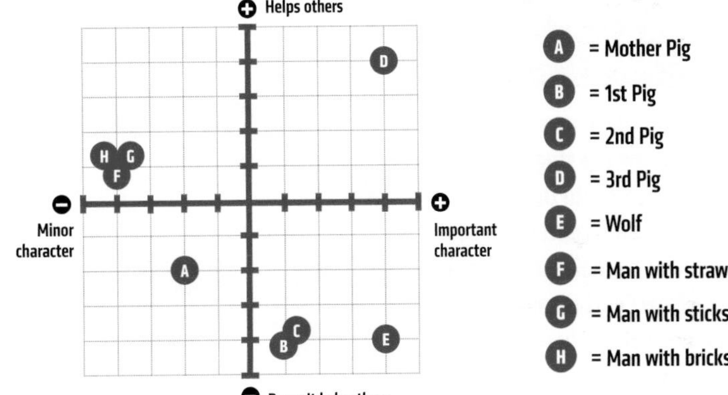

Action

While the split-attention effect might imply that you write the names of the characters within the grid itself, that would cause problems: it would be hard to know exactly where the character's assigned position was, and the overall effect would be of a confusing picture. So, create a key nearby and start to plot the characters. As you can see above, there can still be a problem when several characters occupy the same position.

TYPE | **SEQUENCE**

FLOW CHART

Clarify the correct order of steps or events in a process

The Flow Chart is one of the more simple graphic organisers. Placing the stages or steps of an event or process into the correct sequence allows you to reach conclusions and make predictions. Don't be fooled into thinking that constructing a Flow Chart is easy because of its simple structure. Follow these steps to get the most out of its use.

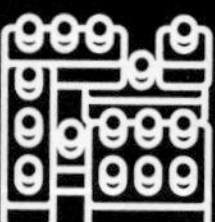

Construction instruction

1 | Collect the events

Purpose

The simple structure of the Flow Chart can mask the challenge some students encounter when constructing one. Avoid inaccurate thinking and cognitive overload by breaking down the construction of the Flow Chart into its constituent parts.

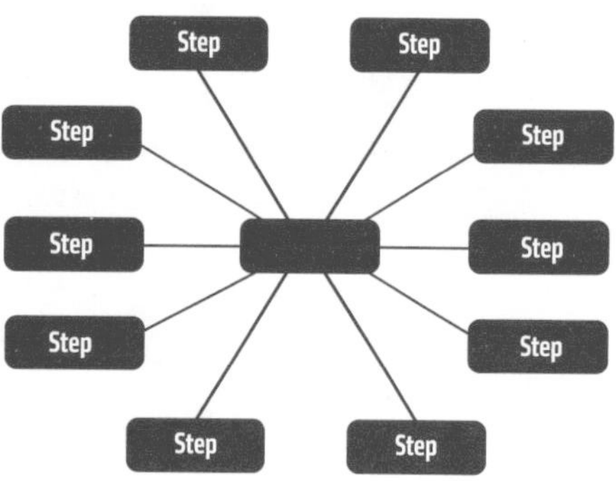

Action

To capture the events or steps of the process in mind, use a Spray Map. You can use sticky notes or text boxes on a screen, but the urge to arrange them sequentially might arise. Resist the temptation by concentrating on capturing the events or steps only.

2 | Cull

Purpose

When there are around eight or more steps to a process, it might become difficult for your students to follow. After careful consideration, try to cull those steps that are not necessary. If you are unable to cull the content into seven steps, consider using a Flow Spray instead.

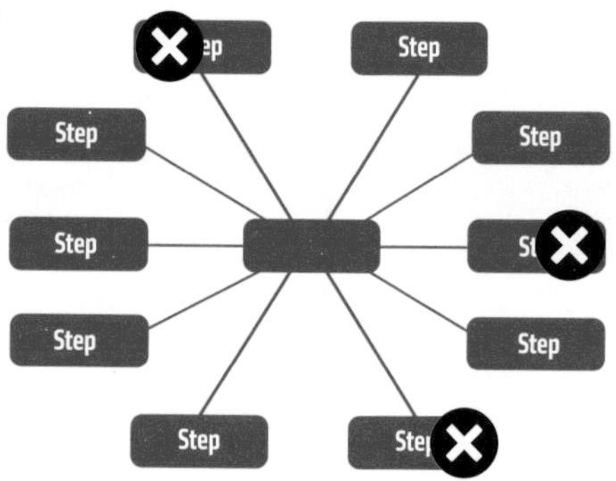

Action

Cross out (cull) those events or steps that are not necessary. Such a process might be a useful stimulus for class discussion and checking for understanding.

3 | Sequence the events and draw the Flow Chart

Purpose

You are now ready to construct the Flow Chart. With the content collected and culled, the focus changes to temporal relations. The correct sequential arrangement of steps or events helps you reach conclusions about past events and make predictions or prepare for future events.

LRRH walks to Gran's house
LRRH speaks to the wolf in woods
The wolf eats Gran
LRRH arrives at Gran's house
The wolf eats LRRH
The woodsman arrives at Gran's
Woodsman kills wolf & LRRH is saved

Action

The content needs arranging into a sequence. Although it might seem like extra work, you might find it advantageous to transfer your identified events or steps on to sticky notes. By doing so, you can arrange and rearrange them effortlessly. Start with the first step and write it down. Decide on the next step, write it down and draw an arrow to it from the first step. Continue the process until you have mapped all the steps.

TYPE | **SEQUENCE**

FLOW SPRAY

Overcome the limitations of a Flow Chart by chunking steps into mini-maps

You know that breaking content down helps to reduce cognitive overload. But what happens when there are too many individual pieces? The students who need content breaking down are likely to be overwhelmed if there are too many new pieces. A Flow Spray chunks the steps or stages of a process or event into bite-sized mini-maps, greatly reducing the risk of cognitive overload.

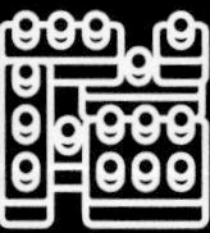

Construction instruction

1 | Select the key steps

Purpose

Follow steps 1 and 2 of Flow Chart construction (see previous spread). If you cannot cull the content into fewer than six steps, you need to chunk it into mini-maps – you need to construct a Flow Spray.

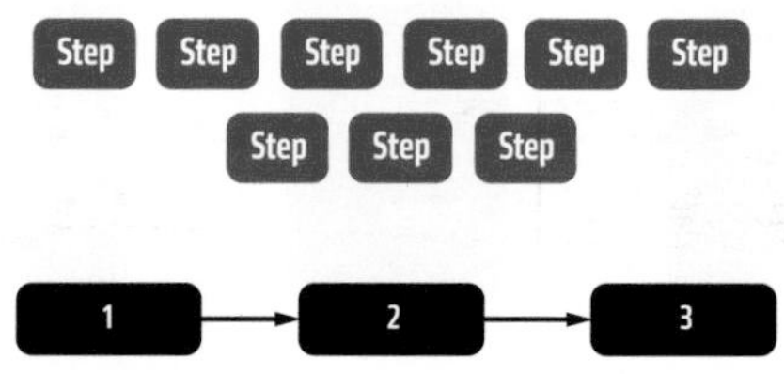

Action

Explore whether any events in your Flow Chart are more significant than the rest. Create a smaller Flow Chart – no more than five steps – with the events you identified as being significant. Temporarily place the remaining events to one side.

2 | Group events

Purpose

The students who need content breaking down are the same students who are easily overwhelmed by too many pieces of information. The Flow Spray rescues such students by chunking the stages or steps of an event or process into mini-maps.

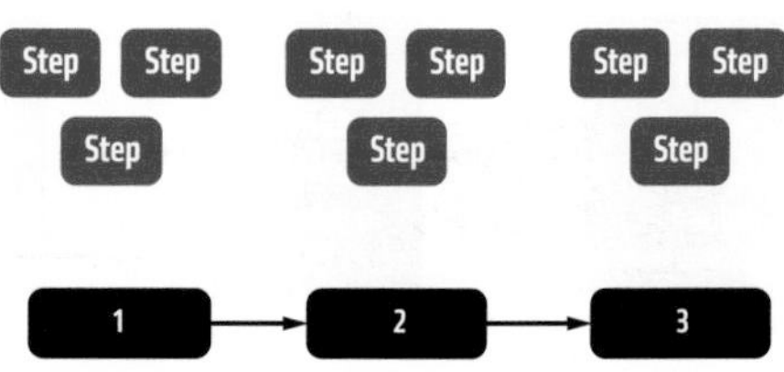

Action

Group the stages or steps into chunks and find a name that captures the meaning of each mini-map. Label your existing Flow Chart with the names you create. Leave the chunked events to one side.

3 | Draw the Flow Spray

Purpose

Creating a Flow Spray by chunking events overcomes the limitations of a Flow Chart. The central spine of your Flow Spray reveals the most significant events. The attached events add further clarity, allowing you to reach conclusions or make predictions.

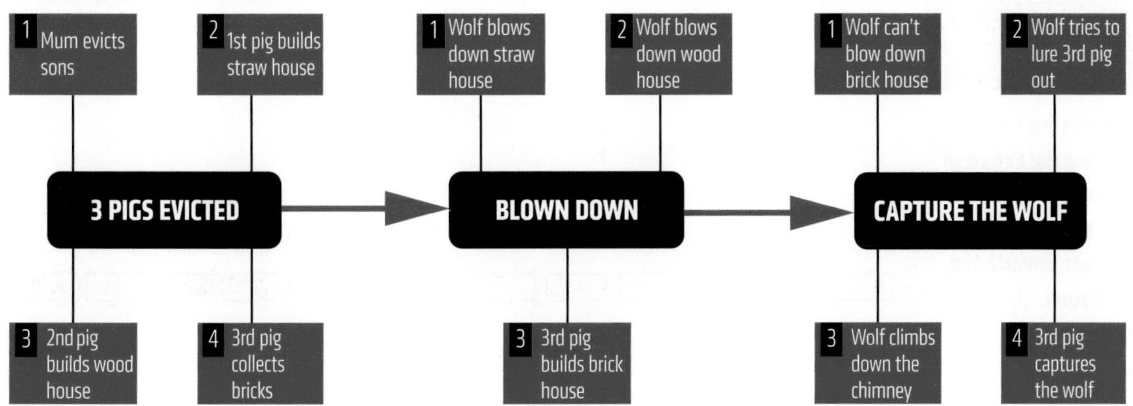

Action

Connect each of the individual steps to the main central events of your Flow Chart. If there is a particular reading route for each of the mini-maps, be sure to indicate this, as we have. Numbers or letters of the alphabet work well for this. When introducing your Flow Spray, do so step by step. Remember, you have chunked the temporal information to make it less of a burden for your students' working memory. Don't undo your hard work by sharing with them the completed version and consequently overwhelming them.

TYPE | **CAUSE & EFFECT**

FISHBONE DIAGRAM

Explicitly depict the causes behind a situation and their magnitude of influence

Move away from superficially listing causes to grouping them and analysing the extent of their influence on an outcome. The Fishbone Diagram is visually simple. Its value resides in the construction process, as you unearth the causal relationships of a situation.

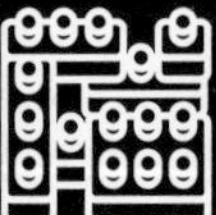

Construction instruction

1 | List causes

Purpose

As with all graphic organisers, the collection of content presents an opportunity for retrieval practice or selecting material from texts. The initial collection or selection of ideas should be divorced from any organising to avoid overloading your students.

cause cause cause cause cause cause
cause cause cause cause cause cause

Action

Begin by collecting the causes of a situation you are studying, writing each on an individual sticky note or text box on a screen. Doing so will allow you to group the individual causes with ease in the following steps.

2 | Group causes

Purpose

The grouping of causes offers greater clarity and a deeper understanding. Why? Because you analyse the shared characteristics between each cause. By arranging causes into groups, you begin to unearth causal patterns, leading to deeper understanding.

Title 1		Title 2		Title 3	
cause	cause	cause	cause	cause	cause
cause	cause	cause	cause	cause	cause

Action

Make an Affinity Map with the sticky notes or text boxes you created in step one. Physically group the causes that seem to belong together because of shared attributes. Give each group a title that captures the commonality of the categorised causes.

3 | Draw the Fishbone Diagram

Purpose

The Fishbone Diagram appears deceptively simple. As with most graphic organisers, it is the process, not the finished product, that elicits meaningful learning. The finished product serves to support extended writing and classroom discussions. An advanced version of the Fishbone Diagram is detailed in step 4.

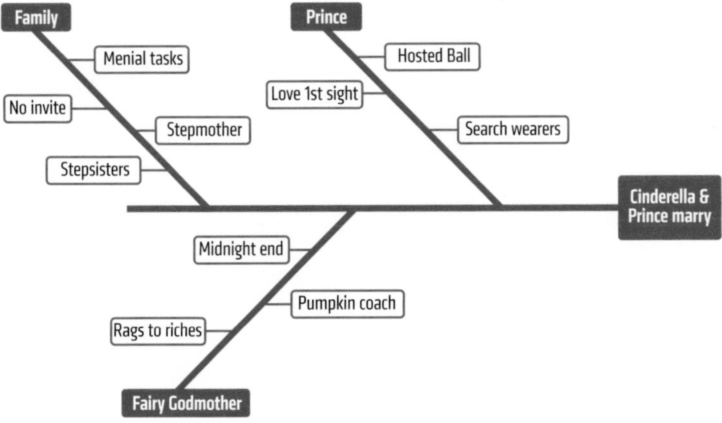

Action

Construct the Fishbone Diagram by drawing diagonally the same number of branches as there are categories. Attach the diagonal branches to a central, horizontal line. Place the outcome to be analysed at the far right of the horizontal line. At the end of each diagonal branch, write the titles for each of the identified categories. Write each cause on horizontal lines attached to the main diagonal branch of their appropriate group.

4 | Advanced Fishbone Diagram

Purpose

The advanced Fishbone Diagram arranges causes in order of magnitude of influence. Such a configuration requires you to analyse which forces are most responsible for the outcome being studied.

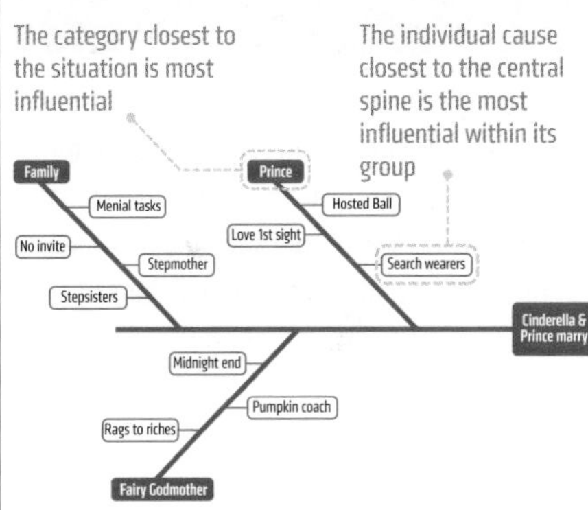

Action

Decide which category has the most influence on the situation. Place this category on the branch closest to the outcome. Within each group, analyse which individual cause is most influential. Place this on the horizontal line nearest the central spine.

TYPE | **CAUSE & EFFECT**

INPUT-OUTPUT DIAGRAM

Depict the cause-and-effect dynamic and the catalyst it is centred around

Developing your students' understanding of cause-and-effect dynamics can be challenging. Identifying the catalyst around which the dynamic pivots allows you to depict the complex cause-and-effect relationships.

Construction instruction

1 | Capture the preceding events

Purpose

Capturing the causes and effects in separate steps is beneficial for many reasons. Firstly, and most obviously, it reduces the risk of cognitive overload. It allows you to evaluate the cause-and-effect factors and to retain those that are valid. Finally, greater attention is given to the pivotal event on which the cause-and-effect relationship hinges.

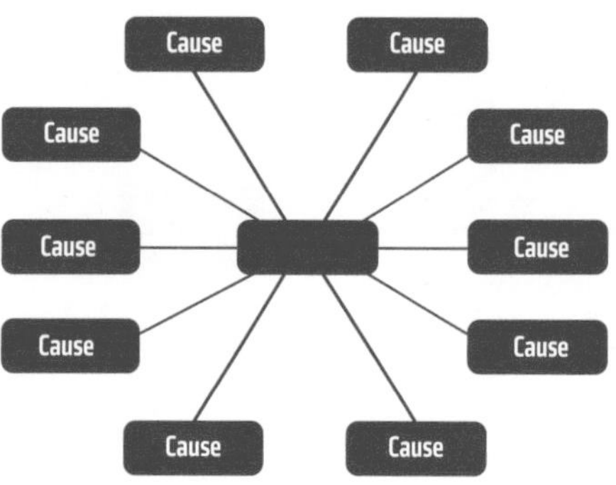

Action

Identify the pivotal event to be studied. Using a Spray Map, capture all the potential causes preceding the decisive event. Focus on causal events, discarding those that are only temporal.

2 | Capture the after events

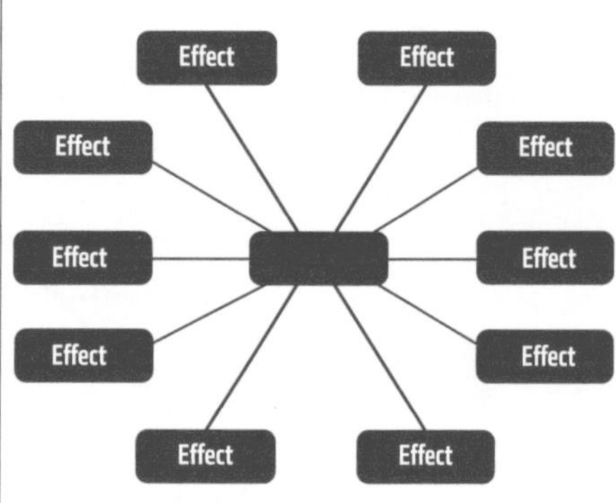

Action

Using a separate Spray Map, capture the events following the pivotal event. Discard any event that isn't dependent upon the decisive event. You should only identify causal links.

3 | Construct the diagram

Purpose

The diagram is a simple visual metaphor for the purpose it serves. The Input-Output Diagram helps you and your students identify the pre- and post-connections of a pivotal event. As such, the diagram can help shape your students' thinking about critical events.

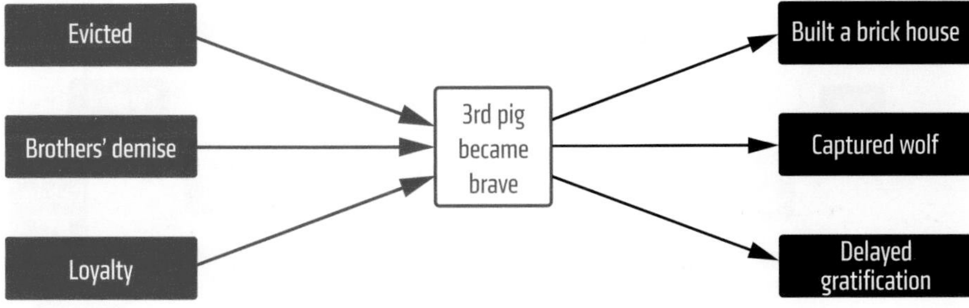

Action

Place the causes in a vertical arrangement on the left-hand side of the diagram. To emphasise the significance of the pivotal event, place it in the centre of the diagram. Use a different colour, further emphasising its importance. Draw arrows from the causes to the pivotal event. On the right-hand side, vertically arrange the effects. Draw individual arrows from the pivotal event to each effect.

TYPE | **CAUSE & EFFECT**

RELATIONS DIAGRAM

Elements relate to each other in a number of ways other than in a hierarchy

Identifying potential causes or, at least, forces of influence and connecting them together is a complex process – one that will overwhelm your working memory. By breaking down the process into three distinct parts, using three different diagrams, this danger is avoided and a map of the network of causal relations is captured.

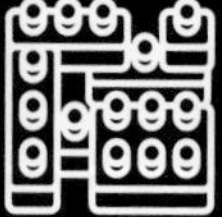

Construction instruction

1 | Create a Single Spray

Purpose

As with so many processes, the collection and capture of ideas is critical here. The Single Spray is perfect for this purpose, with all triggered thoughts emanating from the centre. Yes, a list does the same job if that is better suited to your participants.

Action

From a central issue, capture, in radiant fashion, the ideas that surface. At this stage there is no editing or evaluative function to the process. Capture should be your sole concern.

2 | Expand into a Cluster

Purpose

Having made a start with a Single Spray, the intention now is to expand and discover all linked associations.

Action

The emphasis remains on generating content rather than evaluating it. A Cluster – with its non-hierarchical format, perhaps familiar to students through a creative writing module – helps stimulate this exploration.

3 | Reconfigure into a Relations Diagram

Purpose

We now arrive at the creation of the Relations Diagram itself. With the content generated, the focus changes to causal links.

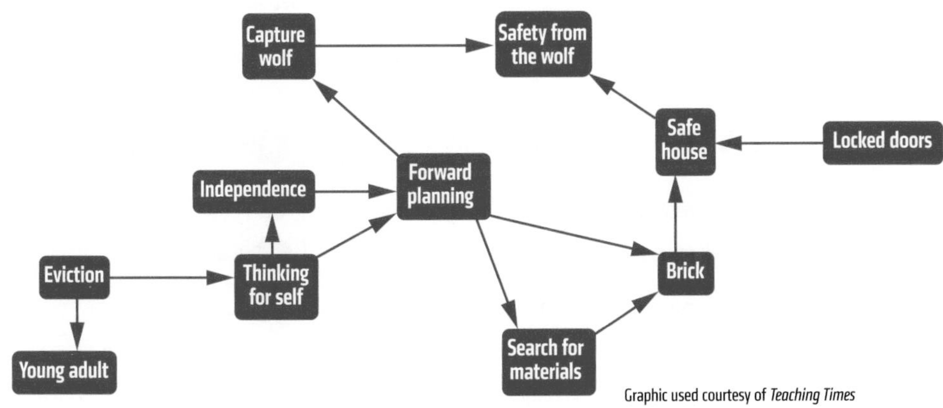

Graphic used courtesy of *Teaching Times*

Action

The content needs to be reconfigured into a network of causal links. These are established by asking of each element which of the others can be seen as causal in some way. Arrows are drawn between the two elements, in the direction of the causal impact. Sticky notes are useful here, in order to avoid a graphically messy and confusing diagram where many arrows cross over each other.

TYPE | **CAUSE & EFFECT**

FLOWSCAPE

A novel graphic approach to identifying the source and development of our perceptions

Flowscape is a three-step process that leads to insights into the architecture of the perceptions and thoughts that often determine many of our actions. It surfaces responses to our environment and others that are mostly unconscious – until we put the spotlight on them and how they interrelate.

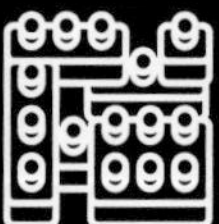

Construction instruction

1 | Identify the elements

Purpose

Identify the elements of your thoughts and feelings regarding the particular situation you want to analyse. List them and, by the side, allocate a letter (or number), as below.

A | Eviction
B | Self-regulation
C | Planning
D | Patience
E | Courage
F | Building skills
G | Knowledge of danger
H | Independent thinking
I | Hunger

2 | Expand into a Cluster

Purpose

Starting with the first element in the list, consider which other single element it most relates to. This relationship, Edward de Bono explains, must be a "*flow*" from one to the other (hence *Flowscape*). Then continue with the second element in the list in the same way. It is critical to note that elements can be chosen several times, as shown below.

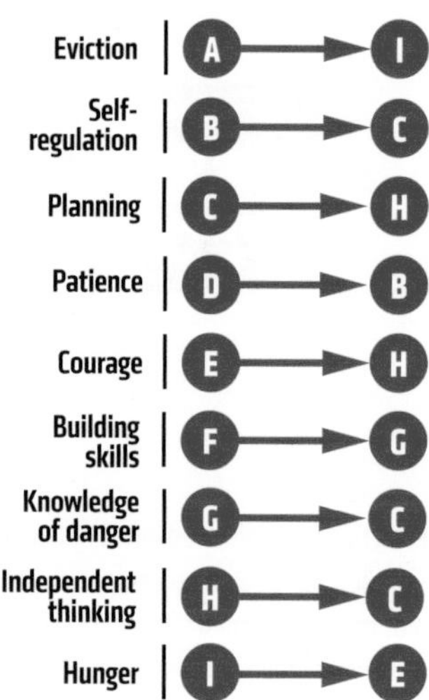

3 | Map the relationships

Purpose

Surveying the pairs, start to map them out. Because some elements can – and invariably will – be chosen several times, the mapping can become rather complex. In order to avoid a confusing picture and, instead, to show with clarity the nature of the emerging patterns, it is far easier to work with sticky notes, or their digital equivalent. This aids in experimenting with different configurations, where crossed lines are avoided. While all Flowscape maps will differ, the one below shows a typical range of patterns, each of which is listed in the key in step 4.

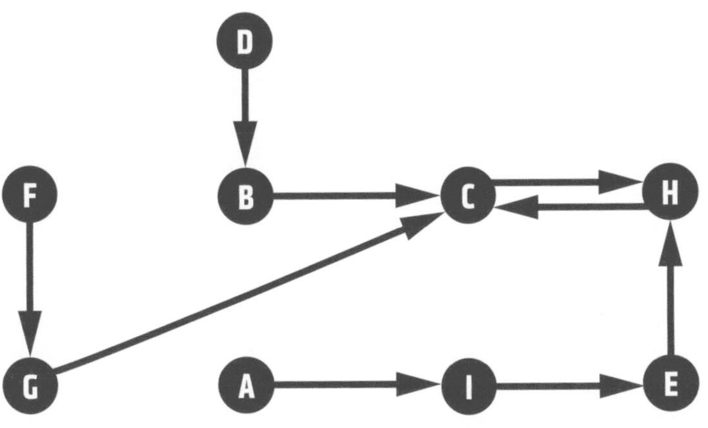

4 | Read the map

Purpose

Using the key below, you are armed to interpret the patterns you see in your map. Which elements feature at the centre of several arrows? Why are certain elements seemingly self-contained within their own loop? Does the sequence signify anything? What is the nature of two elements with reciprocating arrows?

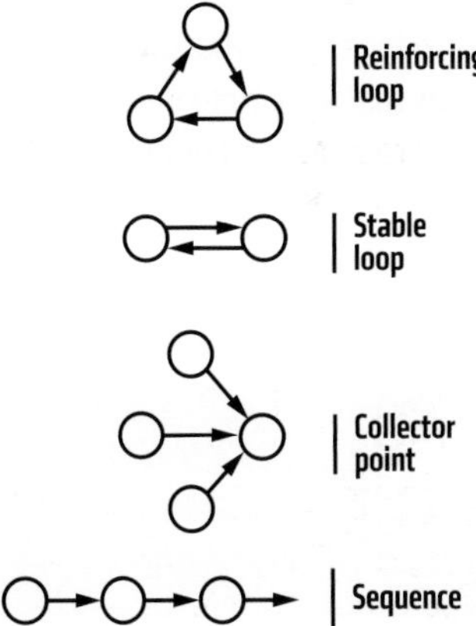

TYPE | **CAUSE & EFFECT**

CONSEQUENCES MAP

A diagram to curb enthusiasm by looking further ahead into possible chains of consequences

We tend to devalue what we call *pessimists* when, in reality, we ought to embrace their concerns. The Consequences Map is devoted to the search for all potential problems, via a chain of links that arise from the strategies chosen to achieve the aims of the project.

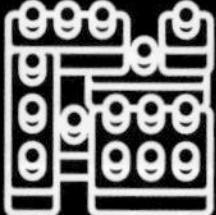

Construction instruction

1 | Identify the strategies to realise the aim

Purpose

State the specific strategies chosen to deliver the promises of the project.

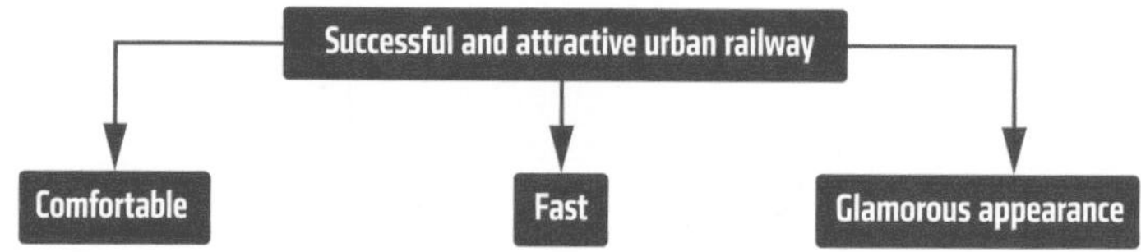

Action

A sticky note approach is best for this early work. Position the strategies along the top in anticipation of a wider array of consequences lower down.

2 | Identify the chain of consequences

Purpose

The real work starts here, anticipating the unintended but foreseeable chain of consequences arising from the strategies.

Successful and attractive urban railway
Comfortable
Fast
Glamorous appearance
Passengers: all seated
High acceleration & deceleration
Ends of train given streamlined shape
Lightweight carriages
Coupling & shunting difficult
Wide-gauge track for stability
Lightweight motors Aluminium wheels
Breakdowns harder to handle

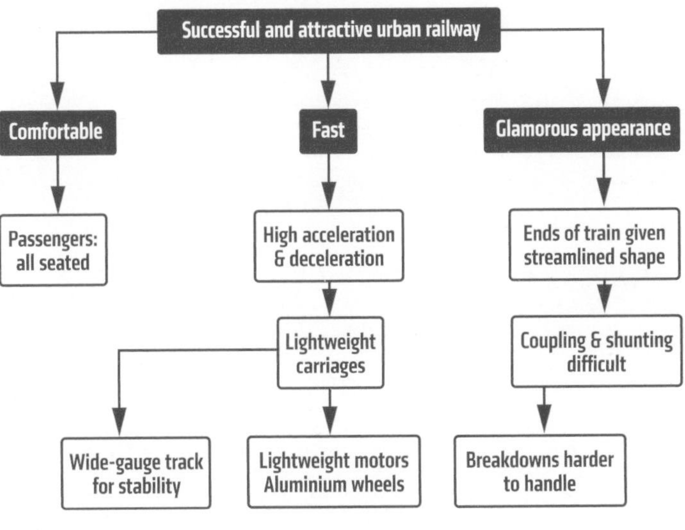

Action

Methodically and objectively, look into the future and imagine what might be the range of consequences of the adopted strategies. Place them below the associated strategies. Continue the chain to further consequences if they arise. Some may have several further consequences. Link them.

3 | Identify the resultant problems

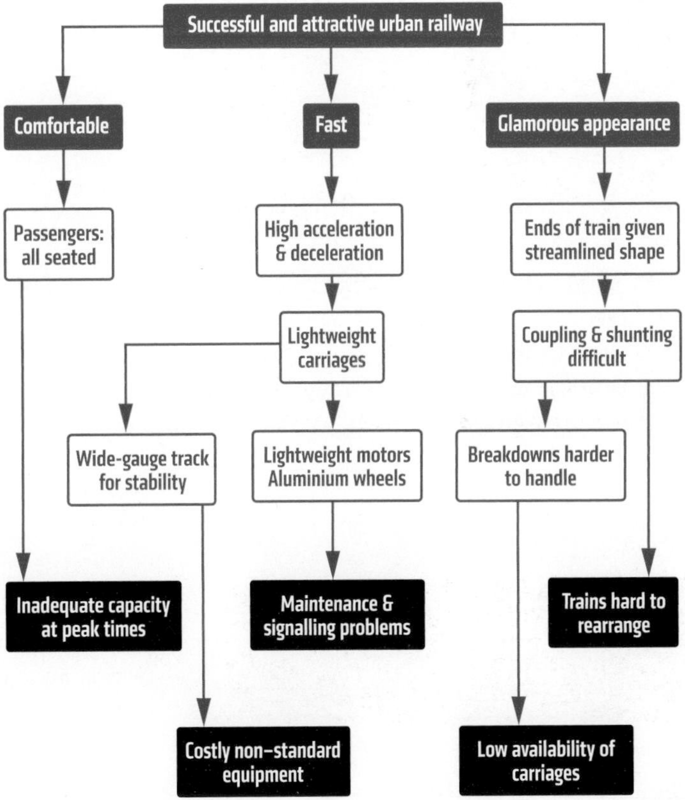

Successful and attractive urban railway
Comfortable
Fast
Glamorous appearance
Passengers: all seated
High acceleration & deceleration
Ends of train given streamlined shape
Lightweight carriages
Coupling & shunting difficult
Wide-gauge track for stability
Lightweight motors Aluminium wheels
Breakdowns harder to handle
Inadequate capacity at peak times
Maintenance & signalling problems
Trains hard to rearrange
Costly non-standard equipment
Low availability of carriages

Graphic organisers of all sorts by teachers of different age groups across an assortment of subjects — and all with fascinating and personal accounts of why and how they were used in real classrooms.

Chapters

AYELLET MCDONNELL

BEN NORRIS

BEN RANSON

BRETT KINGSBURY

CATHERINE ACTON

CAROL HARIRAM

CHARLOTTE HAWTHORNE

CHRISTIAN MOORE ANDERSON

CLARE MADDEN

DAN RODRIGUEZ-CLARK

DAVID KING

DAVID MORGAN

DEEPU ASOK

ELLIOT MORGAN

EMMA SLADE

EVE CAIRNS VOLLANS

FAHEEMAH VACHHIAT

FRAZER THORPE

GEORGE VLACHONIKOLIS

HELEN REYNOLDS

JANCKE DUNN

JJ WILSON

JOE BURKMAR

JOHN ETTY

JOHN HOUGH

JUSTIN WAKEFIELD

KELLY PEPPIN

LOUISE CASS

LUKE TAYLER

MADELEINE EVANS

MATT STONE

MEGAN BOWS

NICKY BLACKFORD

PETER RICHARDSON

PETER STOYKO

RACHEL WONG

SAM STEELE

SARAH JONES

SARAH LALLY

SARAH SANDEY

SELINA CHADWICK

SHAUN STEVENSON

SIMON BEALE

SIMON FLYNN

TIM BEATTIE

TOM HANSON

TOM ODDY

TOM SIMS

ZEPH BENNETT

AYELLET MCDONNELL

Graphic organisers help children organise ideas, build and extend connections, and embed knowledge in long-term memory.

Current job: Assistant headteacher and Year 6 teacher
Subject: All areas of primary curriculum
Age phase: Primary (7-11)
Organisation: Hartford Junior School

Why did you choose the graphic organiser in your example?

The graphic organiser in my example is a Mind Map. The subject content determined the type of organiser required. Using this graphic organiser provides a sound structure for students, defining the whole-part relationships within the subject. By breaking down the knowledge into its key components and illustrating the links between them, we can zoom in on different areas within the subject. This reduces cognitive load and enables students to organise the information, increasing the chances of it being encoded into long-term memory. In return, it makes it easier for them to retrieve and use the information in working memory.

How did you teach it to your students?

My students have not been explicitly taught how to use graphic organisers and although it is likely they have previously come across a variety of these, they would not know which organiser to use for which purpose. We needed to expose them to different types of organisers and their guiding principles. The first one was this Mind Map.

Introducing the Mind Map to students in its entirety would have caused cognitive overload. Instead, we introduced each main branch separately and explained to students the aim of creating a graphic organiser. I used the strategies presented by Oliver, asking students to copy the Mind Map as I revealed each element. I explained each piece of the Mind Map, capitalising on Allan Paivio's dual coding theory. Students were asked to trace their maps with their index finger while we repeated the information. The process was then repeated for each branch, so that by the end students had developed a rich understanding of their entire Mind Map.

Using this graphic organiser provides a sound structure for students, defining the whole-part relationships within the subject.

The result was high-quality writing by all, including those considered not strong writers.

How did you use the graphic organiser in conjunction with other strategies?

Initially, I used the Mind Map for retrieval practice, applying the Recount & Redraw strategy found in Oliver's *Dual Coding With Teachers*. Following Barak Rosenshine's weekly and monthly review principle (2012), I made sure students revisited the Mind Map each lesson to retrieve and rehearse the knowledge.

Revisiting the graphic organiser frequently enabled students to retrieve knowledge with relative ease over time. I combined the use of the graphic organiser with Judith C. Hochman and Natalie Wexler's strategies from their book *The Writing Revolution* (2017). The strategies helped students structure an explanation of their map. Because knowledge was embedded, students could focus on structuring and reasoning their writing as they linked the newly learnt knowledge to previously learnt content. The result was high-quality writing by all, including those considered not strong writers.

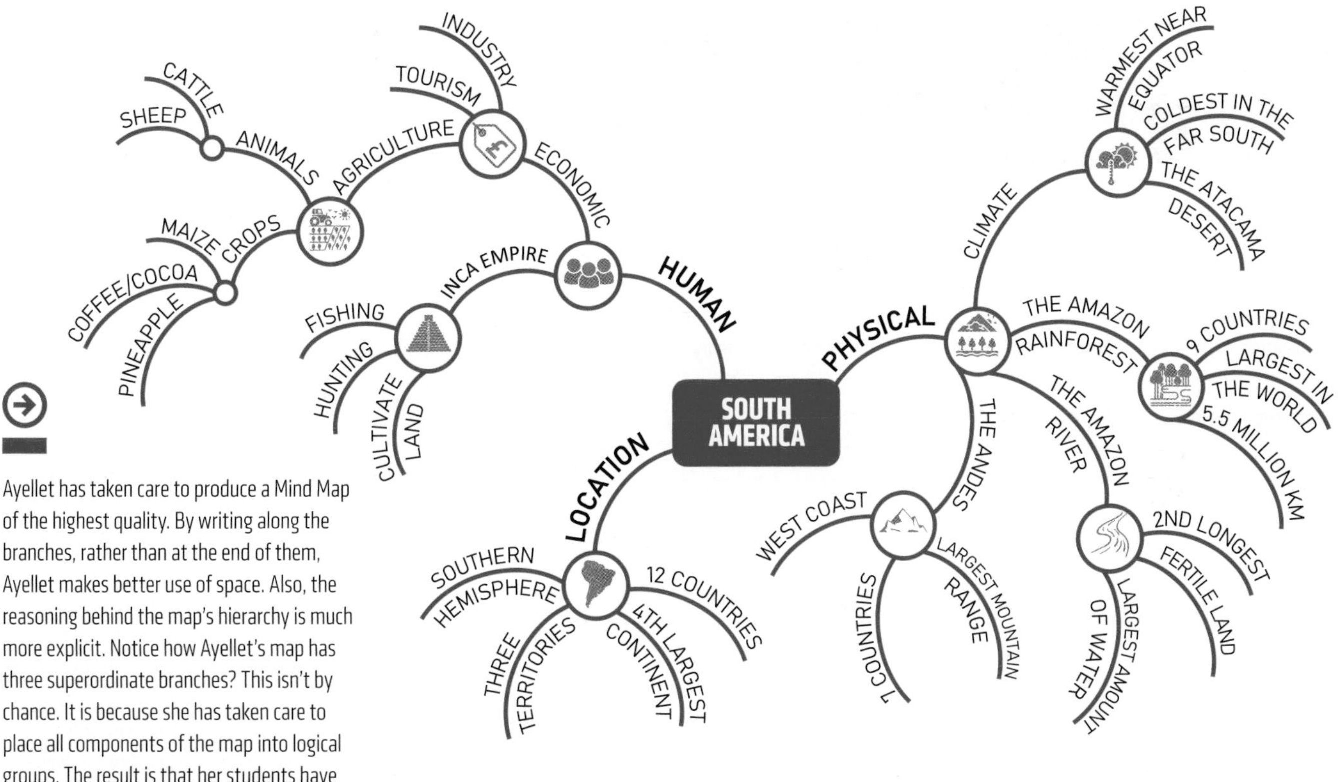

Ayellet has taken care to produce a Mind Map of the highest quality. By writing along the branches, rather than at the end of them, Ayellet makes better use of space. Also, the reasoning behind the map's hierarchy is much more explicit. Notice how Ayellet's map has three superordinate branches? This isn't by chance. It is because she has taken care to place all components of the map into logical groups. The result is that her students have organised their knowledge, making it more memorable and usable.

BEN NORRIS & JJ WILSON

Visual tools improve shared understanding within collaborative work by increasing the clarity of complex processes.

Current job: Phase leader
Age phase: Primary
Organisation: Shakespeare Primary School

Current job: Head of school
Age phase: Primary
Organisation: St Dominic Primary School

What problem did you face?

Our schools, like all others across the country, had been working hard to come to terms with the challenges presented by the global pandemic. We knew the problems that we faced in supporting pupils to access new curriculum learning along with what we wanted to offer. A myriad of decisions and logistical problems stood in our way, especially with ever-changing guidance and the needs of the school community. Following a questionnaire of our parents and carers, we quickly established that every household found itself in a different situation – e.g. lack of broadband, lack of available devices, lack of confidence. We needed a whole-school approach so that any stakeholder across the community could receive and understand the offer along with their responsibility.

The Flow Chart we have designed enables its user – leader, teacher, parent – to arrive at any one required solution.

Why did you choose this graphic organiser?

The problem we faced was unlike any other. Such was its complexity that it was almost impossible to distil into a coherent narrative – one that would support school leaders, teachers and parents to realise the full potential of our remote curriculum offer. The Flow Chart we have designed enables its user – leader, teacher, parent – to arrive at any one required solution. It allows for key pathways to be highlighted and exemplified.

How did you construct your graphic organiser?

In order to represent our ideas clearly, we used Post-it notes so that each thought became an object to work with. Through a series of questions, it became easier to manipulate in view than when abstract and in head. In short, the model enabled us to hack the limits of working memory, so that we could free up space to find the best curriculum solution for our schools and the communities they serve.

How does this Flow Chart support the successful outcome of a remote learning strategy?

We have been able to successfully develop a whole-school strategy, using our model for clarity in explanation and practical delivery. One benefit of the Flow Chart is that specific pathways can be isolated to exemplify expectations for a specific child, class or teacher. An ever-changing environment meant we needed all stakeholders to be prepared for every possible eventuality. Presenting our strategy using this graphic organiser enabled all stakeholders to understand their roles within the process, reducing misconceptions and offering adaptability if a child's personal circumstances were to change. It will allow for a transition to remote learning to take place in a formulaic, coherent and succinct way. This will mean that all children, regardless of personal circumstances, can access new learning.

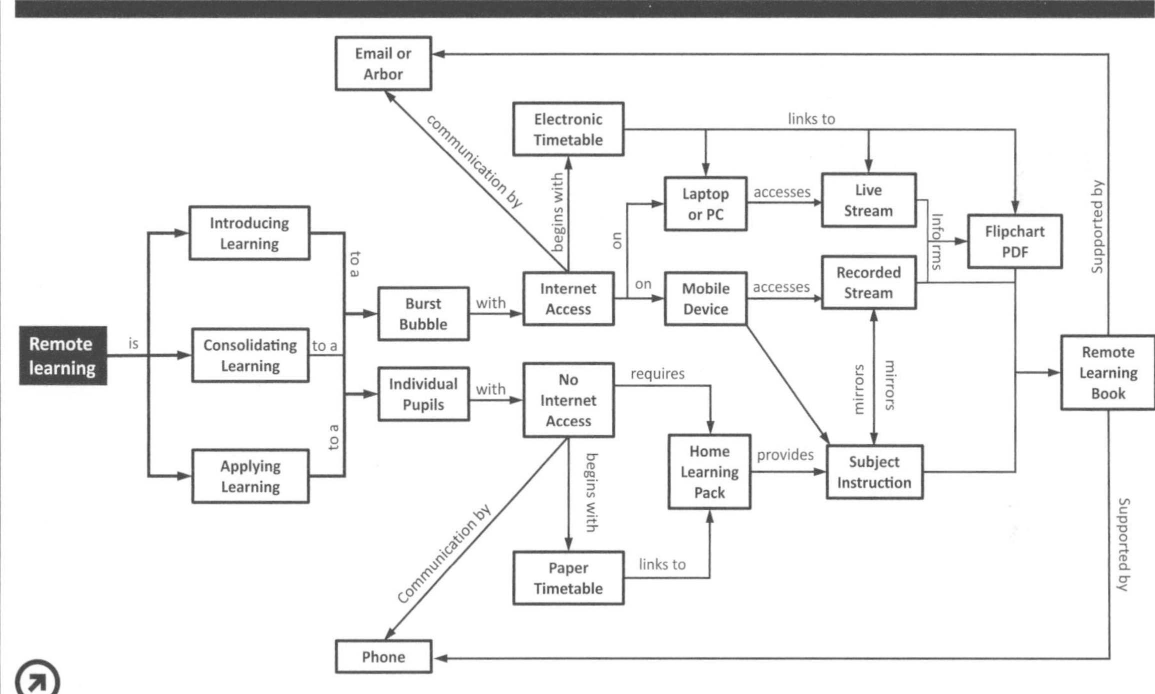

Ben and JJ's organiser goes by different names: Algorithm, decision tree, Flow Chart and process map. Their graphic represents possible alternative routes through a variety of options. The organiser helps teachers, students and parents bypass the obstacles of remote learning – the challenges and their solutions are in full view for all to see. When a situation has three to five individual components, you might get to grips with it, but one with any more than that is beyond most people's cognitive capabilities. When reading a diagram like Ben and JJ's, the reader can look at the problem from different angles and search for the heart of the matter with efficiency.

BEN RANSON

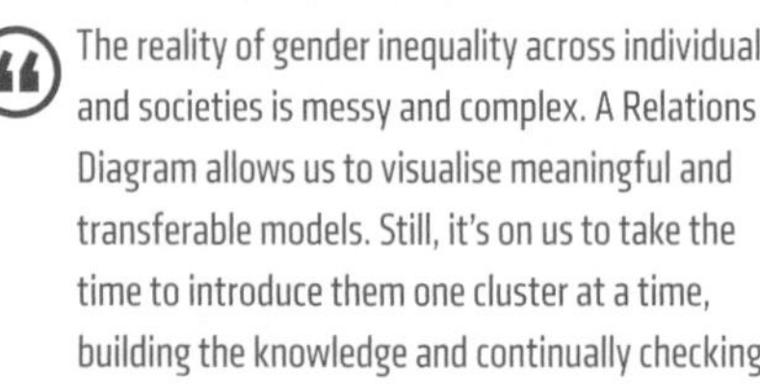

The reality of gender inequality across individuals and societies is messy and complex. A Relations Diagram allows us to visualise meaningful and transferable models. Still, it's on us to take the time to introduce them one cluster at a time, building the knowledge and continually checking for understanding.

Current job: Assistant headteacher (KS3)
Subject: Geography
Age phase: Secondary (11-16)
Organisation: El Alsson British International School, Cairo, Egypt

---

Isn't your completed Relations Diagram complex to look at?

Yes. Absolutely. But that's precisely the point. The factors that contribute to Nigeria's high rate of population growth are complex and interconnected. It takes a lot of unpacking to get a real understanding of why. A Relations Diagram is the perfect tool for showing how these factors lead into one another and contribute to a systemic limitation of women's opportunities and the perpetuation of child marriage. It takes time for students to grasp what's at work here. No one looks at the entirety of the Relations Diagram without a secure understanding of the noun-factors first. We need students' working memories to be free to see how the puzzle pieces fit together. If they're struggling with what a dowry payment is or what colonial legacy is, then we've not done a good enough job of managing cognitive load.

How do you go about introducing it?

Piece by piece, step by step. Cause and effect. Beginning with the end. We know that the fertility rate in Nigeria is high – it's measurable. We also know that Nigeria isn't alone in having a high fertility rate. So, we ask:

- How would secure access to contraception affect this?
- How would lowering the likelihood of conception result in a lower fertility rate?
- Why would we expect fertility rates to be lower in areas where young people are educated about sexual and reproductive health?
- What if those young people didn't have access to that education?
- What if funding family planning clinics wasn't a high priority in the government's budget?
- Why might it be more of a priority if there were more women in government?

Oluyemi Oloyede

The national average of women's political participation in Nigeria has remained 6.7 percent in elective and appointive positions, which is far below the Global Average of 22.5 percent.

Oloyede, 2016

Is this just about Nigeria?

What we're developing through cause-and-effect chains is a mental model. A process of linking actions and their consequences, intended or otherwise. Through modelling how to think through demographic data, we're supporting students in developing a framework for investigating gender equality. While the convergence of gender inequality is expressed through high fertility rates in Nigeria, it can and will be manifested differently in different places. To take part in the wider conversations of humankind, our students need a model that supersedes the Nigeria organiser and can be applied to question the value placed on girls' education, opportunities and freedom anywhere and everywhere.

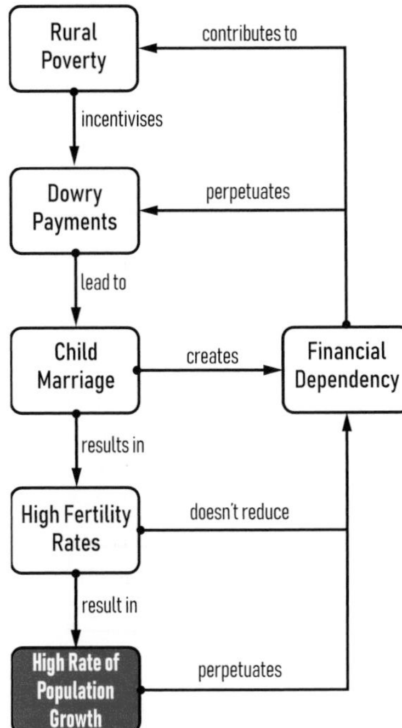

To give you an appreciation for Ben's scrupulous planning and insight into how he introduces graphic organisers, we thought it best to reveal his Relations Diagram in clusters, similar to how he does with his students.

How do you mine it for all it's worth?

Several weeks are spent building students' understanding of the issues involved before they're in a position to make meaning from the interplay between them. Having taken the time to design the whole Relations Diagram, it's rewarding for me as the teacher to be able to use individual strands as precursors. The ideas of inequality, poverty, rural isolation, governmental priorities, patriarchal values and colonial legacies are big and complex. Introducing each one as its own chain of cause and effect increases our students' familiarity with the visual organisation of noun-factors. The graphic organiser also acts as an aide-memoire for my planning. I can hold myself to account against each of the strands. What might we need to retrieve from earlier in the year to be successful in that lesson? It helps me to think about sequencing, making sure we're introducing ideas early enough that we can recall them later.

How do you share it with students when they're ready?

Printed on paper. Analogue. The Relations Diagram is chock-full of information and there's a lot to work with. We start by examining its

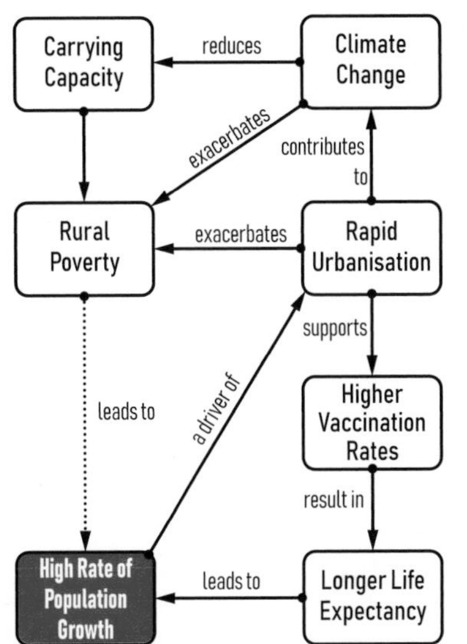

With each new cluster that Ben introduces, the level of complexity increases. But he avoids the risk of cognitive overload by cautiously revealing content in manageable batches.

organisation. Why are colonial legacies and patriarchal values centred and bordered in red? What does this say about their influence and significance? Once students are comfortable that the diagram radiates from the centre and converges on high fertility rates, then we're ready to start unpacking some of the ideas and examining the connections. I typically spend an entire lesson on this, with each student annotating their copy of the graphic organiser while I check for understanding.

How does its layout support checking for understanding?

Each verb-connector offers up so many questions. The first is to explain what we mean by each of the ideas. What is rural poverty? What might be its indicators? How could we measure it? How would it be different from urban poverty? Then I can ask the students about the link. Why does rural poverty incentivise dowry payments? Why does child marriage create financial dependency? I can ask challenging questions of syntax in verb-connectors: why is the influence of colonial legacies and patriarchal values on dowry payments to *perpetuate* them, but to *promote* child marriage? I've found examining these verb-connector choices a rewarding rabbit hole, and it's a question that necessitates hard thinking. How is *promoting* different from *perpetuating*? What alternative synonyms could we use? I can ask students to group similar themes, recognising how environmental noun-factors are disconnected from educational policy decisions but still contribute to the same outcome. I don't think it's possible to communicate this idea in any other format while taking into account students' working memory.

What do they do with this understanding?

Ideally, they take a stand for the international standard that people should have equal rights and opportunities regardless of gender. In a more immediate timeframe, students use the Relations Diagram to support their writing. Simply, why does Nigeria have a high rate of population growth? Having the noun-factors and verb-connectors laid out in the diagram outsources much of the cognitive demand of writing structure. This, in turn, frees up students' working memory to focus on sentence formation and expanding the noun-factor fragments. The results speak for themselves.

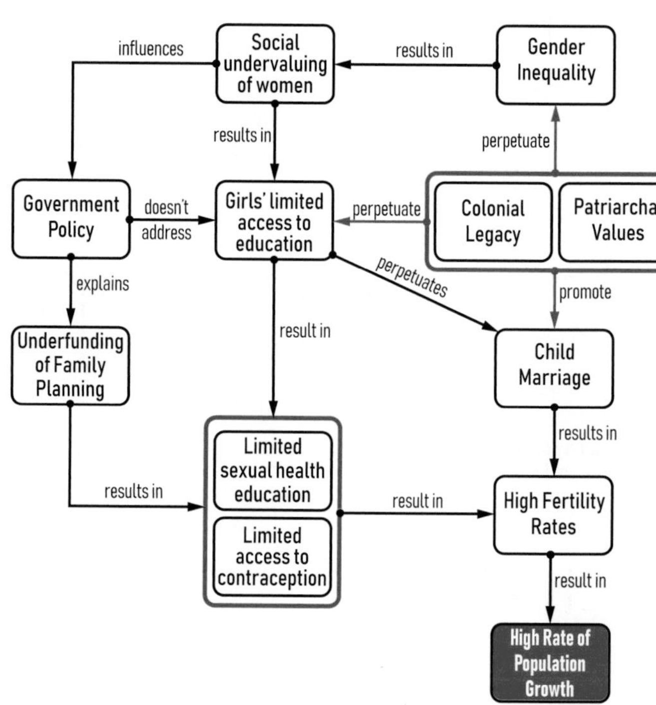

Geography is a subject founded on interdisciplinary knowledge. Using a graphic organiser can help students identify and construct rich associations between big ideas. The content represented in Ben's diagram is complex. We commend him for his ingenuity in depicting it in such a manner. While his Relations Diagram is stunning, what is clear is that for Ben, the process of its use is more important than the finished product. And rightly so. While some might fear such graphic

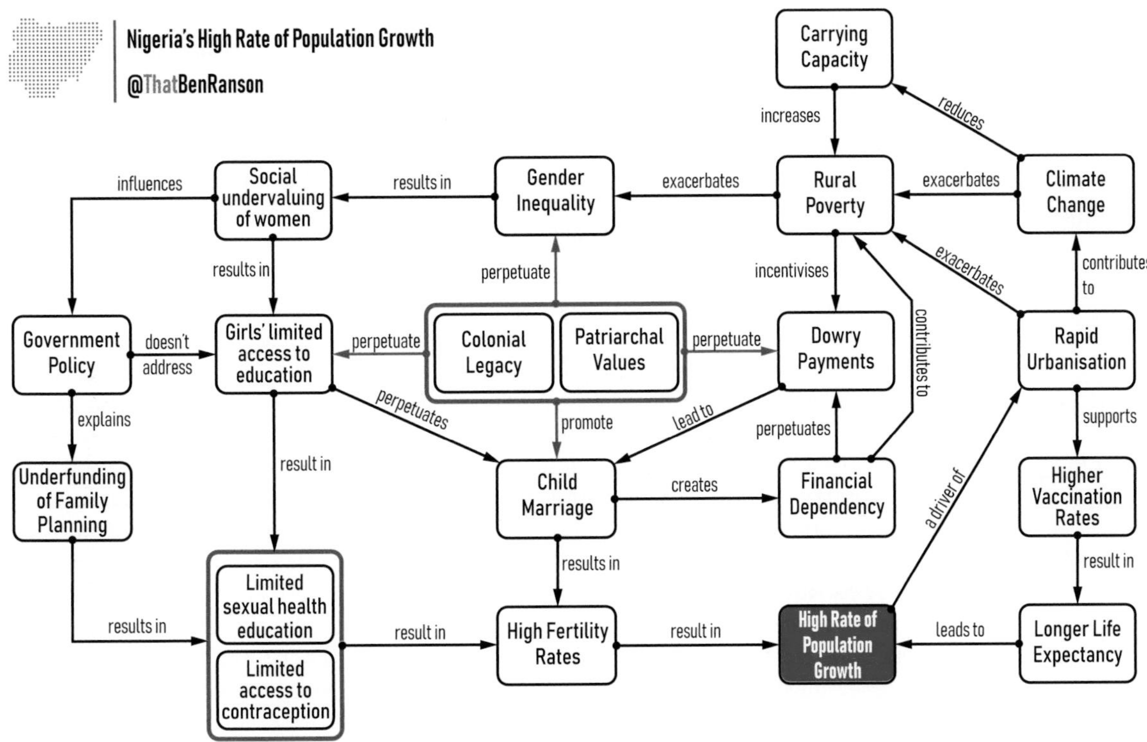

organisers are reductionist, remember the product is not the learning – it is an access point to meaning. Given the complexity of the big ideas and the myriad connections, it would be difficult for anyone who is not a subject expert to arrive at the same meaning conveyed by this diagram using prose alone. That is to say, the Relations Diagram allows Ben's students to gain insight into how he organises knowledge. As is to be expected by someone who has invested a lot of time in thinking about his organiser's construction, Ben has respected the principles of cut, chunk, align and restrain. He has an eye for sophisticated graphic design.

BRETT KINGSBURY

Graphic organisers help manage the load as students juggle the selection of appropriate sentence structures with retrieval of recently acquired knowledge.

Current job: Deputy faculty leader of science
Subject: Biology
Age phase: Secondary and FE (11-18)
Organisation: City of Norwich School

Why and how did you choose this graphic organiser?

Comparisons are a common organisation of knowledge in biology, owing both to the huge diversity in living organisms and to the fact that they have evolved over time from a single common ancestor around 3.9 billion years ago. This results in biological components that living organisms share and precise differences in those components that result in the classification of different species.

In my example comparison, it is now understood that single circulatory systems, similar to that found in modern fish, were the precursors of double circulatory systems found in birds and mammals. They share similarities that make them both circulatory systems, but they have key differences that distinguish them as examples of single or double systems. For single-continua comparisons like this, the best choice of graphic organiser is between a Venn Diagram and a Double Spray. While most students are familiar with Venn Diagrams, I've found many issues with students using them – from poor construction (such as drawing very small circles that barely overlap, leaving little room for content) to interpretation issues (some students just don't get the meaning of the different compartments). Double Sprays are an improvement on Venn Diagrams for two reasons. Firstly, the use of lines directly joining the similarity/difference to the items being compared makes the connection more concrete to the student. Secondly, they encourage further organisation of the similarities/differences, in that they can be shown hierarchically or in comparable pairs.

How did you introduce this graphic organiser in your lessons?

The ubiquity of comparisons in biology means graphic organisers like Double Sprays are of high utility in my subject and well worth the short time needed to teach students how to construct and interpret them. I think this is one of the easiest graphic organisers to teach students to use independently, as the spatial arrangement remains the same as that of the familiar Venn Diagram (central similarities and peripheral differences) and only connections to two items are under consideration. Initially, I would construct the Double Spray in chunks during the instructional phase, explaining the similarities and differences of the more concrete aspects first (the structure of the heart) before moving to the more abstract (differences in systemic pressure). Students have then seen a clear model of construction and use of the graphic organiser, meaning I can use it for retrieval practice later in the teaching sequence or via self-quizzing homework.

How did you use the graphic organiser to support other strategies?

Beyond initial instruction of the content and later retrieval practice, I also utilise the further organisation element of a Double Spray as a support for students in writing comparative sentences. Due to the spatial arrangement of the differences, they can be arranged to form comparable pairs. I then model how these are used to write comparative sentences – e.g. *The heart in a fish circulatory system has two chambers, whereas there are four chambers in the heart of a human*. The organiser can be annotated to show the different comparative vocabulary that can be used when comparing similarities (both, in common, similarly) or differences (whereas, however, while).

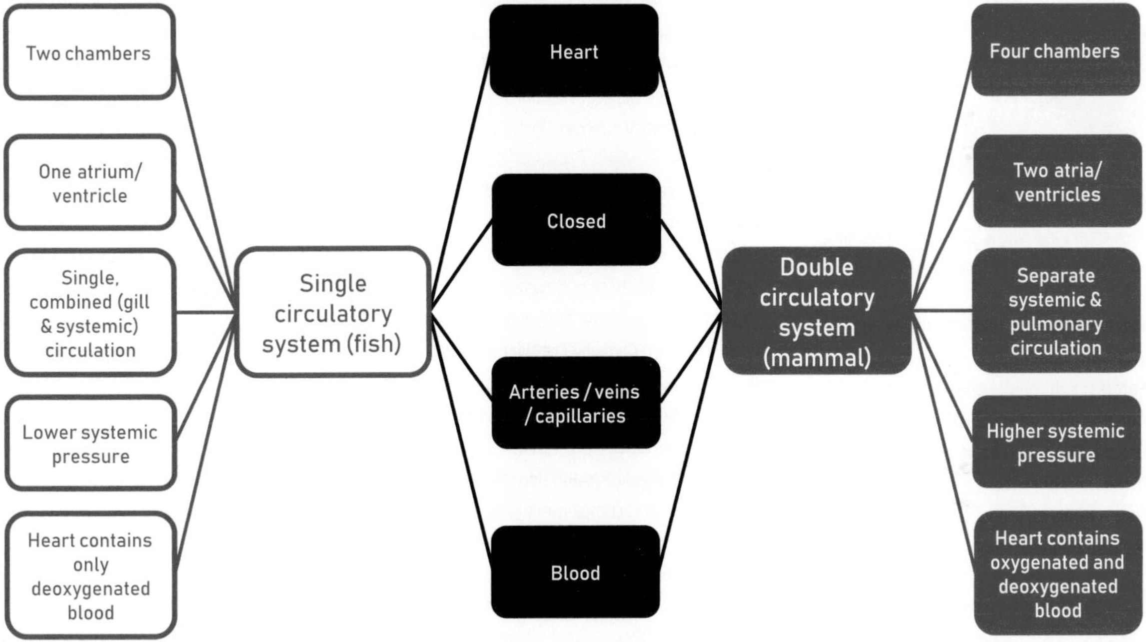

Two chambers

One atrium/ ventricle

Single, combined (gill & systemic) circulation

Lower systemic pressure

Heart contains only deoxygenated blood

Single circulatory system (fish)

Heart

Closed

Arteries / veins / capillaries

Blood

Double circulatory system (mammal)

Four chambers

Two atria/ ventricles

Separate systemic & pulmonary circulation

Higher systemic pressure

Heart contains oxygenated and deoxygenated blood

Brett's Double Spray is expertly crafted. Double Spray organisers show which attributes are similar and which are different. The centrally linked characteristics are those that are similar. Brett has made similarities and differences more noticeable with his effective use of colour. He has also used the principle of alignment, spatially arranging comparable pairs. In doing so, Brett helps his students organise their knowledge according to its intended use – students will be able to write comparative sentences.

CATHERINE ACTON

Parents in our community are focusing on how their child's learning is organised to enhance memory and create conversations of interest.

Current job: Class teacher, writing and grammar leader
Subject: Community engagement
Age phase: Primary (3-11)
Organisation: Mayflower Community Academy
In partnership with
Isaura Roberts: Higher-level teaching assistant
Melissa Palmer: School parent

Why did you choose to introduce graphic organisers into your community?

Teachers use graphic organisers in school. Why should these be kept a secret? By giving our parents access to the most effective methods of learning, our intention is that we will work in partnership with parents and create a culture of collective responsibility for pupil outcomes. Introducing graphic organisers into our community has allowed us to become more transparent in our teaching techniques. These techniques enable our learners to transfer the knowledge taught in school beyond the classroom and into conversations at home.

How are graphic organisers used within the community?

Our remote learning strategy centres around pupils being able to select, organise and integrate their learning. We primarily chose to do this through our subject-driver: history. In order to expand children's depth of understanding, we have combined graphic organisers with two other reference tools (knowledge organisers and tiered vocabulary). These three tools complement each other by enabling pupils to move away from seeing knowledge as isolated lists of information and towards identifying new learning and locating it within their cross-subject schema. These tools stimulate subject-related conversations between pupils, peers, teachers and parents. Expanding on the work in school, and through tailored online workshops, teachers have empowered parents to support their children to select, organise and integrate learning at home.

ISAURA ROBERTS

MELISSA PALMER

These tools stimulate subject-related conversations between pupils, peers, teachers and parents.

How has using graphic organisers impacted the community?

As a result of our community engagement, pupils are able to recall their subject knowledge of a certain area of the curriculum at home with increased confidence – and their curiosity is stimulated, along with their parents' curiosity. Parents have been able to identify the importance of organising ideas on a page in a way that makes links between prior knowledge and new knowledge. Our hope now is that parents will be able to use this process to instigate and meaningfully engage with their children, taking an informed role in the process of selecting, organising and integrating learning. However, most importantly, introducing graphic organisers into our community has enabled parents to support their child and connect school and home together for a considered approach to learning. Parents have become empowered to teach, share and celebrate their new skills, with many parents now feeling ready to run their own workshops.

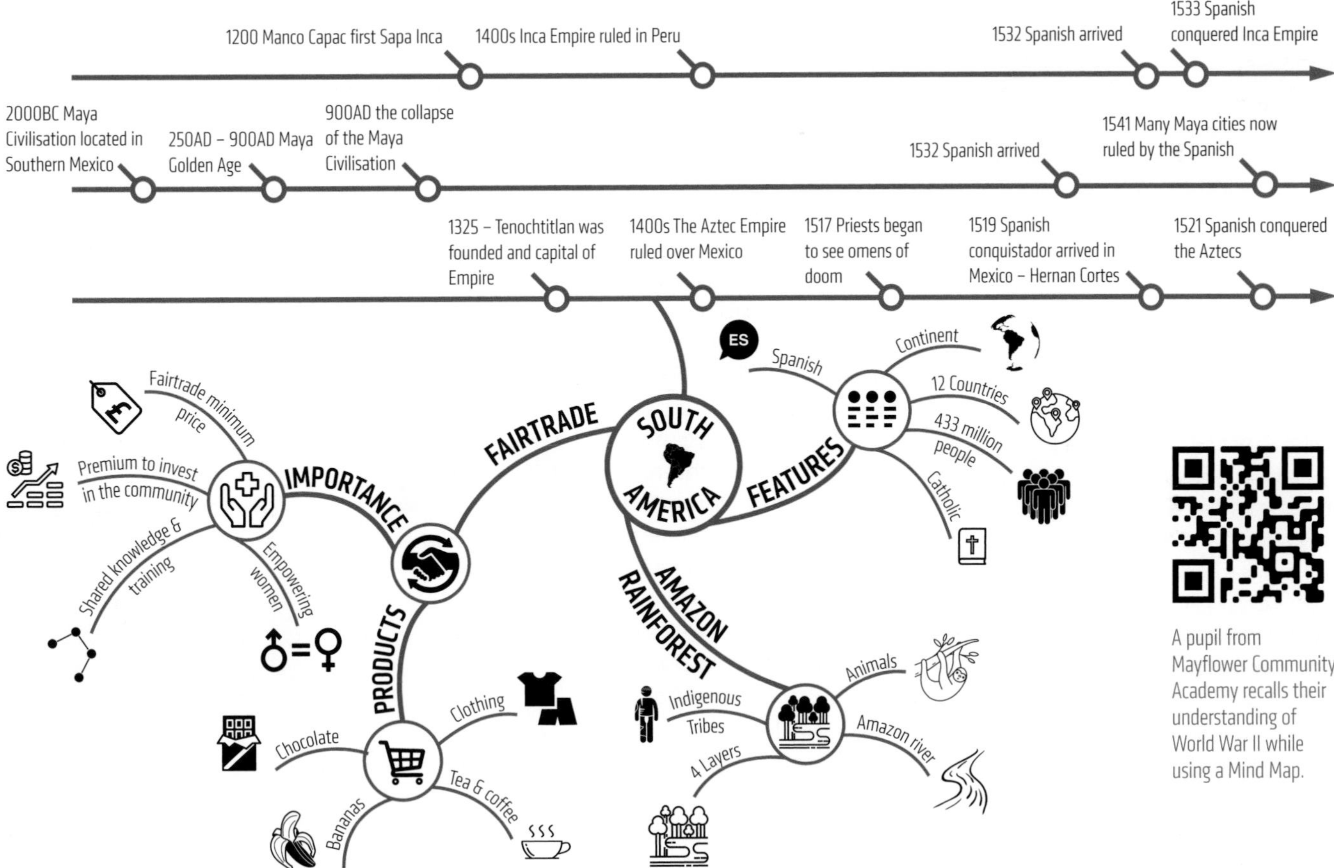

A pupil from Mayflower Community Academy recalls their understanding of World War II while using a Mind Map.

CAROL HARIRAM

Carol Hariram taught with Oliver at Woodlands special (SLD) school in Chelmsford, Essex. She died in 2016. This is a tribute to her skills and commitment.

Avoiding overload

Carol taught the full age range, from 3-19. The maps on the opposite page are from a series of maps she used when teaching in the further education department. One problem Carol faced was in covering all the content for a PSH topic and, at the same time, avoiding overloading the students. A canny way around this was in using nested maps. The top map shows the *big picture* of what the particular PSH topic would cover. Lower down is how one aspect of the topic (hygiene) is developed in more detail. In this way, Carol was able to zoom out and then zoom in.

Nested maps

In Frederick Reif's *Applying Cognitive Science to Education* (2008) he writes about how we are all familiar with this strategy, giving the example of geographic maps. He explains that, initially, one would show a map of the US, pinpointing the area to pursue in more detail. This is then followed by a map of California, where the particular village in question is situated. Finally, out comes a map showing the details of the village and surrounding areas. With exactly the same approach, Carol showed her students the big ideas of their PSH study. This was then followed by a series of maps that expanded these ideas with increasing fidelity. Critical to the success of this approach was that Carol put the maps on the walls after their introduction. By doing this, she was able to continually point and refer to the larger map when investigating with her students details of the most recent map. This enabled Carol's students to navigate and connect a far greater volume of information than could otherwise have been thought possible.

David Ausubel

Advance organizers are designed to favour meaningful learning.

Ausubel, 1978

Advance organisers

Another way in which this strategy can be framed is David Ausubel's advance organisers (1960). With the accent on meaningful learning and its retention, Ausubel argued and researched the benefit of giving students the major concepts or principles at the very start. Thus, when students encountered the subsequent details, those details were *housed*, so to speak, in the appropriate places. Technically, this was termed *subsumption* and it is close in meaning to Jean Piaget's explanation of schema development (1952).

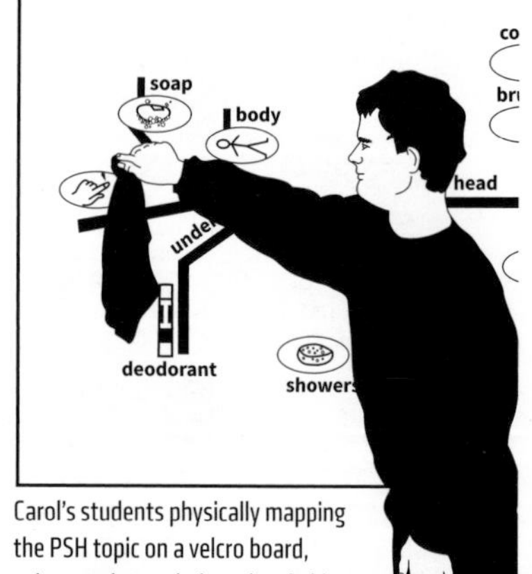

Carol's students physically mapping the PSH topic on a velcro board, using words, symbols and real objects.

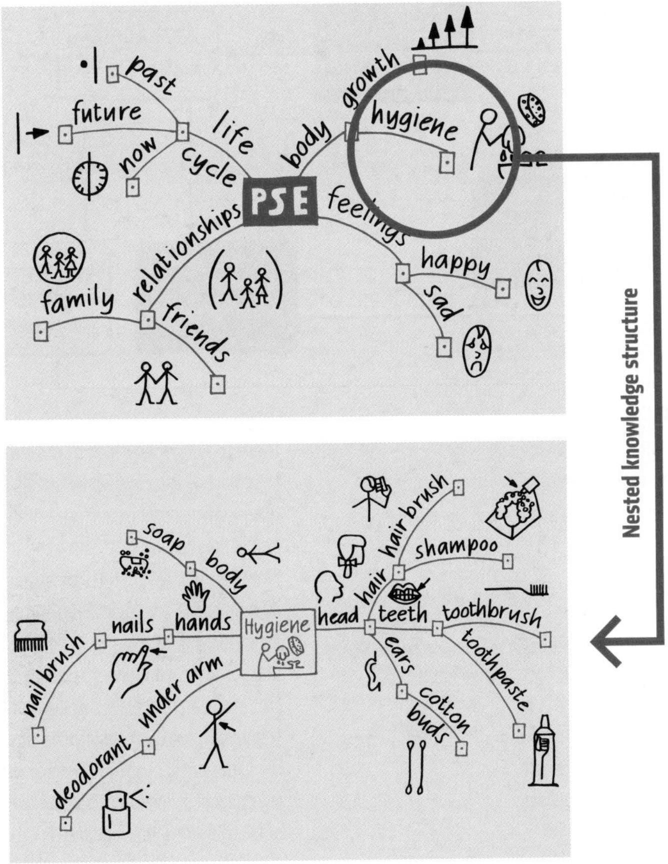

PSE
life cycle
past
future
now
body
growth
hygiene
feelings
happy
sad
relationships
family
friends

Hygiene
soap
body
hands
nails
nail brush
under arm
deodorant
head
hair
hair brush
shampoo
teeth
toothbrush
toothpaste
ears
cotton buds

Nested knowledge structure

In a 2006 article for *Special Children* magazine, Oliver and Tina Detheridge discussed linear use of symbols in special schools. But Carol's practice showed symbols could more profitably be used in non-linear fashion. The diagram to the left exemplifies this.

Making ideas come alive

Symbols have become a mainstay of communication in special schools and are increasingly finding a place in mainstream settings. Here, **Oliver Caviglioli** and **Tina Detheridge** explain why and discuss how these 'visual tools' might be used in the future

CHARLOTTE HAWTHORNE

> Mathematics is a huge interconnected web of ideas – sometimes you can take a small part of this and explicitly show these connections to students. This is where I feel graphic organisers can be so powerful in mathematics.

Current job: Second in faculty
Subject: Mathematics
Age phase: Secondary and FE (11-18)
Organisation: St John Fisher Catholic School

Do you need to work out an unknown angle or side length?

SIDE

Have you been given the length of two of the sides?

✔ Use your knowledge of **Pythagoras** to work out the value of the missing side

✘ Do you know one side length and one angle other than the right angle?

✔ Using your knowledge of **Trigonometry**, work out the value of the missing side or angle

✘ Look for more information in the problem or a different way to solve

ANGLE

Do you know the length of at least two of the sides?

✔ Using your knowledge of **Trigonometry**, work out the value of the missing side or angle

✘ Look for more information in the problem or a different way to solve

Why did you chose to use graphic organisers in your lessons?

Although I hate the thought of my beautiful subject being reduced to a string of processes, the use and production of GOs is not about that for me. It's about making visual the times where processes, decisions or comparisons are useful. Mathematics is such a wonderfully connected subject. I choose to use GOs to make those connections explicit to students, prompting them to look for and create their own diagrams to connecting topics. I use decision trees to help students with method selection in topics like Pythagoras and trigonometry.

How did you teach this to your students?

When I teach linear sequences or linear graphs, I always draw connections between the two. The mathematics behind each of these areas can be very similar but we use different terminology. This can lead students to believe that they need to learn different maths for these topics, when much of it is the same.

> **I chose to use GOs to make those connections explicit to students.**

I use part of the Flow Spray alongside a few examples of sequences or equations of lines and, when appropriate, show the connected Flow Spray to reveal the similarities and differences in the topics. Method selection is an important part of the journey of learning mathematics and having a basic GO that students can use, elaborate on and then extend seems to have huge benefits in this area, in my experience. I use Tree Diagrams to help my students develop this skill. My Pythagoras or trigonometry decision tree is rather basic

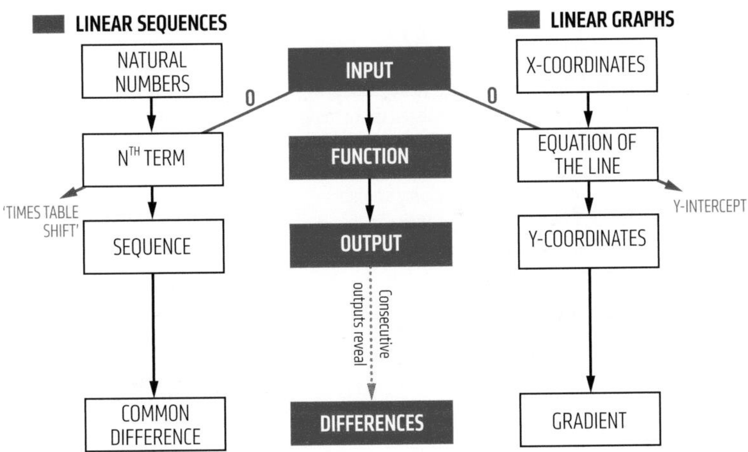

and doesn't go into detail, but I've found that once students have seen and used this GO they can then go on to create their own trees – one for Pythagoras and one for trigonometry. The type of questions that students see in practice or in the exam are sometimes more complex than just a triangle. I encourage them to think about how they can add to the GO with the features they look for to spot a right-angled triangle. Common additions made by students include the diagonal of a rectangle or the height of a parallelogram.

How and why do you introduce students to graphic organisers and their structure?

I've used both of the graphic organisers shown above with my students after they have spent time on the topics in question. These GOs are not definitive or exhaustive. They are used as the basis of discussion with students, to help them structure their thought processes for method selection, or to make obvious the connections between other areas of maths. I hand-draw many diagrams like these in lessons when I feel they are the best way to communicate some of my schema to students. My aim is for them to know about all the different structures of graphic organisers and what they are used for, so that they can use them in their own way.

Charlotte shares the same concern we have heard many times: graphic organisers communicate ideas too effectively. But Charlotte is experienced enough to know that graphic organisers serve the learning process. They are not the learning itself. Both of Charlotte's organisers help students navigate mathematical sequences in their external memory fields. As a result, their minds are free to attend to the mathematical problems – they are not burdened by having to recall the steps, too. This is not to say that being able to recall the steps isn't important. It is. But the organisers act as a scaffold to help students until they can retrieve the steps on demand. Also, Charlotte's GOs explicitly reveal how two sequences from different topics are similar. As such, Charlotte is activating her students' prior knowledge to increase the chances of new material being successfully encoded. Charlotte is sharing her expert schema with her students.

CHRISTIAN MOORE ANDERSON

Novakian Concept Maps allow students to see, or force them to reflect on, not just connections, but how concepts can be subsumed under more fundamental and more encompassing concepts.

Current job: Teacher
Subject: Biology
Age phase: Secondary and FE (11-18)
Organisation: Oak House School

Why do you use graphic organisers?

Biology is a subject perpetually overloaded by content, especially the names and functions of components, which can distract from the underlying meaning. It is often the case that these details are what translate to gaining marks in standardised exams. So I find I have two major pressures: ensuring my students learn new content, but also find meaning within it. I have found Novakian concept mapping to be a fantastic and pragmatic tool for the job.

How do you create Concept Maps?

Joseph Novak invented the Concept Map when attempting to understand student thinking under the framework of David Ausubel's theory of learning. As such, Novakian Concept Maps are much more than just connecting things with arrows. They are also organised into a hierarchy of concepts, from the more general and encompassing to the more detailed (which are *subsumed* by the former).

How does concept mapping support your students?

In my biology classes, I am constantly asking probing questions of my students about prior knowledge and the content of the current lesson. However, with so many questions and so much content, I noticed that my students would often lose the thread of what I was trying to achieve: the connection of concepts. At some point I realised that I could employ Concept Maps as live organisers, helping students organise in the moment. This way, through my extended questioning, the connections between concepts could be held together by a Concept Map developed on the whiteboard. Students are now able to follow the reasoning behind my questioning and maybe see connections they hadn't thought of before. The live maps also serve as regular modelling, especially of the need to reflect on their construction – I often restructure them here and there as they develop.

At some point I realised that I could employ Concept Maps as live organisers, helping students organise in the moment.

Students are now able to follow the reasoning behind my questioning and maybe see connections they hadn't thought of before.

How has concept mapping helped your students gain a broader understanding of your subject?

Biology is a subject that is fond of causal mechanisms, the steps in a process that lead from a cause to an effect. These are generally displayed as Flow Charts. However, deep at the centre of Ausubel's theory is that students who do not connect their knowledge achieve not much more than rote learning. They can recall verbatim, but without being able to explain what it all means, how it connects. Consequently, another benefit I have found with using live maps is to draw students' attention away from the Flow Chart of a causal mechanism, to see how the content of the lesson can be organised conceptually rather than as a series of steps. I have found that this has been a good way to help students connect the process to the more encompassing or fundamental patterns found in biology.

Glucose in glycogen
Insulin
Glucagon
Glucose in blood
Glucose in tissues
Feeding
uptake

Blood glucose
is controlled by
Pancreas
secretes
secretes
Glucagon
responds to
Insulin
reduces
reduces
causes
Hypoglycemia
Hyperglycemia
Storage of Glucose
causes
causes
as
in
Low energy Flow
Tissue Damage
Glycogen
Liver Muscle

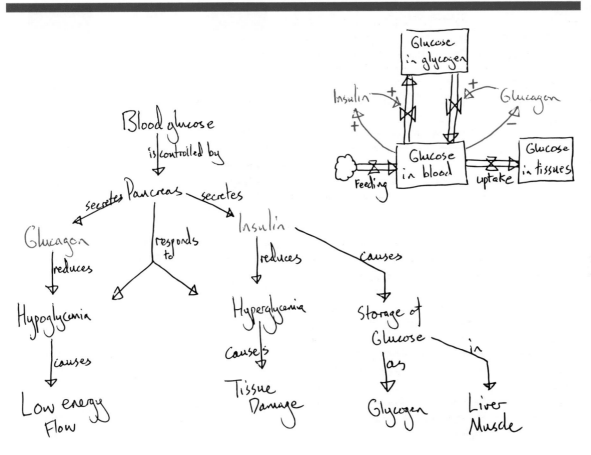

Christian uses Concept Maps as a metacognitive tool. By concept mapping live, he makes visible to students his expert thinking. Christian's students are immersed in his iterative cognitive loop, where he frequently refines and improves his ideas. For Christian and his students, it would be almost impossible to perform this level of cognition internally.

CLARE MADDEN

Using GOs in English helps students pull abstract concepts, arguments and ideas down from their minds and organise them on the page.

Current job: Teacher
Subject: English
Age phase: Secondary and FE (11-18)
Organisation: Glanmire Community College, Republic of Ireland

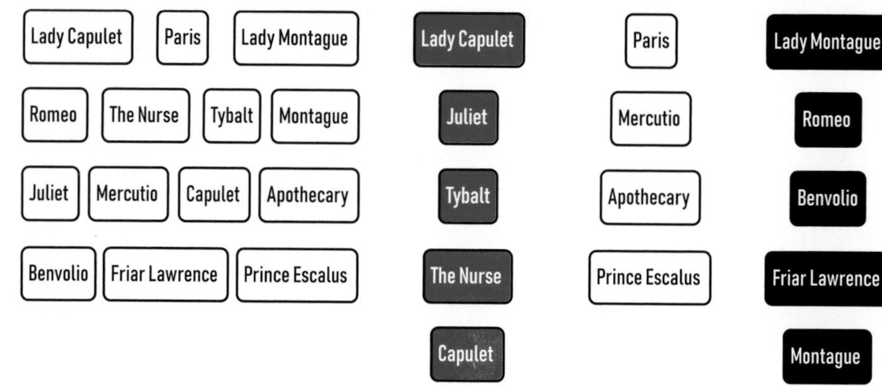

Step 1 Collect character names

Step 2 Categorise

Why do you use this graphic organiser?

The graphic organiser in my example is a Concept Map and I use it after the reading of any type of literature text: a play, a novel or a film. To understand the world of a literature text is a complex undertaking. Students must grapple with the physical, social and cultural setting of the text and the resulting social hierarchy. They also must contend with a variety of interconnected characters and how they are impacted by the setting. To avoid cognitive overload, I use this diagram to visually organise the world of the text.

How do you use this graphic organiser in the classroom?

1. List: I write every character's name on a Post-it note. I stick each Post-it on the board.

2. Categorise: I ask students to think about grouping the characters together. What links the characters together? Family? Friendship? Religion? Race? Job? We come to a consensus and arrange the Post-its on the board to reflect our decisions.

> **To avoid cognitive overload, I use this diagram to visually organise the world of the text.**

3. Hierarchy: I ask the students to consider the social hierarchy of the text. Who holds the most power? The least? Do gender, race or religion determine the places of certain characters in the hierarchy? We come to a consensus and arrange the Post-its on the board to reflect our discussion, keeping the characters within their categories or groups.

4. Links: We look at the relationships/links between all the characters. A line is drawn for each connection and the relationship is named. Students then create their own version of their graphic organiser using the model we have

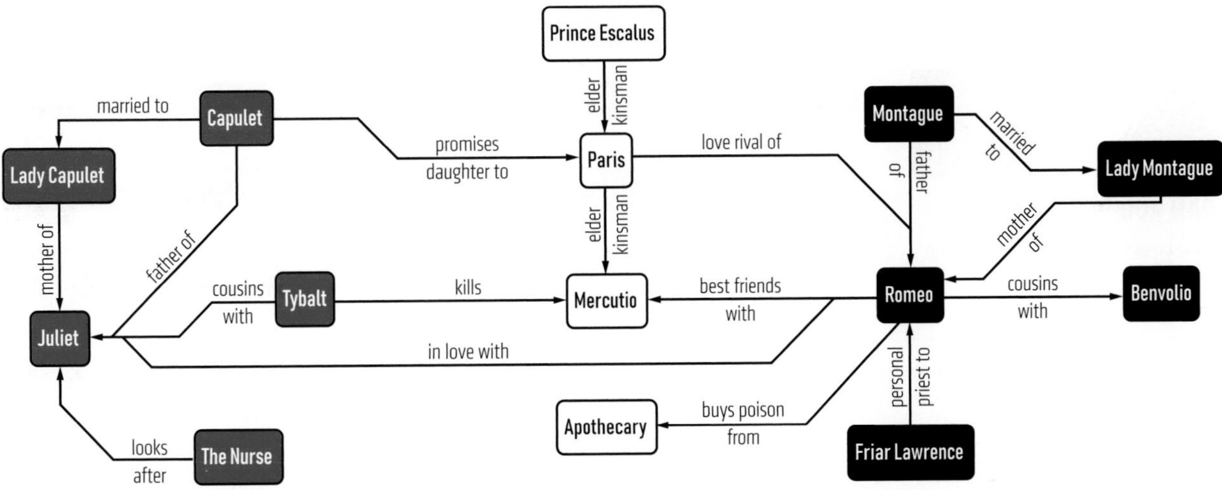

Step 3 & 4 Establish hierarchy and link

created together. At this point we discuss the use of icons and colour if they are necessary to the meaning of the text.

What is the impact of using this graphic organiser?

Students must understand and engage with every aspect of the world of the text and think deeply to create their graphic organiser. The process of creating the graphic organiser lightens the cognitive load on students. They thereafter have the cognitive bandwidth to think about the bigger questions of the text and are better equipped to analyse them in-depth.

How do you use this graphic organiser once it is completed?

My students use their text maps frequently in conjunction with retrieval practice. One of the retrieval strategies I use is to get students to resketch the text map from memory. When they have finished, I ask them to return to their original organiser and to add anything they have missed in a different colour. They then have a clear visual representation of what they do know and what they still need to know. For students who need extra support, I may give them a partially completed text map to fill in. The completed sections may trigger a memory cue and enable them to retrieve and complete the organiser. This is repeated at spaced intervals to maximise its effects.

DAN RODRIGUEZ-CLARK

A Flow Spray breaks a complicated process into manageable steps, and forces the teacher to identify the constituent steps.

Current job: Teaching and learning coordinator
Subject: Maths
Age phase: Secondary and FE (11-18)
Organisation: Markham College

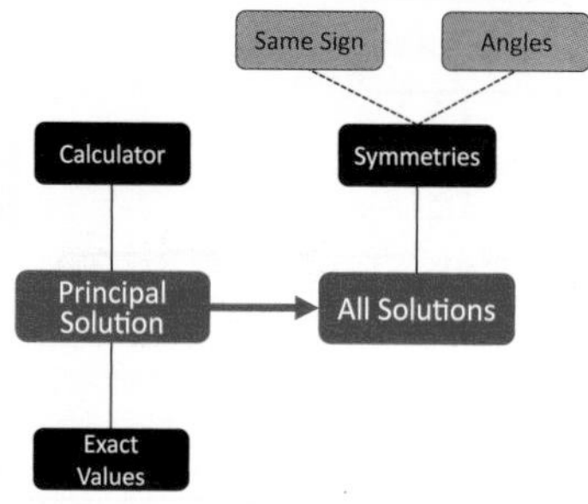

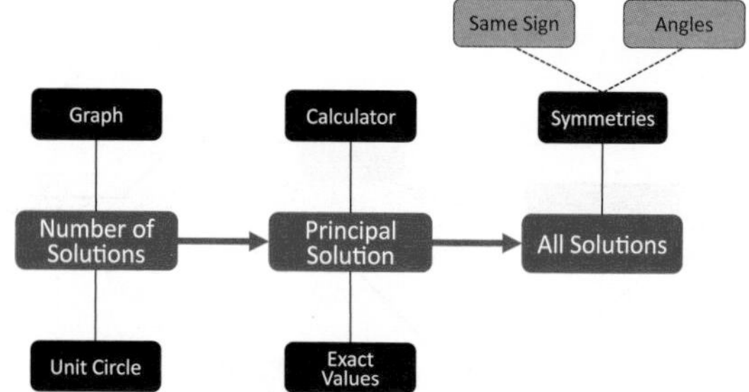

Why did you choose this graphic organiser?

This GO is a Flow Spray. It was chosen as it suits the purposes of what I wanted to convey to students. In this case, I am explaining the stages of solving a trigonometric equation, a traditionally quite complicated process. The Flow Spray enables me to break the whole process into four linked sections, each of which has minor aspects to it. It is a forward-facing GO as well, as I designed it to be able to be reduced and slowly built up to the whole picture. In breaking up this complicated process, I was aiming to reduce the excess strain put on students' working memory.

How did you use this organiser in class?

The GO was organised so that I could build it up over several lessons, taking a complicated process and showing how it is an extension of more simple ideas. Initially, I taught students how to solve the most simple trigonometric equation, which only involved some of the GO (shown above). In teaching this, I started by revealing the boxes one at a time, talking through the stages. I then paired this with a worked example, using gestures to link each stage of the example to the relevant part of the GO. Students then practised questions of this type. The next stage of the process was to look at equations over different ranges, which have differing numbers of solutions. By adding a single element to the beginning of what students had already seen, I was attempting to make it clear that this was the same concept, but just with an extra aspect to it (shown above). I taught it to students in the same way as the first part of the process. As students gained confidence with this level of the process, I introduced the last section one step at a time, as the three parts of "*Simplify*" are each different aspects of the *simplify* stage. Initially we looked at "*Inner functions*", adding these to the diagram, and then "*Quadratics*" and "*Identities*".

How do you combine this organiser with other strategies?

The Flow Spray method for showing a mathematical process is an excellent way to enable students to partake in retrieval practice and elaboration. Using the Recount & Redraw process from Tom Sherrington and Oliver's *Teaching WalkThrus*, students were encouraged to trace their fingers over the completed diagram while explaining to their partner what it meant.

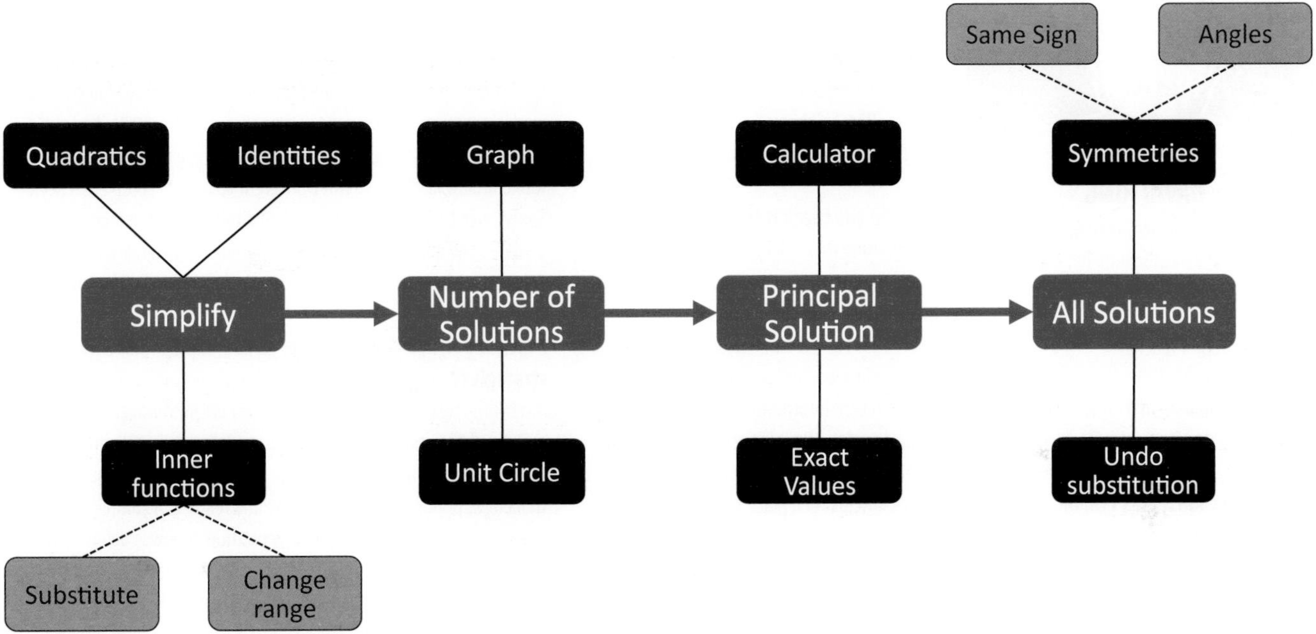

Same Sign
Angles
Quadratics
Identities
Graph
Calculator
Symmetries
Simplify → Number of Solutions → Principal Solution → All Solutions
Inner functions
Unit Circle
Exact Values
Undo substitution
Substitute
Change range

Maths is a subject full of complex processes. Dan knows this and helps his students by using a Flow Spray as a visual instruction plan. In Dan's organiser, the process is broken up. He has chunked each step into a manageable block, making trigonometry accessible to his students. Dan achieves clarity by aligning all elements, giving his text space to breathe, and using a readable typeface. Dan uses arrows as a visual metaphor, guiding his students through each step of the sequence. It is easy to see how Dan's organiser serves the learning process — we commend his thoughtful design.

DAVID KING

A GO allows the reader to understand the importance of the most minute detail by embedding it in an easily accessible schema.

Current job: Year 4 teacher
Subject: History
Age phase: Primary (5-11)
Organisation: Wainscott Primary School

Why did you choose this graphic organiser?

The graphic organiser in my example is a Double Spray. The national curriculum asks children studying history in key stage 1 to "*study the lives of significant individuals in the past who have contributed to national and international achievements*". It elaborates upon this to note that "*some should be used to compare aspects of life in different periods*". I chose to use a Double Spray organiser to compare Tim Peake and Neil Armstrong.

This organiser provides children with a clear visual cue to identify similarities and differences between two items. Through understanding only the position of a piece of information, children can identify whether or not it is unique to that item.

How did you teach it to your students?

Before using this graphic organiser, children would have used a Spray Map (a "chunking" graphic organiser) to support their recording of information about Tim Peake. At another point in time, they would have used another Spray Map to record information on Neil Armstrong. I introduced the Double Spray by explaining that we could put all our information from two places into just one place to help us recall and compare it.

I provided children with a blank Double Spray and we added our two items to each section: Tim Peake and Neil Armstrong. Having done this, children were asked to use their Spray Maps to find a certain piece of information about each astronaut. For example, they were asked to find where each astronaut was from; upon the realisation that they were from different places, I used a visualiser to record these pieces of information as differences on the outsides of the Double Spray. Another child noticed that both men had been pilots, so I used the visualiser to show that we would record this similarity in the inside of the Double Spray. We continued this through our Spray Map information, working in mixed-ability pairs or small groups. The similarities and differences were shared again as a class at the end of the lesson. I have found it beneficial to use three different colours to complete a Double Spray. I use two colours to show the factors that are unique to their owner – the differences. I use one final colour to signal similar factors. This further helps the reader identify similarities and differences.

How did you use this graphic organiser alongside other strategies?

As children record their information, they are encouraged to use icons to prompt their recall (which again is modelled through a visualiser). This is especially useful in key stage 1, where we may still be having challenges phonetically with spelling and reading of complicated terms. The iconography, alongside choral repetition of new vocabulary when introduced, helps children to share their knowledge. If we have built a graphic organiser together, I will regularly use the Recount & Redraw technique, where children are asked to trace their graphic organiser with their finger as they explain it to a partner, before attempting to redraw the organiser without seeing it again. You will also notice that my example includes a Time Line graphic organiser along the bottom.

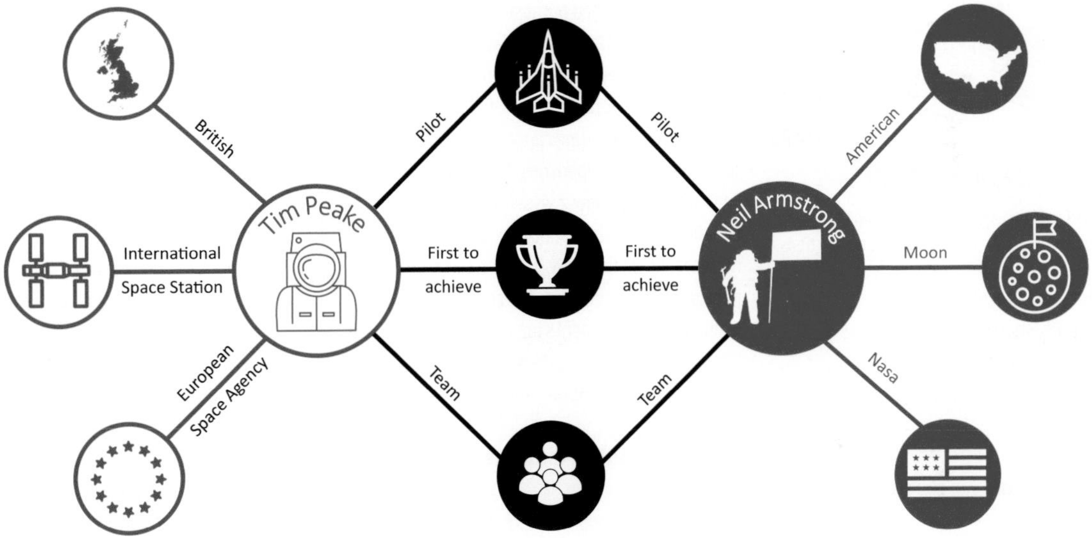

British
International Space Station
European Space Agency
Tim Peake
Pilot
First to achieve
Team
Pilot
First to achieve
Team
Neil Armstrong
American
Moon
Nasa

1930 1958 1969 1972 1975 2000 2015 2020

David has created a beautifully clear Double Spray diagram, accompanied by a Time Line. David describes how initially, students construct two separate Spray Maps, before uniting them to fulfil one of our most fundamental learning strategies – drawing comparisons. He has made overt something which is often implicit. To add further clarity, David uses colour to his advantage. Notice how the external differences use the same colours but in reverse, while the inner similarities are all one colour. This is by design. David is guiding his students to meaning.

DAVID MORGAN

Coherent graphics give learners the opportunity to embed key concepts through visible connections.

Current job: Curriculum leader
Subject: PE, sport and dance
Age phase: Secondary (11-16)
Organisation: St Edmund Arrowsmith Catholic High School

Why and how did you choose this graphic organiser?

When considering which graphic organiser to use, my main aim was to overcome misconceptions and show separate lists of information that can be learnt together to strengthen schema. I wanted the students to be able to chunk information together while comparing and creating links between two different areas. I decided to use a hybrid model, combining a Double Spray and a Concept Map. I think the key is not to be afraid to adapt and customise a graphic organiser. You need to make it fit the desired purpose so you do not lose the intended impact. The Double Spray shows the different elements separately while illustrating similar features. The Concept Map links the elements using connective language to reinforce the comparisons. Not only do the lines and arrows show a visual link between the benefits and drawbacks, but the alignment also makes it simple to follow, with the comparisons populating the same level. The connective language shows students how to use the information to answer extended writing questions while promoting literacy efficacy.

How did you initially introduce this graphic organiser?

I introduced it to pupils in its entirety in their work booklets, displayed on the whiteboard and reinforced by my explanation. I feel that this combination, acting as a supporting scaffold, is essential in embedding an understanding of key concepts. The information and explanations had already been shared with learners in previous lessons, with the organiser establishing links. Students can annotate the organiser from the teacher commentary, directed questions and responses. I am an avid user of a visualiser when modelling how to annotate a graphic organiser.

You need to make it fit the desired purpose so you do not lose the intended impact.

My students have previously seen graphic organisers that relayed simple concepts of curriculum content. This was the first one that delved into more complex subject matter while not being unfamiliar in its structure. I chose not to formally introduce the use of graphic organisers with this class; however, this will not be the case going forward. I feel it would be beneficial for students to understand their use and how they can effectively strengthen learning.

I feel it would be beneficial for students to understand the use of graphic organisers and how they can effectively strengthen learning.

Do you use graphic organisers with any other strategies in your repertoire?

As seen in Kate Jones's book *Retrieval Practice* (2019), we discover the significance of tasks designed to recall information from long-term memory. A framed approach can be used, giving the graphic without words for students to populate, gradually working towards the students drawing it from memory. I have previously used icons with this graphic to reinforce the information, but the integration of images should be well thought out and used only if it enhances learning. In later lessons, the text can be replaced with icons so students recall information linked to the picture, giving an alternative retrieval practice.

David has created a hybrid organiser. His design utilises features of a comparison matrix and a Concept Map. David has aligned all the to-be-compared features and connected them with arrows and lines. Additionally, his subtle use of colour and overall restraint makes for a clear and sophisticated design. When considering which organiser to use, David thought carefully about its intended use – hence his unity of a comparison matrix and a Concept Map. A traditional Concept Map is rich in connections and concepts can be linked more than once. They also have an observable hierarchy. While David's design doesn't have vast connections or an obvious hierarchy, it does contain the kernel sentences associated with concept mapping. Each of the to-be-compared elements links to create kernel sentences. David has used conjunctions to help his students write comparative essays.

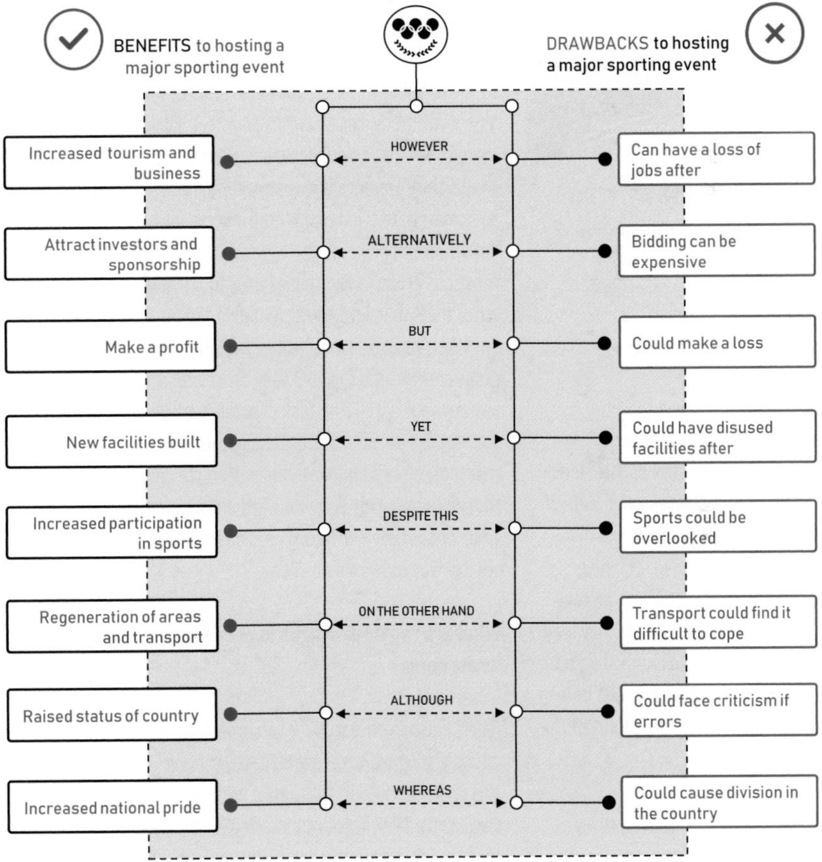

BENEFITS to hosting a major sporting event		DRAWBACKS **to hosting a major sporting event**
Increased tourism and business	HOWEVER	Can have a loss of jobs after
Attract investors and sponsorship	ALTERNATIVELY	Bidding can be expensive
Make a profit	BUT	Could make a loss
New facilities built	YET	Could have disused facilities after
Increased participation in sports	DESPITE THIS	Sports could be overlooked
Regeneration of areas and transport	ON THE OTHER HAND	Transport could find it difficult to cope
Raised status of country	ALTHOUGH	Could face criticism if errors
Increased national pride	WHEREAS	Could cause division in the country

DEEPU ASOK

True understanding is the conversion of information into conceptual knowledge and the linking of conceptual knowledge into mental models.

Current job: Portfolio ops manager
Organisation: Pfizer

What does your diagram represent?

Reading something is easy, but understanding something you have read takes work. When was the last time you read a book and then, a few weeks later, all you could remember was a one-sentence summary? The average reader highlights key sections while they read a book or makes notes in the margin of a book. However, most of these highlights and notes are never revisited and hence lost forever. The solution: *smart notes.*

What are smart notes?

Smart notes is a note-taking system popularized by the book *How to Take Smart Notes* by Sönke Ahrens (2017). The book is based on the slip box methodology developed by the sociologist Niklas Luhmann. According to him, it was this unique system of note-taking that allowed him to publish over 70 books. So what's the difference between regular notes and smart notes? In regular note-taking, each note is an independent entity. There is no conscious effort to link these notes to previous notes that you might have created in the past. But when you take smart notes, the individual notes are revisited to see if they are related to any previous notes. The task of actively making connections between notes requires you to think critically about ideas. It has been proven that elaborating ideas as you read and making connections between heterogeneous ideas is a reliable way to learn something.

When you take smart notes, the individual notes are revisited to see if they are related to any previous notes.

What are the three stages of creating smart notes?

1. Take notes

Albert Einstein once said, *"If you can't explain it simply, you don't understand it well enough."* This is why it's important to take notes in your own words. The goal of note-taking is not to copy the ideas from the book. The goal is to actively think about these ideas as you read them so that you can translate knowledge into understanding. It is also important to write these notes as you read the material, so that you don't forget what you meant while you were reading the material.

2. Connect related ideas

Having a note-taking system allows us to build an external system to think and connect ideas. When you actively take notes, you are using writing as a tool to think about these ideas and generate new ones. Another reason to take notes is that thinking happens on paper as much as it happens inside your own head. The neuroscientist Neil Levy wrote, *"Notes on paper, or on a computer screen ... do not make contemporary physics or other kinds of intellectual endeavor easier, they make it possible."*

The task of actively making connections between notes requires you to think critically about ideas.

3. Build mental models

As you start taking smart notes, you start building new mental models. Mental models are internal representations of how things work in the world. By connecting new ideas with the old, you are forced to actively think about how new ideas support, contradict or add to

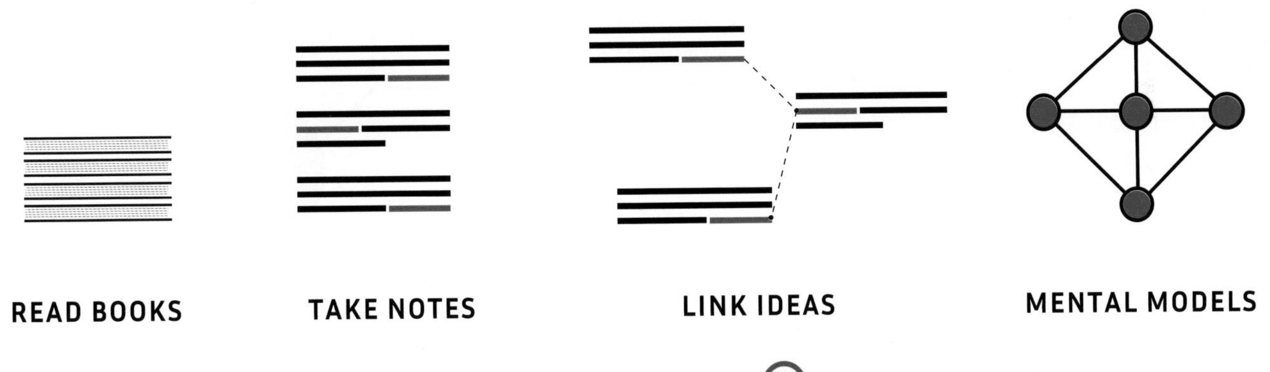

the existing ideas embedded in your existing mental models. Over time you will see clusters of related ideas emerge around a certain topic. Having this archive of notes means that you will never have to start from scratch for writing an essay or giving a talk. You can simply go back to your note-taking system and pick up the ideas that are most relevant to your essay or talk and organise them for presentation. Taking smart notes is the no. 1 way to compound your knowledge and remove writer's block. Without a note-taking system, your ideas get lost in the chaos of your mind. As they say, *the faintest ink is more powerful than the strongest memory.*

It is easy to see how what Deepu explains has the potential to expand your students' capacity for note-taking. You will see in the When? section how kernel sentences take discrete unitary items and connect them to reveal meaning. If you aren't convinced, read what Sönke Ahrens, via Deepu, has to say about meaningful note-taking. Deepu's diagram beautifully captures the transformation of external linear information into an internal, non-linear representation. Using a word-diagram bypasses the complexities of syntax and reveals connections by way of spatial relations. When clustering a note-taking system with word-diagrams, you provide your students with powerful meaning-making tools.

ELLIOT MORGAN

Graphic organisers are a means through which intricate and complex relationships can be revealed – the unseen becomes seen.

Current job: Lead practitioner
Subject: History
Age phase: Primary (6-7)
Organisation: St Vincent's Primary School

Why did you choose the graphic organiser in your example?

As a school, we acknowledged that disciplinary knowledge in the foundation subjects was not emphasised enough and we wanted to address this throughout our units of learning. For younger children, this posed a significant challenge: how can we make abstract concepts (i.e. cause and effect) comprehensible? I chose to use a Fishbone Diagram. By taking something abstract and making it visual, I believed pupils would find it easier to understand, even at the age of 6 studying the Great Fire of London. I needed something that could simultaneously organise a lot of information and demonstrate links between the information, which would make it easier to encode. I was focusing on the concept of cause and effect, but I need to reduce the complexity of the language associated with it to make it easier to comprehend. The Fishbone Diagram was suitable for this because it has a *computational advantage* over simple text and it can group causes into similar themes to indicate a more subtle sphere of influence. It is perfect for uniting individual pieces of knowledge learnt throughout the unit into one schema bound by commonality. After all, the better organised this information is, the more likely pupils will remember it.

How did you initially introduce this GO?

Throughout the unit, we kept referring back to the question *Why did the fire spread?* and referencing the different factors that contributed to it. Because of the pupils' lack of familiarity with a Fishbone Diagram and the historical concept of cause and effect, I first introduced the children to a converging radial diagram (see above). It achieves the

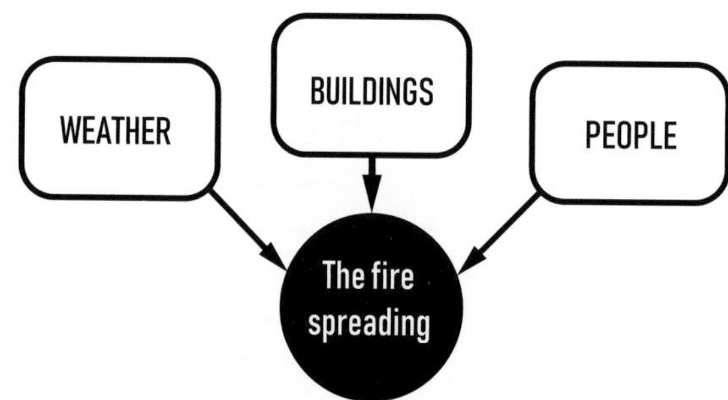

same representation of information but on a broader scale, ignoring the individual pieces of information about how the buildings, weather and people contributed to the fire and instead just focusing on the overarching factors themselves. The converging radial provides a more condensed version of the information and serves as a starting point for understanding the relationship between the different causes. Introducing this first made the zoom-in approach enacted later on much easier for the pupils. Pupils then completed a scaffolded, pre-set diagram for their task. Over time, the intention would be to let pupils create their own diagram independently.

Was there a sequence to your introduction of graphic organisers?

Yes, there was. I showed them four graphic organisers throughout the unit. I started with organisers that were easier to grasp and slowly built up to the more complex Fishbone Diagram. In the first session, I used a Flow Chart to sequence the events of the fire in order to demonstrate the

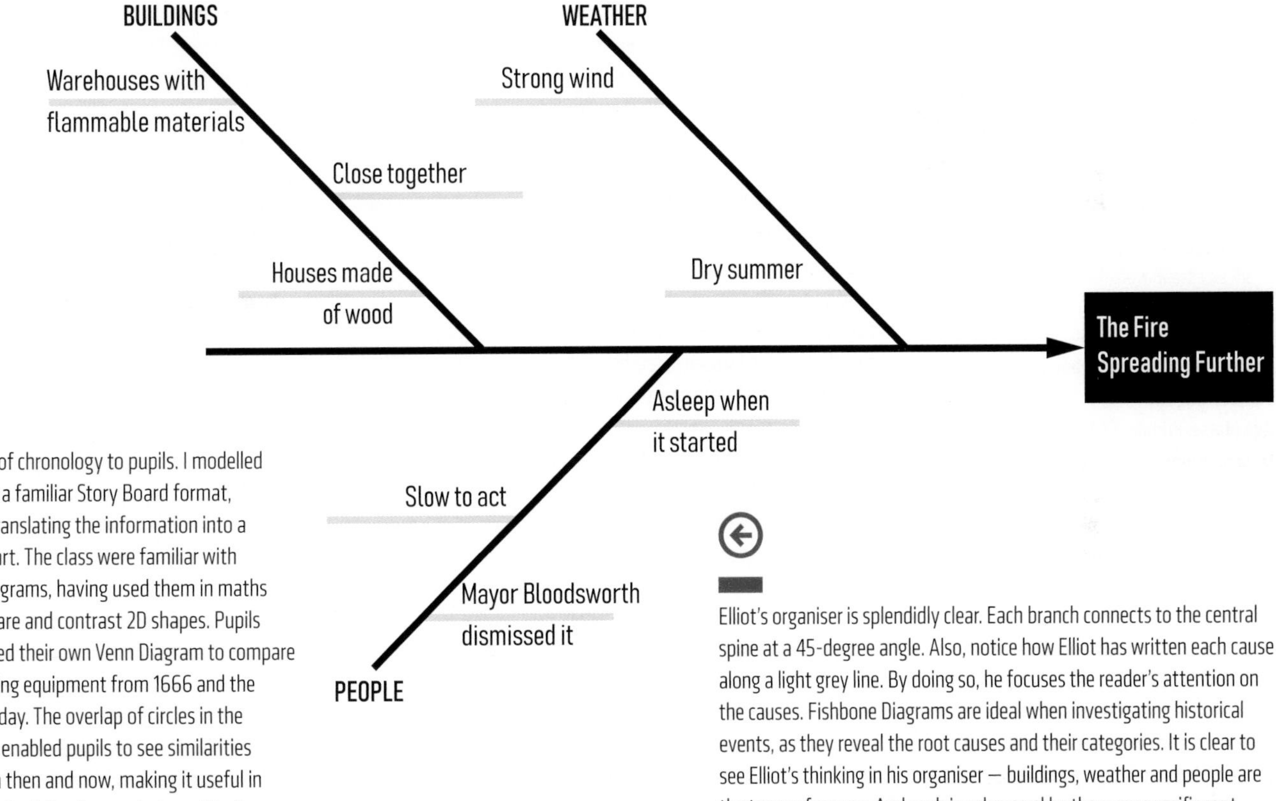

concept of chronology to pupils. I modelled it first in a familiar Story Board format, before translating the information into a Flow Chart. The class were familiar with Venn Diagrams, having used them in maths to compare and contrast 2D shapes. Pupils completed their own Venn Diagram to compare firefighting equipment from 1666 and the modern day. The overlap of circles in the diagram enabled pupils to see similarities between then and now, making it useful in meeting the following curriculum objective: "*events beyond living memory that are significant nationally or globally*".

Elliot's organiser is splendidly clear. Each branch connects to the central spine at a 45-degree angle. Also, notice how Elliot has written each cause along a light grey line. By doing so, he focuses the reader's attention on the causes. Fishbone Diagrams are ideal when investigating historical events, as they reveal the root causes and their categories. It is clear to see Elliot's thinking in his organiser – buildings, weather and people are the types of causes. And each is subsumed by the more specific root causes. It would be difficult for primary-aged students to arrive at the same meaning using prose alone.

EMMA SLADE

Graphic organisers – at all levels of education – are an essential element of effective teaching, resulting in long-term learning.

Current job: Assistant headteacher
Subject: English
Age phase: Primary (7-11)
Organisation: Hartford Junior School

What prompted you to use graphic organisers for reading lessons?

I began to use graphic organisers alongside the introduction of a complex canon of children's classic literature as part of our English curriculum a year ago. High expectations for all pupils to access these inspirational and foundational texts meant it was vital that the selection and design of visuals supported children's understanding of high-level texts and reduced the cognitive load produced by such ambitious expectations. Graphic organisers have played a significant part in enabling all pupils in my class to read books above their assessed reading level, and to not only make sense of the texts but to learn knowledge from them and organise it in meaningful ways.

How do you use Flow Spray organisers to support reading?

Flow Spray organisers, at their most basic level of use, can simply allow pupils to track the main events of the storyline. However, applied carefully, they can be used in teaching children knowledge of how to summarise, understand complex temporal narratives and make analytical predictions based on Flow Sprays of previous chapters. For example, removing parts of the graphic organiser allows for quick retrieval and revisiting of previous knowledge of the main events. Asking children to complete blank Flow Sprays engineers opportunities for them to pinpoint the main events and use these as prompts to write complex summary sentences. Flow Sprays work exceptionally well in tracking and visually representing books with alternate or co-existing timelines, allowing for children to reap the benefits of reading highly complex novels without losing track.

Graphic organisers have played a significant part in enabling all pupils in my class to read books above their assessed reading level.

Careful application of this Flow Spray resulted in efficient use of lesson time and supported all pupils in remembering the book.

What impact did this Flow Spray have when teaching *The Lion, the Witch and the Wardrobe*?

This Flow Spray was used for Year 3 and was introduced at the end of a series of chapters as a pre-completed graphic organiser. At the beginning of lessons, the GO was revisited and used as a quizzing tool. After reading each chapter, teacher support was gradually reduced, so that ultimately children were able to extract the main events from a whole chapter, order them and utilise the GO to write summary sentences or to prompt oral recall.

When producing summative essays, it was incredibly gratifying to see that children could, in many impressive instances, recall key events and corresponding chapters simply from memory. All pupils could revisit their Flow Sprays to independently identify evidence, resulting in increased autonomy when planning writing. This particular sequence of Flow Sprays was also invaluable in addressing gaps in knowledge when children were absent for key reading lessons, or for bringing cover teachers up to speed with the narrative so that they could effectively deliver subsequent lessons. Furthermore, careful application of this Flow

Spray resulted in efficient use of lesson time and supported all pupils in remembering the book so well that working memory could be used for application of knowledge and writing practice, as opposed to trying to remember events.

The Lion, the Witch and the Wardrobe
by C S Lewis

CHAPTER 7
A DAY WITH THE BEAVERS

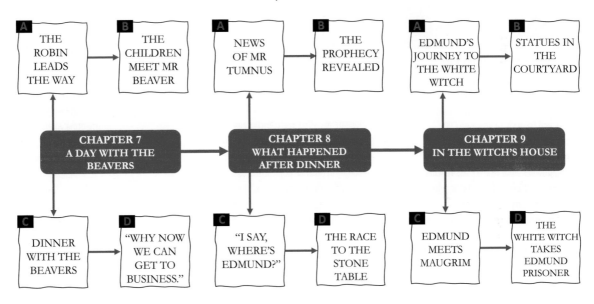

- A: THE ROBIN LEADS THE WAY → B: THE CHILDREN MEET MR BEAVER
- C: DINNER WITH THE BEAVERS → D: "WHY NOW WE CAN GET TO BUSINESS."

CHAPTER 8
WHAT HAPPENED AFTER DINNER

- A: NEWS OF MR TUMNUS → B: THE PROPHECY REVEALED
- C: "I SAY, WHERE'S EDMUND?" → D: THE RACE TO THE STONE TABLE

CHAPTER 9
IN THE WITCH'S HOUSE

- A: EDMUND'S JOURNEY TO THE WHITE WITCH → B: STATUES IN THE COURTYARD
- C: EDMUND MEETS MAUGRIM → D: THE WHITE WITCH TAKES EDMUND PRISONER

Emma has created a Flow Spray to chunk the main events of a novel into manageable sections. Rather charmingly, Emma has made the individual textboxes look like the pages of a story. What is even more admirable is that despite this fancy graphic touch, Emma has resisted the temptation to use gimmicky fonts and overuse colour. Arrows used correctly are a physical metaphor to indicate movement. In Emma's design, she uses them effectively to chart the reader's path. Also, at each of the main events, Emma orientates the reader by using the letters A-D — a shrewd move.

EVE CAIRNS VOLLANS

Using the Flow Spray graphic organiser has helped me to clarify my thoughts. It's a great tool to talk through. I feel I can now select, organise and be ready to integrate CPD.

Current job: Research/CPD lead, reading/phonics lead, Year 4 class teacher
Subject: Continuing professional development
Age phase: Primary (3-11)
Organisation: Mayflower Community Academy

Why and how did you choose your graphic organiser?

Cognitive overload applies to adults as well as children. How many times have you listened to new information and retained little? If asked, could you summarise the learning? At Mayflower, we have designed a new CPD (continuing professional development) programme for all members of staff to be involved in. There is a lot of information, beginning with the theories and research, before staff begin to study new modules of learning. The Mayflower CPD approach has been designed specifically to allow for time and space through a spiral method of learning. New learning is introduced, imbedded, tested and innovated. It is a planned sequence of learning.

It is imperative that all members of staff understand the CPD sequence of learning, as the ultimate aim is for us to encourage "*interdependency*" (Covey, 2013) and professional and personal autonomy in our staff, resulting in positive pupil outcomes. To enable staff to clearly understand the sequence of learning, without causing undue cognitive overload, I have chosen to use the Flow Spray graphic organiser.

The design for the organiser was split into the four main stages of the sequence: introduce, imbed, test and innovate. These four stages are sequential – you need to be secure in each stage before moving to the next. The Flow Spray clearly shows the four main parts through the middle of the graphic organiser, and directional arrows showing progression. Sprouting from the four main parts are the contributing factors that explain the processes to be introduced, imbedded and tested before finally allowing for innovation. These also have directional arrows, showing that these contributing factors are sequential. One cannot be successful without the other.

Cognitive overload applies to adults as well as children.

How did you initially introduce this graphic organiser?

To begin with, I held a whole-staff remote meeting where I virtually presented the main parts of the CPD approach and spiral diagram, alongside the planned CPD calendar for the year ahead and pre-reading suggestions. The following week, I presented the Flow Spray CPD overview to the staff at face-to-face departmental phase meetings.

Feedback from the staff has been positive when using the Flow Spray graphic organiser as a reference tool.

How did using the Flow Spray graphic organiser impact staff understanding of the new CPD approach?

Feedback from the staff has been positive when using the Flow Spray graphic organiser as a reference tool. Staff felt that having the graphic organiser alongside the spiral approach diagram enhanced their clarity and understanding of the new learning. They were able to discuss the sequence of CPD and articulate each of the four main stages, conferring and clarifying expectations. Staff have requested that future new learning is explained via graphic organisers.

INTRODUCE → **IMBED** → **TEST** → **INNOVATE**

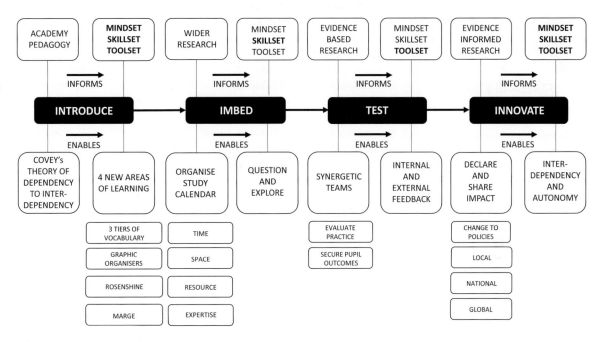

	INTRODUCE	IMBED	TEST	INNOVATE
INFORMS →	ACADEMY PEDAGOGY → **MINDSET SKILLSET TOOLSET**	WIDER RESEARCH → MINDSET **SKILLSET** TOOLSET	EVIDENCE BASED RESEARCH → MINDSET SKILLSET **TOOLSET**	EVIDENCE INFORMED RESEARCH → **MINDSET SKILLSET TOOLSET**
ENABLES →	COVEY's THEORY OF DEPENDENCY TO INTER-DEPENDENCY → 4 NEW AREAS OF LEARNING	ORGANISE STUDY CALENDAR → QUESTION AND EXPLORE	SYNERGETIC TEAMS → INTERNAL AND EXTERNAL FEEDBACK	DECLARE AND SHARE IMPACT → INTER-DEPENDENCY AND AUTONOMY
	3 TIERS OF VOCABULARY; GRAPHIC ORGANISERS; ROSENSHINE; MARGE	TIME; SPACE; RESOURCE; EXPERTISE	EVALUATE PRACTICE; SECURE PUPIL OUTCOMES	CHANGE TO POLICIES; LOCAL; NATIONAL; GLOBAL

By displaying content using a Flow Spray diagram, Eve rescues her readers from the risk of information being transient. Eve has been guided by the principles of space, alignment and typography, elevating her design. The result is a diagram with immense clarity. Only the essential information is represented, further reducing the risk of cognitive overload. The arrows give a clear signal to follow the flow of information. The use of bold capital letters and one typeface makes for a coherent design. Eve's design admirably captures the message she wishes to convey.

FAHEEMAH VACHHIAT

Graphic organisers empower students to classify and organise their ideas on a visual display, enabling them to make deeper connections within their learning.

Current job: Year 4 teacher
Subject: English
Age phase: Primary (7-11)
Organisation: Joseph Cash Primary School

What prompted you to use graphic organisers in your reading sessions?

During guided reading sessions, students found it challenging to classify ideas and communicate effectively without any visual input. Therefore, I introduced graphic organisers to further engage students and increase their curiosity around the text they are studying. This has improved students' abilities to make valid connections and sensible inferences based on what they are reading.

How have you used the Input-Output Diagram in your reading sessions?

An Input-Output Diagram enables students to examine the main events from a text that would have an impact on a character's development. When applied properly, the organiser helps to sequence the character's experiences and identify the consequences of each. This method teaches children how to connect causal links and the effects. Presenting a pre-completed GO in the earlier sessions can help teachers gauge how well students recall their previous knowledge of the main events. Asking students to identify causes and effects creates an opportunity for them to highlight key parts of the text and use them as a guide in their discussion. This facilitates classroom debates around how these events have had an impact on a character. Input-Output Diagrams work exceptionally well in allowing students to compare their ideas with their peers, promoting increased engagement.

How has the Input-Output Diagram helped your students?

The Input-Output Diagram was implemented for a Year 4 class while reading a series of chapters. It was introduced as a pre-completed organiser, with the headings displayed and the question displayed above. I facilitated a discussion, asking open-ended questions to support students in articulating their insights and ideas, enabling them to build knowledge together. The students were able to extract the main events of the chapter and discuss how each event had an impact on the character's development. The handwriting displayed on the GO is the information I would expect my students to discuss and extract. For example, children would identify and discuss how maltreatment had an impact on Harry Potter's physical appearance.

Input-Output Diagrams work exceptionally well in allowing students to compare their ideas with their peers, promoting increased engagement.

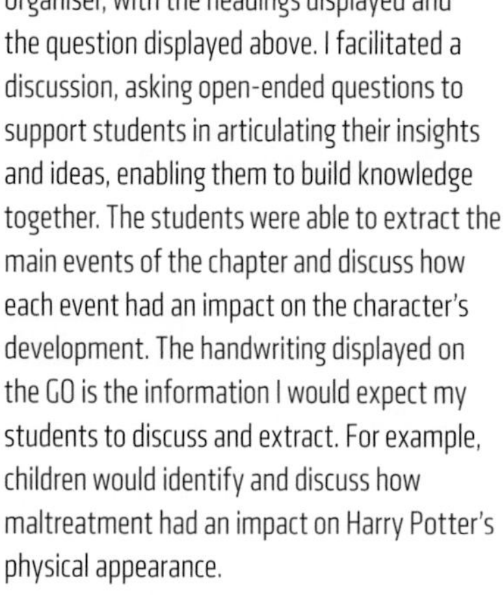

During the sessions, it was incredibly rewarding to see pupils recalling key events and making successful inferences using evidence from the text, with the GO the only tool used to collate their thoughts. Overall, proper application of this GO supported all pupils to voice their opinions and initiate positive discussions with their peers. It allowed the teacher and the students to build knowledge together.

This method teaches children how to connect causal links and the effects.

Harry Potter and the Philosopher's Stone by J.K Rowling

What effect does Harry's upbringing have on his character?

Harry is neglected

Harry is neglected by his aunty and uncle, often being given less food and made to sleep under the stairs.

Harry isn't treated equally

Doesn't receive the same treatment as Dudley. Never had a birthday Celebration.

Family is scared of his powers

Glass disappears at the zoo. Ends up on the roof when Dudley chases him.

Bullied by his cousin

He struggles to make friends or find anyone who he can relate to.

Considered small for his age

Described as "small and skinny for his age", with a thin face and knobbly knees.

Feels unsure of his abilities

Often questions his own abilities. He mentions to Hagrid he is sure to be sorted in Hufflepuff because it is the house for "a' duffers" (Pg.90) and later to Ron when sitting on the train to Hogwarts: "I bet I'm the worst in the class" (Pg.112).

Brave

Learned to defend himself against Dudley's and Malfoy's threats. Saved Hogwarts and obtained the Philosopher's Stone

Faheemah has created a beautiful Input-Output Diagram. We think it is charming and fitting for the content she presents and her audience (primary-age students). Equally impressive is how Faheemah uses it as a tool to increase her students' confidence in sharing their ideas publicly. Faheemah's organiser helps shape her students' thinking about critical events, supporting them to identify the pre-and post-connections.

DR FRAZER THORPE

Graphic organisers provide access to complex and dynamic ideas with simple clarity. Understanding is built by highlighting what is important and how the pieces fit together.

Current job: Professional learning lead
Subject: Biology
Age phase: 5-18 years, tertiary and teacher
Organisation: Zoos Victoria, Melbourne, Australia

Why are you using graphic organisers?

Zoos Victoria are creating a future rich in wildlife, with a focus on 27 endemic and endangered Fighting Extinction species. These species' conservation stories and research have been used to create case studies to support teaching and learning biology for young people aged 16-18. We developed a collection of online graphic organisers to portray the conservation case studies, enabling easy access to real-world science and complex curriculum content knowledge and ideas through a conservation lens.

How are these Fighting Extinction (FE) species case studies being used?

The graphic organiser is part of an FE case study that includes a short video of conservation scientists introducing the species, followed by explicit explanations voicing over the graphic organiser while gradually revealing the next steps and their significance. Teachers and students can access the videos and graphic organisers online. They are provided with completed graphic organisers and modifiable partially completed versions for students to complete/develop/devise. We aim to support teachers in their classroom and student learning, providing real-world examples that enrich the curriculum and increase understanding of conservation. Graphic organisers depict the interdependence within an ecosystem with a clarity that could not be achieved with text alone.

How do you use graphic organisers with other strategies?

In addition to the completed and partially completed graphic organisers, and online explainer videos, we have also provided video transcripts and a *How to Use* teacher guide that includes mini quizzes. We designed these graphic organisers to allow teachers to use the videos, GOs, transcripts and quizzes in flexible and varied ways to enhance student understanding. We suggest ways GOs can be used to support excursions to Zoos Victoria, integrating the case studies with experience-based learning and practical investigation activities. We are also offering coaching and teacher professional learning programmes in how to make effective use of the FE case studies in their specific contexts.

Graphic organisers depict the interdependence within an ecosystem with a clarity that could not be achieved with text alone.

Teachers and students can access the graphic organisers online.

Frazer has created a food web. This sort of organiser is common in biology and geography curriculums. The taxonomy of species in Frazer's diagram is explicit due to its hierarchical structure. Such a level of clarity would not be achievable with text alone. That is to say, the graphic organiser is computationally efficient. Frazer alleviates some of the confusion of lines crossing by making them partially transparent where they intersect.

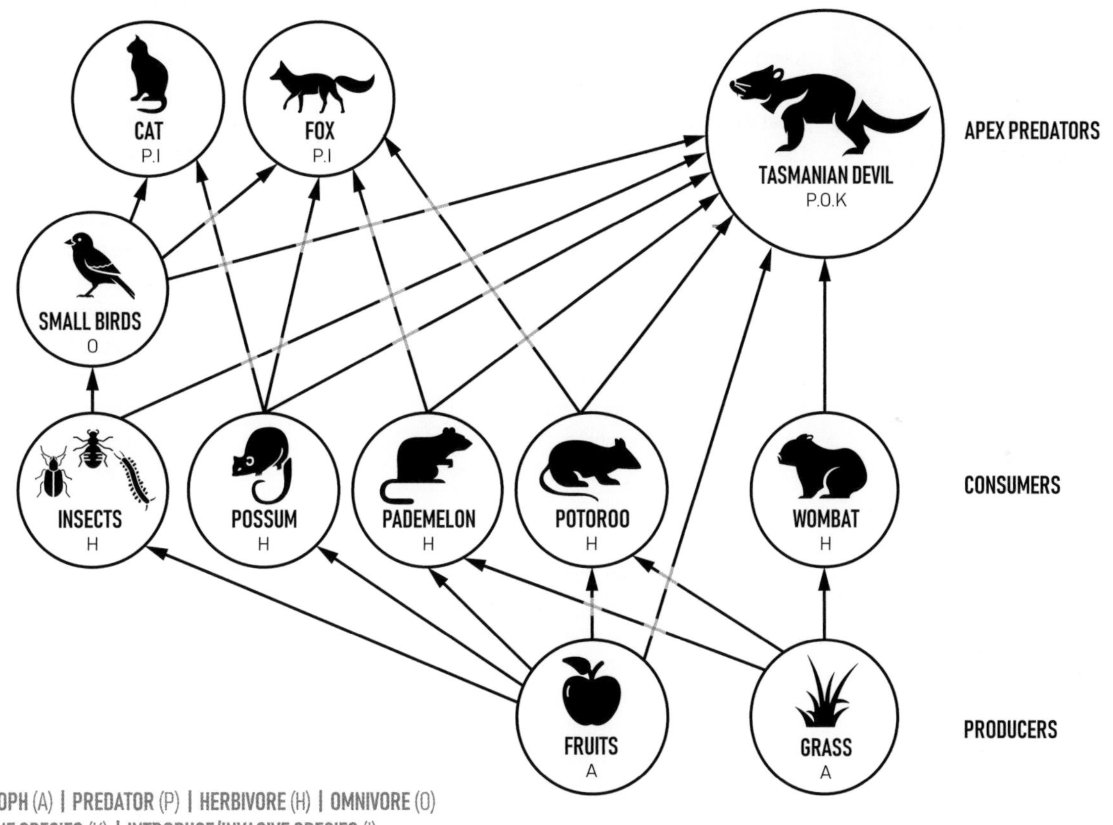

AUTOTROPH (A) | **PREDATOR** (P) | **HERBIVORE** (H) | **OMNIVORE** (O)
KEYSTONE SPECIES (K) | **INTRODUCE/INVASIVE SPECIES** (I)

GEORGE VLACHONIKOLIS

I see graphic organisers as a communication tool. They convey important concepts in simple yet effective terms. The user can fill in the detail later.

Current job: Head of department, professional tutor
Subject: Economics
Age phase: Secondary and FE (16-18)
Organisation: Headington School

Have you always used graphic organisers?

I spent nearly seven years in the Army before becoming a teacher. During military planning cycles, we would always develop what we called an *effects schematic*. This is similar to a graphic organiser in the sense that it is a single visual image that communicates all the key elements of a military operation. There are certain symbols, for example, that designate the size of force, and others that show the synchronisation of decisive movements on the battlefield in relation to one another. A good effects schematic will communicate information quickly without losing vital components.

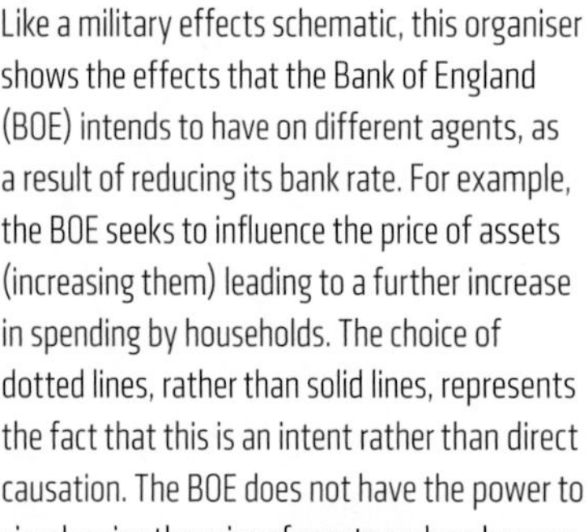

What does this graphic organiser show?

Like a military effects schematic, this organiser shows the effects that the Bank of England (BOE) intends to have on different agents, as a result of reducing its bank rate. For example, the BOE seeks to influence the price of assets (increasing them) leading to a further increase in spending by households. The choice of dotted lines, rather than solid lines, represents the fact that this is an intent rather than direct causation. The BOE does not have the power to simply raise the price of assets such as houses – it can only influence them.

A good effects schematic will communicate information quickly without losing vital components.

How would you use it in your teaching?

I use this model at the end of the topic on monetary policy. It acts as a good summary of our learning, as well as a good revision tool for any future summative assessment. I'm not the first person who's ever attempted to illustrate monetary policy via a Flow Chart-type model, but my contribution is strongly influenced by military schematics. I believe there are significant uses of the organiser that can support retrieval practice. For example:

This model acts as a good summary of our learning, as well as a good revision tool for any future summative assessment.

- I have used the ABC mnemonic to aid memory of various agents. Military personnel love mnemonics.
- The red dots (large and small) all represent points of the process that could break down. This is similar to representing "the enemy" in a military schematic. Students who use this organiser to revise from should be testing themselves about the evaluation points they could make in an essay. For example, a reduced bank rate may lead to a currency depreciation, but this depends on a range of other factors that may affect the exchange rate.
- The dotted lines represent an "intent" rather than direct causation.
- The use of icons helps students to retain knowledge.
- The effects are CAPITALISED to emphasise decisive action.
- The arrows represent the progression from the start line to the final objective.

BOE INTEREST RATE DECREASE

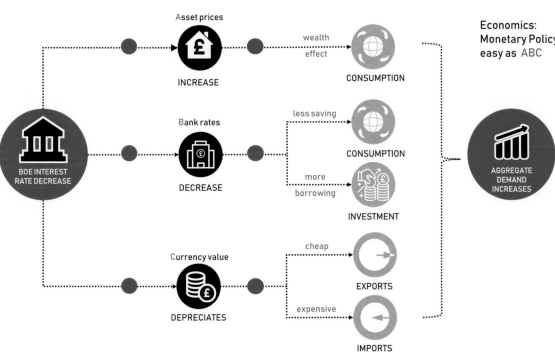

Asset prices
INCREASE
wealth effect
CONSUMPTION

Bank rates
DECREASE
less saving
CONSUMPTION
more borrowing
INVESTMENT

Currency value
DEPRECIATES
cheap
EXPORTS
expensive
IMPORTS

AGGREGATE DEMAND INCREASES

Economics: Monetary Policy, easy as ABC

George's narrative reveals how other industries have cottoned on to the potential of diagrams to convey meaning. Business and other sectors have known for a long time that when ideas are made public, a shared understanding is more likely. Structurally, George's diagram doesn't fit into one of our four categories, making it a hybrid diagram. His use of subtle graphic features offers a more direct route to meaning than prose alone.

HELEN REYNOLDS

A Concept Map that maps the "territory" of a subject gives students a tool to zoom in and out. Seeing connections supports meaning-making, which helps to build more robust schema.

Current job: Teacher
Subject: Physics
Age phase: High school (8th grade)
Organisation: The Gregory School, Tucson, Arizona, US

Why did you make this graphic organiser?

This is an advance organiser Concept Map of the whole GCSE/HS physics course that I teach. I made it after reading about the idea of *zooming in, zooming out* in various books and blogs about cognitive science principles. I wanted my students to see how I see the course: a series of topics taught sequentially out of necessity, but all interconnected and building on each other. I chose the Concept Map format for that reason. The work involved in thinking about the *so you can* sections helped to clarify the rationale for making links between topic areas.

How did you use this graphic organiser?

I spent some time at the start of the course discussing learning and memory with students. I showed them a graphic about working memory and long-term memory, and talked about retrieval practice. I introduced the idea of schema, at which point I showed them this graphic organiser with just the headings. Each student filled in boxes with things that they already knew. I brought it back out periodically to pull together the topics in their minds, and set them the task of making their own Concept Maps of topics to build up to their own graphic organiser of the course.

One unanticipated benefit was that the action of creating it reminded me to make the connections more explicit as I introduced new topics. I included explicit retrieval practice — the action of building up this map illustrated the importance of bringing to mind information from different areas. Making the organiser also reminded me to do more spaced practice.

I wanted my students to see how I see the course: a series of topics taught sequentially out of necessity, but all interconnected.

Making the organiser reminded me to do more spaced practice.

How do you plan to use this in the future?

My initial plan had been to build up this graphic organiser as a wall display with detachable boxes and arrows. At the start of the year, I would talk through it as I put it on the wall, and then take it all down again. As we completed topics, I would add them to the display, and have some blank boxes on which we could agree "critical points" they had learned. Periodically I would take it all down and we would build it back up again.

For too long, teachers haven't known the best way to share with their students how they organise knowledge. Helen's beautiful advance organiser affords her students the same privilege as Dorothy in *The Wizard of Oz* — they get to peep behind the curtain. By making the associations of her subject explicit to her students, Helen helps them to see how the knowledge is organised. By providing her students with an advance organiser, Helen isn't reducing her subject — she is making it more inclusive for all students.

MAP OF PHYSICS

Why are we learning this?

Physics is concerned with explaining and predicting the phenomena that we see or can detect, or make happen. The areas of study are interconnected as shown below.

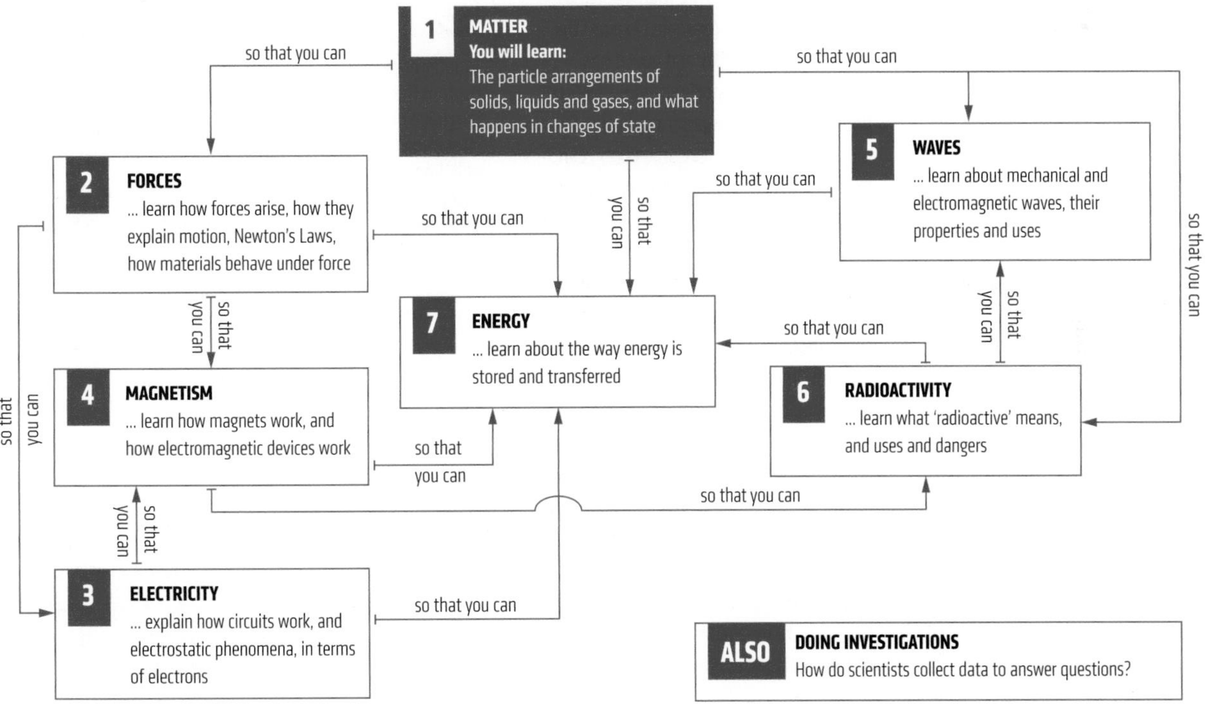

JANCKE DUNN

Graphic organisers distil complex information with clarity, demonstrating the relationships between abstract ideas in a powerful way.

Current job: Lead practitioner
Subject: English
Age phase: Secondary and FE (11-18)
Organisation: Al Yasmina Academy, Abu Dhabi

Why do you use graphic organisers?

Graphic organisers have been a natural development for my teaching practice since learning of the value of visual coding to support working memory and limit cognitive overload. The journey began with dual coding, which I have utilised in the design to support recall and, in my international context, EAL learners. Graphic organisers capture the transient language of the classroom and solidify nebulous information within structural simplicity.

How did you introduce your GO to your students?

We begin with clearly defined concepts, especially if they are more abstract. These are then broken down into their *ingredients* or conventions, which are more concrete for students. In this example I explore the conventions of *tragedy* and how it has developed from Aristotle's traditional Greek drama to Shakespearean tragedy and, lastly, modern drama. At A-level, these texts are taught as separate units: *Othello*, *King Lear* and *A Streetcar Named Desire* to name a few. However, I wanted students to understand the cause-and-effect relationship that spans the genre, so as to appreciate the wider conventions and development of tragedy through time. I believe this is a crucial part of developing a closely interconnected and sound schema. I will explicitly model these relationships for students at the beginning, but as their foundational schema grows, we often co-create GOs based on comparing, sequencing or establishing hierarchies in our texts. We do this for everything from plot structures to pyramidal evaluation for essay writing. A visualiser is an invaluable tool in this process and the discussions that arise from co-developing GOs are always stimulating.

Graphic organisers capture the transient language of the classroom and solidify nebulous information within structural simplicity.

This has been revelatory for supporting EAL students: paring back colour, font and gawdy images to retrain focus on the important information.

What other strategies did you pair it with?

Graphic organisers and dual coding make natural allies. Both have shaped my practice and ensure design enhances the information presented rather than hindering it. This has been revelatory for supporting EAL students: paring back colour, font and gaudy images to retrain focus on the important information. Dual coding can be used to activate prior knowledge, so more knowledge can be nested within a GO without an expanse of text.

Jancke has done a fine job of chunking the convention of tragedy and showing how it has developed over time. Breaking concepts down into their constituent parts is crucial, but it is likely that the same students who require things broken down are the same ones who are easily overwhelmed. Jancke has artfully coalesced the features of a Flow Spray diagram to create a chunked Time Line.

LITERARY CONVENTIONS: Aspects of Tragedy

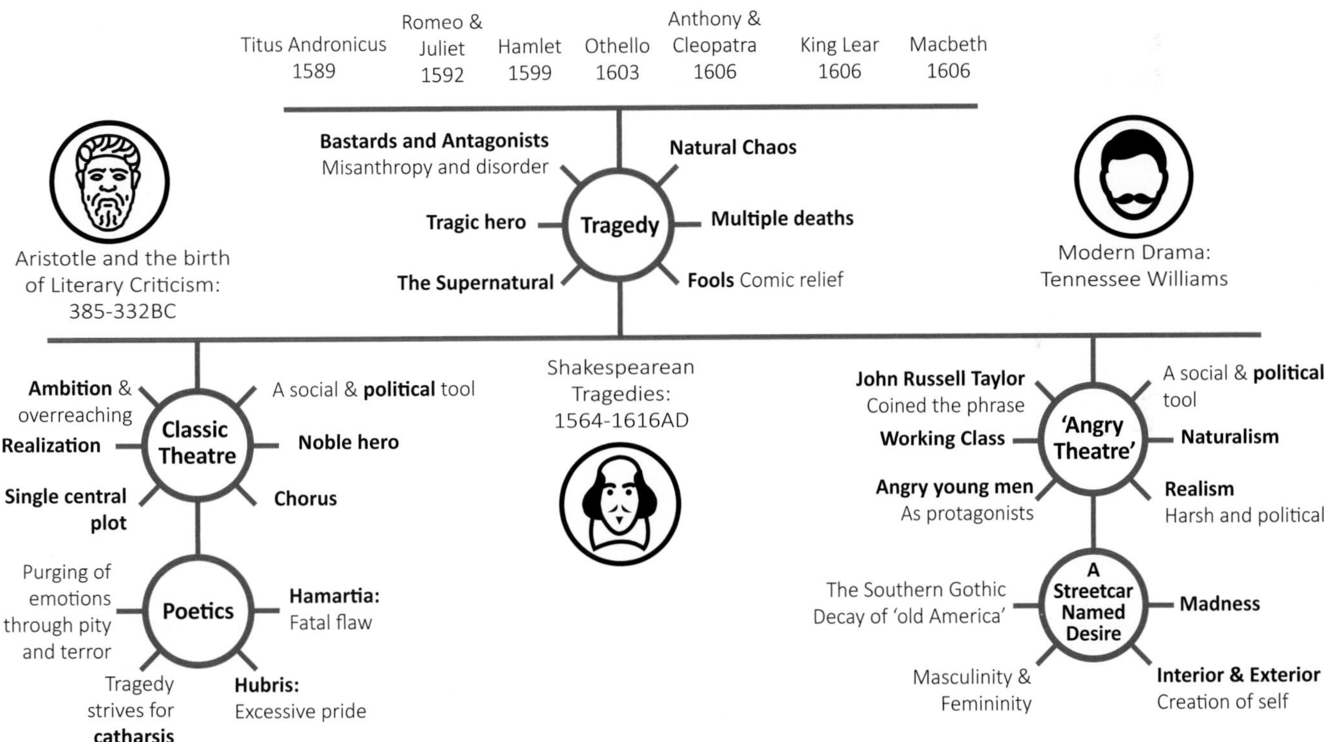
Titus Andronicus
1589
Romeo &
Juliet
1592
Hamlet
1599
Othello
1603
Anthony &
Cleopatra
1606
King Lear
1606
Macbeth
1606
Tragedy
Bastards and Antagonists
Misanthropy and disorder
Natural Chaos
Tragic hero
Multiple deaths
The Supernatural
Fools Comic relief
Aristotle and the birth
of Literary Criticism:
385-332BC
Modern Drama:
Tennessee Williams
Shakespearean
Tragedies:
1564-1616AD
Classic
Theatre
Ambition &
overreaching
A social & political tool
Realization
Noble hero
Single central
plot
Chorus
Poetics
Purging of
emotions
through pity
and terror
Hamartia:
Fatal flaw
Tragedy
strives for
catharsis
Hubris:
Excessive pride
'Angry
Theatre'
John Russell Taylor
Coined the phrase
A social & political
tool
Working Class
Naturalism
Angry young men
As protagonists
Realism
Harsh and political
A
Streetcar
Named
Desire
The Southern Gothic
Decay of 'old America'
Madness
Masculinity &
Femininity
Interior & Exterior
Creation of self

JOE BURKMAR

This type of diagram allowed me to share my schema with Year 7 and check for understanding throughout. When concept mapping, students gain a better sense of how ideas are connected.

Current job: SCITT partnership director
Subject: History
Age phase: Secondary (11-16)
Organisation: Poole High School

Why did you choose the graphic organiser in your example?

I wanted to demonstrate how the plight of the Huguenots was multifaceted and complex, while focusing the students on key areas. The linking verbs allowed me to support the lower-ability students with sentence structures, and aid their understanding of how the main elements of the map are linked. They also allowed me to link the different aspects together accurately.

How did you teach it to the students?

The lesson started by sharing a completed version with students. I asked them to highlight words they didn't know or understand in the context. I then addressed misconceptions, such as what a Protestant was and what the Reformation meant. Next I used animations on PowerPoint to focus the students' attention to key areas of the Concept Map. I began by introducing what life was like for people in France. At the end of the first section, I directed students to complete a question using their Concept Map as a writing frame. I repeated the process, revealing one segment of the Concept Map followed by a student question until the Concept Map was complete. I used Think-Pair-Share to help the process and check for understanding.

What is the impact of this on your organisation?

I taught this lesson to two groups of Year 7 students. One group used the concept mapping activity as described and the other a more traditional teaching approach. I did this as I wanted to compare how much recall there was and the accuracy of that recall between the two groups. The recall among the graphic organiser group was significantly better than among their peers. The most impressive aspect of this was the recall of students who had lower reading ages. Students were able to recall key dates, key events and infer the impact of these events from memory two weeks after the lesson (with a half-term in between).

The linking verbs allowed me to support the lower-ability students with sentence structures, and aid their understanding of how the main elements of the map are linked.

Students were able to recall key dates, key events and infer the impact of these events from memory two weeks after the lesson (with a half-term in between).

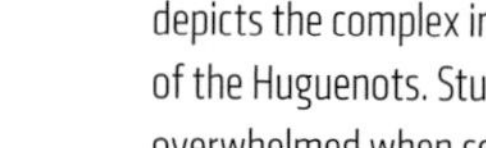

Joe has produced a Concept Map that depicts the complex interconnected nature of the Huguenots. Students can become overwhelmed when concept mapping if there are too many connections. Joe relieves some of the cognitive burden by introducing each element one by one. He also describes how he assigns a writing task after each section of the map is made public. Joe uses kernel sentences to mitigate the limitations of his students' working memory and provide sentence-level writing practice.

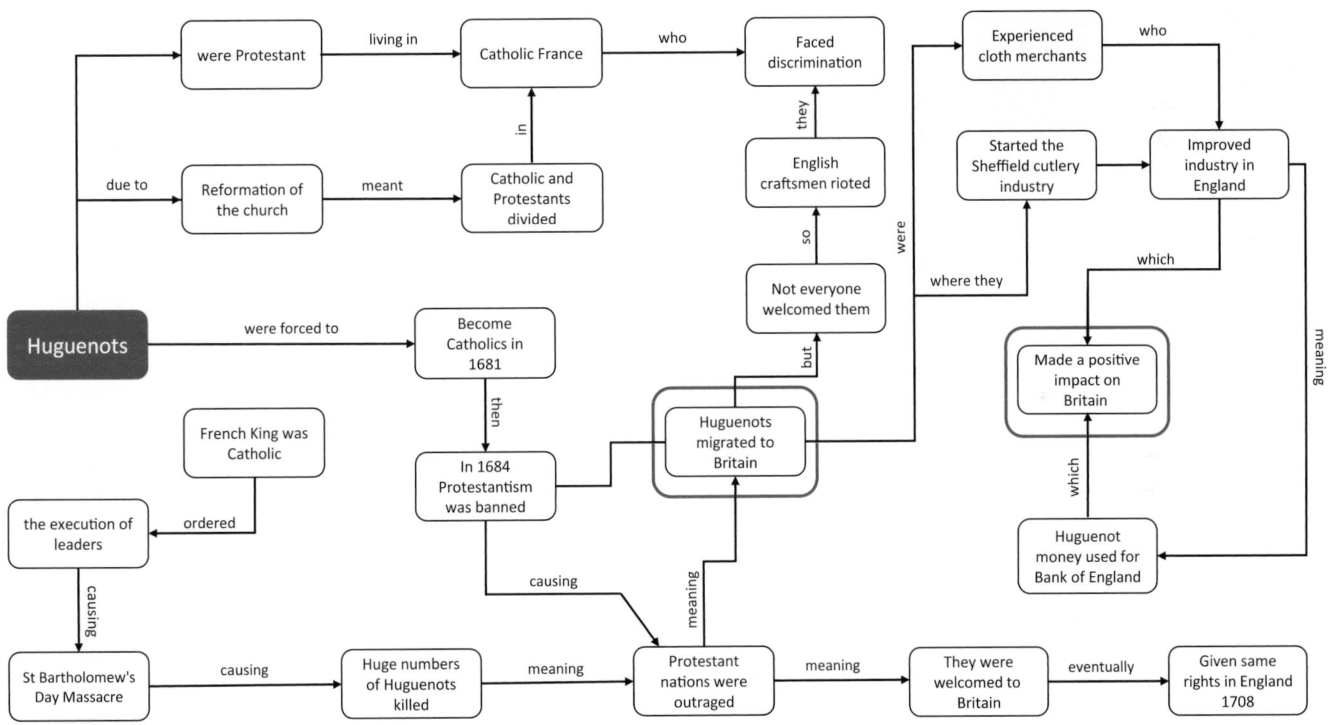
Huguenots
due to
were Protestant
living in
Catholic France
who
Faced discrimination
Reformation of the church
meant
Catholic and Protestants divided
in
they
English craftsmen rioted
so
Not everyone welcomed them
but
were forced to
Become Catholics in 1681
then
In 1684 Protestantism was banned
Huguenots migrated to Britain
were
Experienced cloth merchants
who
Improved industry in England
Started the Sheffield cutlery industry
where they
which
Made a positive impact on Britain
which
meaning
Huguenot money used for Bank of England
French King was Catholic
ordered
the execution of leaders
causing
St Bartholomew's Day Massacre
causing
Huge numbers of Huguenots killed
meaning
Protestant nations were outraged
causing
meaning
meaning
They were welcomed to Britain
eventually
Given same rights in England 1708

JOHN ETTY

This method for uncovering the structure of an historian's argument helps my students to break down and summarise complex texts.

Current job: Associate headmaster
Subject: History
Age phase: Secondary and FE (11-18)
Organisation: Auckland Grammar School, New Zealand

Why do you use graphic organisers?

Analysing historians' arguments in extended texts has been challenging for some of my A-level history students. Some have found explanations in long texts overwhelming; some have misread and over-inferred, or overlooked important clauses; others have foundered at word-level and these errors of comprehension have led to profound misconceptions about what the historian is saying. Over the years I have recommended various strategies for finding the main ideas in texts, but these strategies tend to describe how experts approach texts, rather than giving students a reliable method for breaking down a long extract. This graphic organiser enables students to uncover the structure of an historical argument.

How does the graphic organiser help your students?

This graphic organiser combines tiers of Input-Output Diagrams. Each tier represents the construction of a complex key claim. The intention is that students identify:

- The evidence (red boxes);
- Reasoning (red-outlined boxes);
- Sub-claims (black boxes); and
- Main messages (black-outlined boxes) without losing sight of how they fit together.

The claims making up the historian's argument are constructed in text, so they are linear. The tiers of the finished graphic organiser reflect this, but dividing the page into a grid allows students to add notes in any order. Concentrating on one element at a time helps them to manage the cognitive load intrinsic in the task.

Once all the historian's claims are mapped out, the completed graphic organiser visualises the relationships between different elements in the text. The key claims arranged horizontally form a Relations Diagram. Summarising the argument from a long text is difficult for novices, but the diagram visualises the structure of the argument so that condensing the four or five key claims becomes more manageable.

How do you teach students to use this graphic organiser?

Students work on selections from historians' writing. This example comes from pp.276-277 in Vladislav Zubok and Constantine Pleshakov's *Inside the Kremlin's Cold War*. At first, we read an extract, discuss, and map the argument together. Using my visualiser, I live-model the annotations, writing on a laminated A3 template, blank except for the headings *Evidence*, *Reasoning*, *Sub-claims* and *Main messages*. Meanwhile, my students work on paper copies. We analyse extracts in order of publication. Contextual knowledge is essential, so before asking students to analyse a new extract, I introduce them to key developments in the historiography of the topic, the leading historians and their main arguments, and different historical methods used in each period.

Working on a new extract each time, I vary the conditions of practice (by providing part-worked examples instead of modelling, for instance) and gradually withdraw the support. By the end of term, my students are mapping arguments with little teacher input. Before I started using this graphic organiser, the classroom conversations were corrective; now the discussion centres on the historian's evidence and reasoning, or which of the historian's claims are subordinate.

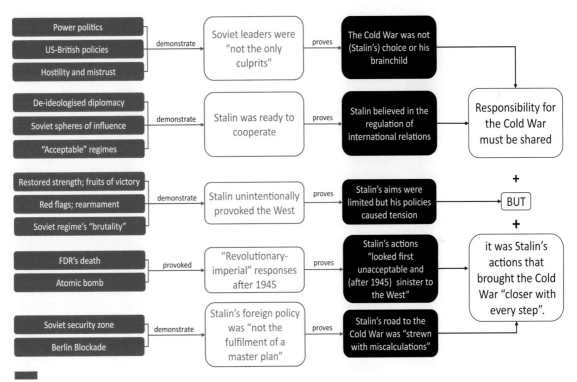

Power politics
US-British policies
Hostility and mistrust
demonstrate
Soviet leaders were "not the only culprits"
proves
The Cold War was not (Stalin's) choice or his brainchild

De-ideologised diplomacy
Soviet spheres of influence
"Acceptable" regimes
demonstrate
Stalin was ready to cooperate
proves
Stalin believed in the regulation of international relations

Responsibility for the Cold War must be shared

\+

BUT

\+

Restored strength; fruits of victory
Red flags; rearmament
Soviet regime's "brutality"
demonstrate
Stalin unintentionally provoked the West
proves
Stalin's aims were limited but his policies caused tension

FDR's death
Atomic bomb
provoked
"Revolutionary-imperial" responses after 1945
proves
Stalin's actions "looked first unacceptable and (after 1945) sinister to the West"

it was Stalin's actions that brought the Cold War "closer with every step".

Soviet security zone
Berlin Blockade
demonstrate
Stalin's foreign policy was "not the fulfilment of a master plan"
proves
Stalin's road to the Cold War was "strewn with miscalculations"

John's Relations Diagram is a perfect example of how graphic organisers can support students when engaging with demanding text. His use of graphic organisers has changed the discourse in his classroom. Since John began using graphic organisers, he has seen his students spend more time interrogating historical evidence and reasoning — they have a new tool in their learning arsenal. The value of John's organiser is boosted by its immeasurable clarity. Text boxes are aligned, arrows signal lines of influence, and he has shown restraint. Here is a high-quality design with immense utility.

JOHN HOUGH

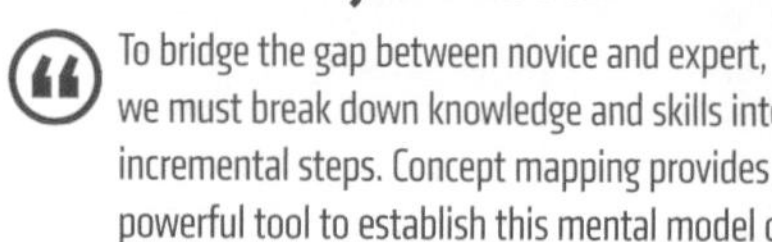

To bridge the gap between novice and expert, we must break down knowledge and skills into incremental steps. Concept mapping provides a powerful tool to establish this mental model of the complex.

Current job: Associate assistant principal
Subject: History
Age phase: Secondary and FE (11-18)
Organisation: Hope Academy Sixth Form

What was your thought process when designing this graphic organiser?

Achieving simplicity and alignment. The design is governed by the subject, and a Concept Map is the most effective way to represent the relationships between success criteria, teaching and techniques. From left to right, it follows the thought process from aim to outcome. This example is the colleague version, but to make it student-friendly I change *teach with* to *learn with*. For students, this sets out what they aim to do: how to break down the thinking into aspects of significance; how to represent this thinking on the page and then transform this thinking into sentences. Overarching the Concept Map is a thread that explores the nature of significance and how analysis, categorisation and explanation are key skills that support understanding historical significance. These three skills are taught to students in isolation first. Underpinning the first two columns are the definitions of analysis and assessment as a reminder, and a visual that shows short- and long-term significance can be explored within all other aspects.

What purpose does this graphic organiser serve?

It is a tool to better understand what historians mean by *significance*. The skills and concepts of history are complex, and they rarely have a shared meaning across classrooms, departments and schools. Students could encounter very different explanations of what *significance* is and, more importantly, how they *do it*. This does not support the establishment of a mental model. For my team, this GO acts as a guide for less experienced staff and a skeleton for department discussion for more experienced staff. This clarity across the team has had a profound impact in the classroom: we use a shared language, taking the students from *basic* to *complex* through activities that always end with writing techniques. In our department, where deliberately and incrementally closing the gap between novice and expert is our aim, GOs are essential.

In our department, where deliberately and incrementally closing the gap between novice and expert is our aim, GOs are essential.

The visual clarity of the graphic organiser reduces extraneous load on the working memory, providing the space and simplicity required to understand the complex nature of historical enquiry.

Why are graphic organisers important in history?

They allow us to break down complex substantive knowledge, concepts and skills into incremental building blocks that can be mastered with a high success rate. The visual clarity of the GO reduces extraneous load on the working memory, providing the space and simplicity required to understand the complex nature of historical enquiry. When reacquainted with the other *historical skill* graphic organisers and my curriculum, they go some of the way to establishing what Daisy Christodoulou calls a "*progression model*" in *Making Good Progress?* (2017). This model prioritises formative assessment in the classroom, allowing for responsive teaching. Breaking down complex skills into incremental steps towards those skills is fundamental to this model. Each incremental skill is so specific that it allows for incisive immediate feedback, where misconceptions and errors of thought can be quickly corrected. Graphic organisers provide these steps with clarity.

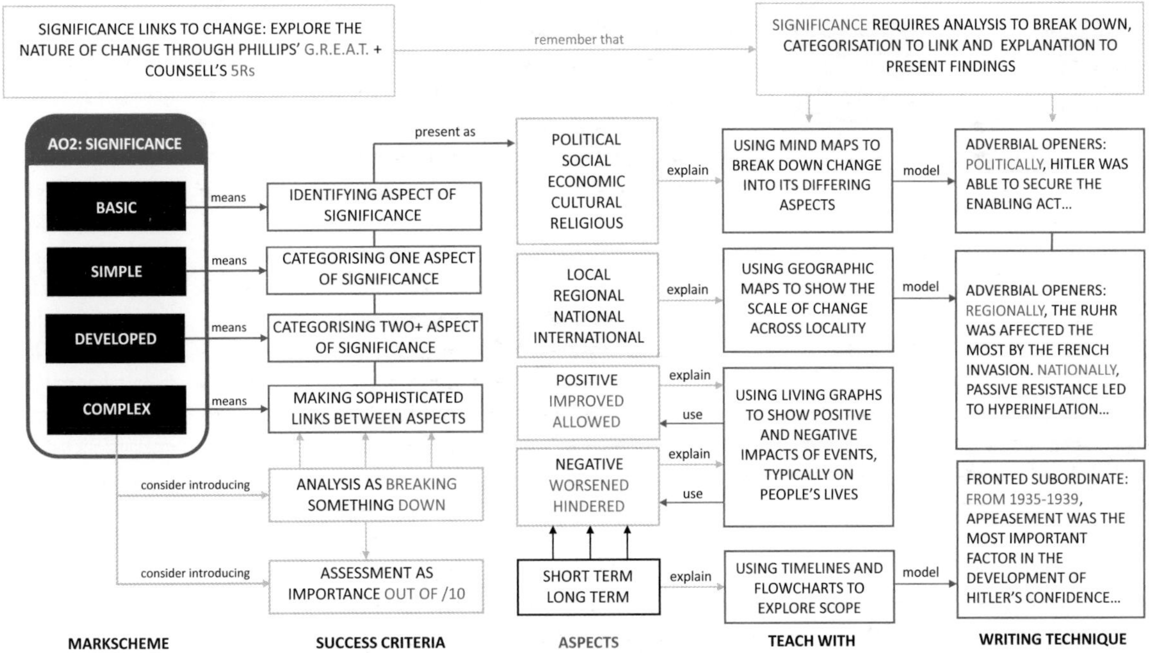

SIGNIFICANCE LINKS TO CHANGE: EXPLORE THE NATURE OF CHANGE THROUGH PHILLIPS' G.R.E.A.T. + COUNSELL'S 5Rs

remember that

SIGNIFICANCE REQUIRES ANALYSIS TO BREAK DOWN, CATEGORISATION TO LINK AND EXPLANATION TO PRESENT FINDINGS

AO2: SIGNIFICANCE

- BASIC — means — IDENTIFYING ASPECT OF SIGNIFICANCE
- SIMPLE — means — CATEGORISING ONE ASPECT OF SIGNIFICANCE
- DEVELOPED — means — CATEGORISING TWO+ ASPECT OF SIGNIFICANCE
- COMPLEX — means — MAKING SOPHISTICATED LINKS BETWEEN ASPECTS

present as

consider introducing — ANALYSIS AS BREAKING SOMETHING DOWN

consider introducing — ASSESSMENT AS IMPORTANCE OUT OF /10

POLITICAL SOCIAL ECONOMIC CULTURAL RELIGIOUS — explain — USING MIND MAPS TO BREAK DOWN CHANGE INTO ITS DIFFERING ASPECTS — model — ADVERBIAL OPENERS: POLITICALLY, HITLER WAS ABLE TO SECURE THE ENABLING ACT...

LOCAL REGIONAL NATIONAL INTERNATIONAL — explain — USING GEOGRAPHIC MAPS TO SHOW THE SCALE OF CHANGE ACROSS LOCALITY — model — ADVERBIAL OPENERS: REGIONALLY, THE RUHR WAS AFFECTED THE MOST BY THE FRENCH INVASION. NATIONALLY, PASSIVE RESISTANCE LED TO HYPERINFLATION...

POSITIVE IMPROVED ALLOWED — explain / use

NEGATIVE WORSENED HINDERED — explain / use

USING LIVING GRAPHS TO SHOW POSITIVE AND NEGATIVE IMPACTS OF EVENTS, TYPICALLY ON PEOPLE'S LIVES

SHORT TERM LONG TERM — explain — USING TIMELINES AND FLOWCHARTS TO EXPLORE SCOPE — model — FRONTED SUBORDINATE: FROM 1935-1939, APPEASEMENT WAS THE MOST IMPORTANT FACTOR IN THE DEVELOPMENT OF HITLER'S CONFIDENCE...

MARKSCHEME | **SUCCESS CRITERIA** | **ASPECTS** | **TEACH WITH** | **WRITING TECHNIQUE**

John has created a Concept Map of the highest quality. His graphic organiser is based on his extensive knowledge of his subject, and it is a useful tool for colleagues and students. For his department, the Concept Map acts as a third point of contact during professional conversations. John and his team have capitalised on the visual clarity his diagram affords, helping to build a lingua franca – a common language. Students get to peep behind the curtain – they are not left guessing how knowledge is organised in history.

JUSTIN WAKEFIELD

Graphic organisers help provide visual clarity, enabling colleagues to foresee the stages of development that a teacher may traverse when making the journey from novice to expert.

Current job: Director of a Teaching School
Subject: PE
Age phase: Secondary (11-16)
Organisation: Healing School and the Humber Teaching School

Tell us about your graphic organiser?

The development of skill, acquisition and application of knowledge, and routine reflection and evaluation cycles are vital elements that aid successful teacher delivery and development. Successful teachers identify opportunities for growth, ensuring that ample time is invested in the rehearsal and refinement of their delivery. However, the development of this golden thread can take colleagues significant time to develop, sometimes resulting in educational settings not providing significant development opportunities for their staff. This graphic organiser explores the various stages of teacher development and its intricacies, showing how these are connected and also how they can be developed and supported effectively, primarily through following Jim Knight's instructional coaching cycle (2017). This schema is then used to help build CPD opportunities for educators within the region that the Teaching School serves.

Why did you choose to present the information using a graphic organiser?

A key role of a Teaching School is to provide development opportunities for educators at a variety of different career points. This ranges from initial teacher training all the way to leadership level (executive leadership). Clarity and depth of understanding are vital when sharing and discussing information with any key stakeholders. This graphic organiser ensures that colleagues retain and embed the material. It is essential that a student is shown the path of progression within their learning – and educators are no different. For stakeholders, this enables developed, detailed discussions to occur that critique and improve the professional development offer provided for the region, while showing leadership teams how they may effectively build a cross-pollination support for their teams.

How does your organiser help establish a lingua franca for your organisation?

Due to the vast array of partners that my team interact with, commonality is hugely important. It is essential that all stakeholders and colleagues associated with the Teaching School fully understand how we operate and embrace the visions and values that we believe in. No matter what type of background or industry, a lingua franca ensures that ideas become projects, communication connects discussions to actions, and visions are realised. This organiser includes key terminology linked to national policy (Department for Education) and research (evidence base). This ensures there is still commonality for the teacher development being performed from regional level to national level. This shared language will expose teachers to key terms and information from national frameworks/research, to ensure that they start making a link between the work within their individual classroom and the work performed at a much wider scale (national). Having this consistency results in a very clear operational intent and implementation, while supporting the needs of colleagues within the region.

How do you use your organiser?

The graphic organiser can be used in a variety of different ways that are bespoke to the institution and individual. Primarily, its core function is to map the several stages of teacher development, showing how every development stage enhances and can improve provision. This graphic organiser is very powerful when having professional dialogue with teachers. The organiser acts as a third point of communication. With mentor and mentee sat side by side as mutuals, and with the organiser as a point of reference, feedback feels less personal for the recipient.

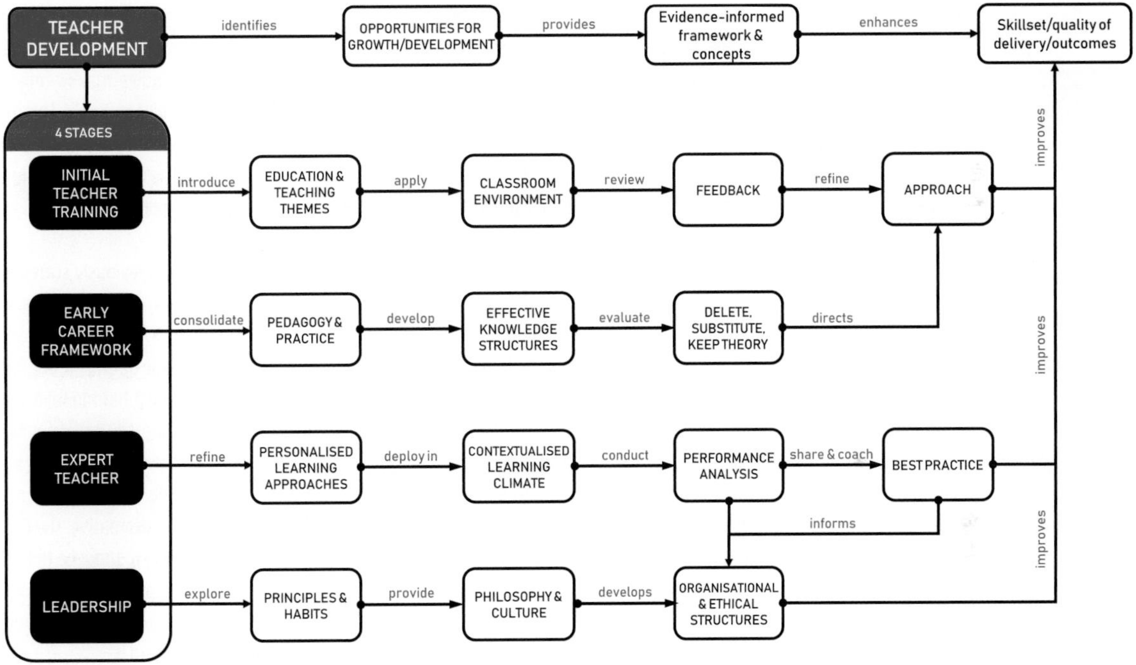

TEACHER DEVELOPMENT — identifies → OPPORTUNITIES FOR GROWTH/DEVELOPMENT — provides → Evidence-informed framework & concepts — enhances → Skillset/quality of delivery/outcomes

4 STAGES

- **INITIAL TEACHER TRAINING** — introduce → EDUCATION & TEACHING THEMES — apply → CLASSROOM ENVIRONMENT — review → FEEDBACK — refine → APPROACH — improves → Skillset/quality of delivery/outcomes
- **EARLY CAREER FRAMEWORK** — consolidate → PEDAGOGY & PRACTICE — develop → EFFECTIVE KNOWLEDGE STRUCTURES — evaluate → DELETE, SUBSTITUTE, KEEP THEORY — directs → APPROACH
- **EXPERT TEACHER** — refine → PERSONALISED LEARNING APPROACHES — deploy in → CONTEXTUALISED LEARNING CLIMATE — conduct → PERFORMANCE ANALYSIS — share & coach → BEST PRACTICE — improves → Skillset/quality of delivery/outcomes; BEST PRACTICE — informs → ORGANISATIONAL & ETHICAL STRUCTURES
- **LEADERSHIP** — explore → PRINCIPLES & HABITS — provide → PHILOSOPHY & CULTURE — develops → ORGANISATIONAL & ETHICAL STRUCTURES — improves → Skillset/quality of delivery/outcomes

Justin's Concept Map and narrative embody one of the core messages of this book. The organiser doesn't replace prose – far from it. It enhances the reader's chance of arriving at meaning. Given that Justin is responsible for teacher training across a large region, he must communicate with absolute clarity. As he describes, this organiser is versatile and can be used in different ways. Its versatility and clarity reside in its careful design. Speaking with Justin, we were delighted to hear how he used sticky notes to capture his initial ideas before arranging them into a coherent structure. Such meticulous planning has resulted in a high-quality design.

KELLY PEPPIN

It can be challenging to transfer thoughts to paper. This is why graphic organisers are so valuable. They provide a basic structure so students can, instead, focus on making connections between their thoughts.

Current job: Assistant subject lead
Subject: Geography
Age phase: Secondary (11-16)
Organisation: Greenbank High School

Why did you choose the graphic organiser in your example?

My decision to use a Double Spray graphic organiser was driven by the nature of the subject content as well as practical application of skills. The study of place is an important aspect of geography. Students are required to explore location examples, case studies, in accordance with subject content. This means students need to understand and compare statistics between various case studies, in order to apply their knowledge and understanding before drawing conclusions. Most commonly, when comparing case studies, students are drawn to Venn Diagrams due to familiarity. However, I find this type of graphic organiser discourages deep thinking when used to write essay-style questions. One advantage of a Double Spray organiser is that it encourages students to compare and analyse statistics, alongside subject content, prior to adding the information to the template. The content can be broken down further with the support of statistics to encourage deeper analysis, rather than writing down generic similarities and differences. This type of graphic organiser allows students to select the most appropriate content, filtering that which is irrelevant/not applicable. The Double Spray organiser limits the amount of content students can include, providing space in their working memory to process the information and apply their knowledge and understanding.

How did you introduce this graphic organiser to your students?

My use of graphic organisers depends on the content and skill(s) I want students to learn and practice. In this instance, I want students to draw comparisons between case studies, making reference to statistics – independently. This means students need to identify applicable content, select that which is the most appropriate/relevant, organise it and apply prior learning.

My decision to use a Double Spray graphic organiser was driven by the nature of the subject content.

As previously stated, students are familiar with Venn Diagrams. We briefly discuss the advantages and disadvantages of using this type of graphic organiser, revealing that some find it hard to follow when used as a scaffold for essay writing, while others recognised the risk of including irrelevant or generic information. It is here that I would introduce an alternative, the Double Spray. I would model how to produce the graphic organiser with the help of a student exemplar, including how to select appropriate information and how to record it.

This type of graphic organiser allows students to select the most appropriate content.

With low-ability students, I often provide the information alongside the graphic organiser. At this stage I am emphasising the process of organising comparative thoughts, and don't want the students overwhelmed by having to conduct research, too.

Hurricane Irma, 2017

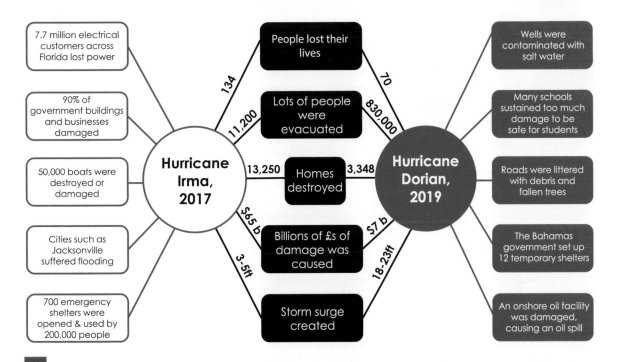

- 7.7 million electrical customers across Florida lost power
- 90% of government buildings and businesses damaged
- 50,000 boats were destroyed or damaged
- Cities such as Jacksonville suffered flooding
- 700 emergency shelters were opened & used by 200,000 people

Hurricane Irma, 2017		Hurricane Dorian, 2019
134	People lost their lives	70
11,200	Lots of people were evacuated	830,000
13,250	Homes destroyed	3,348
$65 b	Billions of £s of damage was caused	$7 b
3-5ft	Storm surge created	18-23ft

Hurricane Dorian, 2019

- Wells were contaminated with salt water
- Many schools sustained too much damage to be safe for students
- Roads were littered with debris and fallen trees
- The Bahamas government set up 12 temporary shelters
- An onshore oil facility was damaged, causing an oil spill

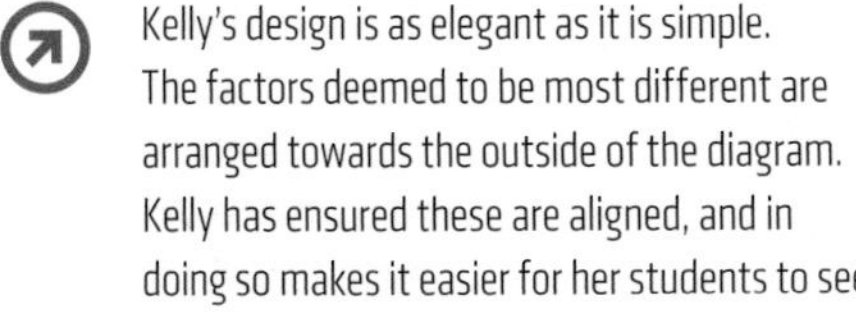

Kelly's design is as elegant as it is simple. The factors deemed to be most different are arranged towards the outside of the diagram. Kelly has ensured these are aligned, and in doing so makes it easier for her students to see how the two tropical storms were different.

The centrally connected statements represent similar factors. Kelly, rather shrewdly, positions the statistics for each along their respective branches. For her students, there can be no confusion as to which statistic relates to which tropical storm. Kelly has created an organiser that allows her students to consider more challenging questions. They can see the similarities and differences easily. As such, they can begin to conclude and speculate upon the reasons for why one storm was more deadly than the other.

LOUISE CASS

An advance organiser zooms in on the most important ideas of a scheme of learning and forces the creator to reflect on their own knowledge structures.

Current job: Lead practitioner
Subject: Science
Age phase: Secondary (11-16)
Organisation: Havelock Academy

Why did you decide to create this graphic organiser?

I was asked by Phoenix Park Academy, a pupil referral unit, to help create their science curriculum. Before working with the PRU, they had a limited science offer and teaching staff with a minimal scientific background. The advance organiser I have created was given to staff in advance of teaching a new sequence of lessons. For non-specialist teachers, the curriculum can be voluminous. While using an unfamiliar scheme of learning, a non-specialist is likely to feel a cognitive burden. To reduce the load, I created a Flow Spray diagram. The Flow Spray explicitly presents in sequence the core elements to be taught during the unit of work.

How do you use the graphic organiser?

The Flow Spray is a useful tool when having curriculum discussions. The diagram's power resides in its visual clarity – the potential to see the individual elements and the whole. Using an advance organiser as a servant to a curriculum document is more efficient than a scheme of learning on its own. My Flow Spray emphasises the core and most important concepts/ideas to be taught. It selects and organises these concepts in a way that a non-specialist might not be able to do when using the scheme of learning on its own.

How do you see your colleagues expanding their use of GOs?

Having created this advance organiser for the PRU, the natural progression is to work with them to help construct their own. Working with the PRU team, I will model my thought process while creating a graphic organiser. To help the PRU create advance organisers, I will make one with them. Using Post-it notes, I will direct the team to extract what they perceive to be the core ideas from a scheme of learning – one idea per note. The notes will then be grouped and sequenced into a logical order. At this stage, we can interrogate our thinking and explore where there are authentic links. Working with the PRU, I hope to help them develop their subject expertise and confidence. We know graphic organisers can help disadvantaged students to read and write. If the teachers at Phoenix Park are confident in organising their knowledge, they can begin to explore using graphic organisers with students.

The diagram's power resides in its visual clarity – the potential to see the individual elements and the whole.

My Flow Spray selects and organises the concepts in a way that a non-specialist might not be able to do when using the scheme of learning on its own.

Louise has created a Flow Spray advance organiser with admirable clarity. As an advance organiser, the Flow Spray explicitly details a sequence of learning and to-be-taught concepts. Louise's use of capital letters, subtle graphic elements and minimal colour allows her to display a lot of content with clarity – her readers are not overwhelmed.

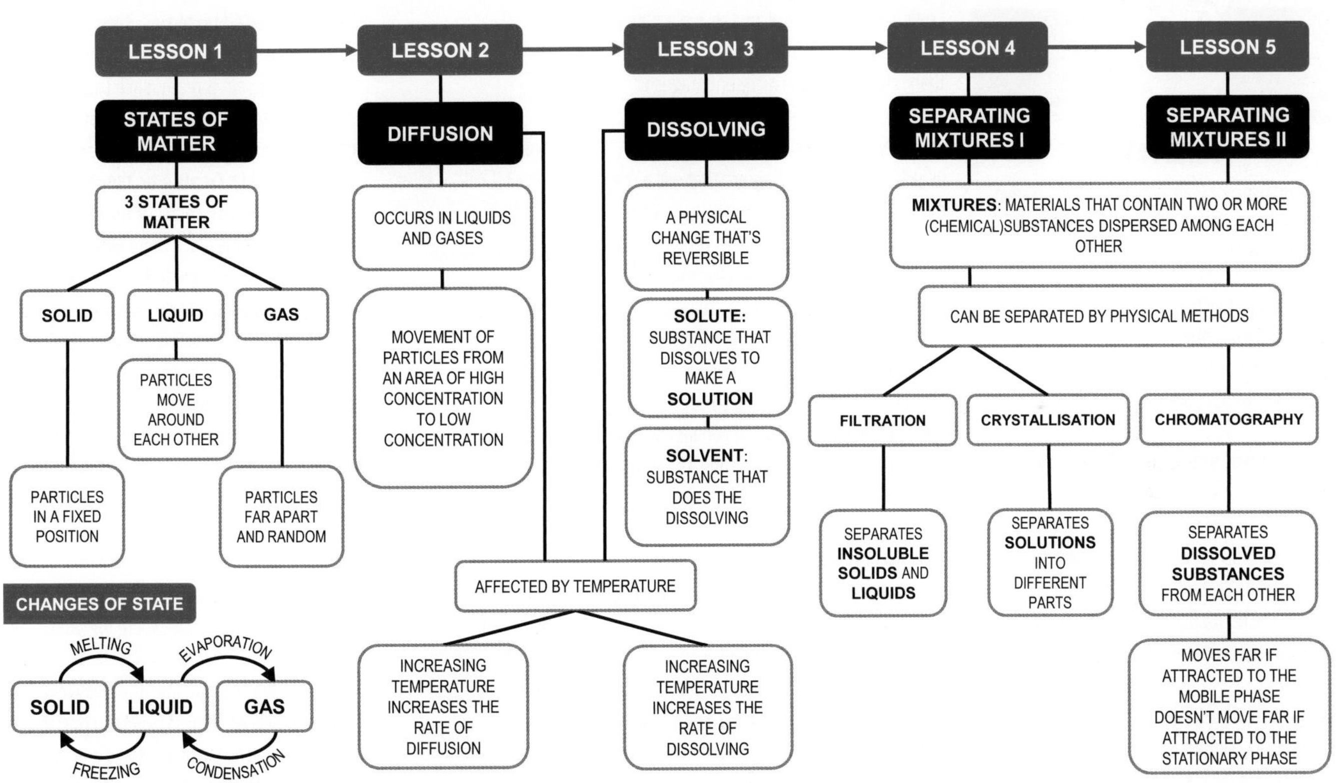
LESSON 1
LESSON 2
LESSON 3
LESSON 4
LESSON 5
STATES OF MATTER
DIFFUSION
DISSOLVING
SEPARATING MIXTURES I
SEPARATING MIXTURES II
3 STATES OF MATTER
SOLID
LIQUID
GAS
PARTICLES MOVE AROUND EACH OTHER
PARTICLES IN A FIXED POSITION
PARTICLES FAR APART AND RANDOM
CHANGES OF STATE
MELTING
EVAPORATION
SOLID
LIQUID
GAS
FREEZING
CONDENSATION
OCCURS IN LIQUIDS AND GASES
MOVEMENT OF PARTICLES FROM AN AREA OF HIGH CONCENTRATION TO LOW CONCENTRATION
A PHYSICAL CHANGE THAT'S REVERSIBLE
SOLUTE: SUBSTANCE THAT DISSOLVES TO MAKE A SOLUTION
SOLVENT: SUBSTANCE THAT DOES THE DISSOLVING
AFFECTED BY TEMPERATURE
INCREASING TEMPERATURE INCREASES THE RATE OF DIFFUSION
INCREASING TEMPERATURE INCREASES THE RATE OF DISSOLVING
MIXTURES: MATERIALS THAT CONTAIN TWO OR MORE (CHEMICAL)SUBSTANCES DISPERSED AMONG EACH OTHER
CAN BE SEPARATED BY PHYSICAL METHODS
FILTRATION
CRYSTALLISATION
CHROMATOGRAPHY
SEPARATES INSOLUBLE SOLIDS AND LIQUIDS
SEPARATES SOLUTIONS INTO DIFFERENT PARTS
SEPARATES DISSOLVED SUBSTANCES FROM EACH OTHER
MOVES FAR IF ATTRACTED TO THE MOBILE PHASE DOESN'T MOVE FAR IF ATTRACTED TO THE STATIONARY PHASE

LUKE TAYLER

A hybrid Concept Map allows students to keep track of how different parts of a diagram are interconnected.

Current job: Teacher
Subject: Geography
Age phase: Secondary and FE (11-18)
Organisation: St Christopher's School, Bahrain

What type of graphic organiser have you chosen?

My graphic organiser is a hybrid diagram. It is a Concept Map set with a diagrammatic cross-section of a coastal feature. The Concept Map reveals the relationship between the different facets of that coastal feature.

Why are they useful?

In physical geography, much of what we study can be described through a diagram of a particular process or feature. Students soon become familiar with the *classic* diagrams, such as a Destructive Plate Margin or a Meander Cross-Section. When using these diagrams, teachers will usually show the diagram and then talk through the different stages or sections. Given the interconnected nature of these geographical features, there are usually sections of a diagram that will link with multiple other parts, meaning the teacher will need to keep referring back to various areas of the diagram. The expert teacher can see these connections and finds it easy to make the links. The novice student is only now learning about the parts of the diagram, as well as having to listen to how they are connected. Overlaying the diagram with a series of connections allows the student to keep track of how the different parts are linked.

Overlaying the diagram with a series of connections allows the student to keep track of how the different parts are linked.

How do you make hybrid Concept Maps?

There is no set way to make either a Concept Map or a hybrid Concept Map. However, there are few stages that I follow...

Draw the background diagram. This is usually the *classic* geography diagram. Keep it simple and be prepared to edit as you start to add on the Concept Map. A good tip is to find an existing diagram and to trace over it with a polyline tool. It is important that the diagram doesn't dominate the Concept Map or detract from the overlaid textboxes. Keep the drawing as simple as possible and the colours subtle. Once the diagram is ready, save that slide as a .PNG file before uploading it as the background image to your Concept Map. Decide on the key terms to include. Create a textbox for each one (don't worry too much about formatting yet) and either roughly place them where they fit on to the diagram, or leave them to one side of the slide if it isn't immediately clear where to put them. I tend to have a few relevant textbooks open at this stage to remind me what to include. Start moving the words around and fitting them into position. Be prepared to make lots of adjustments. Having a background diagram at this stage can be a real help with positioning, but it can also be restrictive if you have several keywords that relate to a specific part of a diagram. I also try to keep text boxes aligned and a similar size where possible.

I find that my knowledge of the particular topic is enriched by this process of synthesising the various components.

Although time-consuming, it is really rewarding when it finally all comes together. I find that my knowledge of the particular topic is enriched by this process of synthesising the various components.

FROST ACTION
PLANT ROOTS
HYDRATION
SALT CRYSTALS

PRECIPITATION,
VEGETATION &
HUMAN ACTIVITY

including

influences

EROSIONAL LANDFORMS

leads to

SUB-AERIAL PROCESSES

WEATHERING

MASS MOVEMENT

leads to

CLIFF RECESSION

such as

SLUMPING ROCK FALL

leads to

at

MARINE EROSION

CORROSION

WAVE QUARRYING

ABRASION

affects

CLIFF FACE

of

results in

GEOLOGY

beneath

WAVE-CUT NOTCH

causes

uses

DENUDED MATERIAL

determines

WAVE-CUT PLATFORM

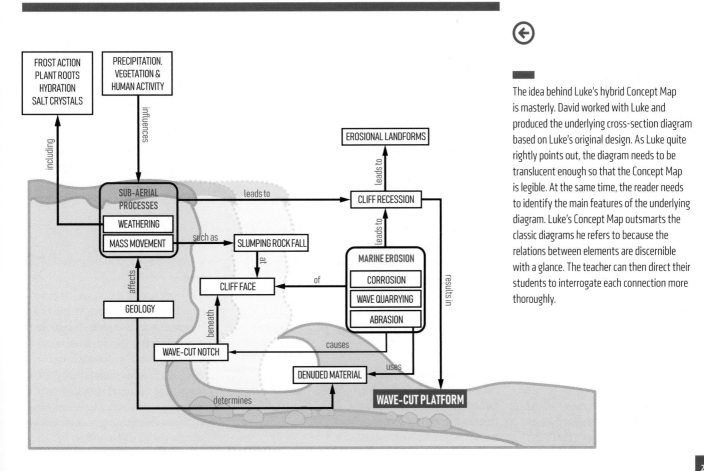

The idea behind Luke's hybrid Concept Map is masterly. David worked with Luke and produced the underlying cross-section diagram based on Luke's original design. As Luke quite rightly points out, the diagram needs to be translucent enough so that the Concept Map is legible. At the same time, the reader needs to identify the main features of the underlying diagram. Luke's Concept Map outsmarts the classic diagrams he refers to because the relations between elements are discernible with a glance. The teacher can then direct their students to interrogate each connection more thoroughly.

Crossed Continua encourage students into more than just a simple ranking exercise, and are great for a visual comparison of factors.

What are the benefits of a Crossed Continua?

One of the key skills students learn in geography is the ability to evaluate. They are regularly asked in lessons and exams to assess the relative importance of various factors, or to discuss the extent to which they agree with a point of view. More often than not, these discussions or questions begin with looking at a range of factors, which are then analysed and assessed. The Crossed Continua is a means of clearly displaying these factors so that students can start to make judgements about the relative importance of each one. Without the visual *bigger picture,* students can sometimes get lost in the detail without appreciating the wider context.

What about this particular example?

This particular exercise was used with A-level students and works well for the very reason described above. The common misconception with earthquakes is that a greater magnitude leads to more deaths, so I wanted students to consider the role played by a place's vulnerability. In the past I might have just provided a list of various earthquakes and asked students to compare their Human Development Index (HDI) scores. A simple ranking exercise forces students to compare each one, but ranking them on the Crossed Continua lets the students easily compare magnitude with HDI. The eye is quickly drawn to see whether the countries fit in the same place on each organiser, helping students build up an overall picture of their judgement. When I subsequently mark the students' written assessment of the relative importance of the two factors, I am able to refer back to their Crossed Continua. If a student's paragraph is not especially clear, then I can see the *working* from their diagrams. In the same way that examiners like to see an essay plan before an exam answer, I can use the Crossed Continua to comment on how the student developed their initial ideas into a piece of extended writing.

How did you teach it to your students?

I have found that the use of graphic organisers is a new experience for many students. Therefore the introduction, presentation and explanation of the Crossed Continua is important. Taking the time to illustrate the benefits of graphic organisers prior to their use helps make them seem more than *just another task*. My students love hearing about cognitive load theory and how graphic organisers can make their learning more effective. It also helps students appreciate the rationale for using methods like the Crossed Continua. One of my aims is for the students themselves to develop their skills and understanding to the point where they suggest using specific types of graphic organiser. We're not quite there yet!

I can use the Crossed Continua to comment on how the student developed their initial ideas into a piece of extended writing.

My students love hearing about cognitive load theory and how graphic organisers can make their learning more effective.

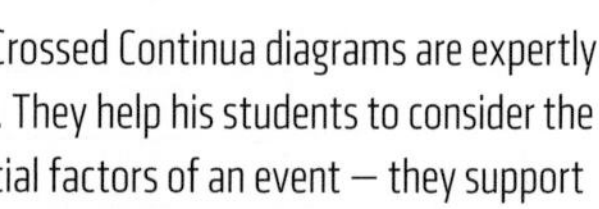

Luke's Crossed Continua diagrams are expertly crafted. They help his students to consider the influential factors of an event – they support analytical thinking. Students sometimes view facts disconnected from any real context. When Luke guides his students through the construction of a Crossed Continua, he is making the context explicit. His students begin to compare the significance of events, judging which factors are most responsible.

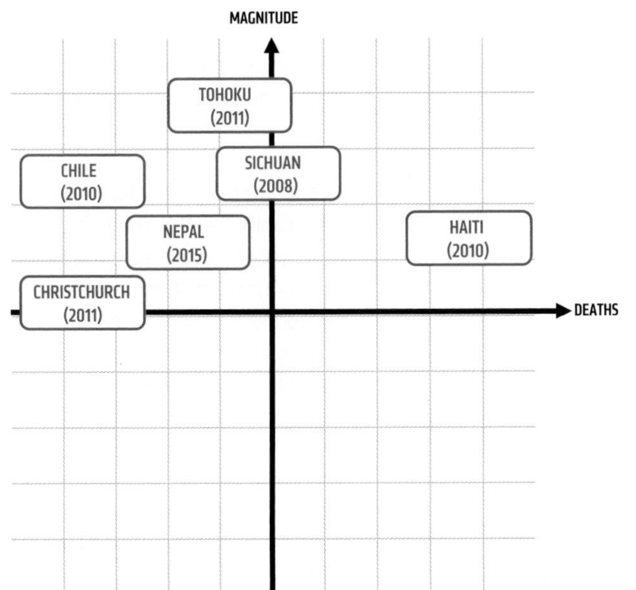
MAGNITUDE
TOHOKU
(2011)
SICHUAN
(2008)
CHILE
(2010)
NEPAL
(2015)
HAITI
(2010)
CHRISTCHURCH
(2011)
DEATHS

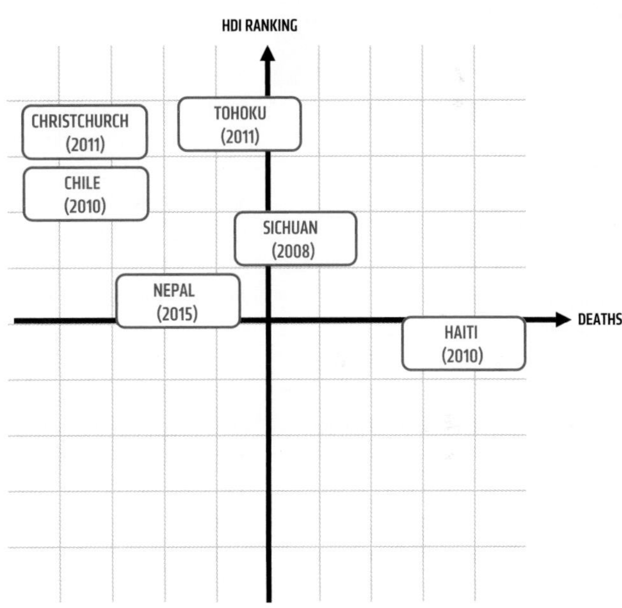
HDI RANKING
CHRISTCHURCH
(2011)
TOHOKU
(2011)
CHILE
(2010)
SICHUAN
(2008)
NEPAL
(2015)
DEATHS
HAITI
(2010)

MADELEINE EVANS

To reduce the feeling of being overwhelmed, a Concept Map quickly provides visual clarity. It can also spark curiosity and encourage independent study.

Current job: Parent, teacher
Subject: Various
Age phase: KS2-4

Why did you choose a Concept Map for your example?

Concept Maps are an effective tool to help students find a detailed answer to a specific question. They allow concepts to be logically represented, showing connections between them and guiding extended writing. They also provide teachers with a concrete way of assessing students' understanding, by gaining an insight into their internal schema and identifying knowledge gaps.

How did you teach it?

My son, who is in Year 9, was asked to summarise his knowledge of the role of enzymes in digestion. I thought this would be the perfect opportunity to introduce him to a Concept Map. First, I wrote 12 key concepts linked to the topic on the front of small cards. Then, I asked him to retrieve as much as he could about each concept on the cards. He used his exercise book for the concepts he struggled to retrieve.

A different coloured pen was used to identify which information was or wasn't from memory.

How did the student have to *think hard*?

I instructed my son to try to find relationships between two or more cards and explain the links he had identified. He soon discovered many links, which generated further questions and ideas. I then explained that it was possible to link them all together into a navigable map. I provided a template containing 12 empty boxes with connecting lines. I explained that he needed to decide where to put each card, with the general concepts shown at the top and the more detailed retrieval underneath. His hard thinking was made visible as he decided where each card should go while verbalising his thought process – creating linking phrases.

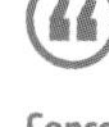

Concept Maps are an effective tool to help students find a detailed answer to a specific question.

My son had visually made sense of his schema and he found it easier to write a well-structured and detailed answer to the key question.

Once the cards were in place, I asked him to write a phrase along each line to represent the relationship between the concepts. To make the tasks more accessible, a bank of linking phrases could have been given.

How did you use the graphic organiser in conjunction with other strategies?

The rationale for adding flaps is two-fold. Firstly, by limiting the text it avoided mapshock, thus reducing cognitive overload. Secondly, the flaps could be used like flashcards supporting retrieval practice, with the added benefit of being able to see the interconnections of knowledge at the same time, rather than standalone chunks of information. My son had visually made sense of his schema and, when presented with the question again, he found it easier to write a well-structured and detailed answer to the key question.

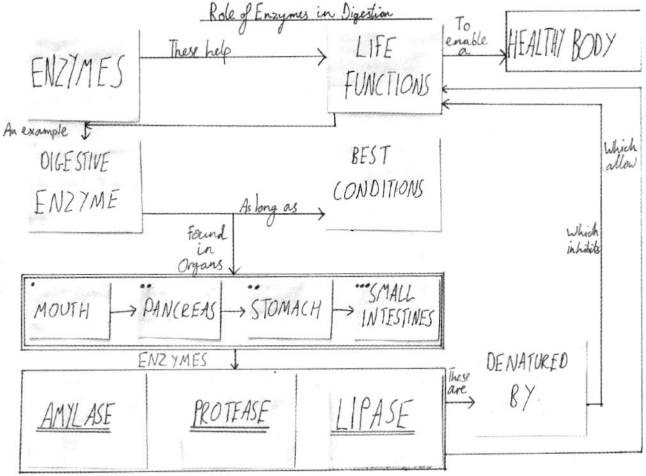

Role of Enzymes in Digestion

ENZYMES
These help
LIFE FUNCTIONS
To enable a
HEALTHY BODY
An example
DIGESTIVE ENZYME
As long as
BEST CONDITIONS
Found in Organs
MOUTH → PANCREAS → STOMACH → SMALL INTESTINES
ENZYMES
AMYLASE
PROTEASE
LIPASE
These are
DENATURED BY
Which allow
Which inhibits

Role of Enzymes i
These help
To enable a
HEALTHY BODY
A type of protein
Break down food molecules
Nutrients easily absorbed by body
Body temperature 37°
Healthy routines: Sleep, fresh air, food
As long as
Which allow
Which inhibits
BREAKS DOWN
Starch and carbohydrates (the substrates)
Produces
Sugars → Allows ENERGY
BREAKS DOWN
Proteins (substrate)
Produces Amino Acids
Allows
Our body to build + repair
BREAKS DOWN
Lipids (substrates)
Fatty acids + glycerol
Heat (cooking food)
Disease
Chemicals and pesticides
These change the shape of the enzyme. The substrate cannot fit the active site of the enzyme so don't work.
These are

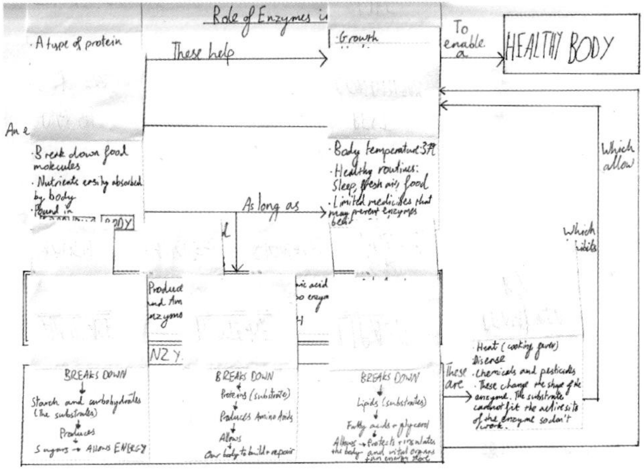

Madeleine has helped her son create a powerful tool for the retrieval of prior learning. The Concept Map offers dual benefits. The individual flaps act as flashcards, which are useful for self-testing. But the power of this resource lies in the explicit linking of concepts. When it comes to meaning-making, a traditional knowledge organiser could not compete with this resource. The process Madeleine describes is well thought through. At each stage, the pitfalls of using a Concept Map are considered and reduced. Using a template provides visual clarity and can lessen the time it takes to construct a Concept Map. Madeleine's son verbally justified his decision-making and went through an iterative process before deciding on his final map configuration. The finished Concept Map acted as an aide-memoire, enhancing his writing. Madeleine's son had little difficulty knowing what to write about and benefited from the structure the Concept Map affords.

MATT STONE

Graphic design can draw attention to the important elements in visual display, avoiding distraction or confusion.

Current job: Assistant headteacher
Subject: English
Age phase: Secondary and FE (11-18)
Organisation: Heolddu Comprehensive School

Why do you advocate the use of graphic organisers for learning and teaching?

Students benefit when information is presented succinctly. They benefit when they are able to offset the cognitive burden of complex material and focus the attention of their working memory on the task in hand. Graphic models used skilfully can help students combat the transient information effect. Graphic design can draw attention to the important elements, avoiding distraction or confusion.

What is the purpose of a Cycle diagram?

The purpose is to provide a simplified view of a complex process, in this case close reading. This may facilitate a more accessible introduction to new learning material, or provide a static model through which to communicate a student's progress through the process. The Cycle model represents a process that has no definitive start or end point. While a Flow Chart is the simplest way to show the flow of a process by a series of factors or events joined by arrows, a Cycle model establishes a one-way direction. Its effect is comparable to a walkthrough, in that it visually depicts the steps of a process and takes the guesswork out of knowing what to do.

How do you use this graphic organiser to support reading, writing and oracy?

This resource is really about supporting the teaching of analysis and evaluation in English. Reading and comprehending ideas in a complex text is challenging, but what many students find tougher still is articulating their understanding in writing. This is particularly the case when dealing with big texts, such as novels, where the mass of information can be overwhelming. Lemov et al (2016) assert that *"successfully analysing meaning requires a solid grasp of the argument; and establishing meaning requires the epiphanies of insight that come from subsequent analysis to justify it"*.

Students benefit when they are able to offset the cognitive burden of complex material and focus the attention of their working memory on the task in hand.

I use the graphic organiser to facilitate a three-point feedback conversation.

I prefer to introduce this resource as the focus of class discussion – students cannot write about what they don't know. Moving through the close reading sequence orally is powerful, using the language of the process (*assertion, observation, context, craft, criticism, judgement*) so that students speak like an essay before they put pen to paper. Then, when supporting students to work independently, I use the graphic organiser to facilitate a three-point feedback conversation where both the student and I refer to the resource as an objective third party, of which we both have a shared understanding.

LINK

Assert a claim that is linked explicitly to the question (using repetition of key words or synonyms).

OBSERVE

Identify where in the text your claim is best supported. Observe and describe significant features.

CONTEXTUALISE

Contextualise your observations through a consideration of narrative, social, historical and/ or literary heritage.

ANALYSE CRAFT

Analyse and evaluate how the writer crafts language and prose techniques to create meaning.

CRITICISE

Discuss alternate or wider critical interpretations of the text.

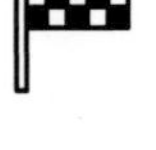

CONCLUDE

Present a critical judgement on your claim and explain how it was reached.

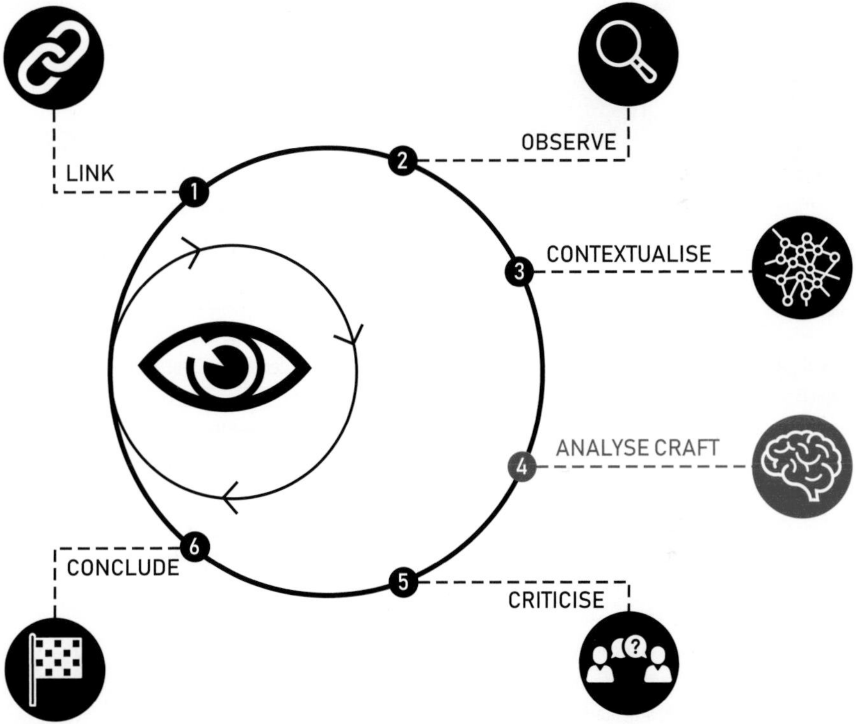

1 LINK

2 OBSERVE

3 CONTEXTUALISE

4 ANALYSE CRAFT

5 CRITICISE

6 CONCLUDE

Matt has broken down the stages of a learning sequence and done so with elegance – this is an accomplished design. What makes Matt's Cycle diagram sophisticated is how the elements are aligned, the concentrated white space and his restraint. By restraint, we mean Matt doesn't make the mistake of trying to be ostentatious with his use of colour or typeface. For his students, Matt has crafted a useful reading and writing tool. His diagram offsets the limitations of his students' working memory. With clearer minds, Matt's students can focus on articulating what they know.

MEGAN BOWS

Why do I use graphic organisers? They are a great tool for presenting prior knowledge to students in a safe way.

Current job: Lead practitioner
Subject: Science
Age phase: Secondary and FE (11-18)
Organisation: Gloucester Academy (Greenshaw Learning Trust)

How did you begin to use graphic organisers?

Over the past 18 months, I have read with interest the theory behind dual coding. I began to consider how graphic organisers could be implemented to help build schema. Graphic organisers are an ideal way of presenting both prior knowledge and the big picture overview. This helps students move from inflexible to more flexible knowledge and develop a secure schema over the long term.

How did you use this graphic organiser to present prior knowledge?

Ausubel (1960) states that the most important single factor influencing learning is what the learner already knows, and suggests it is important to revisit prior knowledge before beginning a new topic. I have used graphic organisers as a way of presenting prior knowledge to students in a format that optimises intrinsic load. This particular organiser presented prerequisite knowledge that students had to understand as a starting point for the topic ahead. We dedicated a lesson to recapping this knowledge and each branch was covered in a specific order to build on existing prior knowledge.

Graphic organisers are an ideal way of presenting both prior knowledge and the big picture overview.

How did you use the graphic organiser to retrieve and link to the bigger picture?

An additional benefit of graphic organisers is that you can use them as a framework for retrieval and refer back to them to make explicit links between prior and current learning. Some examples of how I did this are:

- Giving students a partially filled version where they have to fill in specific details for a purely recall-based activity.
- Scripting a range of retrieval questions based on the graphic organiser, with the intention of extending knowledge recall across a range of contexts or examples.
- Using the organiser periodically within the topic, annotating to make links between new knowledge and previously learnt knowledge.

I have used graphic organisers as a way of presenting prior knowledge to students in a format that optimises intrinsic load.

The above strategies enable students to make meaningful links between different components of their learning. When students are given more regular opportunities to make links between topics, it enables them to build secure schema over the long term.

Megan creates her Mind Maps by hand-drawing them. To help capture her deep thinking and the complexity of the information she presents, David worked in partnership with Megan to create a digital version of her work. Working from the centre outwards, the items on Megan's Mind Map become more specific. All the items in Megan's Mind Map live in a hierarchy, made explicit by her labelling of first- and second-level branches.

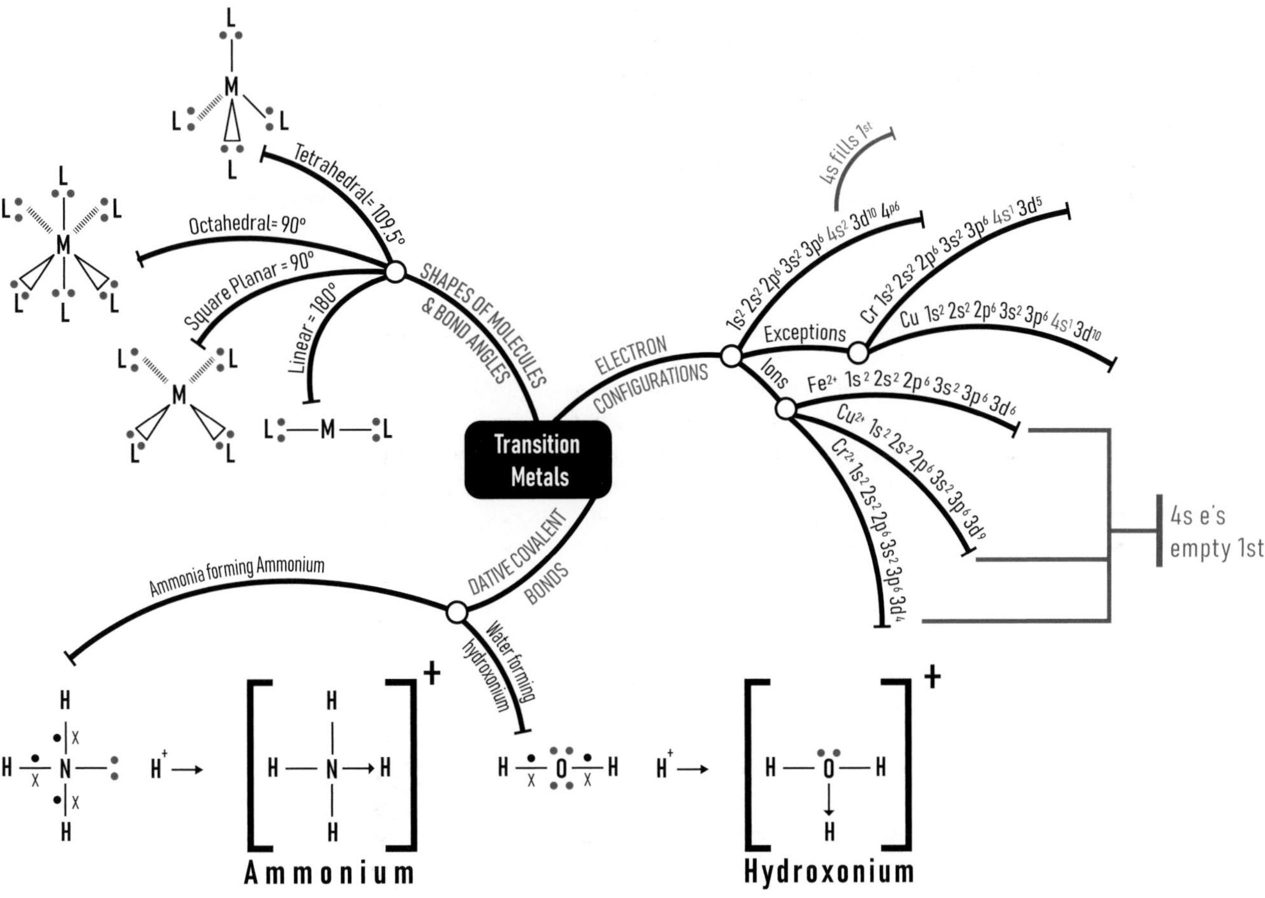
Transition Metals
SHAPES OF MOLECULES & BOND ANGLES
Tetrahedral= 109.5°
Octahedral= 90°
Square Planar = 90°
Linear = 180°
ELECTRON CONFIGURATIONS
1s2 2s2 2p6 3s2 3p6 4s2 3d10 4p6
4s fills 1st
Exceptions
Cr 1s2 2s2 2p6 3s2 3p6 4s1 3d5
Cu 1s2 2s2 2p6 3s2 3p6 4s1 3d10
Ions
Fe2+ 1s2 2s2 2p6 3s2 3p6 3d6
Cu2+ 1s2 2s2 2p6 3s2 3p6 3d9
Cr2+ 1s2 2s2 2p6 3s2 3p6 3d4
4s e's empty 1st
DATIVE COVALENT BONDS
Ammonia forming Ammonium
Water forming hydroxonium
Ammonium
Hydroxonium

NICKY BLACKFORD

Comparing concepts to make distinctions between knowledge more visible, a Venn Diagram provides a powerful visuospatial representation.

Current job: Assistant headteacher
Subject: English and dance
Age phase: Secondary (11-16)
Organisation: Telford Priory School

Why and how did you choose this GO?

Dance genres these days are very seldom in one *pure* style. Whether teaching GCSE, BTEC or A-level dance, ballet is usually featured as the historical foundation from which a multitude of other styles/techniques are derived. Contemporary dance has almost always been used in direct opposition for comparison, due to its liberal nature (where classical ballet is heavily prescriptive in terms of technique). While this postmodern dance style sought to distance itself from its evolutionary roots, many similar technical features/movement concepts remain integral to any form of dance, under the stylistic qualities of dance as a form of art, self-expression and storytelling. A graphic organiser, in this sense a Venn Diagram, compares two ideas with a central space for the mutual/similar features. Students are able to easily separate the differences from the similarities, while appreciating the core elements that fundamentally link them together.

Students are able to easily separate the differences from the similarities, while appreciating the core elements that fundamentally link them together.

Was your selection of organiser based on the language of the content or the title of the content?

To look at the historical context of ballet and contemporary dance would require an enormous amount of research into provenance and evolution – much more than is required pre-higher education. The content for this graphic organiser serves as an introduction, comparing some of the more immediately obvious differences between two styles. The similarities typically will lead back to familiar concepts within the umbrella term *dance*. They will allow students to understand that the majority of styles were born out of something that came before, but they still share the *core beliefs*: dance as shape, movement, self-expression and storytelling, whether the purpose is entertainment or enjoyment or something else entirely.

This graphic organiser allowed the common traits to be distinguished and chunked for a clear explanation in the early phases of learning.

How did you initially introduce this organiser to your students?

Showing students a performance of the dance style(s) they are being introduced to serves as the model. This graphic organiser allowed the common traits to be distinguished and chunked for a clear explanation in the early phases of learning.

How did you ensure that your students thought hard about it?

Some of the historical context of the style(s) was introduced as a threshold concept to incite curiosity and allow students to construct preliminary questions. Upon viewing the *model* (performance) they looked for the identifiable features outlined in the GO: technique/staging, etc. This generated information then led to discussion, connecting the *observable* back to the historical context: societal norms, key figures and pioneers.

Was there a sequence to the introduction of your GO?

In terms of curriculum, depending on the learning outcome (technique, terminology, evolution and influence, etc), the knowledge built on previous learning to allow links to be made from the factual information to the more complex causational information. In terms of learning, the gradual release model (Fisher & Frey, 2008) structured the planning through direct instruction to guided and deliberate practice (using different dance styles). The introduction of this GO was modelled and then repeated, using faded examples for retrieval/spaced practice. Interleaving developed and reinforced this practice to allow students to increasingly make more independent complex connections.

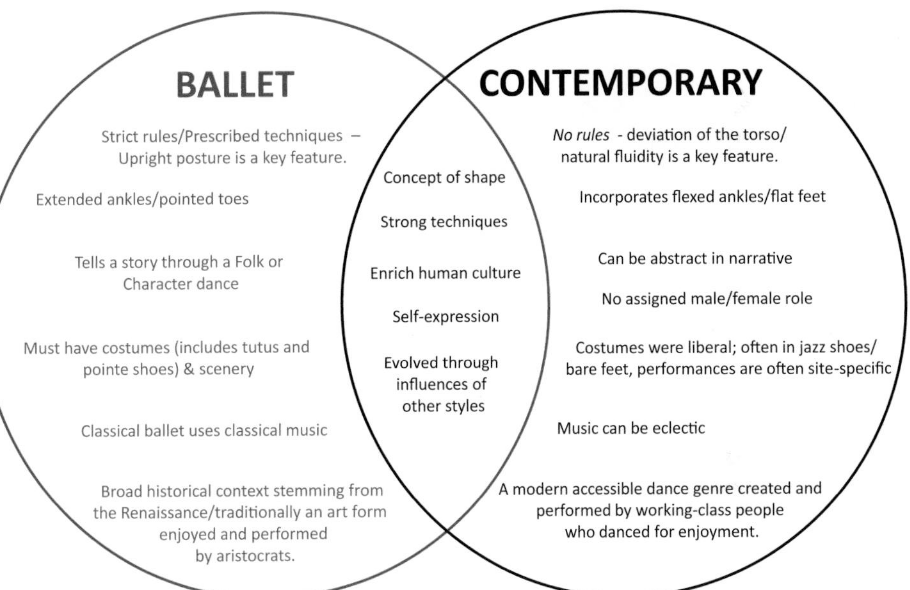
BALLET
Strict rules/Prescribed techniques – Upright posture is a key feature.
Extended ankles/pointed toes
Tells a story through a Folk or Character dance
Must have costumes (includes tutus and pointe shoes) & scenery
Classical ballet uses classical music
Broad historical context stemming from the Renaissance/traditionally an art form enjoyed and performed by aristocrats.
Concept of shape
Strong techniques
Enrich human culture
Self-expression
Evolved through influences of other styles
CONTEMPORARY
No rules - deviation of the torso/ natural fluidity is a key feature.
Incorporates flexed ankles/flat feet
Can be abstract in narrative
No assigned male/female role
Costumes were liberal; often in jazz shoes/ bare feet, performances are often site-specific
Music can be eclectic
A modern accessible dance genre created and performed by working-class people who danced for enjoyment.

Nicky's Venn Diagram is beautifully simple. The similarities and differences between the two types of dance are visually apparent. For students, trying to identify such a large number of similarities and differences would have been challenging with text alone. Nicky introduced the diagram by modelling it, step by step. By doing this, she reduced the likelihood that her students would feel overwhelmed. Careful consideration of what Nicky wanted her students to achieve – understanding how dance types evolve from previous forms – has allowed her to get the most from her graphic organiser.

PETER RICHARDSON

With the depth of thought required to fully make sense of ideas and concepts, the use of spatial organisation is integral for children and teachers alike.

Current job: Deputy head and Year 3 teacher
Subject: Teacher CPD
Age phase: Primary
Organisation: Walton-le-Dale Primary School

Where do graphic organisers fit in your school's pedagogical approach?

We have developed a cognitive science-led, knowledge-led approach to our curriculum. With an increased focus on knowledge – and specifically on understanding that knowledge – adopting Fiorella and Mayer's generative SOI (select-organise-integrate) model has been a natural fit. Alongside this, I've been really excited to integrate Barbara Tversky's idea that "*the mind regards ideas as objects*" into our approach, with the aim of developing children's visible schema.

To support children's working memory, we have previously developed staff knowledge of dual coding, but what I've recently come to realise is that with working memory so restricted, having children chunk and develop ideas using their external memory field really enables them to think so much harder about the content and, crucially, their understanding of it. Graphic organisers are the vehicle that helps achieve synergy between all these concepts.

How are you developing staff use of graphic organisers?

The first step was to come up with a solution to Frederick Reif's argument that "*students don't know how to organise their knowledge effectively*" (2008). To get our primary-aged children to effectively create their own graphic organisers, I wanted them to be systematically introduced at the most appropriate age, so they were useful and understood. This also stops Relations Diagrams, for example, being unnecessarily taught from scratch three years in a row. Subsequently, I was able to create a series of CPD videos, one about each of the main graphic organisers: generative learning; a refresher on dual coding; spatial organisation and the place of graphic organisers in the classroom. After initially introducing staff to these resources over a series of weeks, we switched back to using Dylan Wiliam's "*teacher learning community*" as our bottom-up model for CPD, hopefully empowering staff to go back and deepen their understanding over time.

Graphic organisers are the vehicle that helps achieve synergy between all these concepts.

The goal was for staff to understand my hidden schema and mental representation of the big picture, which I have found incredibly difficult to articulate in linear speech or text.

Why did you choose the graphic organiser in your example?

I could have chosen a Flow Spray, but that would have simply grouped and sequenced the content we would cover. The goal was for staff to understand my hidden schema and mental representation of the big picture, which I have found incredibly difficult to articulate in linear speech or text. In particular, I wanted to highlight the importance of generative learning and how spatial organisation takes us beyond dual coding. Lakoff and Johnson state that "*most of our fundamental concepts are organised in terms of one or more spatialisation metaphors*" (1980). I felt a deceptively simple Tree Diagram would be the most effective spatial metaphor to represent how I saw these concepts relate.

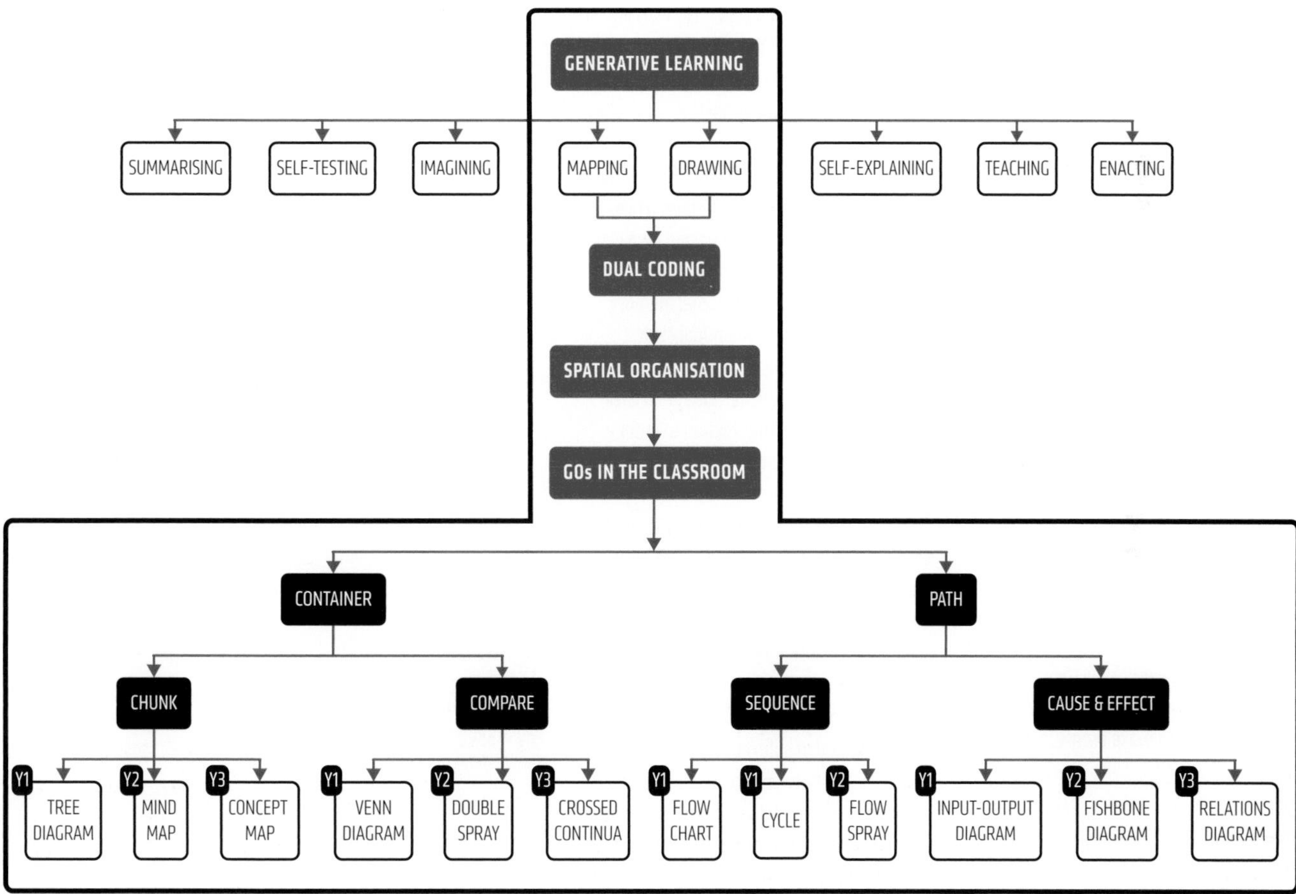
GENERATIVE LEARNING
SUMMARISING
SELF-TESTING
IMAGINING
MAPPING
DRAWING
SELF-EXPLAINING
TEACHING
ENACTING
DUAL CODING
SPATIAL ORGANISATION
GOs IN THE CLASSROOM
CONTAINER
PATH
CHUNK
COMPARE
SEQUENCE
CAUSE & EFFECT
Y1 TREE DIAGRAM
Y2 MIND MAP
Y3 CONCEPT MAP
Y1 VENN DIAGRAM
Y2 DOUBLE SPRAY
Y3 CROSSED CONTINUA
Y1 FLOW CHART
Y1 CYCLE
Y2 FLOW SPRAY
Y1 INPUT-OUTPUT DIAGRAM
Y2 FISHBONE DIAGRAM
Y3 RELATIONS DIAGRAM

You can't underestimate the power of a novice making their growing schema visual. Spatial organisation has enormous potential to impact on learning in the arms of a well-trained student.

Why did you choose the graphic organiser in your example?

I chose a Flow Spray graphic organiser based on the vocabulary in the title of the content: Column Addition Written Method. The trigger word is *method*, a process, which tells me the appropriate model is Path. There are elements of cause and effect, but owing to the age of the children and the complexity of the content, I prioritised sequencing. A Flow Spray is initially simple, while incredibly flexible, with the ability to touch on cause and effect and the Container model.

What support did you give your students through the process?

This was the second Flow Spray they would create, so I asked them to visualise their first, which covered how to make bronze. I then used a worked example. While I was conscious of the SOI model, there was potential for cognitive overload due to the relative complexity of the content. I determined that the selecting and organising of the nodes held more learning potential than that of the core, so went through possible core collection names and their order with the whole class.

Pairs of children were given blank Post-it notes to select and subsequently organise. Their conversations were fascinating and involved really deep thinking and significant cognitive load. Without using their external memory field, this load would have undoubtedly inhibited their learning. As this phase developed, I shared specific nodes and their organisation, compelling children to enter a cognitive loop by evaluating their own spatial arrangements.

Without using their external memory field, this load would have undoubtedly inhibited children's learning.

How did the creation of the children's graphic organisers support their future learning?

One reason I wanted the children to create graphic organisers for this content was to relate it to our subsequent learning on the written method of subtraction, integrating the similarities between the two processes into their schemas. Children firstly engaged in retrieval practice, recreating their Flow Sprays. They were then each given a copy of the Flow Spray example and asked to take turns tracing the nodes as they explained the process to their partners. Using tracing was transformational: in addition to being fully engaged with this process, several children uncovered a vital node that needed to be made more explicit – adding any exchange. When modelling written subtraction, children saw multiple common nodes and organisational similarities. This resulted in much faster grasping of written subtraction than in previous years, where similarities were explained with lineal speech.

When modelling written subtraction, children saw multiple common nodes and organisational similarities.

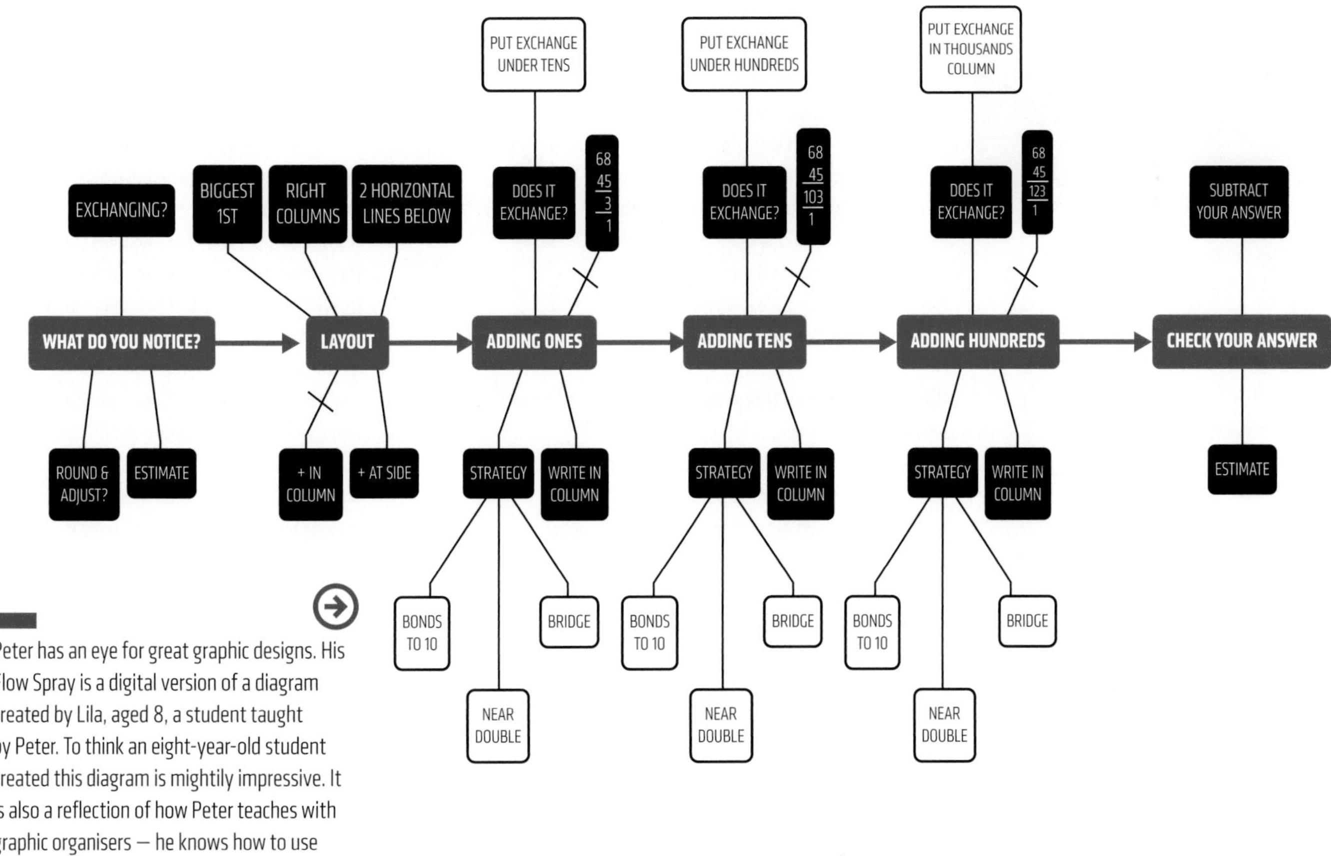

Peter has an eye for great graphic designs. His Flow Spray is a digital version of a diagram created by Lila, aged 8, a student taught by Peter. To think an eight-year-old student created this diagram is mightily impressive. It is also a reflection of how Peter teaches with graphic organisers — he knows how to use them and pair them with other strategies.

PETER STOYKO

More ideas can be juggled analytically by mapping them. This is crucial for the study of complex systems, given all the moving parts.

Current job: Researcher and information designer
Subject: Services and governance
Age phase: Further education
Organisation: Elanica

Why did you choose the graphic organiser in your example?

I have been cataloguing diagramming methods and visual shorthands for mapping systems. The compendium, part of a larger project called SystemViz, includes everything from medieval cosmograms to the schematic dashboards of nuclear power plants. Systems thinking has become a highly valued skill. Yet complex systems (such as ecosystems and societies) are difficult to study holistically without a visual organising device. There are too many moving parts, too many dynamics between parts, to juggle otherwise. That said, maps get cluttered very quickly as items are added. Moreover, every mapping approach contains an implicit (and under-theorised) model of what a system is and how it works. That influences what gets noticed and prioritised. The perfect general-purpose method remains elusive. Nonetheless, a few serve a narrow analytical purpose reasonably well.

What purpose does this graphic organiser serve?

This is a radial flow map. It focuses attention on a central activity (or topic), showing its knock-on effects on other activities, some of which *knock back* as system dynamics. Lines radiate outwards or gravitate inwards to show those relations. Some system effects can be hard to attribute to a specific activity because they happen far away in time or space. Concentric circles organise near and far impacts. In the example shown, a pulp and paper mill causes all sorts of benefits and harms. The full implications are difficult to grasp without situating the factory within a web of systemic relations operating at different scales. By focusing on one activity at a time, the graphic organiser shows a meaningful slice of how a system works while not becoming overwhelming.

This radial flow map focuses attention on a central activity (or topic), showing its knock-on effects on other activities, some of which *knock back* as system dynamics.

The trick is to use a tidy organising structure that avoids messy, spaghetti-like tangles of lines, even if the systems are complex tangles in reality.

Why are graphic organisers important for systems thinking?

My first instinct is to draw systems using lots of illustrations to engage the viewer's imagination. System diagramming methods and visual shorthands were created so that people lacking drawing skills could map systems too. Basic symbols replace illustrations. In some professional specialisations, large banks of cryptic symbols are used, posing a different barrier to sense-making for some. Graphic organisers using mostly text labels fulfil two needs. First, they make the analysis of systems approachable to a wider audience. Insofar as jargon is used, it is in the service of vocabulary-building and analytical precision. Second, most attempts to map a system take the form of a graphic organiser at some point. The trick is to use a tidy organising structure that avoids messy, spaghetti-like tangles of lines, even if the systems are complex tangles in reality.

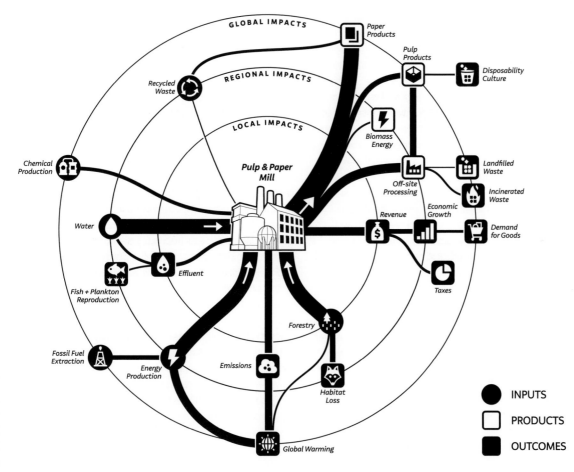

GLOBAL IMPACTS
REGIONAL IMPACTS
LOCAL IMPACTS

Pulp & Paper Mill

Paper Products
Pulp Products
Disposability Culture
Recycled Waste
Biomass Energy
Chemical Production
Off-site Processing
Landfilled Waste
Incinerated Waste
Economic Growth
Revenue
Water
Demand for Goods
Effluent
Fish + Plankton Reproduction
Taxes
Forestry
Fossil Fuel Extraction
Energy Production
Emissions
Habitat Loss
Global Warming

INPUTS
PRODUCTS
OUTCOMES

In a flow map, line thickness signifies the magnitude of effects. Colour coding and line styles can differentiate types of effects. Subtle white gaps show where lines feed into objects and distinguish overlapping lines with a mock shadow. Shapes enclosing icons can indicate the type of object. Geographic scale is signified by concentric circles that also work for timescales. Compact, custom icons give the eye a visual target and a glanceable placeholder of meaning. Text labels alone work in a pinch (and are better than generic, off-the-shelf icons of dubious fit).

RACHEL WONG

Graphic organisers allow retrieval of knowledge and the forming of synoptic links to look at the bigger picture.

Current job: Biology teacher
Subject: Science (biology specialism)
Age phase: Secondary and FE (11-18)
Organisation: Beechen Cliff School

Why did you choose this graphic organiser?

The graphic organiser I have chosen is a Mind Map that summarises the essential information of this topic on one page. It shows the differences between various transport mechanisms used by cells in moving substances in and out of them. Pupils often get confused in this content-heavy topic; therefore, I have used this Mind Map to help them distinguish between the mechanisms and introduce keywords.

How did you use it to teach your students?

I always draw this Mind Map live under the visualiser as part of my explicit explanation of the content. I find this is better than giving it to students as a photocopy of notes, as otherwise they do not go through the thinking process necessary in building this Mind Map. I introduce each section one at a time and ask questions to elicit students' existing understanding, adding the information they have into the Mind Map as we go along.

This is a Mind Map used with sixth-form students. In the past I have often taught it as a revision summary in the last lesson of the topic. It allows students to organise their understanding as a conclusion to the topic, which presents a chance to test their understanding and iron out any misconceptions. However, I've begun to explore using a basic version of the Mind Map as an advance organiser in the first lesson. The benefit is that it helps students connect prior knowledge in GCSE to the new, to-be-learnt material. And it provides an opportunity for spaced retrieval when we go through the topic in more detail later on. During the introduction or starter of those more detailed lessons, I typically direct students back to the relevant branches on their Mind Map, helping them recall and connect the information they have received in the first lesson. The more they refer back to the Mind Map, the more successful they will be at retrieving knowledge.

Tell us more about your use of graphic organisers?

As I gained experience in teaching biology, I realised how difficult it is for pupils to process and understand such a large volume of content, let alone form links. I have used some graphic organisers unknowingly in my lessons before, to help overcome such problems – for example, using a two- or three-way Venn Diagram to allow pupils to compare different processes, such as photosynthesis, aerobic and anaerobic respiration. I have also drawn various topic overviews using Flow Charts and Cycle diagrams, but I did not fully understand the benefits – I simply thought the topics made more sense that way. I explained to the students (with my limited knowledge of the matter) that drawing these diagrams would help them form synoptic links between topics, gaining a better understanding of how the science behind them works while doing retrieval practice on their understanding of the topic.

It wasn't until I attended a researchEd Home talk by Oliver on dual coding and graphic organisers that I understood the difference between and the importance of the two strategies in teaching. I have not explicitly taught my students the different types of graphic organisers and how and when they should be used, but that is something I can potentially do from now on, to help them facilitate their own learning.

Rachel has created a Mind Map using the deductive method: working from the centre to the outside edge, the content gets more specific. Rachel constructs her Mind Maps, drawing them by hand and under a visualiser. By doing so, she can narrate the whole process, checking for understanding and lessening the chances of cognitive overload. For Rachel's students to understand the concept of transport mechanisms, they must figure out its attributes. Thus, her use of a Mind Map to classify said attributes is textbook.

- **TRANSPORT MECHANISMS**
  - passive / no energy
    - **DIFFUSION**
      - factors increasing rate
        - thinner membrane
        - higher SA:V
        - higher temperature
        - steeper concentration gradient
      - no barrier required — **SIMPLE DIFFUSION**
      - required channel/ carrier proteins — **FACILITATED DIFFUSION**
    - **OSMOSIS**
      - animals
        - **HYPOTONIC** — burst (lysis)
        - **HYPERTONIC** — shrivelled crenation
      - plants
        - **HYPOTONIC** — turgid
        - **ISOTONIC** — flaccid
        - **HYPERTONIC** — plasmolysed
  - active / requires energy
    - **ACTIVE TRANSPORT**
    - **BULK TRANSPORT**
      - into cell — **ENDOCYTOSIS**
        - solid — **PHAGOCYTOSIS**
        - liquid — **PINOCYTOSIS**
      - out of cell — **EXOCYTOSIS**

- **Bulk Transport** is for large molecules and whole cells
- **Active Transport** is for smaller molecules

SAM STEELE

Graphic organisers focus my teaching and help my students understand large and complex bodies of information.

Current job: Curriculum leader for maths
Subject: History
Age phase: Primary
Organisation: The British School of Brussels, Belgium

Why did you choose the graphic organiser in your example?

The Concept Map shows the main activities of major groups in ancient Egyptian society and begins to show how they interact, through taxes and in sacrifice to the gods. The map links elements with verbs to form simple subject-verb-object sentences. It also reveals the content's hierarchy – critical for organising knowledge.

How did you use the graphic organiser?

There are many boxes in this map, so I used PowerPoint to reveal branches slowly, narrating as I did so. The oral text from me is most important, but the map ensures the information doesn't become transient. A more general point to be made here is that graphic organisers can also help teachers to craft the curriculum. They provide not only a means of effectively and efficiently conveying ideas in the classroom, but a lens through which teachers are encouraged to distinguish between core knowledge and hinterland.

How did you use the graphic organiser in conjunction with other strategies?

Before introducing the Concept Map, students read a text laden with images of farmers and craftsmen, and we watched short videos on the everyday lives of these groups of people. This preparatory work established the hinterland for the limited and specific core knowledge in this map that I wanted children to know. Later in the unit of work, I wanted students to look more closely at the role of the Pharaoh and to study particular Pharaohs in depth. This graphic organiser provided background context in terms of the Pharaoh's relationship with the rest of Egyptian society.

Graphic organisers are a lens through which teachers are encouraged to distinguish between core knowledge and hinterland.

The map links elements with verbs to form simple subject-verb-object sentences. It also reveals the content's hierarchy – critical for organising knowledge.

Concept Maps represent hierarchical knowledge structures. Traditionally, they are arranged with the more general ideas displayed at the top and the more specific subsumed under these broad concepts. Sam has arranged his Concept Map from left to right. By doing so, he retains the hierarchical structure while making it more natural for the reader – Western cultures read from left to right. The map's hierarchy is signalled to the reader by Sam's use of colour, both for the text boxes and connecting lines. Note how Sam reduces the likelihood of his students experiencing *mapshock*. He carefully reveals each element one by one and coordinates this with a scripted explanation. Each proposition – subject-verb-object sentence – unearths the concepts that lie behind the subject knowledge. When explicitly sharing said propositions, Sam is manifesting his schema. And he is making it public, visual and accessible to his students.

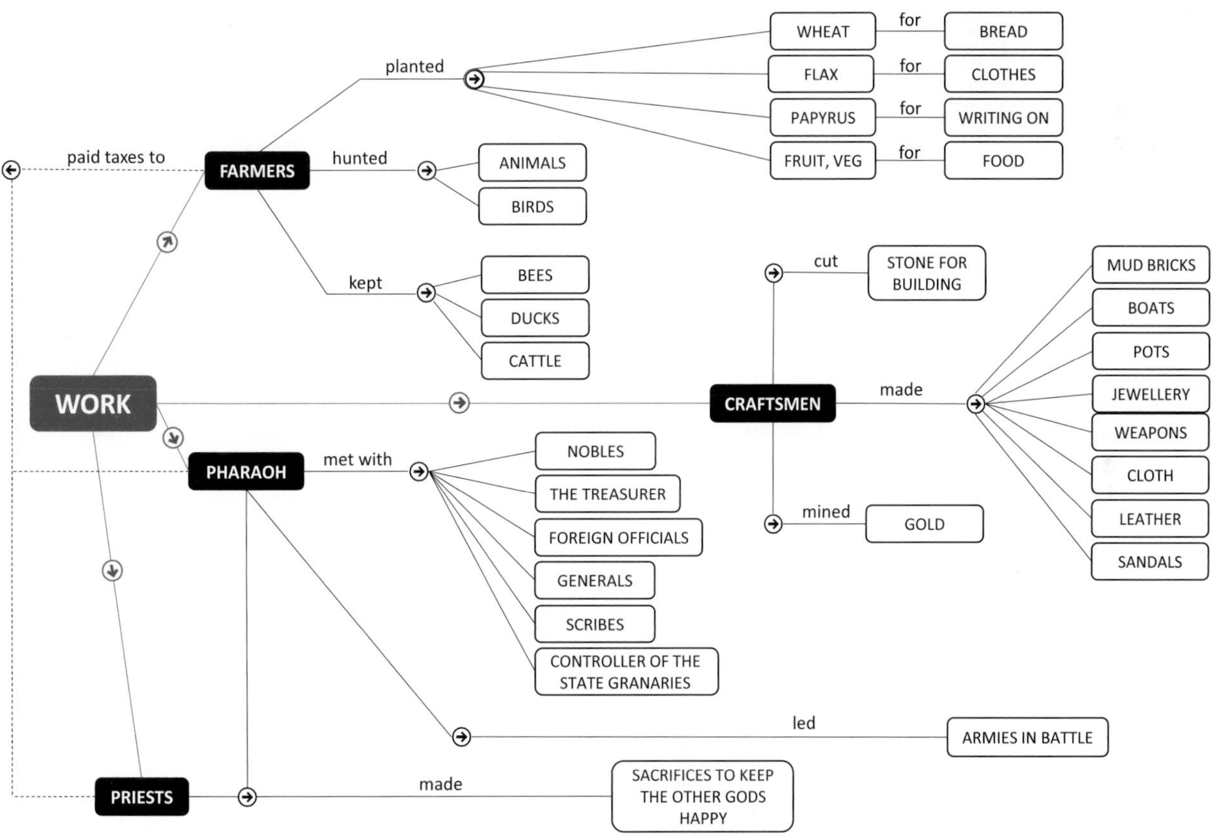
WORK
FARMERS
paid taxes to
planted
WHEAT
for
BREAD
FLAX
for
CLOTHES
PAPYRUS
for
WRITING ON
FRUIT, VEG
for
FOOD
hunted
ANIMALS
BIRDS
kept
BEES
DUCKS
CATTLE
CRAFTSMEN
cut
STONE FOR BUILDING
made
MUD BRICKS
BOATS
POTS
JEWELLERY
WEAPONS
CLOTH
LEATHER
SANDALS
mined
GOLD
PHARAOH
met with
NOBLES
THE TREASURER
FOREIGN OFFICIALS
GENERALS
SCRIBES
CONTROLLER OF THE STATE GRANARIES
led
ARMIES IN BATTLE
PRIESTS
made
SACRIFICES TO KEEP THE OTHER GODS HAPPY

SARAH JONES

Becoming an economist involves learning to think like an economist. My macro-map helps me to convey my thinking to A-level students so we can think, talk and write about economies together.

Current job: Subject leader and SLE
Subject: Business, economics and finance
Age phase: Secondary and FE (14-18)
Organisation: Redborne Upper School and Community College

Why did you choose the graphic organiser in your example?

I chose this organiser as it represents my own schema. I think about, analyse and evaluate macroeconomic causes, effects and policies by using my own mental map of an economy. I am keen for students to arrange their thinking in the same way. I work to develop a shared understanding of my mental map and ways of thinking with students, so they can learn from me how to engage in macroeconomic analysis and evaluation for themselves. I have selected an Input-Output Diagram because my priority is to direct students to channel their explanations via the aggregate demand | short-run aggregate supply | long-run aggregate supply model. I have placed those names in the centre of the organiser. I show the factors affecting them as feeding into them and the results of shifts in the curves flowing out. This provides a basic skeleton outline of how an economy works and displays the framework in which I arrange almost all my macroeconomic thinking.

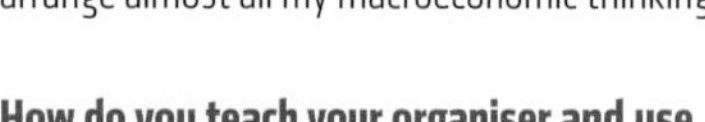

How do you teach your organiser and use it to aid learning?

I do not present this organiser at all to begin with. I teach this organiser in a jigsaw fashion. I initially display only the main component factors affecting aggregate demand (consumption, investment, etc). I then explore consumption (consumer spending by households) in more depth, tracing back through the factors that affect it. I gradually continue to teach and connect further factors and parts of the economy, piece by piece, until students are ready to cope with seeing and using the full organiser. Much of my remaining teaching on macroeconomics then embellishes this picture with details about how particular chains of analysis occur, and additional specific information about certain types of inflation, unemployment, growth, etc.

This organiser provides a basic skeleton outline of how an economy works and displays the framework in which I arrange my thinking.

I connect factors and parts of the economy, piece by piece, until students are ready to cope with seeing and using the full organiser.

I think about a national economic system in a very similar way to how I think about the London tube map. I use this analogy to help students develop chains of analysis (routes) using this map. As their understanding develops, they are able to analyse increasingly complicated chains and use the map in a flexible manner (eventually from memory) in order to identify causes and explain effects of changes in variables and policy initiatives. I frequently annotate projections of the map on a whiteboard to show the routes of my thinking and how this orderly thinking can then be converted into logical written analytical and evaluative paragraphs.

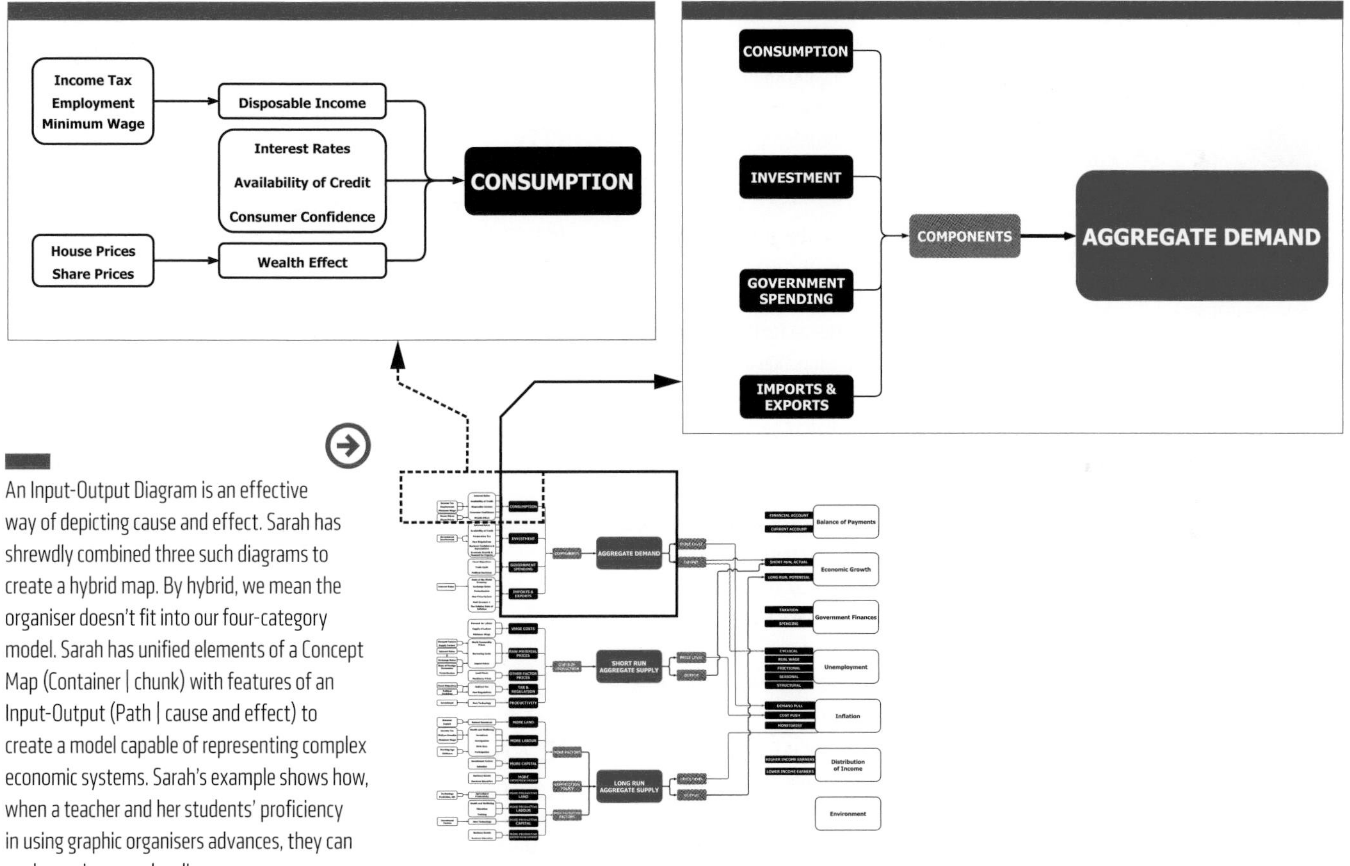

An Input-Output Diagram is an effective way of depicting cause and effect. Sarah has shrewdly combined three such diagrams to create a hybrid map. By hybrid, we mean the organiser doesn't fit into our four-category model. Sarah has unified elements of a Concept Map (Container | chunk) with features of an Input-Output (Path | cause and effect) to create a model capable of representing complex economic systems. Sarah's example shows how, when a teacher and her students' proficiency in using graphic organisers advances, they can explore using complex diagrams.

SARAH LALLY

Graphic organisers can reduce the cognitive load needed to link together seemingly disparate pieces of information.

Current job: Head of Year 12
Subject: Science
Age phase: Secondary and FE (11-18)
Organisation: Deyes High School

Why did you choose this graphic organiser?

I find that students' most significant stumbling block is the overwhelming amount of recall knowledge. I have therefore spent time considering how best to present key concepts to aid memory. The given reactions are key to students' ability to relate the various fundamental concepts and gain a better idea of the bigger picture. This Relations Diagram uses fundamental concepts in the names of the functional groups and links them to the reactions they observe. This minimises the cognitive load by summarising it in one simple image. Presenting the information in this way to the students, many years ago, and modelling how I pictured the information, I saw the impact on recall and understanding.

How did you use the graphic organiser?

I always introduce this graphic organiser early in students' first A-level year, once they have mastered the schema for the structures and properties of the functional groups. This allows me to limit the diagram to contain the fewest possible words. Before seeing the Relations Diagram, students will undertake the test tube reactions, so they can observe how the positive reactions in the diagram appear. I then make a point of questioning the students to see how well they can make connections between the reactions, and they always struggle.

I draw the organiser piece by piece under a visualiser. I explain each step, relating it to the reactions the students have seen. Frequent questioning allows me to make sure they understand and can follow the diagram. The difference is always marked, with students able to understand how the functional groups relate. They are then more than capable of using the diagram to help them design experiments and understand the importance of negative results. They also discover the benefits of using graphic organisers to organise and present information.

I draw the organiser piece by piece under a visualiser. I explain each step, relating it to the reactions the students have seen.

What strategies do you use with the graphic organiser?

I have found that using graphic organisers makes my explanations clear and concise. I find students are more engaged, and because the information isn't presented all at once, students are less overwhelmed. By breaking content down and capitalising on dual coding theory, I can then give them a copy of the completed, more complex graphic organiser and many practice questions to apply their new understanding. The students can become reliant on the graphic organisers, so I initially test them with factual recall-based quizzes shortly after the lesson.

Using graphic organisers makes my explanations clear and concise.

Some students like to memorise their graphic organisers as an aid in an exam. This diagram also allows students to picture and predict synthetic pathways, a considerable and significant skill in chemistry.

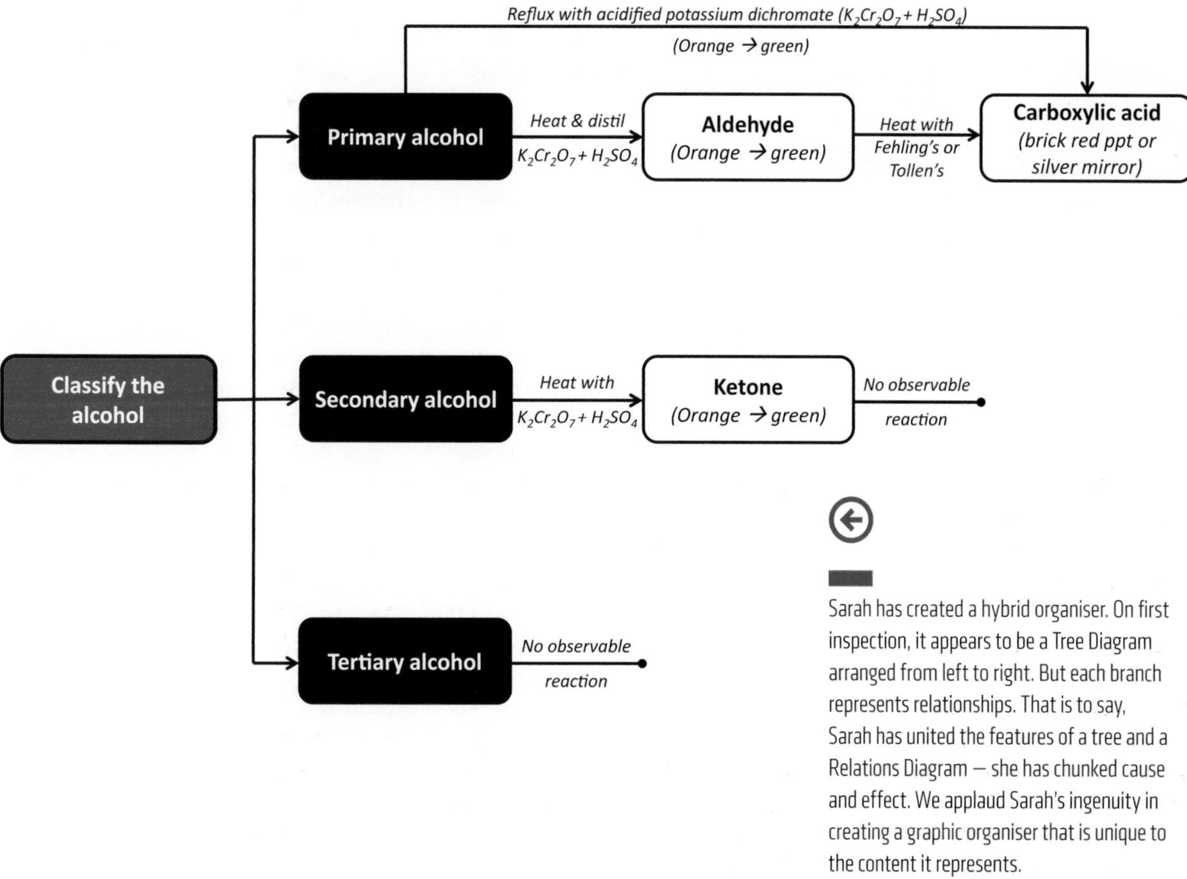

Sarah has created a hybrid organiser. On first inspection, it appears to be a Tree Diagram arranged from left to right. But each branch represents relationships. That is to say, Sarah has united the features of a tree and a Relations Diagram – she has chunked cause and effect. We applaud Sarah's ingenuity in creating a graphic organiser that is unique to the content it represents.

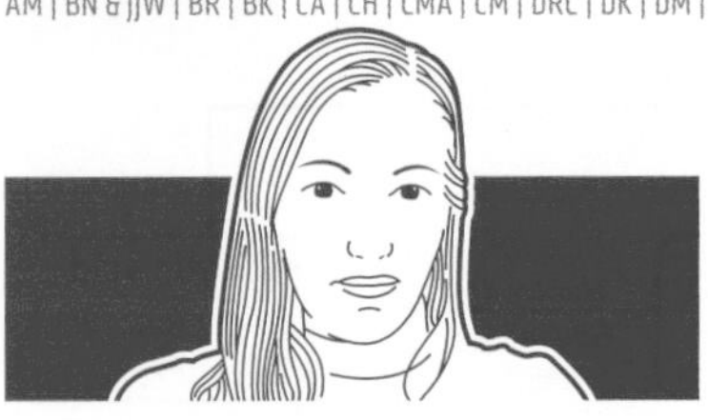

SARAH SANDEY

Graphic organisers are an integral tool in enabling pupils to select, organise and integrate their learning. They provide students with an "access point" in retrieving key information with logic and coherence.

Current job: Headteacher and Year 6 teacher
Subject: History
Age phase: Primary (7-11)
Organisation: Mayflower Community Academy

Why and how did you choose your graphic organiser?

Although we use a variety of graphic organisers for different reasons within the curriculum (and beyond), one of the key areas in which we use them on a daily basis is historical study. History is one of our key driving subjects and we use the Mind Map graphic organiser as a tool to chunk different items contained within the overall topic. The historical topic content supports the need for a hierarchical model, emphasising the weighting on the central theme and radiating outwards for expansion.

How did you create your graphic organiser and how did you use it with your students?

The initial creation of the graphic organiser really depends on the intended outcome. For example, when creating a graphic organiser for historical study, we have found it most effective for the teachers to initially prepare the organiser for the pupils – working deductively from the main theme and branching out into each contained item. This way, the teacher holds the autonomy for what is being taught and the organiser provides a road map of expected knowledge, directing pupils through their topic. Therefore, even though pupils may (and should) expand on the content of the initial organiser, the non-negotiable items are carefully considered, logically organised and accessible to all.

It is important to remember that this is not a test – pupils are encouraged to interact with the graphic organiser as they recall information and expand on each item. Pupils will physically follow the lines of the graphic organiser with their finger as it directs them from one item to the next, and often a facilitator will assist in the recall. We have found that this facilitator (a teacher, parent or peer) actively enhances the process by prompting and probing the retriever.

How did you use the graphic organiser in conjunction with other strategies?

When looking at Martin Robinson's work on trivium in the 21st century, it is clear where the graphic organiser can aid the first stage of recall (grammar), as well as the second stage of question and explore (dialect). However, we have also seen the impact of the graphic organiser as a tool for the third and final stage – communication (rhetoric). This final aspect, for us, is when pupils are able to independently and coherently share the knowledge presented in the graphic organiser, as well as the schematic design they have constructed from it. One method is in the form of our final topical essay: the Justification of Opinion.

At the end of term, pupils at Mayflower answer their "topic question" (which is posed at the start of the term) by forming a justified opinion on the topic at hand. This is presented as a formal essay. In order to structure the content of their essay, pupils create their own plan in the form of a Flow Spray diagram, owing to the sequential nature of the essay structure. They transfer content from their original Mind Map organiser, while also inputting additional information they have learnt throughout the term. Thus, they produce a coherent and logical plan to follow for their independent writing.

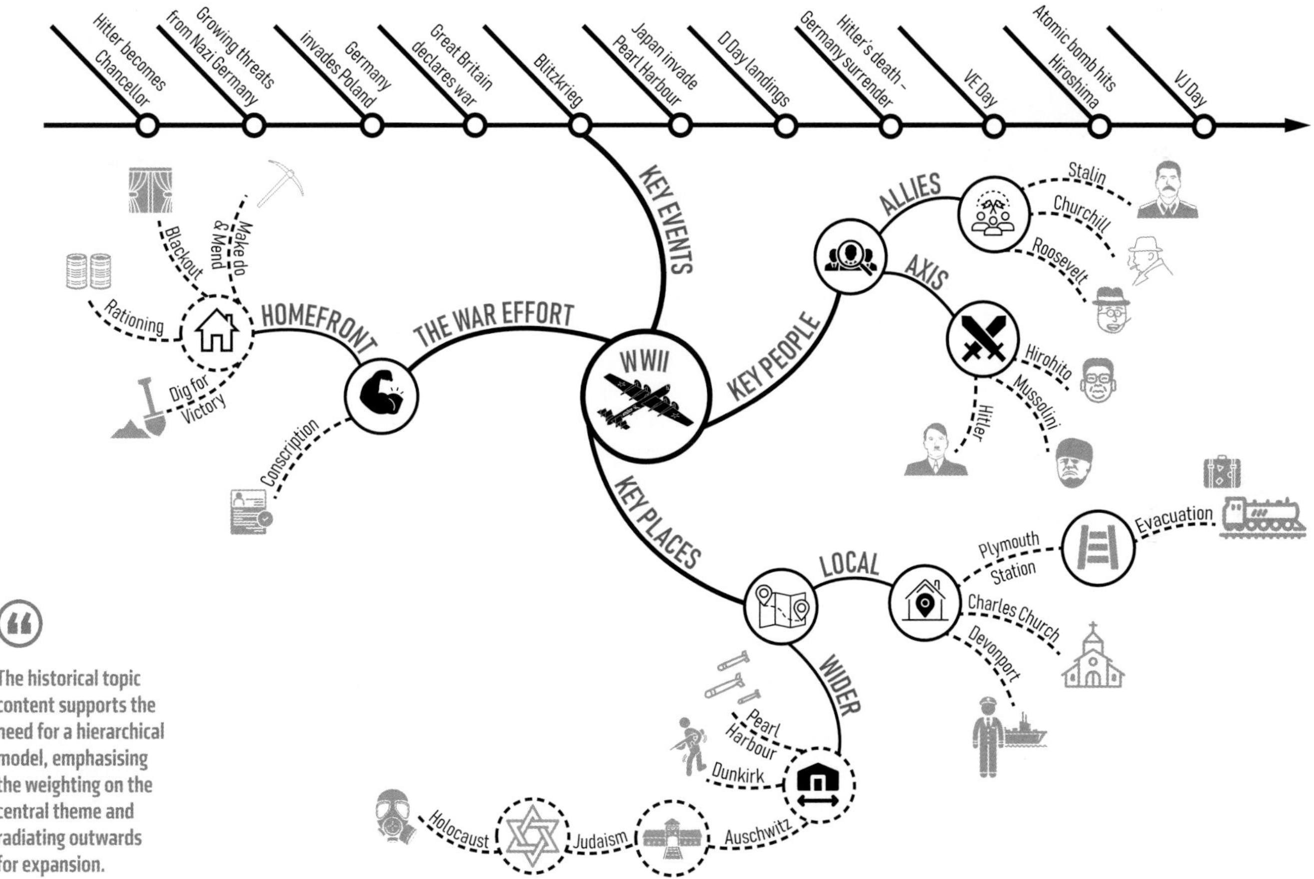

The historical topic content supports the need for a hierarchical model, emphasising the weighting on the central theme and radiating outwards for expansion.

SELINA CHADWICK

Visuals are the most effective method of disseminating information. They're everywhere: road signs, emojis, symbols, flat-pack furniture instructions, etc. It makes sense to use visuals in the classroom.

Current job: Head of department
Subject: Product design
Age phase: Secondary and FE (11-18)
Organisation: St Philomena's Catholic High School for Girls

How did the need arise for this graphic organiser?

Sustainability is a key topic in design and technology and in science, particularly lifecycle assessment/analysis. Students need to understand how a product's lifecycle can impact the environment. This topic often features as an extended response question in exams. For extended response questions, students sometimes forget to adequately plan their responses or feel intimidated by writing an answer that fills a vast space. Consequently, their response lacks structure, is repetitive, is vague or deviates from the question.

What was the process of creating this graphic organiser?

The first step is to examine the knowledge that needs teaching and pare this down into something manageable and memorable. A lifecycle analysis has several stages that can be condensed into three: manufacture, use and disposal (MUD). Acronyms are useful to make content stick. If the abbreviation can relate to its definition, this makes it easier to remember. The second step is to consider which type of graphic organiser would be best to represent this knowledge: if the themes overlap or contrast, if there is a sequence of events, cause and effect, etc. The final step is to merge the knowledge and graphic organiser. Using icons can help improve the visual clarity of the information presented. A word of caution about using icons: their purpose is not to make your resource look pretty; the aim is to reduce cognitive overload. The combination of words and visuals makes digesting the communication more effective. The Noun Project (thenounproject.com) is an excellent starting point for choosing icons. Even Microsoft is aware of how powerful dual coding is and has included icon graphics that can be inserted into your PowerPoint resources, as you would with shapes and symbols.

The first step is to examine the knowledge that needs teaching and pare this down into something manageable and memorable.

A word of caution about using icons: their purpose is not to make your resource look pretty; the aim is to reduce cognitive overload.

How is this graphic organiser used in lessons?

I ask students to recall their prior knowledge and explain what they think a lifecycle is. The majority of students remember a tadpole growing into a frog, which leads to a discussion about lifecycles in the context of products and how the stages of a product's existence affect the environment. This discussion leads to a modelled example of how the manufacture, use and disposal of a generic product, such as a plastic bottle, can impact the environment.

What happens next?

The students are given a lifecycle analysis exam question and asked to plan their response using the Flow Spray organiser. Once students have planned their responses, they can write their answers. The final consolidation is for students to keep practising this technique, increasing their confidence to plan and answer the question in timed conditions. MUD is the foundation of understanding sustainability issues surrounding products. When students understand this concept, this leads to more complex problem-solving, such as designing responsibly and shifting products from a linear to a circular economy.

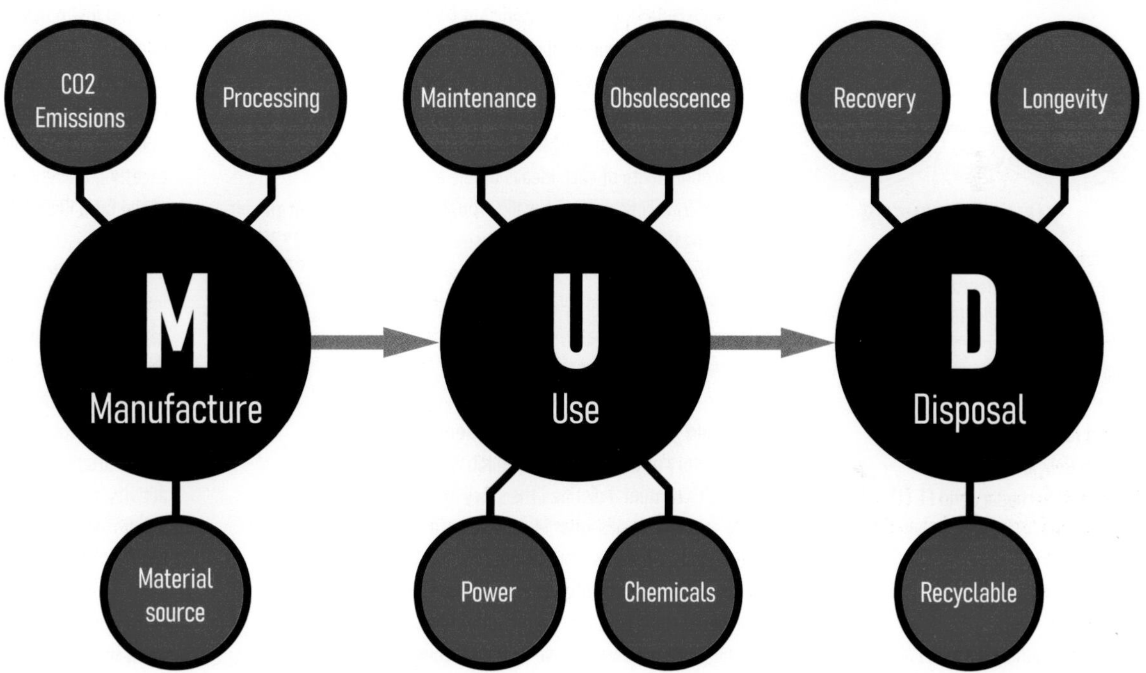

Selina has created a Flow Spray diagram that is stylish and useful. Her students are more likely to remember the subject content as they have created an acronym for the superordinate terms and chunked the process into three stages. The chunking of information is only possible for most people when they do so in their cognitive workspace, the external memory field. It is clear to see how, as a writing tool, Selina's Flow Spray increases the chances of her students creating longer trains of thought. Because their thinking is visible, they can refine ideas and add these back into their workspace. This iterative process helps Selina's students write with greater clarity.

SHAUN STEVENSON

Graphic organisers are remarkable for their ability to visually represent elements of information as both discrete and connected, without any loss to conceptual clarity, intricacy and depth.

Current job: Teacher
Subject: Religious education
Age phase: Secondary and FE (11-18)
Organisation: Worcester University

Why did you choose this graphic organiser?

I find that graphic organisers are an effective way to present complex information in manageable chunks. Ideas grouped in this way are easier for students to sequence. Presenting these chunks diagrammatically allows for a narrative to unfold. Students can follow a sequential narrative through the structure of a walkthrough. In creating a story, students can build strong links between the chronological ideas they are exploring. Walkthroughs not only encourage students to develop a narrative, but they also present a physical map of those ideas. The interconnectivity of each idea is visible at a glance. Travelling along the walkthrough by following it with one's finger can also embed the information through embodied cognition. I have found walkthroughs to be invaluable. They present information as a narrative journey to be explored and retold.

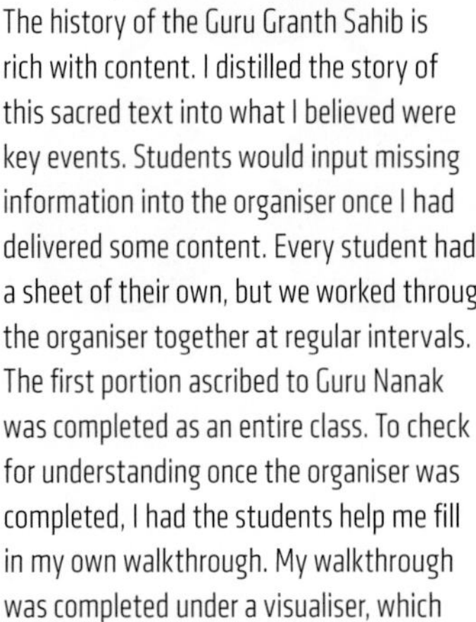

How did you teach it to your students?

The history of the Guru Granth Sahib is rich with content. I distilled the story of this sacred text into what I believed were key events. Students would input missing information into the organiser once I had delivered some content. Every student had a sheet of their own, but we worked through the organiser together at regular intervals. The first portion ascribed to Guru Nanak was completed as an entire class. To check for understanding once the organiser was completed, I had the students help me fill in my own walkthrough. My walkthrough was completed under a visualiser, which allowed me to model the completion of the organiser. Modelling the work was a boon to those students who still struggled with the concept or had written erroneous entries. Once we had completed the walkthrough together, students recounted the history of the Guru Granth Sahib to one another. To retell the history, students talked through the narrative while following its path with their finger. Retelling this story highlighted links between elements of the narrative. Following the walkthrough path also helped embody the learning physically, as though students were following a route on a map. I was encouraged by the students' engagement throughout the activity, as well as the speed at which they understood and could describe the history of the Guru Granth Sahib.

I find that graphic organisers are an effective way to present complex information in manageable chunks.

GOs can assist in the effective and immediate delineation of complex concepts by presenting information diagrammatically.

Where else could graphic organisers be used in your subject?

Students are often exposed to complex and sophisticated concepts in RE that can require considerable breaking down. GOs can assist in the effective and immediate delineation of such concepts by presenting information diagrammatically. Larkin and Simon (1987) argue that diagrammatic representation of information is more computationally efficient than sentential representations – I believe GOs illustrate this well. Difficult ideas benefit from such a sagacious delivery.

SIKHISM
also called
SIKHI
founded
GURU NANAK — FIRST GURU
succeeded by
GURU ARJUN — FIFTH GURU
succeeded by
GURU GOBIND SINGH — TENTH GURU
born in
INDIA
in the year
1469
died in
1539
collected
TEACHINGS AND HYMNS
in the
ADI GRANTH
which means
FIRST BOOK
who is announced
THE LAST GURU
which is
GURU GRANTH SAHIB — LAST GURU
the last
HUMAN GURU

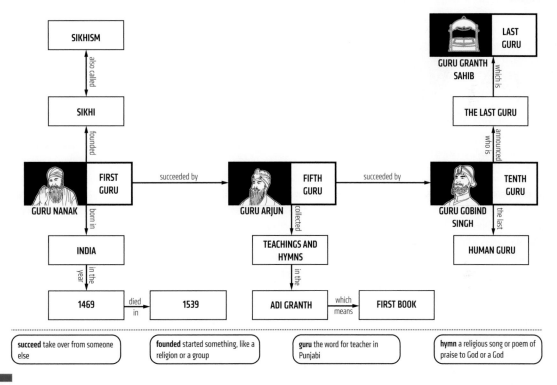

succeed take over from someone else

founded started something, like a religion or a group

guru the word for teacher in Punjabi

hymn a religious song or poem of praise to God or a God

Shaun's Relations Diagram is a splendid example of how well-formed diagrams offer computational efficiency. The linked arrows show causal links. When using this organiser, Shaun's students will find it less cognitively challenging to find causal relationships than using text alone. On each connecting arrow, Shaun specifies the relationship between each element by including a verb. Each subject-verb-object connection fashions a kernel sentence. Kernel sentences have the potential to be more memorable than regular prose as they are terse and unambiguous. As such, Shaun can introduce his students to the rich content his subject affords.

SIMON BEALE

Graphic organisers are an essential tool for teachers in making abstract concepts and their connections more visible to students.

Current job: Associate assistant headteacher
Subject: History
Age phase: Secondary and FE (11-18)
Organisation: Vyners School

Why did you create this graphic organiser?

History requires students to develop a complex framework of events. We expect them to develop an intimate understanding of specific events while also having an awareness of long-term trends. This is problematic for students because they do not have a developed schema to organise information when they start learning a new topic; often they are still lacking it at the end of a unit. I have also found that there can be a lack of awareness of how events affect each other. I wanted to create a graphic organiser that existed in the micro and the macro of history – a chance to focus on a specific year but also show the long-term trends across a set period. Combining a variety of understood spatial concepts around architecture, such as floors, capstones and skylines, provided a clear visual that allowed me to borrow from that conceptual schema and lighten the students' cognitive load.

How is it used?

Students first categorise the events of a given year. This gives them a chance to consider the particular events of a year and the broad themes that are at play. They then write a short synopsis of the key issues of that year, using a predetermined set of themes to provide a framework. This is repeated for every year in the course of study or the period in question. Students finish by summarising the skyline that the Time Line towers create.

Why does this help students?

Students have commented on how much more secure their knowledge of the period is after this activity. They can see how events build up within a year and have an impact the following year because of the growing thematic tensions. The activity gives them a way to consider whole decades and periods in order to make broader judgements. The satisfaction of categorisation at every stage has led to more nuance in students' answers in class, because they are able to access breadth and depth in the same resource.

Students have commented on how much more secure their knowledge of the period is after using this activity.

The satisfaction of categorisation at every stage has led to more nuance in students' answers in class, because they are able to access breadth and depth in the same resource.

How could it be applied across subjects?

Wherever you require students to focus on a process at the micro and macro level. A Time Line could easily be replaced by a sequence of actions or processes. It could be used to consider the developments across acts of a play, the processes of the water cycle or planning an essay.

Simon has taken a simple Time Line and created something quite beautiful – a visual metaphor to capture the causal relations. Simon is using the construction of Time Line towers to illustrate the build-up of tension. Equally pleasing is how Simon extracts added value from his Time Line.

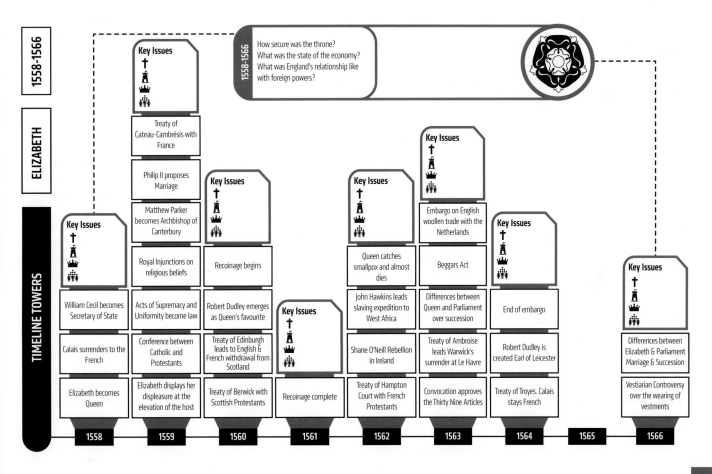

TIMELINE TOWERS

ELIZABETH

1558-1566

1558-1566

How secure was the throne?
What was the state of the economy?
What was England's relationship like with foreign powers?

1558

Key Issues

- William Cecil becomes Secretary of State
- Calais surrenders to the French
- Elizabeth becomes Queen

1559

Key Issues

- Treaty of Cateau-Cambrésis with France
- Philip II proposes Marriage
- Matthew Parker becomes Archbishop of Canterbury
- Royal Injunctions on religious beliefs
- Acts of Supremacy and Uniformity become law
- Conference between Catholic and Protestants
- Elizabeth displays her displeasure at the elevation of the host

1560

Key Issues

- Recoinage begins
- Robert Dudley emerges as Queen's favourite
- Treaty of Edinburgh leads to English & French withdrawal from Scotland
- Treaty of Berwick with Scottish Protestants

1561

Key Issues

- Recoinage complete

1562

Key Issues

- Queen catches smallpox and almost dies
- John Hawkins leads slaving expedition to West Africa
- Shane O'Neill Rebellion in Ireland
- Treaty of Hampton Court with French Protestants

1563

Key Issues

- Embargo on English woollen trade with the Netherlands
- Beggars Act
- Differences between Queen and Parliament over succession
- Treaty of Ambroise leads Warwick's surrender at Le Havre
- Convocation approves the Thirty Nine Articles

1564

Key Issues

- End of embargo
- Robert Dudley is created Earl of Leicester
- Treaty of Troyes. Calais stays French

1565

1566

Key Issues

- Differences between Elizabeth & Parliament Marriage & Succession
- Vestiarian Controversy over the wearing of vestments

SIMON FLYNN

GOs help students to identify the key information and understand how it fits together.

Current job: Teacher
Subject: Science/chemistry
Age phase: Secondary and sixth form (11-18)
Organisation: The Camden School for Girls

What prompted you to produce this graphic organiser?

A-level chemistry, and the organic side in particular, is an incredibly connected subject. This is particularly visible when, towards the end of the course, students encounter organic synthesis questions where they have to decipher or suggest a series of reactions that gets us from A to D. Before this, each step in the sequence is a discrete topic. But now, the individual steps merge to form pathways. For the well-prepared, it can be very satisfying. The frustration, however, is in our journey to this point. Throughout Year 12 and much of Year 13, students often find the array of mechanisms bewildering – they fail to see the connections. The graphic organiser I have designed helps students to see the connections in a meaningful way.

How did you use this graphic organiser with your students?

I introduced the organiser early on in the course, when I first taught the idea of organic mechanisms. At this point, nucleophiles and electrophiles are nothing more than definitions. Using PowerPoint to reveal elements and their connections one at a time, the graphic organiser begins to show students how aspects of the course will develop over 18 months. There is a more complete version than the one opposite, which I introduce to students once they are comfortable using graphic organisers.

I have found that concept mapping helps students identify similar features across multiple mechanisms. And having an appreciation of the similarities helps students make sense of new information, as they connect it to prior learning. As a result, I repeatedly refer back to the graphic organiser throughout the course. I often direct students to complete partially completed versions of the organiser throughout the course for retrieval practice. A later challenge is whether students can retrieve and reproduce the organiser in its entirety, with no support.

The graphic organiser I have designed helps students to see the connections in a meaningful way.

I often direct students to complete partially completed versions of the organiser for retrieval practice. A later challenge is whether students can reproduce it with no support.

Is there anything else you want to add about students and graphic organisers?

I have become interested in distributed cognition – how external representations can expand the limitations of working memory. When grappling with questions that require students to have a well-developed schema, graphic organisers act as a tool to reduce cognitive load. Furthermore, in Fiorella and Mayer's *Learning as a Generative Activity*, they list eight strategies that promote understanding. These include mapping, summarising and self-explaining, all of which can be elevated by using a graphic organiser. There is a lot of talk about metacognition at the moment, and rightly so – graphic organisers help to make thinking more visible. Because I have my students refer back to this graphic organiser, I can show them how thinking is an iterative process. I demonstrate how ideas evolve and how they are refined.

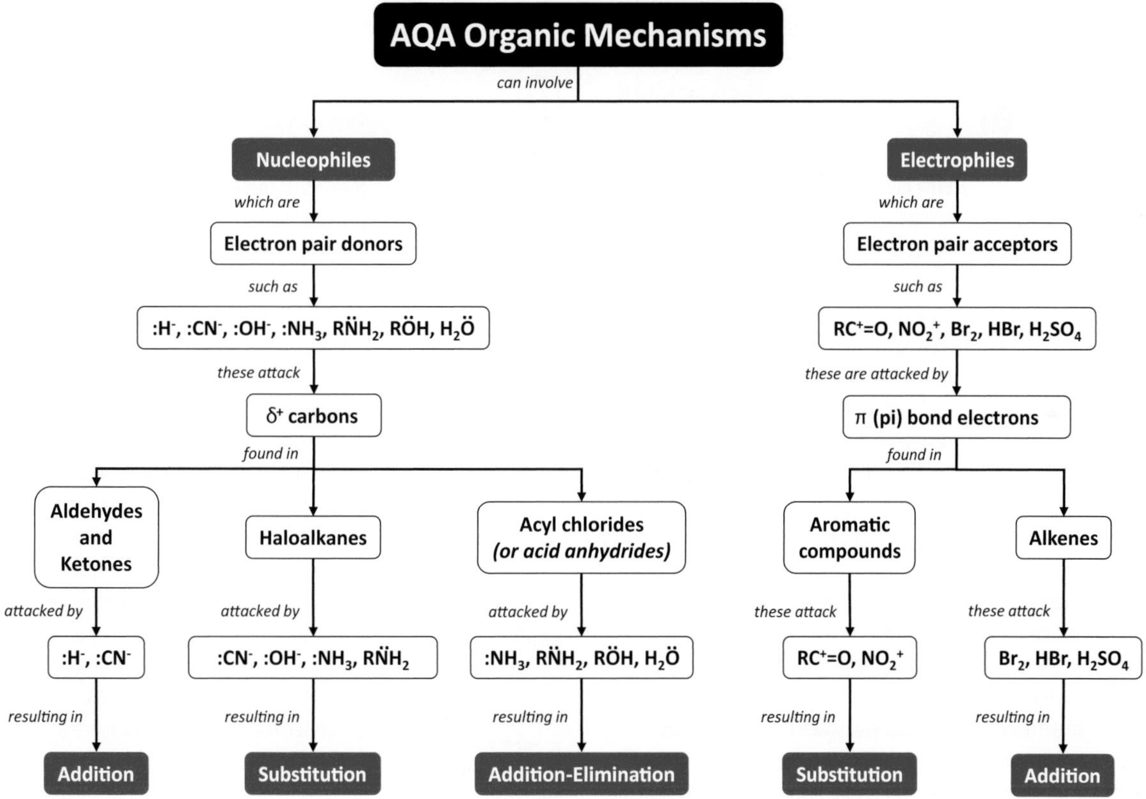

AQA Organic Mechanisms

can involve

Nucleophiles

which are **Electron pair donors**

such as $:H^-$, $:CN^-$, $:OH^-$, $:NH_3$, $R\ddot{N}H_2$, $R\ddot{O}H$, $H_2\ddot{O}$

these attack δ^+ carbons

found in

- **Aldehydes and Ketones** — *attacked by* $:H^-$, $:CN^-$ — *resulting in* **Addition**
- **Haloalkanes** — *attacked by* $:CN^-$, $:OH^-$, $:NH_3$, $R\ddot{N}H_2$ — *resulting in* **Substitution**
- **Acyl chlorides *(or acid anhydrides)*** — *attacked by* $:NH_3$, $R\ddot{N}H_2$, $R\ddot{O}H$, $H_2\ddot{O}$ — *resulting in* **Addition-Elimination**

Electrophiles

which are **Electron pair acceptors**

such as $RC^+{=}O$, NO_2^+, Br_2, HBr, H_2SO_4

these are attacked by π (pi) bond electrons

found in

- **Aromatic compounds** — *these attack* $RC^+{=}O$, NO_2^+ — *resulting in* **Substitution**
- **Alkenes** — *these attack* Br_2, HBr, H_2SO_4 — *resulting in* **Addition**

Simon's graphic organiser is a hybrid diagram. It chunks information under an explicit hierarchy and allows for a comparison of different sequences. Each element in Simon's diagram is aligned. He has also been careful with his use of colour – the result is maximum visual clarity. Simon's organiser is impressive, but more importantly, he knows how to get the most out of its use.

TIM BEATTIE

Graphic organisers act as a metacognitive tool that allow students and teachers to make their thinking visible.

Current job: Principal teacher learning and teaching, DCC pedagogy team
Subject: Religious, moral and philosophical studies
Age phase: Secondary and FE (11-18)
Organisation: Harris Academy, Dundee

Why do you advocate the use of graphic organisers for learning and teaching?

For me, graphic organisers are a powerful tool because they paint the big picture on one page and they support my understanding, grasping and sharing of a metanarrative. I also use them heavily in teaching as a tool to aid direct instruction. For pupils, they are valuable during independent learning. Students can use them to learn domain-specific knowledge, processes and skills that help in the learning process. For other teachers, investing time in using GOs is a no-brainer. But to get the most out of them, you need to understand how they work. If not, you run the risk of their being detrimental to pupil learning.

Why did you choose the graphic organiser in your example?

Pupils often struggle with self-regulation. I want to help my pupils – and those I support across Dundee – improve their planning, monitoring and evaluation of learning.
As teachers, there is a focus on delivering curricular content to our pupils and rightly so. However, we can forget to slow down enough to reinforce the strategies pupils need to navigate their learning themselves. Unfortunately, spoon-feeding domain-specific knowledge is often the status quo. This is such a shame when the research points to metacognitive skills having a significant impact on pupils' learning.

How did you teach it to your pupils?

Firstly, pupils will choose a *topic* – getting this right is vital. Is the theme relevant to the course? An important first question. And, as a teacher, have I provided enough support regarding course content or assessment criteria for pupils to discern this?

Students can use graphic organisers to learn domain-specific knowledge, processes and skills that help in the learning process.

We can forget to slow down enough to reinforce the strategies pupils need to navigate their learning themselves.

Secondly, pupils need to *retrieve* content. Retrieval can be about domain-specific knowledge, procedural knowledge or processes. My go-to is the brain dump/fill. On an A4 sheet of paper, pupils record everything they know about the topic inside a circle – *content recalled*. Next, around the outside, pupils add what they failed to recall, using previously taken notes, teacher talk and textbooks – this is *content missed*. Pupils then *evaluate* the brain dump/fill, ensuring they know the *content recalled* and deciding if they need to review or relearn the *content missed*. The planning and monitoring stages come next and form individual mini-cycles. Using SMART goals, pupils create a checklist (measurable with a tick) for the material that needs to be reviewed or relearnt. If they encounter challenges as they monitor their learning, they will need to reassess their goals using SMART again, until happy they have completed the checklist and the process.

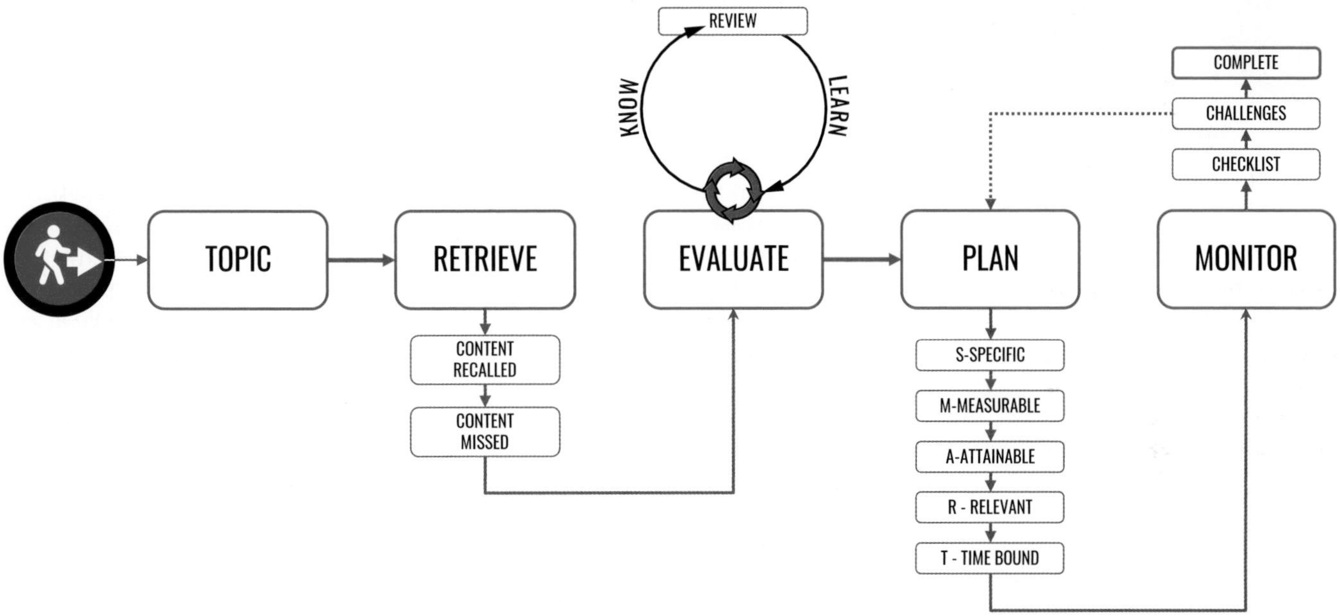

TOPIC → RETRIEVE → EVALUATE → PLAN → MONITOR

RETRIEVE: CONTENT RECALLED → CONTENT MISSED → EVALUATE

EVALUATE: KNOW → REVIEW → LEARN

PLAN: S-SPECIFIC → M-MEASURABLE → A-ATTAINABLE → R - RELEVANT → T - TIME BOUND → MONITOR

MONITOR: CHECKLIST → CHALLENGES → COMPLETE

CHALLENGES → PLAN

Tim has created a Flow Chart with admirable clarity. He has selected appropriate graphics, aligned all elements and restrained his use of colour and typeface. By following the design principles of cut, chunk, align and restrain, Tim has created a powerful visual instruction plan. We have already seen that if the steps aren't sufficiently chunked, the existing steps become lost as new instructions are given. Tim is like the model aeroplane company: instructions are chunked into bitesized, manageable packets.

TOM HANSON

Graphic organisers show students how knowledge is connected. I can also use them to see what students are thinking.

Current job: Teacher
Subject: Geography
Age phase: Secondary and FE (11-18)
Organisation: Allerton Grange School

Why do you use graphic organisers?

I incorporate carefully planned graphic organisers into my practice for two reasons: to share the big picture and to explain how knowledge is connected. Graphic organisers are especially useful for reviewing a sequence of learning to ensure all the individual ideas have been stitched together. It is important to plan a graphic organiser in advance. I need the ideas to be accessible through clear visuals.

Why do you encourage students to use graphic organisers?

Students acquire many individual nodes of knowledge, but we also require them to develop understanding. Asking students to create a graphic organiser, either as a standalone task or as something they return to regularly, is an effective way of assessing the connections they are able to make. I find students deliver better verbal answers after creating a graphic organiser. I also ask students to create graphic organisers before completing extended writing tasks and assessments. This is an opportunity for students to practise explanations and hardwire the connections. As students complete the task, I too receive feedback on the learning that has taken place.

Do students create their own graphic organisers successfully?

It takes time and regular practice. I use a lot of graphic organisers in my lessons, which is also an effective way to model them. By the time students are asked to create their own, they have already seen many examples. Part-complete organisers, or ones that make connections but limit explanations, are a good starting point when students are new to the process. Some students will struggle with the physical layout. In this scenario, I share a template so students can focus on the content rather than the design.

Students acquire many individual nodes of knowledge, but we also require them to develop understanding.

I find students deliver better verbal answers after creating a graphic organiser.

How did you use this organiser?

This graphic organiser was used with an A-level class at the end of a series of lessons investigating ecological succession. As students had already developed their knowledge of the different elements, this organiser was used to review learning before a written assignment. First, I gave students the list of terms and asked them to work in pairs to create their own graphic organiser. Working in pairs promotes discussion and encourages students to think of alternative ways in which knowledge can be connected. Following a class discussion, I shared this model so students had an opportunity to reflect on their own work. Finally, the students were quizzed on their understanding of the key terms and connections.

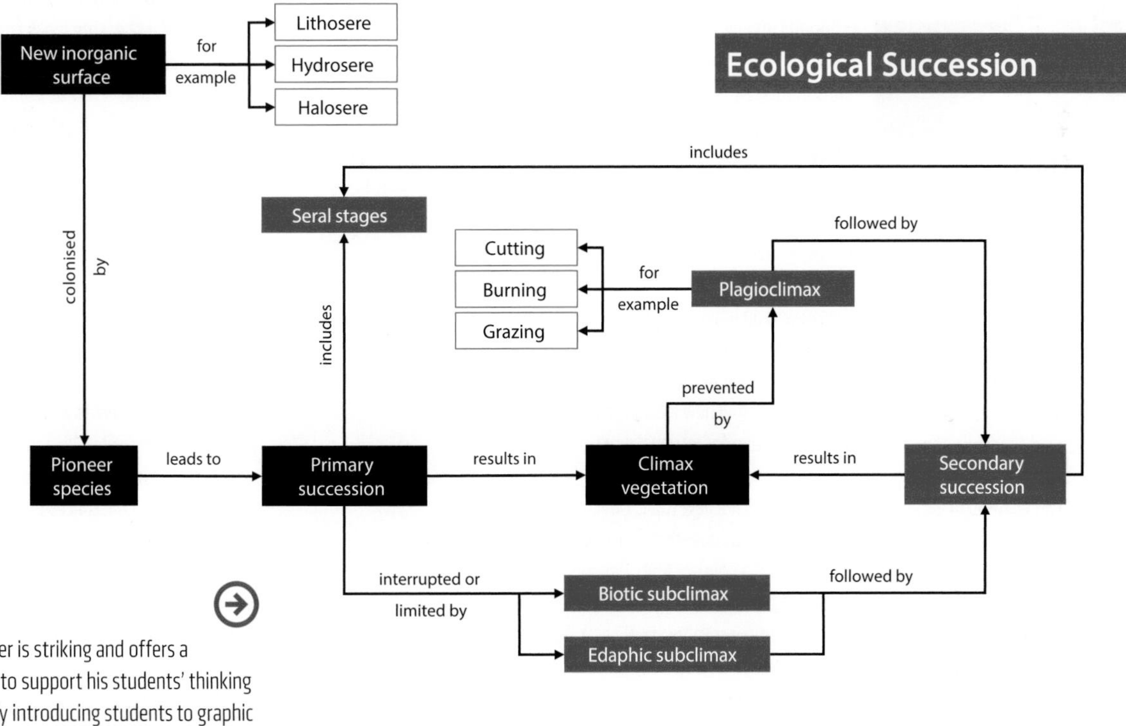

Tom's organiser is striking and offers a powerful tool to support his students' thinking and writing. By introducing students to graphic organisers, Tom is increasing the chances of intellectual discourse. His students become self-assured in their thinking and poised to share ideas verbally.

TOM ODDY

Being able to demonstrate the relationships between various concepts is extremely important in science. Therefore, Concept Maps are often my first call.

Current job: Deputy head of science
Subject: Biology
Age phase: Secondary (11-16)
Organisation: Sheikh Zayed Academy, Abu Dhabi

Why did you choose the graphic organiser in your example?

The graphic organiser I have used is an example of a Concept Map. Concept mapping allows us to convey concepts and ideas and the relationships between them. Being able to demonstrate the relationships between various concepts is extremely important in science. Therefore, Concept Maps are often my first call for introducing and recalling large amounts of information surrounding a particular topic. I have found concept mapping allows students to identify relationships between certain concepts and ideas. And constructing the Concept Map helps students connect new information with prior knowledge.

How do you use Concept Maps in the classroom?

One of the great characteristics of Concept Maps is their diversity in how they can be applied in the classroom. Concept mapping has played an important role in teaching and learning in my classroom for the past four years. I have found they are most effective when connecting new learning to prior knowledge and for retrieval practice.

When we reach a new topic, I will often ask the class a focus question. This is then used to construct a Concept Map. Depending on the ability of the class, this will either be done by the students or collaboratively as a class, often with the use of a visualiser. The construction of the Concept Map allows me to assess students' existing knowledge of the topic and identify any misconceptions they may have; furthermore, it informs my teaching for the rest of the lesson/topic.

The construction of the Concept Map allows me to assess students' existing knowledge of the topic and identify any misconceptions.

There is a misconception that the term *graphic organiser* means icons and images should play a part in their use.

The cognitive science research behind retrieval practice has undoubtedly proven its value in classroom practice. Kate Jones covers this in her book *Retrieval Practice* (2019), in which she mentions that "*every time information is retrieved, or an answer is generated, it changes that original memory to make it stronger*".
I often use concept mapping for retrieval practice, giving students a partial or empty version of the Concept Map they have previously learned and asking them to fill it in. This a great way to test and measure what the students can recall.

What are the benefits of the icons in your graphic organiser?

Although I am an advocate for dual coding, I believe there is a misconception that the term *graphic organiser* means icons and images should play a part in their use. Although I disagree with this misnomer, I do believe that there are instances in which icons or images can be useful when constructing GOs. In my example, I have sparingly used icons to answer some of the questions that may arise for students, such *What is peristalsis?* or *What do proteins, lipids and carbohydrates do?*

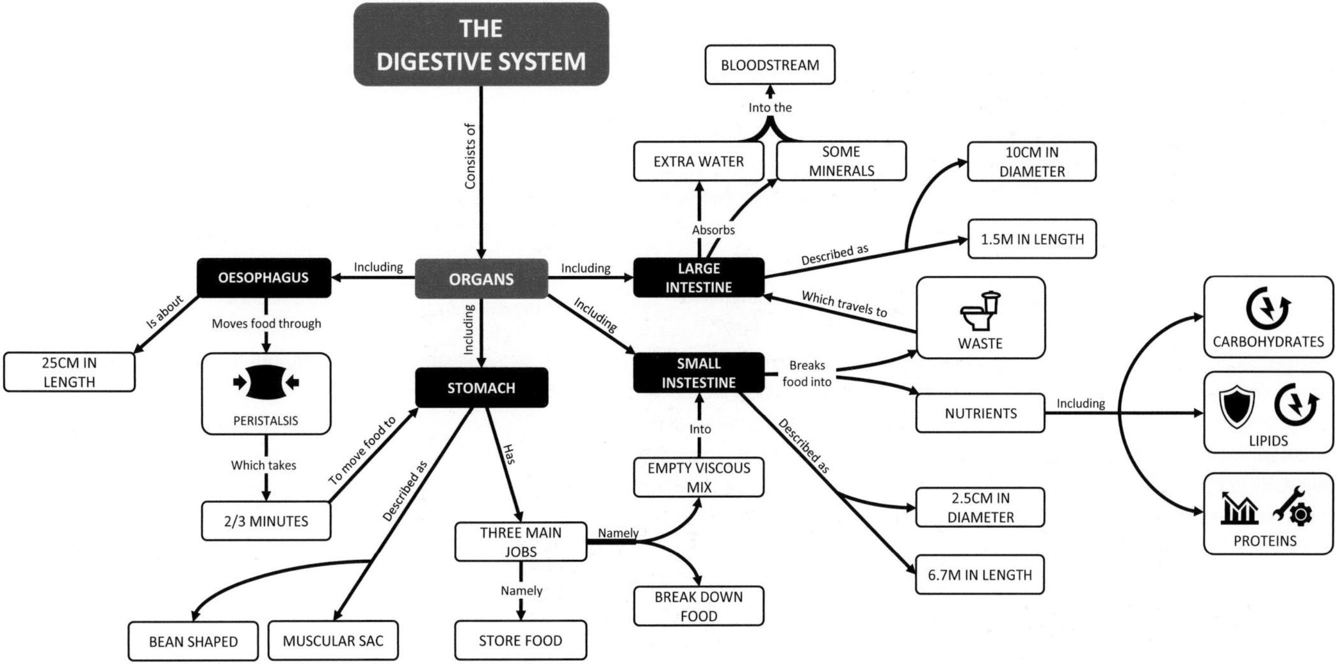

THE DIGESTIVE SYSTEM

Consists of

ORGANS

Including
OESOPHAGUS
Is about
25CM IN LENGTH
Moves food through
PERISTALSIS
Which takes
2/3 MINUTES
To move food to

Including
STOMACH
Described as
BEAN SHAPED
MUSCULAR SAC
Has
THREE MAIN JOBS
Namely
STORE FOOD
BREAK DOWN FOOD
EMPTY VISCOUS MIX
Into

Including
SMALL INSTESTINE
Breaks food into
WASTE
NUTRIENTS
Including
CARBOHYDRATES
LIPIDS
PROTEINS
Described as
2.5CM IN DIAMETER
6.7M IN LENGTH

Including
LARGE INTESTINE
Absorbs
EXTRA WATER
SOME MINERALS
Into the
BLOODSTREAM
Described as
10CM IN DIAMETER
1.5M IN LENGTH
Which travels to

Tom's Concept Map arranges ideas and concepts in a hierarchical structure. The map is made up of mini-sentences. Two elements, linked by an arrow and a verb, form a simple subject-verb-object sentence.

Concept Maps can be difficult to read. Tom has alleviated some of the challenges of reading a Concept Map with his subtle use of colour. The red and black boxes, as well as the arrows, provide a reading route. By creating this Concept Map, Tom has been able to share his schema with his students. As the expert, Tom has made public how he organises and structures knowledge.

TOM SIMS

Graphic organisers allow students to simultaneously view the bigger picture and all its constituent parts. Learners can see instantly how an individual element relates to the larger narrative, providing a powerful visual accompaniment to concepts.

Current job: Classroom teacher
Subject: History and politics
Age phase: Secondary and FE (11-18)
Organisation: The Evolve Trust

What was your thought process when designing the graphic organiser?

I wanted something that would convey to my students the bigger picture connecting each individual lesson in their topic. Graphic organisers such as Concept Maps are fantastic resources to initiate discussion about the relationship between the micro and the macro, and to nimbly shift students' focus between them. Additionally, I wanted to construct the graphic organiser in a way that conveyed both chronology and the relationships between events. In doing so, the graphic organiser provides a visual aid to develop students' understanding of concepts such as cause and consequence – useful second-order concepts in history.

How do you make use of graphic organisers in your teaching?

At the beginning of a new topic, students receive an advance organiser like this one. We then discuss the broad themes of the topic, using the organiser, as well as making links to what they have studied previously. Through questioning, I draw out some of the connections between the vectors – for example, *What sort of challenges will William face when he becomes king?* At the beginning of each subsequent lesson, the relevant section of the graphic organiser is spotlighted on the board, with the rest of the organiser faded. I use this to prompt discussion about what the lesson will cover, and it also provides a good opportunity for retrieval by asking students which previous learning is hidden from view.

Graphic organisers are fantastic resources to initiate discussion about the relationship between the micro and the macro.

I wanted to construct the GO in a way that conveyed both chronology and the relationships between events.

What advice would you give for the construction of a graphic organiser like this?

I have found it really useful to begin by identifying the start and end point of the graphic organiser. This helps to establish parameters, and prevents the scope of the organiser from becoming too large and unfocused. Then, I establish a central thread that runs through the topic – this is easier for a historian, where establishing a narrative or an enquiry is fundamental to the study of the topic. In this case, it is the progression of William, Duke of Normandy, from victor, to conqueror, to ruler. I then add the secondary vectors – those which might be incidental to the main narrative, and the focus of one or two lessons within the broader enquiry – before adding the links between them. This ensures that for any individual lesson, the key elements are close together and can be read with or without the organiser as a whole.

Before 1066

The Conquest of 1066

After 1066

Previous kings were Vikings
supporting the claim of
Harald Hardrada
led an
invasion
won the
Battle of Fulford
lost the
Battle of Stamford Bridge
won the
Harold Godwinson
became
King
promised the throne to
Edward the Confessor
had
No heir to the throne
promised the throne to
William of Normandy
planned an
invasion
lost the
won the
Battle of Hastings
led to
William becoming king
faced
Challenges
took
Land
from
Enemies
to give to
Friends
led to
defeated
Rebellions
led to
built
Castles
led to
Increased control
conducted
Domesday Survey
resolved
Disputes
led to
raised
Money

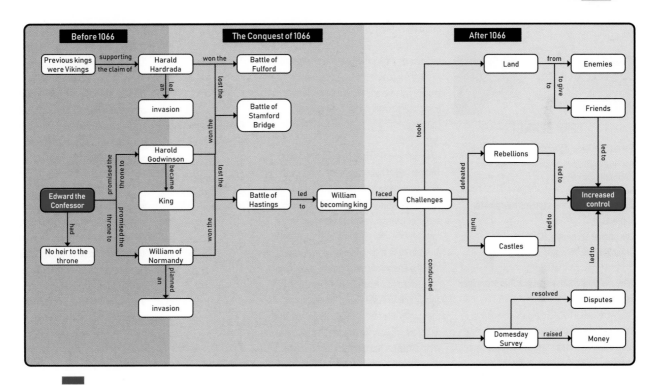

Tom's Concept Map wouldn't look out of place in a published magazine, such is its quality. Individual elements are aligned and chunked based on when they happened, and Tom cunningly uses subtle background colours to indicate where each event belongs within the time period. Tom's advance organiser serves three fundamental stages in the learning process: retrieval of prior learning, making connections, and prompting students to make predictions. The map can prime retrieval practice and support students in predicting what will happen next. Tom has created a tool for meaningful learning.

ZEPH BENNETT

As teachers, we create the visual context for learning instruction. By default we are all information designers.

Current job: Pastoral systems coordinator
Subject: PE
Age phase: Secondary (11-16)
Organisation: Werneth School

Why did you choose the graphic organiser in your example?

I have created a hybrid diagram combining a simple Concept Map and a Flow Chart. My design replicates the stages of an 800m race. The map allows me to represent the bigger picture to my students, but equally, it is chunked to enable key connections to be made between all the components of the 800m race. My map uses colours sparingly to reduce cognitive load. Arrows showing directional flow are kept to a minimum, and the framing of text is defined by colour and an increase in outline thickness. Readers know where to begin because of the *start* symbol, which has an extra-thick outline. For me, graphic organisers require balance and a degree of symmetry, using space to tell a story and define its contents.

How did you teach it to your students?

This particular hybrid organiser works well with a video clip from the BBC's *Tomorrow's World* programme from the 1990s. The video analyses energy systems as the runners complete the race. The organiser is shown in its entirety to give students an overview of how the energy systems change during the race, linked to training zones. Then, using the animations in PowerPoint, I walk through the stages of a race. If students are working remotely, they can reveal the changes in energy requirements step by step. Once the two forms of media are combined, students will have to create a graphic organiser, demonstrating their understanding of the transitions. They can use a Time Line, Flow Chart or Venn Diagram to connect the new information with previously acquired knowledge.

For me, graphic organisers require balance and a degree of symmetry, using space to tell a story and define its contents.

Once students have created their Time Line, they answer short-response questions on different aspects of my organiser.

How did you use the graphic organiser in conjunction with other strategies?

This graphic organiser aims to support students when answering the question, *Analyse how the two energy systems are utilised within a competitive 800m race*. Once students have created their Time Line, they answer short-response questions on different aspects of my organiser. When this knowledge is embedded, they answer the question; for some students the task is scaffolded using the Concept Map, while others answer the question without visual aids. Scaffolding for this task can involve using an answer grid with keywords added to a side column, or an amended graphic organiser that removes some keywords. Feedback is provided for students' answers and then, after a period of time, they revisit the question without the support of the graphic organiser.

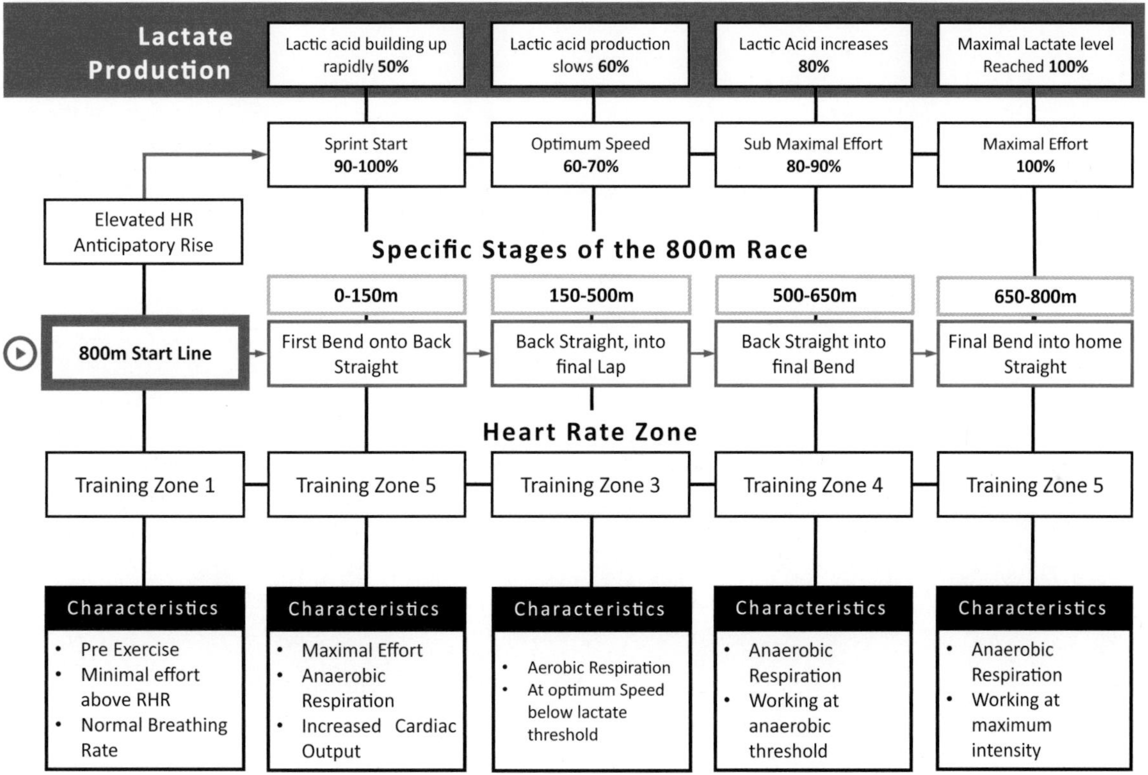

Zeph has created a hybrid organiser that chunks concepts and shows how they change over time – it's as though he has chunked time. In doing so, Zeph reveals his expert mode of thinking. Zeph's organiser is thoughtfully arranged. It is a balanced piece that respects the principles of chunk, cut, restrain and align. His design conveys meaning with absolute clarity.

If graphic organisers are not standalone strategies, then when are they best used and with which other strategies? Here are some examples.

Chapters

SOI MODEL & MAPPING

Graphic organisers are tools for organising. Their full power is only realised when they are used in partnership with, and in service of, other learning strategies.

LET'S GET TO WORK WITH PRODUCTIVE LEARNING STRATEGIES: MAPPING (2021)

Paul A. Kirschner, Mirjam Neelen, Tine Hoof & Tim Surma

Paul Kirschner

As with other productive strategies, the idea behind mapping is that learners go through the SOI model and generate a new product relating to the subject matter in question.

Kirschner et al, 2021

The pure SOI model

Fiorella and Mayer base their 2015 book, *Learning as a Generative Activity*, on their SOI model, shown below. While the direction of attention and the free-flow from working and long-term memory are critical, the key actions that can be directly taught are those of organising information for meaning.

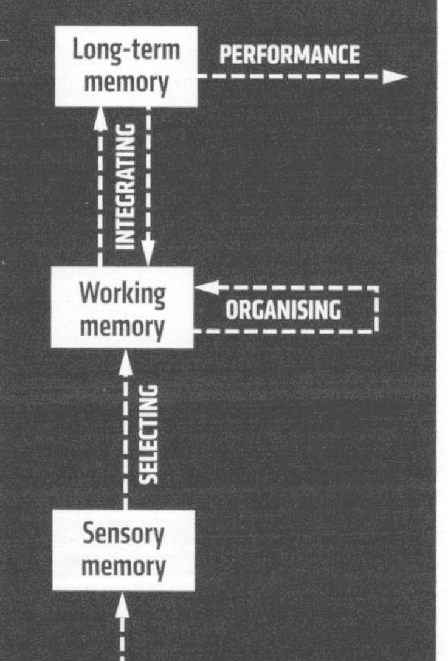

The humanised SOI model

The same model with a more human depiction shows the significance of Merlin Donald's external memory field (EXMF). With the limitations of transient information avoided, the student can work on — generate — the formation of their meaning-making through the selection and development of a GO.

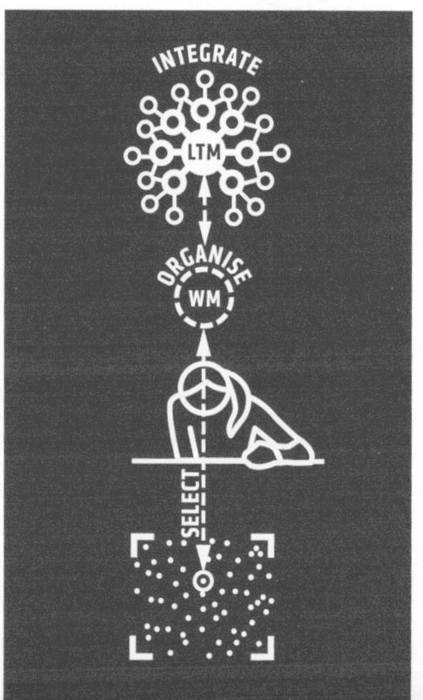

The humanised SOI model in a mapping context

Clark and Lyons, in their 2004 magnum opus *Graphics For Learning*, point out that selecting the correct visual tool is essential for success. And yet a taxonomy of, and instruction about, graphic organisers is mostly missing from most texts about the topic. Consequently, we note with increasing frustration the continued research that omits this factor, as well as treating graphic organisers as a single, standalone strategy. They are not. Their purpose is to aid the process of organising, as a means to create meaning. But that doesn't ever happen in isolation. It is always embedded in a subject context, working as a partner strategy.

Mirjam Neelen

The teacher needs to show learners how to do it and practise using it, show what successful maps look like, and discuss the maps created with learners using epistemic questions.

Kirschner et al. 2021

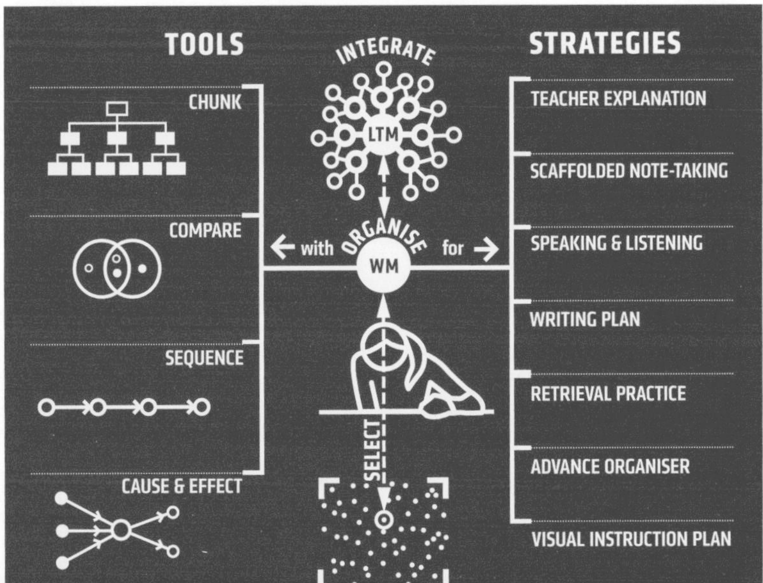

Tine Hoof

Mapping can be used by both the teacher and the learner, in different ways and in different subjects.

Kirschner et al, 2021

Tim Surma

We wouldn't recommend choosing mapping as a sole study strategy.

Kirschner et al. 2021

CLUSTERS

Individual methods are researched, reported on and studied. But, in classrooms, we link them up into a variety of combinations.

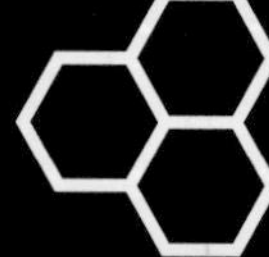

Aristotle

Many things have a plurality of parts and are not merely a complete aggregate but instead some kind of a whole beyond its parts.

The distorting perspective of research

As you would expect from science, teaching techniques are studied one at a time. Variables are eliminated such that there is confidence that what is measured is the sole focus of the study. Then, quite naturally, the single classroom method is reported on and – here is where it gets interesting – *read* by teachers. Their reading is framed by the single-method perspective. No account is given of how the individual approach is integrated into a sequence, yet that is its eventual habitat. Outside the classroom, this practice of combining individual moves into a fluid chain of actions is natural, accepted and assumed. Teaching could do with following this strategy.

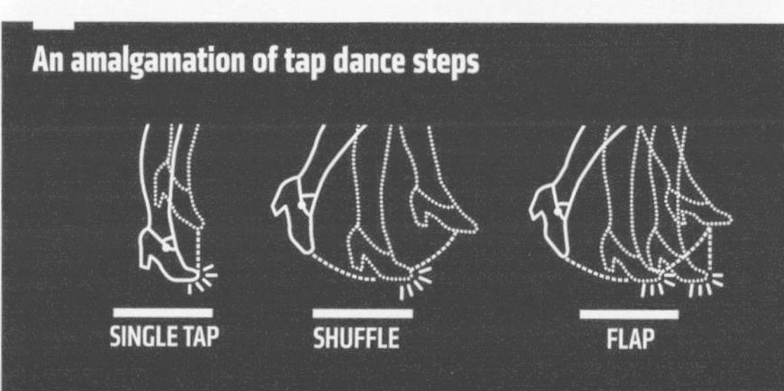

The thinking that glues a sequence together

Bringing individual techniques together into a sequence involves a rationale for its orchestration. Surfacing your reasoning is triggered and structured by the following:

If... Specify what exactly you want your students to do/think/achieve.
Then... Detail the actions needed to achieve that goal.
If you follow this formula and the demands it places on surfacing your reasoning, then you will select and sequence your methods effectively.

Enter the WalkThrus Clusters

The Teaching WalkThrus website has developed cluster hexagons for each of its techniques. While the multimedia versions are for subscribers only, there is a free pack you can download to create your own clusters. Hexagons of graphic organisers are not yet ready, but look out for them in the future.

www.walkthrus.co.uk

Mary Kennedy

Thoughts are intertwined with practice, so if we want to better understand practice, we need to also understand the thoughts that guide practice.

Kennedy, 2008

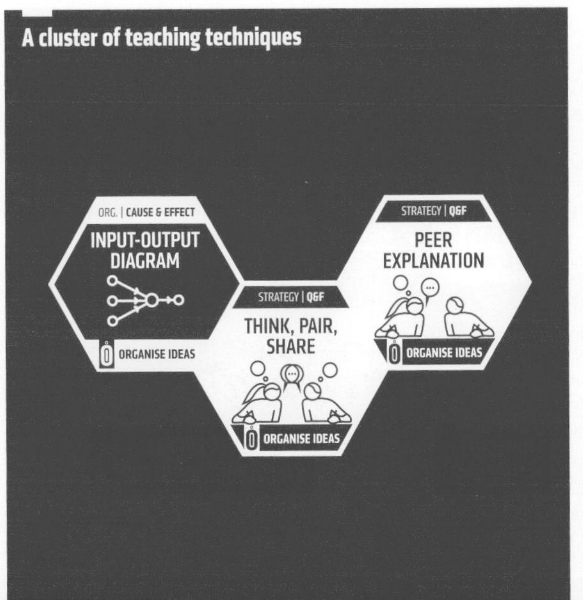

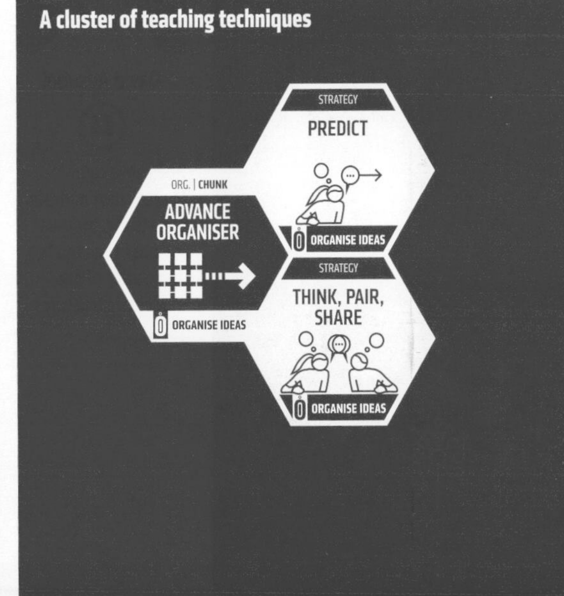

ADVANCE ORGANISERS

Enhance students' capacity to absorb new information by presenting the general concepts first.

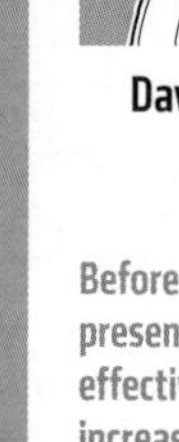

David Ausubel

Before we can present new material effectively, we must increase the stability and clarity of our students' structures.

Ausubel, 1968

Expert knowledge structures

Experts have richly connected and meaningful knowledge structures, which allow them to use knowledge more efficiently and effectively. In contrast, students, who are novices, have sparsely connected knowledge structures as they have not yet developed meaningful ways of organising the information they encounter. The distinction between novices and experts is useful in helping us recognise how best to help our students organise knowledge. The differences between novices and experts are not, however, a distinct binary. It is a continuum that students can move along with careful instruction.

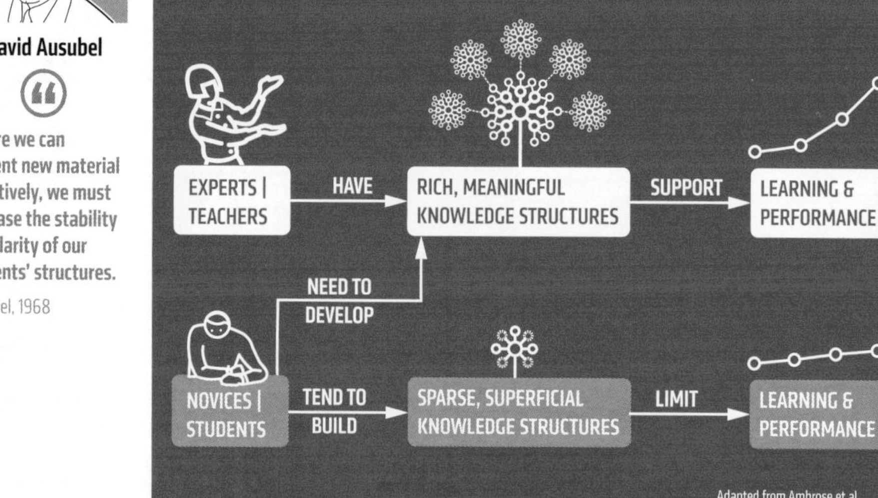

Adapted from Ambrose et al, *How Learning Works*, 2010

Four types AVERAGE EFFECT SIZE

Graphic **1.24**

Transforming an overview into a graphic organiser helps teachers and students identify the key concepts and their links. Expository, narrative and skimming organisers can be supplemented with a graphic organiser.

Expository **0.80**

Describes the new learning to be covered. A teacher could write a short explanation of the key concepts students will learn. Students are nominated to read parts of the description to the whole class.

Skimming **0.71**

Students skim for information before reading a piece of text. To get the most from skimming, demonstrate how to do it. Once students have grasped how to skim-read, direct them to go back and read in great detail.

Narrative **0.53**

Storytelling and personal anecdotes are used to help make connections to the real world. Afterwards, the teacher highlights the main ideas and concepts from the story, capitalising on students' familiarity with narrative genres.

Advance organisers support assimilation of new information

Created by the psychologist David Ausubel (1968), advance organisers provide a conceptual framework for the absorption and retention of new information. They should be presented in advance of a new topic and at a higher level of abstraction than the new learning, providing the general concepts that will act as containers for the storage of new knowledge. There have been many studies into Ausubel's advance organisers, and four types have been identified. Of the four, graphic advance organisers have the largest effect size (see left). Below is an example of a graphic advance organiser created using a framework adapted from Lenz et al's *The Unit Organizer Routine* (1994).

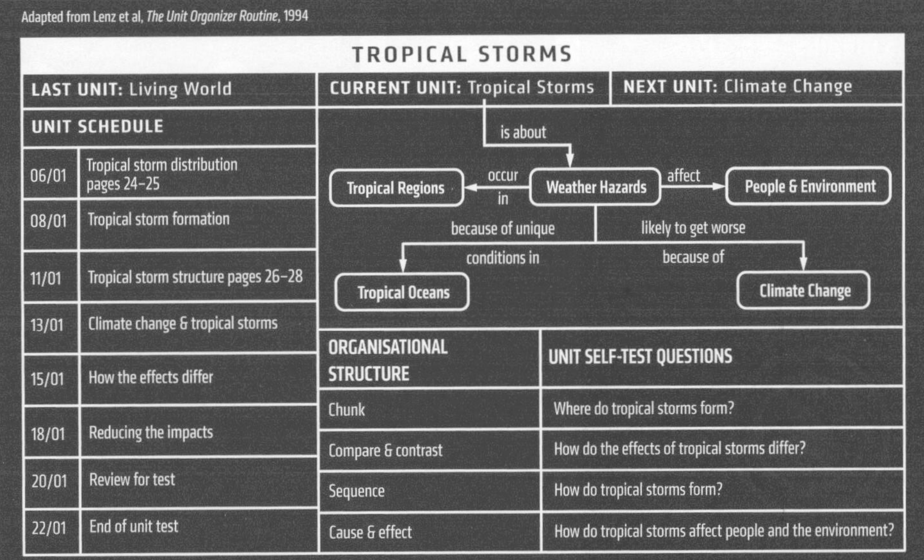

TROPICAL STORMS
LAST UNIT: Living World
CURRENT UNIT: Tropical Storms
NEXT UNIT: Climate Change
UNIT SCHEDULE
06/01 Tropical storm distribution pages 24–25
08/01 Tropical storm formation
11/01 Tropical storm structure pages 26–28
13/01 Climate change & tropical storms
15/01 How the effects differ
18/01 Reducing the impacts
20/01 Review for test
22/01 End of unit test
is about
Weather Hazards
occur in
Tropical Regions
affect
People & Environment
because of unique conditions in
Tropical Oceans
likely to get worse because of
Climate Change
ORGANISATIONAL STRUCTURE
UNIT SELF-TEST QUESTIONS
Chunk
Where do tropical storms form?
Compare & contrast
How do the effects of tropical storms differ?
Sequence
How do tropical storms form?
Cause & effect
How do tropical storms affect people and the environment?

Adapted from Lenz et al, *The Unit Organizer Routine*, 1994

VISUAL INSTRUCTION PLAN

A VIP is a student route map of what they need to know and do at each of its major stages. It is a powerful resource for metacognition and self-regulation.

Fred Jones

If I only had five minutes for a workshop, I'd teach you VIPs – Visual Instructional Plans. One step at a time. A picture for every step.

Jones, 2009

Structure of an empowering VIP

A Flow Spray graphic organiser is unique in its ability to show both process (the Path model) and also content (the Container model). This makes it the perfect vehicle for a visual instruction plan. It is critical to chunk the various steps of the process you want your students to follow into a more manageable number. Past five steps and it begins to become overwhelming. One particular way of arranging the content at each chunked node is to plot the smaller steps above the line of travel, and the necessary facts or strategies to succeed below the line. This gives students the means to identify – and express – where they are and which particular aspect might need addressing.

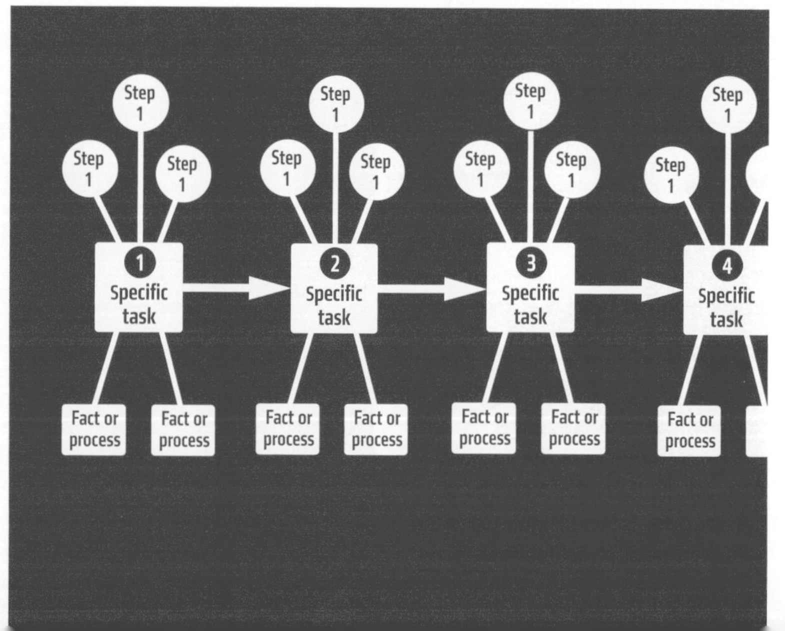

Metacognition and self-regulation model

In order to bring the whole metacognition aspiration down to an operational level, the Education Endowment Foundation model provides a very productive structure. Below, you can see how the teacher might focus a particular combination of metacognitive knowledge and its necessary self-regulation.

Teach students the model

If, as recommended, this model is taught to students, they have a readily accessible method of recognising their responses to the VIP. The combination of both models becomes a type of cognitive radar with which students can navigate their progress and request support at any potential point of difficulty.

Communicate through the model

With teacher and student sharing both models, this joint map of progress allows for more focused and productive conversations. The teacher can request from students a report of their progress, where they are and if they foresee any possible challenges ahead. And students can specify any support needed.

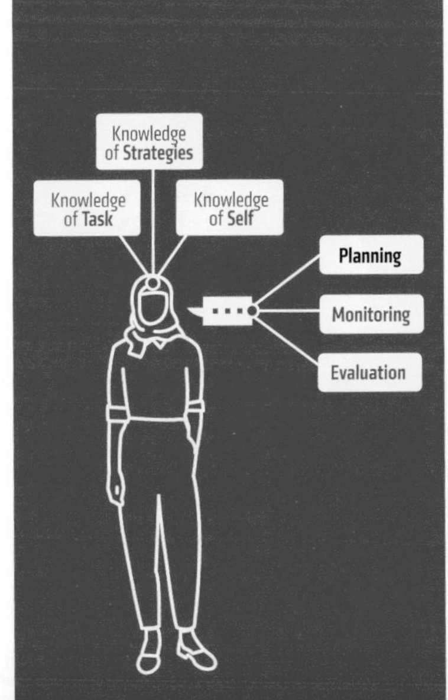

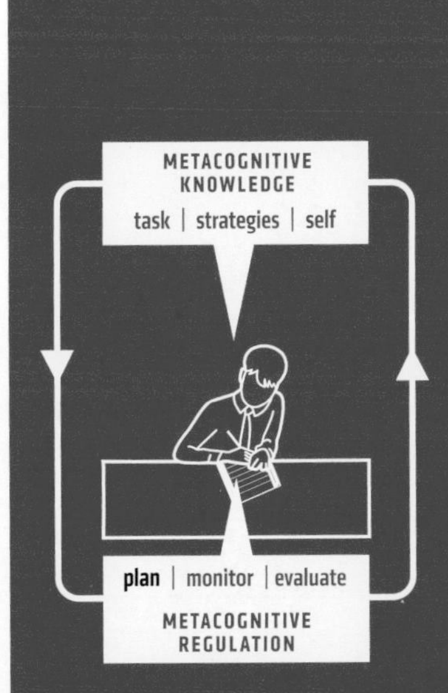

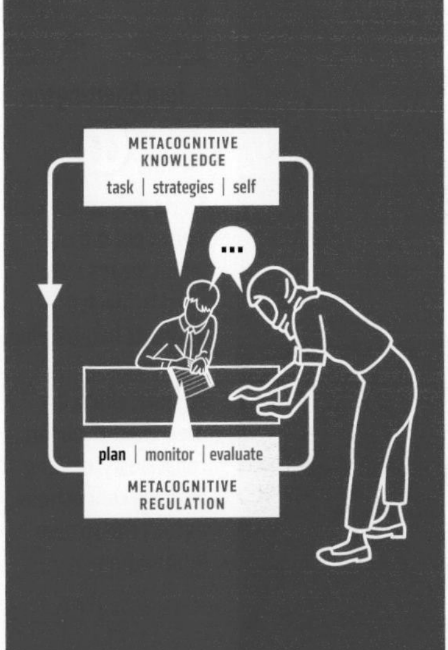

Fred Jones

That is the quickest, simplest thing that accelerates learning, that accelerates understanding – and eliminates helplessness – that I've ever seen.

Jones, 2009

THINK & LINK

Forging associations between concepts and across topics is a powerful method of retrieval practice. Concept mapping enhances this strategy.

Tom Sherrington

These processes need to be generative – which means they need to involve students in retrieving their existing schema, exploring their mental models consciously, making as many connections as they can to new information.

Sherrington, 2020

Direct students to retrieve the ideas and concepts they have learnt during the current topic. Students record what they can remember on the first column of an Affinity Map. If the amount of information an individual can retrieve is be comprehensive, then Think-Pair-Share can stimulate further retrieval.

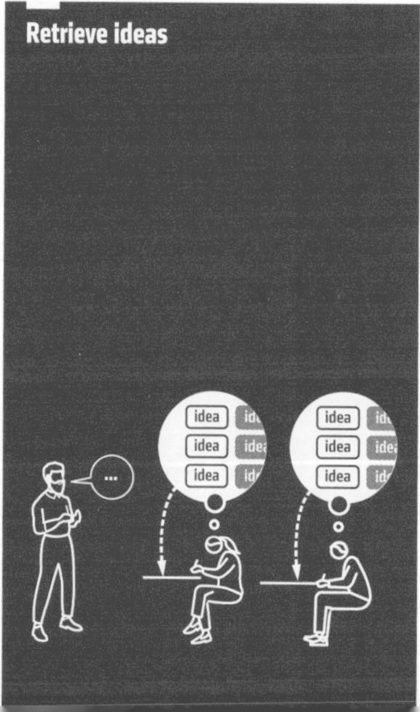

Model to your students how concepts from a previous topic relate to their present learning. Use cold-calling to check they understand the modelling process. Independently, students connect their prior learning to the current topic, recording this in separate columns on the Affinity Map. Limit this to two or three topics.

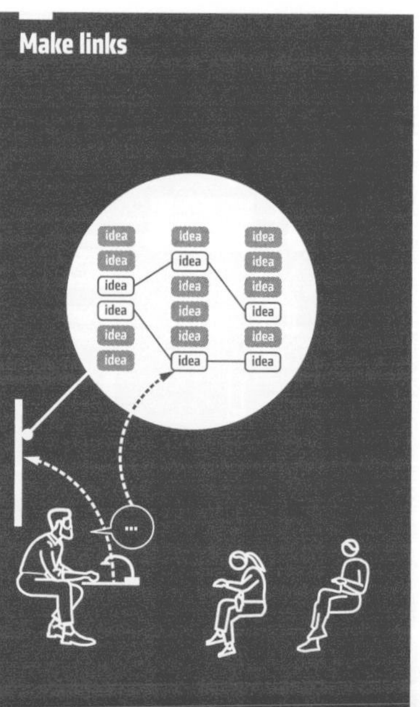

3

To explore the links within and across columns of the Affinity Map, students will need to construct a Concept Map. Demonstrate the first steps of its construction by introducing each element and its connections one by one, each with sufficient explanation. Give students adequate time to complete their Concept Map.

In pairs, students recount the whole visual to their partner. When complete, the pairs switch roles. This provides an opportunity for students to evaluate the accuracy and strength of their map. To encourage deeper thinking, acknowledge those students who made novel connections to what they had previously learnt.

After completing their Concept Maps, students can communicate their understanding through a piece of extended writing. Demonstrate how they can use the organisation of a Concept Map to help structure their paragraphs. Give examples and provide sentence stems to help students write academically.

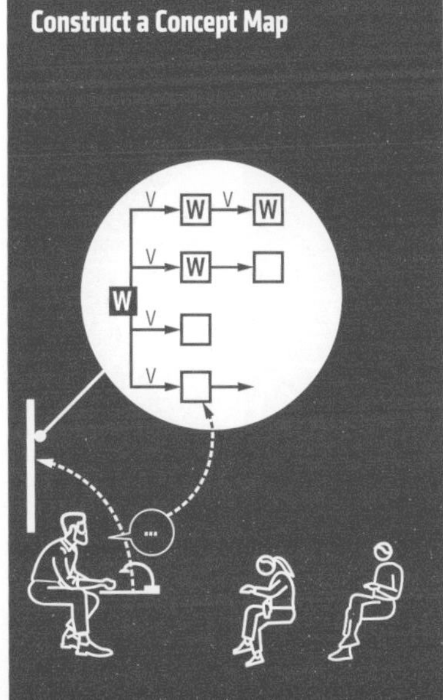

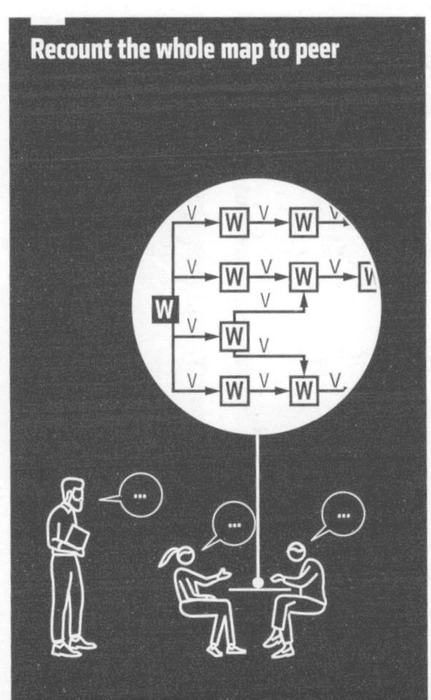

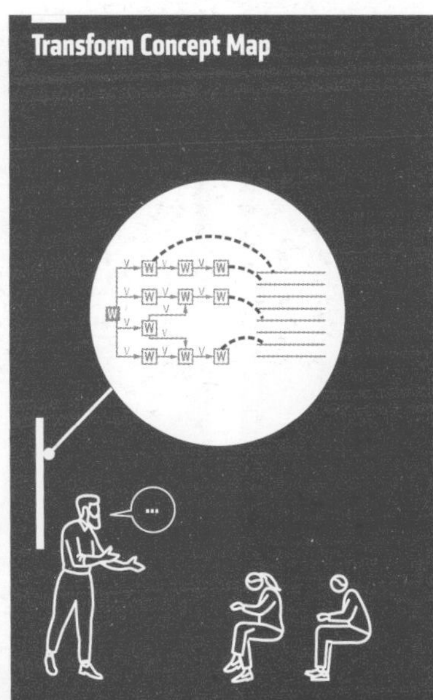

Efrat Furst

I like to define *making meaning* as describing a new concept in terms of other concepts that we already understand, in a way that allows to use it.

Furst, 2019

SPEAKING & LISTENING

Describing something is far easier when you can see it. Word-diagrams provide this concrete, semi-permanent capture of linked ideas.

Attention and meaning-making

Listening to explanations of abstract ideas is difficult, especially if you acknowledge that our interpretations are often inaccurate. As the cognitive psychologist Efrat Furst shows, providing a visual depiction of the abstraction helps focus — and maintain — the attention necessary for understanding.

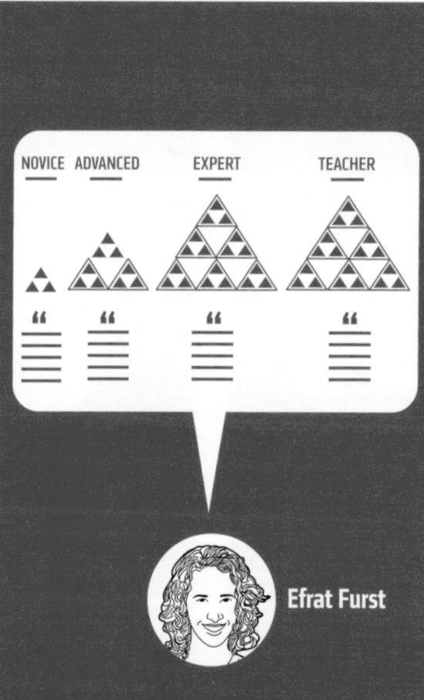

Rehearsal for writing

Transforming a graphic organiser into a verbal narrative requires fluent elaboration and sequencing of the keywords of the diagram — a practical rehearsal for writing. By capturing the transient nature of teacher explanation into visual ideas and concrete connections, the task is made accessible to all students.

Steven Pinker

The metaphor of showing implies that there is something to see. The things in the world the writer is pointing to, then, are concrete.

Pinker, 2014

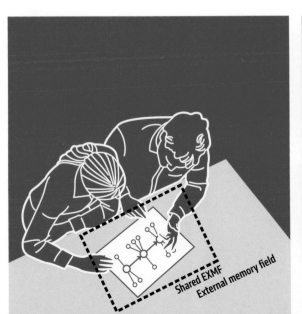

Shared EXMF (external memory field)

When pairs of students use a graphic organiser as a speaking and listening framework, working memory resources can be entirely devoted to creating and listening to their narratives. None is diverted to trying to capture the transient explanations. Any point that needs repeating, elaborating or justifying is easily pointed to. No one gets lost and the dialogue resumes. Always in view, the map is the pair's constant and reliable aide-memoire.

Three-point communication

Contrary to intuition and commonly held notions of effective communication, eye contact – both giving and receiving – can hinder rather than enhance dialogue. It doesn't need a great deal of empathy to realise that the challenge of explaining complex ideas to another person can be personally challenging. Three-point communication is the perfect foil for such anxiety. All communication is directed via the visual. Both sets of eyes remain focused on it, diminishing the personal strain.

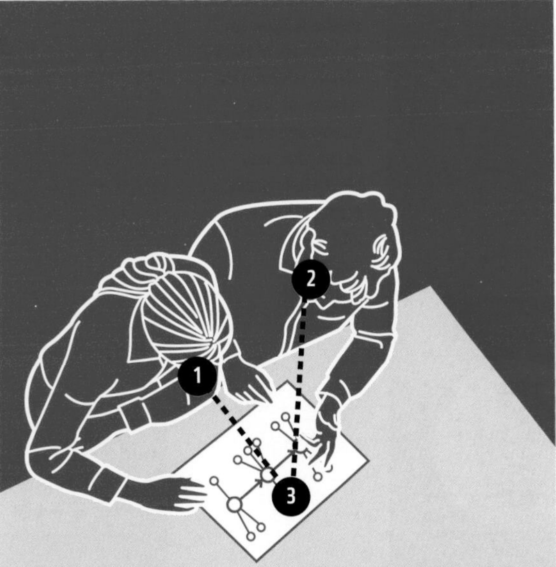

Eric Lunzer

Everyone is looking down and checking what it says. Interactions are therefore object-centred and not person-centred.

Lunzer et al, 1984

VISUAL INSTRUCTION PLAN: WRITING

Jamie Clark explains how to use graphic organisers as visual instruction plans when teaching extended writing.

JAMIE CLARK

Laura Delrose

This study suggests that graphic organisers in conjunction with traditional text-based methods allow for an increase of clarity of new information, relation of new knowledge to prior knowledge, and ability to logically organize thoughts into a coherent sequence.

Delrose, 2011

1

Select the type of writing you want students to produce and break it down into manageable step-by-step instructions. Construct a graphic organiser using containers to establish key headings for the structure. For example, a typical analytical writing framework might include: *topic sentence, evidence, analysis, and purpose*.

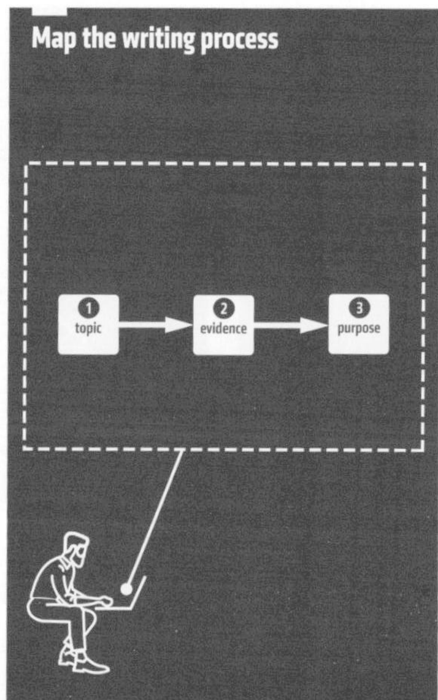

2

Below the headings, add containers with sentence starters to support students' writing. For example: *The language in the text reveals...; The word/phrase ... implies...*

Where necessary, connect arrows to additional containers with *what*, *how* and *why* questions to generate thinking. Create questions like, *What is the writer trying to tell us?*

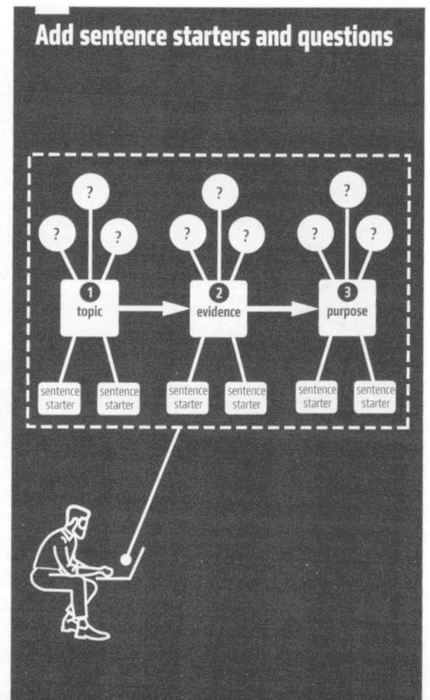

3

To avoid cognitive overload, introduce the graphic organiser to your students by revealing each step section by section. Explain how to apply the steps to the text or topic and check for understanding of the writing conventions required for success. Once students are familiar with the map, distribute hard copies.

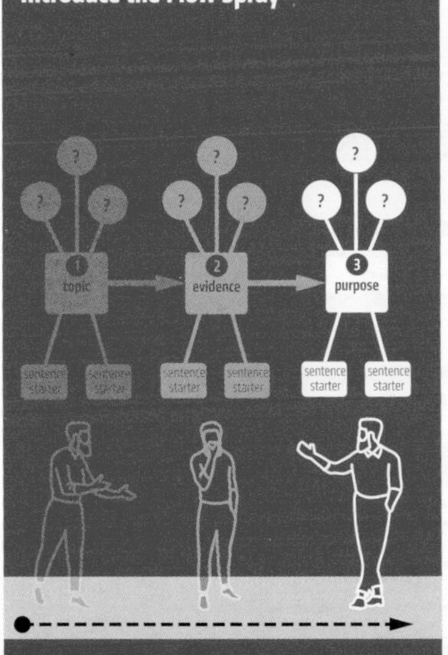

4

Live-model the writing process using the graphic organiser as a guide. If hand-drawn, use a visualiser to make your example visible, and explain your thinking as you write. Direct students to do the writing with you, posing questions to check for understanding. Model how sentence starters from the map can be used or adapted.

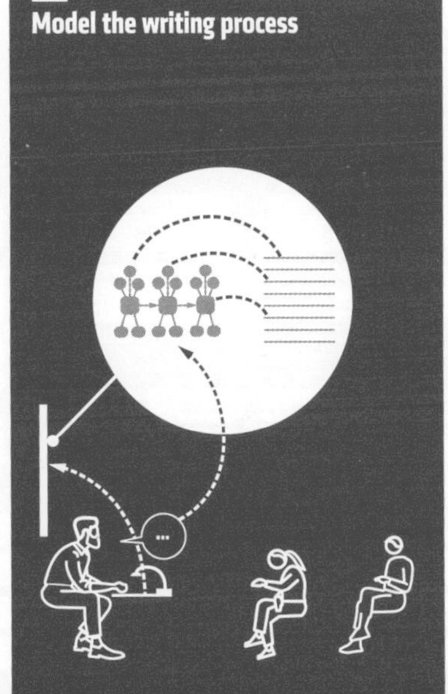

5

As students develop their knowledge of the writing process, the graphic organiser can be gradually removed. Direct students to cover up sections of the map or put it away so it is not in view. Hand over the writing to students to practise independently on a new paragraph or different topic.

Laura Delrose

The results suggest that graphic organizers can be an effective tool used in the writing process to generate sentences and narratives containing more complex structure of syntax and discourse.

Delrose, 2011

On the next spread, Jamie explains the benefits of using a graphic organiser as a visual instruction plan for writing.

VISUAL INSTRUCTION PLAN: WRITING

Jamie Clark explains the benefits of using a graphic organiser as a visual instruction plan when teaching extending writing.

JAMIE CLARK

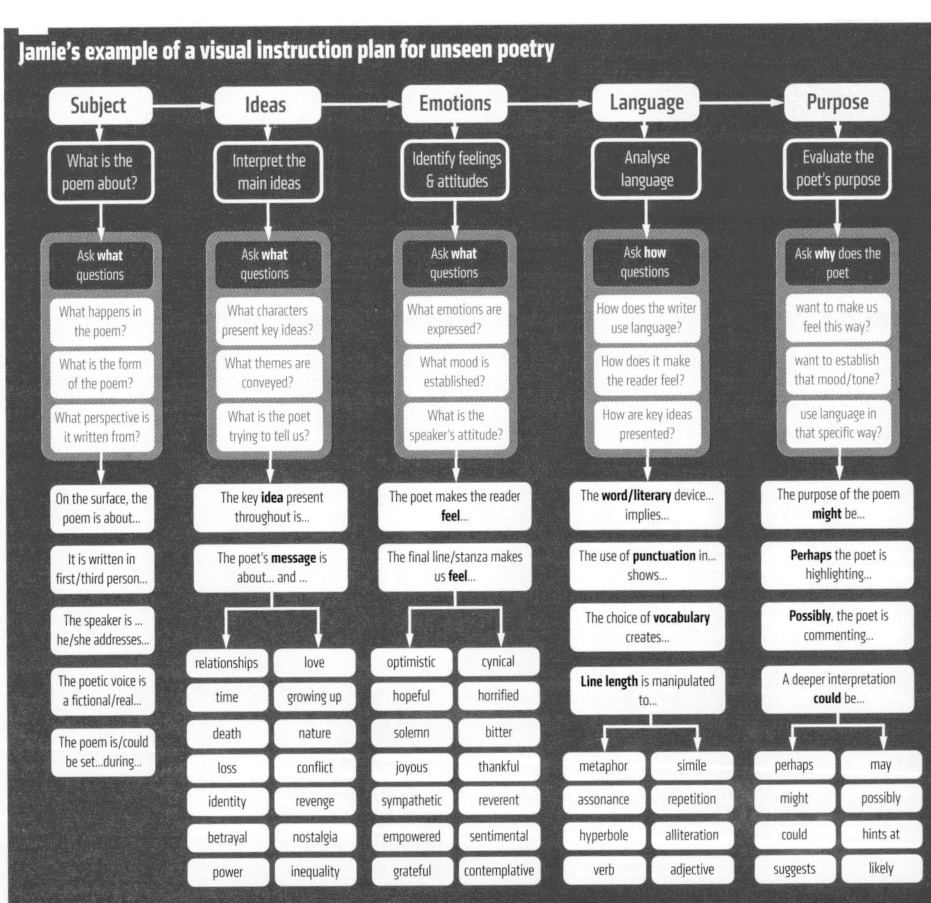

Jamie's example of a visual instruction plan for unseen poetry
Subject
Ideas
Emotions
Language
Purpose
What is the poem about?
Interpret the main ideas
Identify feelings & attitudes
Analyse language
Evaluate the poet's purpose
Ask what questions
What happens in the poem?
What is the form of the poem?
What perspective is it written from?
Ask what questions
What characters present key ideas?
What themes are conveyed?
What is the poet trying to tell us?
Ask what questions
What emotions are expressed?
What mood is established?
What is the speaker's attitude?
Ask how questions
How does the writer use language?
How does it make the reader feel?
How are key ideas presented?
Ask why does the poet
want to make us feel this way?
want to establish that mood/tone?
use language in that specific way?
On the surface, the poem is about...
It is written in first/third person...
The speaker is ... he/she addresses...
The poetic voice is a fictional/real...
The poem is/could be set...during...
The key idea present throughout is...
The poet's message is about... and ...
relationships
love
time
growing up
death
nature
loss
conflict
identity
revenge
betrayal
nostalgia
power
inequality
The poet makes the reader feel...
The final line/stanza makes us feel...
optimistic
cynical
hopeful
horrified
solemn
bitter
joyous
thankful
sympathetic
reverent
empowered
sentimental
grateful
contemplative
The word/literary device... implies...
The use of punctuation in... shows...
The choice of vocabulary creates...
Line length is manipulated to...
metaphor
simile
assonance
repetition
hyperbole
alliteration
verb
adjective
The purpose of the poem might be...
Perhaps the poet is highlighting...
Possibly, the poet is commenting...
A deeper interpretation could be...
perhaps
may
might
possibly
could
hints at
suggests
likely

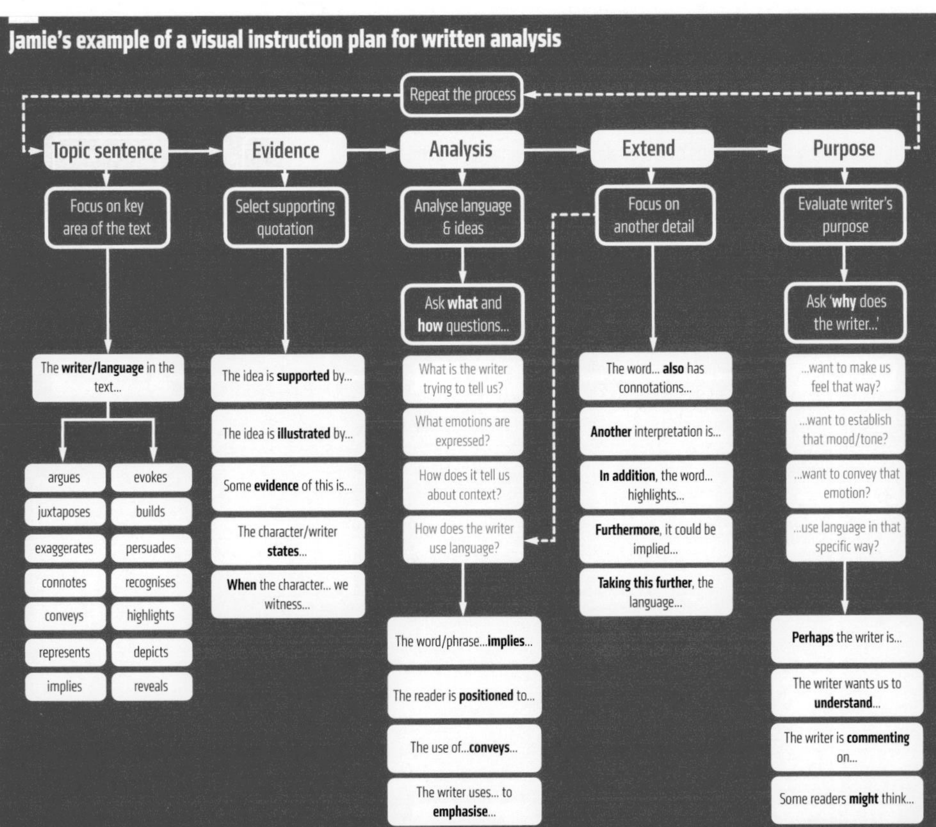

Capturing transient information

Graphic organisers are an effective way of reducing cognitive load as they help to externalise and capture transient information. When teaching analytical writing to English students, Flow Spray maps help my students to externalise the writing process.

The external memory field allows for longer trains of thought

Students engage with their map in their cognitive workspace – the area in front of our eyes that we use to think, which Merlin Donald calls the external memory field. The EXMF aids the working memory by holding content so that students can process and assimilate information without risk of cognitive overload. The maps help optimise intrinsic load by freeing up the working memory so students can incrementally revisit, refine and enhance their ideas. As students practise writing with the map, they add improved thoughts to their visuospatial workspaces, which help them develop more complex thinking and *longer trains of thought*. This results in well-organised and detailed writing with extended points of analysis.

TEACHER VISUAL EXPLANATION

Zeph Bennett explains that a key skill for educators is the ability to communicate complex material in a logical and systematic way – without overloading vital processing capabilities.

ZEPH BENNETT

The dangers of mapshock

Presenting the bigger picture to students is essential for connecting concepts and key themes. But the danger of overwhelming them with too much detail is ever-present. The Concept Map below is a case in point: it shows how the functions of the skeleton are connected to the organs and bones, presenting students with several lines of enquiry. So, the map is only briefly shown, as the six main themes linked by various anatomical parts can feel complex at first sight. The aim is to show the finished puzzle before deconstructing the six interlinking segments.

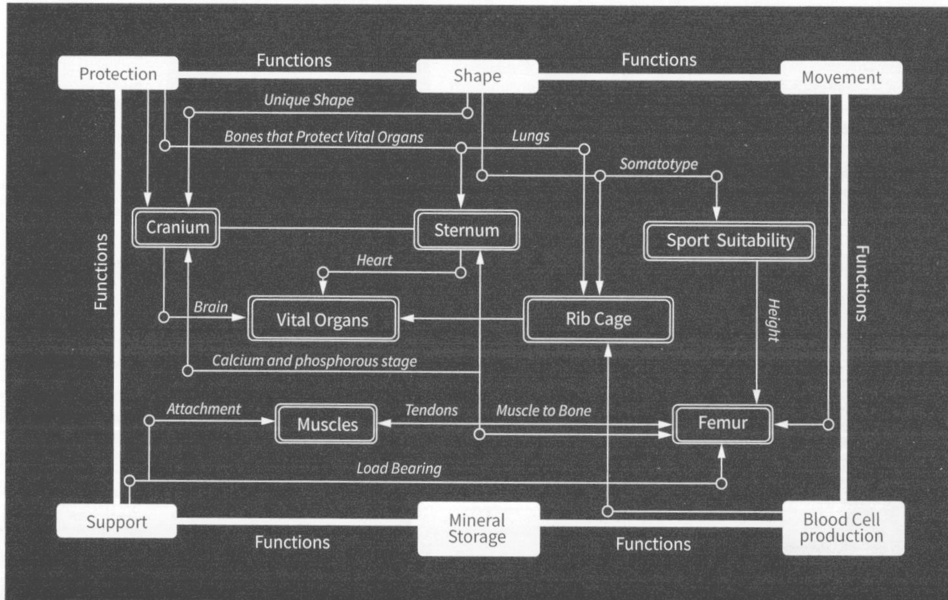

Jeroen van Merriënboer

Splitting up a dynamic presentation into meaningful parts or segments has a positive effect on learning ... [and] learning may be improved if the learner's attention is focused on the critical aspects.

Van Merriënboer & Kester, 2014

Isolate | highlight

The main themes of this Concept Map are the functions of the skeleton around the perimeter of the map. Revealing each function in isolation is necessary for the teacher to investigate how the body uses it effectively. The relevant section *Protection* is highlighted to emphasise its connection to the other functions and components of the full Concept Map. When this is the basis of the lesson, I then emphasise that this will be the sole focus of study.

Extract | enlarge

The next stage of the delivery is to extract the highlighted section out of the bigger picture and enlarge it. Several other opportunities arise at this point, including adding further material, illustrated worked examples and contextual data. Once this process has been repeated for all six functions of the skeleton, each section can then be slotted together and the full Concept Map revealed again – with the intention that students will have encoded the concreted connection between concepts.

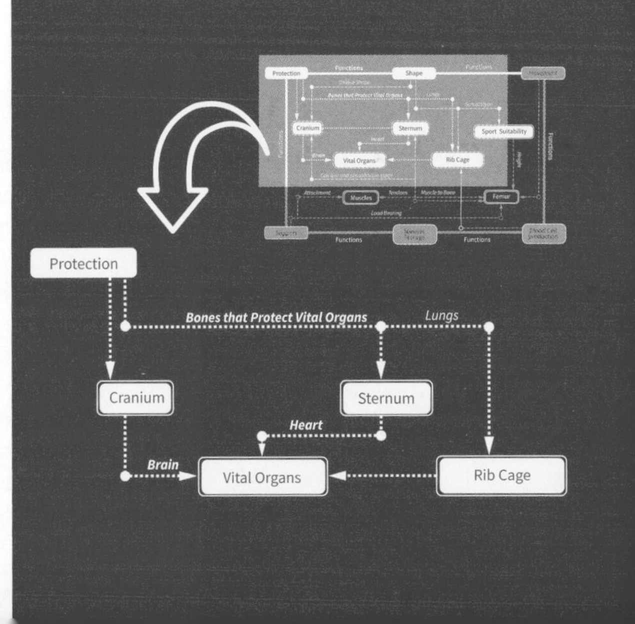

KERNEL SENTENCES 1

Extract more value from a knowledge organiser and create meaningful links during note-taking. Kernel sentences are a halfway house between isolated facts and richly connected knowledge structures.

STRUCTURE	CLARITY	MEANING-MAKING
KNOWLEDGE ORGANISER	DISCRETE UNITS OF INFORMATION – EASY TO REMEMBER.	DISCONNECTED WITH NO MEANING.
KERNEL SENTENCES	PITHY SENTENCES, RETRIEVED THROUGH REHEARSAL.	CONNECTED, REVEALING MEANING.
GRAPHIC ORGANISER	TOO MANY CONNECTIONS CAN CAUSE MAPSHOCK.	COMPLEX ORGANISER REDUCES THE CHANCES OF MEANING-MAKING.

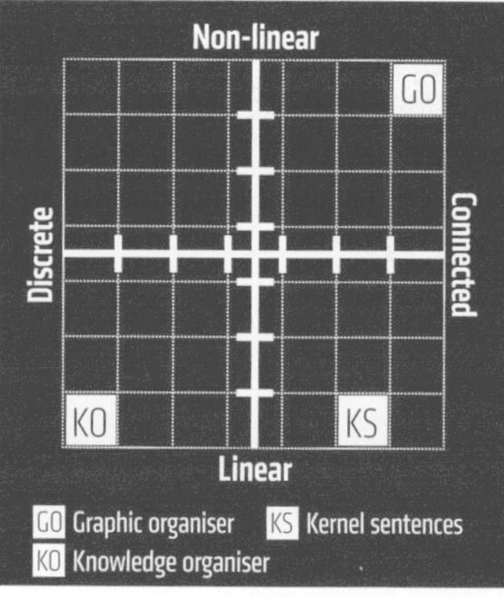

Knowledge organisers are a useful aide

Since their inception, knowledge organisers have grown in popularity. When used effectively, they can assist during retrieval practice and act as a useful aide-memoire for teachers and students. There is no denying their utility in the classroom and we want to avoid the misconception that this is a battle between knowledge and graphic organisers. But knowledge organisers have limits. Knowledge organisers contain discrete unitary items with no propositions and no links between ideas/concepts – they are lists.

Mary Myatt

Knowledge organisers are not good at showing relationships and hierarchies.

Myatt, 2021

Knowledge organisers don't reveal meaning

While lists can be useful for simple recall, they are the lowest organisation structure, says the cognitive scientist Frederick Reif. To a novice, each item on a knowledge organiser stands alone. As such, the user struggles to make meaning of the content. Meaning-making requires ideas to be grouped, ordered and sequenced into a coherent structure.

> Cognitive psychology has shown that the mind best understands facts when they are woven into a conceptual fabric, such as a narrative, mental map, or intuitive theory. Disconnected facts in the mind are like unlinked pages on the Web: they might as well not exist.
>
> Steven Pinker, 2005

Graphic organisers can be complex

Graphic organisers increase the chances of meaning-making as they require the linking of ideas. But if the network of connections becomes complex or too voluminous, the reader might suffer from mapshock.

Kernel sentences provide meaning

Kernel sentences are a midpoint between knowledge organisers and graphic organisers. Kernel sentences are pithy enough to be recalled readily and are easily understood. Both teachers and students can create kernel sentences, but students would benefit from being taught how to write parsimoniously – how to be frugal with words. Follow our four-step process (right) to create kernel sentences with your students.

Constructing kernel sentences

1 Identify 4-5 discrete facts/ideas

From a knowledge organiser, select 4-5 facts/ideas that you would like your students to connect in a meaningful manner.

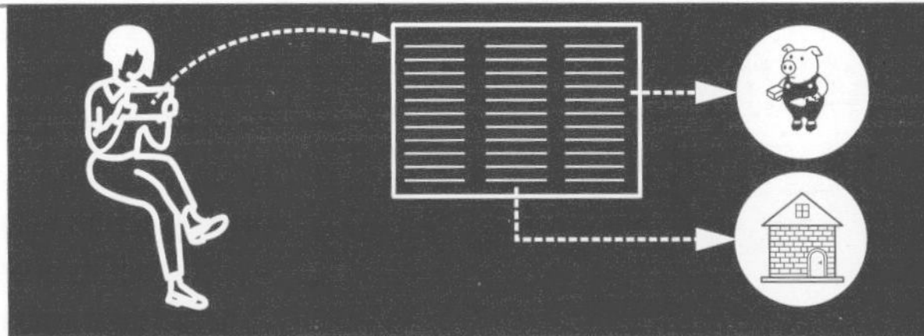

2 Create pithy sentences

For each selected idea/concept, the teacher creates memorable sentences. Replace sophisticated language with everyday language that is easier to recall.

- The 3rd pig was brave.
- The brick house gives safety.
- The wolf was captured.
- The wolf was beaten.

3 Introduce kernel sentences

Introduce each sentence, one at a time. In pairs, students rehearse each sentence until they can recite each by heart. Present each sentence as an individual word-diagram.

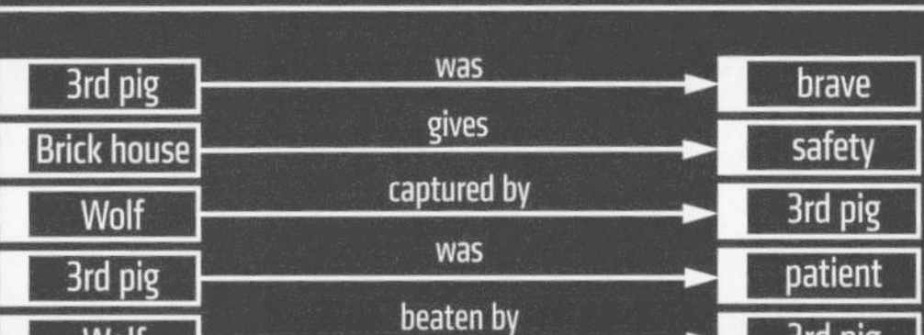

4 Connect kernel sentences

Direct students to identify connections between isolated sentences – use Think-Pair-Share to increase chances of success. The teacher and students create a word-diagram of connected kernel sentences.

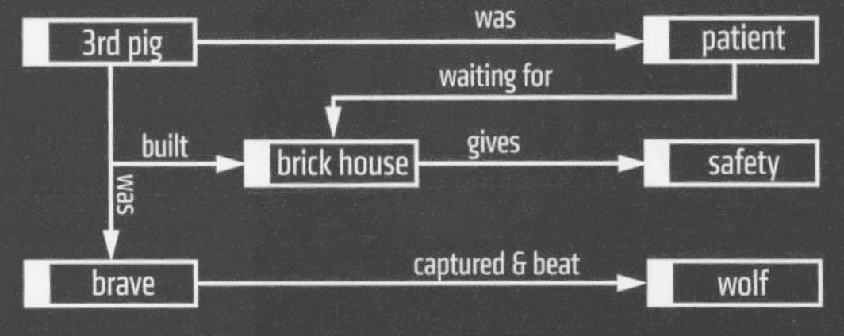

KERNEL SENTENCES 2

Kat Howard explains how kernel sentences help her students connect concepts and, as a result, make meaning.

KAT HOWARD

Connecting knowledge

In the same way that we cannot compose for an orchestra without the hope of musical synchrony, or design narrative tapestry without weaving together warp and weft, we cannot support students to learn knowledge if we do not aid them in making cohesive sense of knowledge within English. Terminology, plot and inference can all become fragmented moments that, if left unattended, provide students with nothing more than shards of disconnected information that lack meaning. Finding sense and sequence is fundamental to learning. It enables students to make connections and recognise recurrence from one moment to the next; to recognise that characters throughout time display similar human attributes that explain the motivations behind their behaviour; to recognise that concepts reoccur and patterns can be traced across the history of literature.

Kernel sentences help make meaning

Kernel sentences act as a springboard for these connections. By drawing student attention to a distilled comprehension of character, plot, themes and considerations, only then can we share connections and relationships between one component of knowledge and the next. Far from being a dilution or disregard for the subject itself, kernel sentences helped me to showcase the power of writing parsimoniously with students. Through careful selection of what is valuable – not just in its isolated form, but in relation to the wider scope of this piece of literature, and even literature a whole – students are liberated to weave together the component parts.

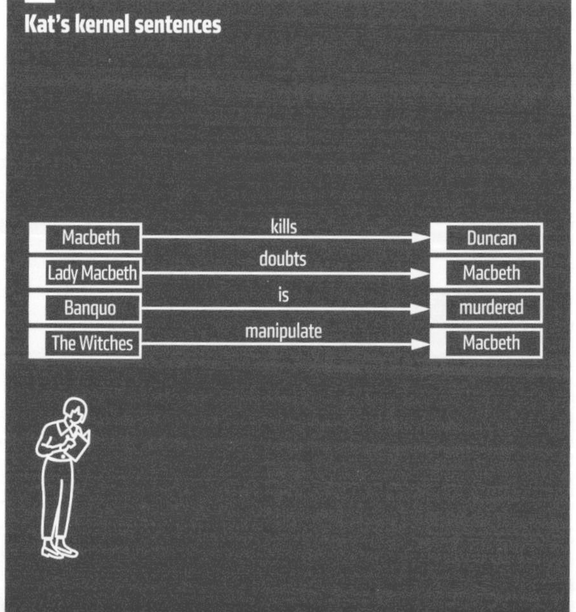

Connecting kernel sentences

I began by plotting out core statements of complete concision, but not at the expense of the text: I pared back to incisive verb use, exposing overarching concepts of the literature itself. Doubt is central to the motivations and choices that characters display in *Macbeth*, and so it made sense to explore the way in which such an idea is webbed across the text through use of character. This presence of doubt evolves into a deep-rooted sense of paranoia, spurring Macbeth to become a victim of his own insecurity. The way in which characters begin to betray or mistrust one another is essential to grasping a deepened understanding of the events that in turn form the narrative behind Macbeth's demise. Lady Macbeth's paranoia eats at her as she realises her husband begins to withhold information from her. The Witches' orchestration of doubt in *Macbeth* is a key catalyst for the actions of others. The kernel sentences act as an interwoven presentation of such knowledge.

Far from being a dilution or disregard for the subject itself, kernel sentences helped me to showcase the power of writing.

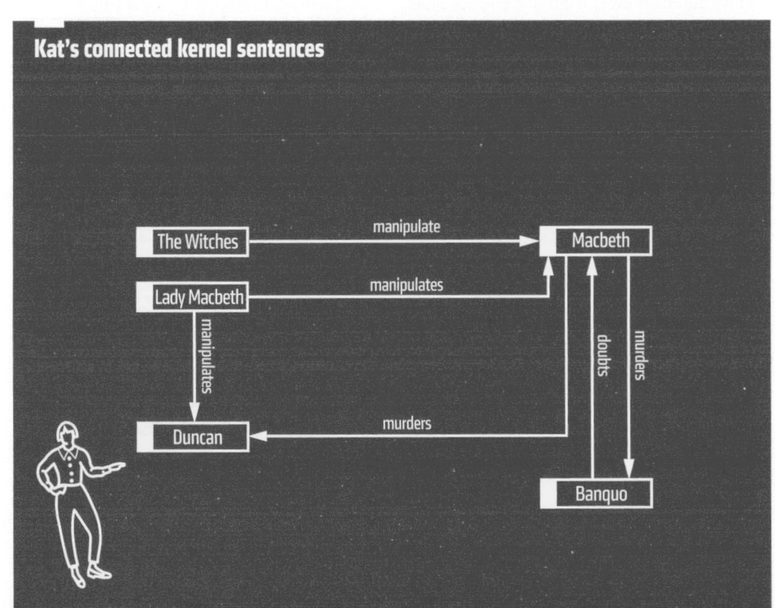

Kernel sentences support spaced retrieval

Over time, the kernel sentences act as a vehicle for demonstrating the recurrence of concepts that present themselves to us within literature: the emergence of power in nature when studying Romanticism is reformed and represented when we come to study the exploitation of power in *Jekyll and Hyde*, or the revolt of power in *Animal Farm*, perhaps. Making these moments explicit enables us to actualise this cohesion for students as they progress through their curriculum journey.

Kernel sentences act as a vehicle for demonstrating the recurrence of concepts that present themselves to us within literature.

MULTIPLE CHOICE QUIZ MAPS 1

Kate Jones explains that word-diagrams are another format to enrich a teacher's retrieval practice repertoire where connections can add meaning to the recall.

KATE JONES

Yana Weinstein

Have students ... create a concept map from memory, draw a diagram from memory.

Weinstein & Sumeracki, 2018

MCQ maps are recognition-based

Multiple-choice questions (MCQs) can be an engaging and workload-friendly retrieval practice task. Their effectiveness depends on the question design and layout. As this is a form of recognition, students identify and select the answer – in contrast to more challenging and effortful free recall. It is vital that we don't shy away from challenge or dilute the act of retrieval. Strike a balance between retrieval success and challenge. An excellent way to do that with MCQs is to combine them with a graphic organiser.

The creation process

Combine MCQs with GOs acting as a cue. This pairing provides opportunities to check for understanding as well as promoting powerful retrieval practice. Create a GO template for the content to be learned. Share the GO with students before the quiz. Or reveal an incomplete GO for students to select the correct answers in order to see the final finished GO. MCQs should focus on core knowledge – as will the GO. Create a duplicate of the GO and select the options to remove (i.e. the answers).

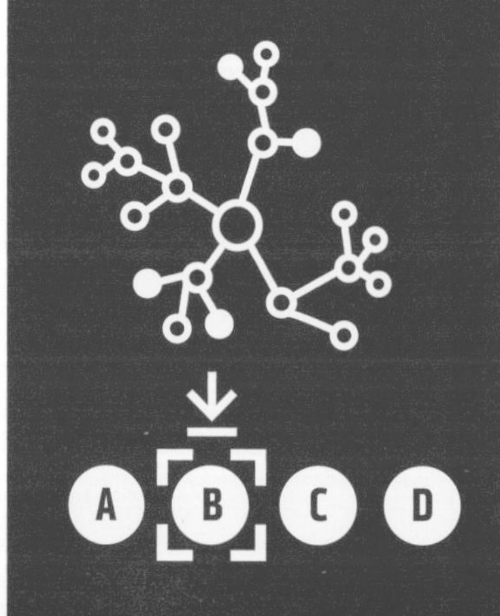

Design principles

The level of challenge can vary according to how much content is removed and how much information is exposed to students. Design MCQs that unearth the missing keywords or concepts on the GO. Effective and desirably difficult MCQs force students to engage with all the options. Keep the number of possible answers to three to four. It's essential that each of the options is a plausible distractor. Aim to provide a link between the options and the correct answers from the GO.

Adapting the map

Multiple sections can be removed from the GO. All the factors removed could form the plausible distractors. That way, if students are able to memorise the original GO – if they have viewed this in advance – then they will also need to be able to recall precise subject knowledge to answer the question carefully. Adapting the MCQ map in this way helps reveal further possibilities. Exploring the relationship between known and targeted knowledge is at the heart of moving from straight retrieval to retrieval and connecting.

Extension ideas

The plausible distractors that link to other key elements of the GO increase the level of challenge. They also allow opportunities for students to elaborate and make connections between linked factors and pieces of information. The MCQ with the GO can be further extended by encouraging students to explain why the answer they selected is correct or why the other answers are incorrect. They can even create MCQs where the incorrect answers become correct.

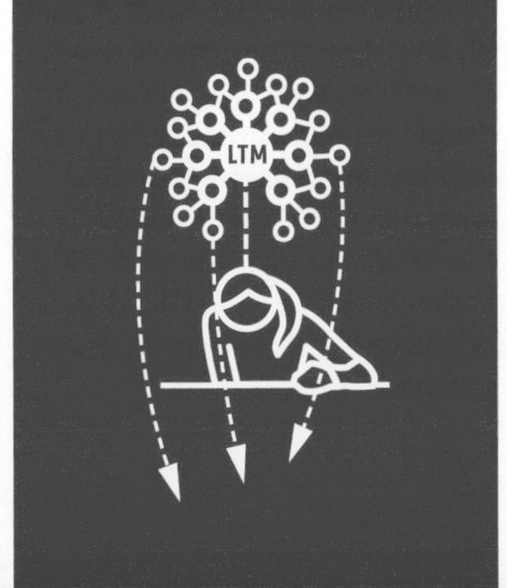

Megan Sumeracki

Learning differences between different retrieval practice formats tend to be small.

Weinstein & Sumeracki, 2018

MULTIPLE CHOICE QUIZ MAPS 2

Bring together multiple-choice questions and graphic organisers to make meaningful associations during retrieval practice.

Blake Harvard

Getting students in the habit of taking a closer look at all responses provided for a multiple-choice question not only may lead to fewer careless mistakes, but can also genuinely change how students cognitively approach these questions.

Harvard, 2018

GOs and MCQs unite for meaningful retrieval practice

Pairing GOs with multiple-choice questions can prove mutually beneficial and afford students meaningful retrieval practice opportunities. Retrieval practice develops students' fluency and accuracy in retrieving knowledge from long-term memory. To maximise the potential of retrieval practice for boosting long-term memory, students must experience making connections between ideas and concepts. While we recognise the utility of quizzing, in a quiz, students answer questions and potentially never make connections between the answers they have given. Pairing MCQs with GOs allows students to see connections and where each answer fits within the knowledge structure. You might also consider this pairing when directing your students to complete complex GOs, as MCQs can help students organise ideas in a more timely manner. MCQs are also a quick strategy for additional checking for understanding, especially if using *show me* boards to check answers.

Create a GO template for the content your students are learning. Identify which keywords and concepts you want your students to engage with and remove these words and concepts from the GO template. When pairing MCQs with GOs for retrieval practice, prime your students, using what Shea (2021) describes as "*warm reactivation*". For example, you might ask your students: *Do you like Winston Churchill?* There is no right or wrong answer to this question, but the memory cells containing information about Winston Churchill would be reactivated.

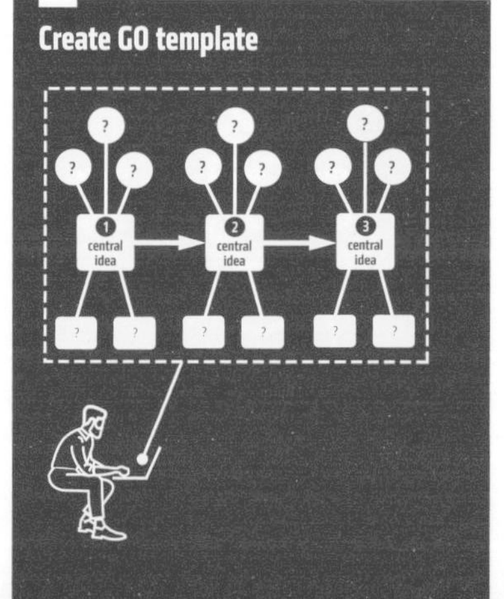

2

Design MCQs that help students identify the missing concepts and keywords on their GO template. Meaningful MCQs force students to engage with all the options. Therefore, keep the number of possible answers to three or four. Make each of the options plausible. Use this as an opportunity to identify any misconceptions students might have by including these as potential answers.

Explore how you might extract more value from your MCQs. Use Think-Pair-Share and cold-calling, asking your students to justify their selections. Consider including more than one correct answer and directing your students to select the *best* correct answer. Again, ask them to articulate their response. Explore having your students engage with incorrect options. For example, you might ask them to design a question or kernel sentence in which an incorrect answer becomes a correct answer.

With the GO complete, have your students use it. This could be via a peer-on-peer explanation. You might direct your students to quiz one another or use their organiser for an extended piece of writing. However your students use their GO, be sure to model the first steps and routinely check for understanding.

Blake Harvard

Providing these sorts of tasks for learners not only leads to more desirable difficulties, but also assists with creating more healthy study habits.

Harvard, 2018

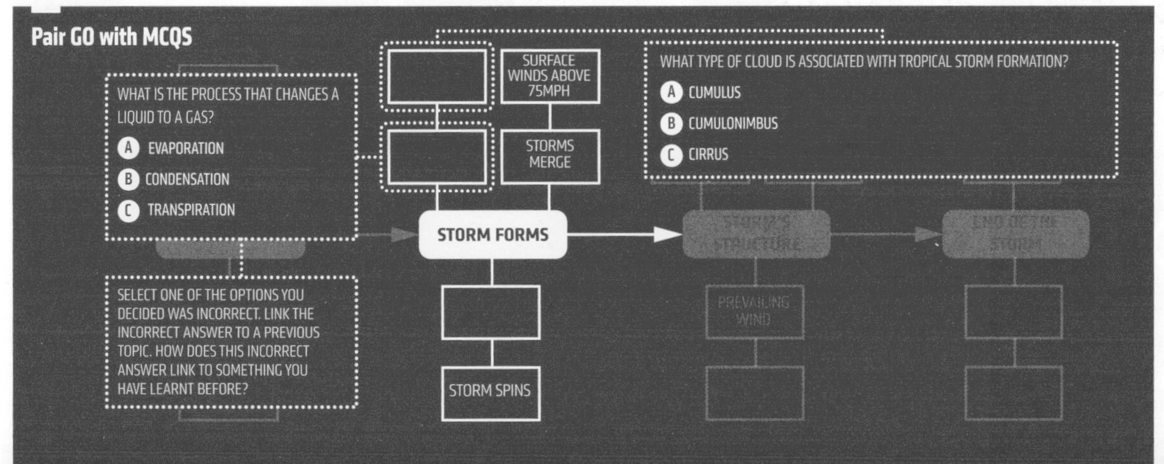
Pair GO with MCQS
WHAT IS THE PROCESS THAT CHANGES A LIQUID TO A GAS?
A EVAPORATION
B CONDENSATION
C TRANSPIRATION
SELECT ONE OF THE OPTIONS YOU DECIDED WAS INCORRECT. LINK THE INCORRECT ANSWER TO A PREVIOUS TOPIC. HOW DOES THIS INCORRECT ANSWER LINK TO SOMETHING YOU HAVE LEARNT BEFORE?
SURFACE WINDS ABOVE 75MPH
STORMS MERGE
STORM FORMS
STORM SPINS
WHAT TYPE OF CLOUD IS ASSOCIATED WITH TROPICAL STORM FORMATION?
A CUMULUS
B CUMULONIMBUS
C CIRRUS
STORM'S STRUCTURE
END OF THE STORM
PREVAILING WIND

RECOUNT & REDRAW

Gesture is a memory-free strategy that, combined with graphic organisers, offers an enhanced retrieval practice strategy.

Fred Paas

Gesture and object manipulation are sensorimotor experiences that could be considered as sources of biologically primary information and have been shown to assist in the acquisition of biologically secondary information.

Paas & Sweller, 2012

Draw a graphic organiser one branch at a time. As you construct it, explain your thinking regarding its connections and hierarchy. When the branch, or part, of the diagram is complete, direct your students to copy it into their books.

Direct students to work in pairs, one explaining the diagram to the other. Establish a rule that each keyword on the visual has to be explained with a minimum of two, or three, full sentences. Pairs swap roles, with the explainer becoming the listener and vice versa.

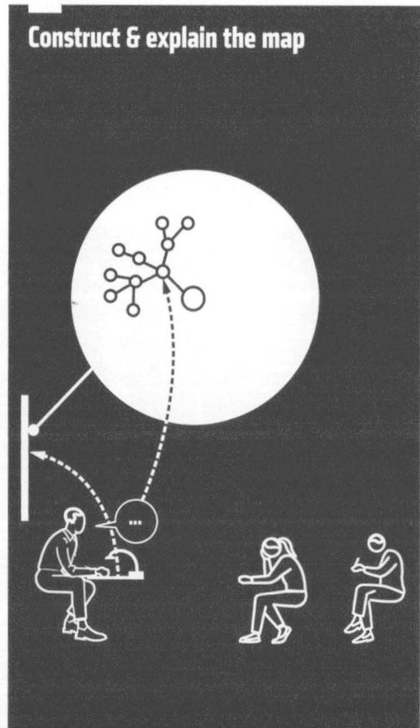

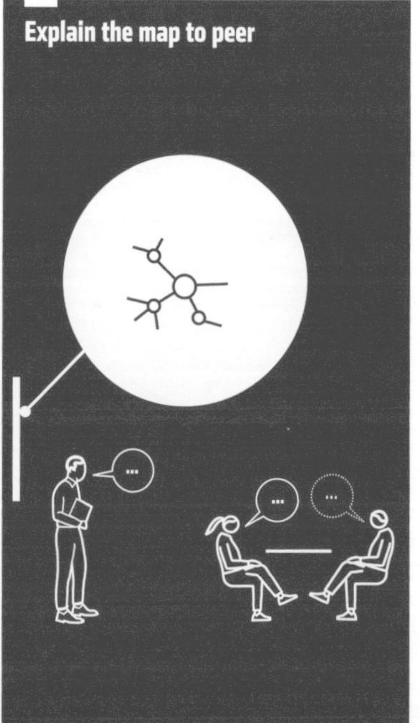

3

Continue to explain the topic at hand, its underlying structure and how it is arranged spatially in the diagram. Repeat the process where the students copy the branch and explain it back to their peer, until the whole diagram is complete.

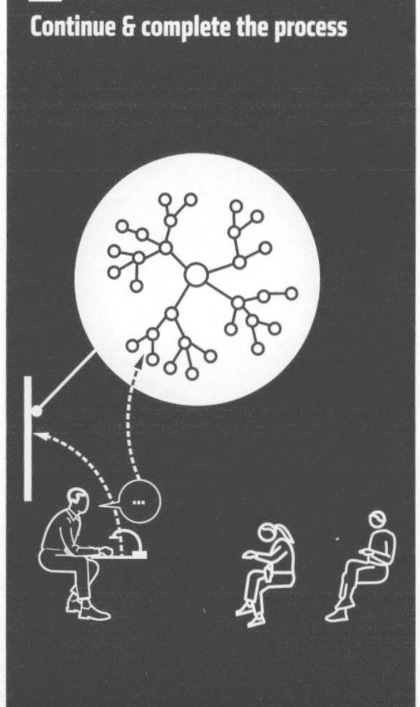

4

In pairs, students recount the whole visual to their partner. When complete, the pairs switch roles. The listener can ask questions – the *How?* and *Why?* of elaborative interrogation. But before they start, direct the students to trace the line with their index finger as they elaborate on the keywords of a particular part.

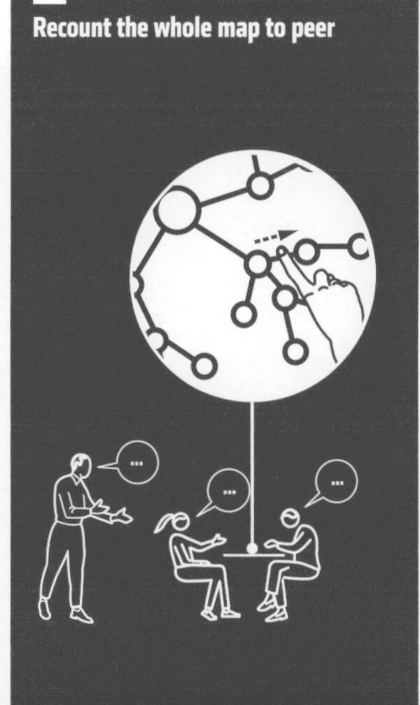

Ensure all copies of the map – yours and theirs – are put away, not in view. Direct the students to work alone and redraw the map completely from memory. Suggest they can attempt to replay their explanations in their minds, as well as tracing their index finger on the paper, to stimulate recall.

Redraw the map from memory

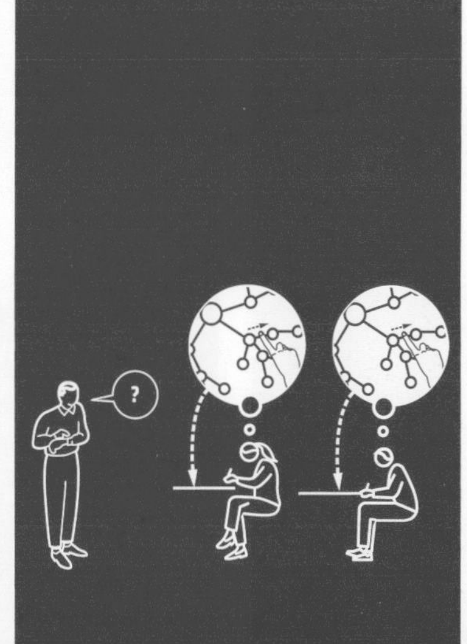

John Sweller

Both gesturing and object manipulation may be very old, very well-developed skills that are acquired easily and can be used with a minimal working memory load.

Paas & Sweller, 2012

SCAFFOLDING GRAPHIC ORGANISERS

Visual scaffolds introduce students to structural analysis of text and can be a powerful aid to learning if used in the service of other approaches.

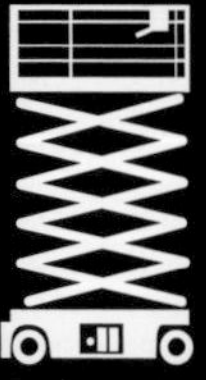

Introducing graphic organisers

Graphic organisers are visual metaphors that reveal the underlying structure of the knowledge they represent. The language of the text being studied, the question being asked and the nature of the task govern which organiser to use. It is all in the language. Explain to your students that there are associate words that signal which organiser to use. When David helped his daughter, aged 9, with her marine mammal project, they analysed the language of the task. Maddison's project required her to provide an **overview** of her chosen mammal, including the **characteristics** and **attributes**. When shown a list of associate words for each of the four graphic organiser types, she was able to identify that she would need to use an organiser from the Chunk category.

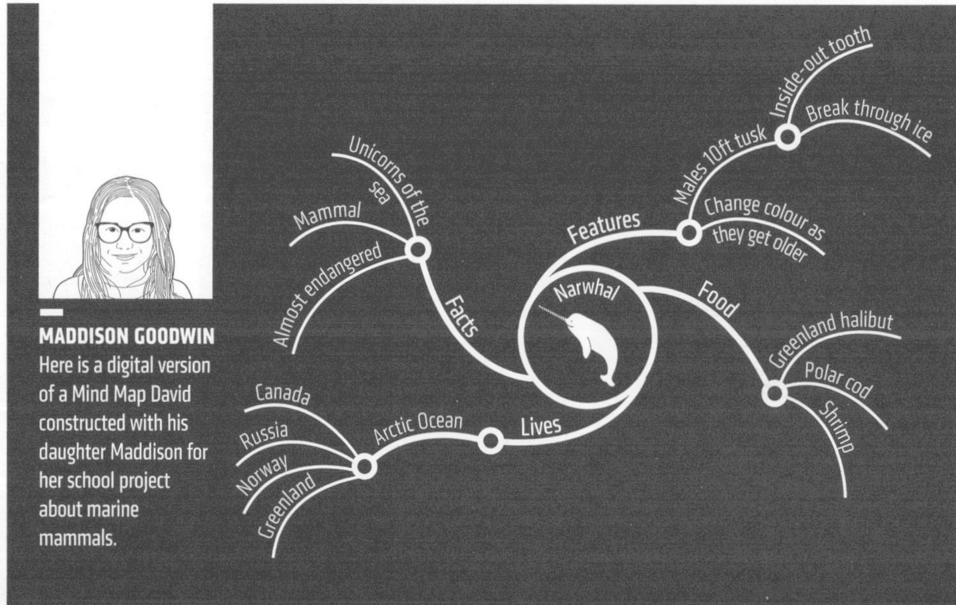

MADDISON GOODWIN

Here is a digital version of a Mind Map David constructed with his daughter Maddison for her school project about marine mammals.

Scaffold graphic organisers

Having students organise knowledge independently takes practice. Your students' learning propensities and their experience of using graphic organisers will determine how much practice and scaffolding they will require. To scaffold the construction of a graphic organiser for your students, create a template. Below is a template David created when helping his daughter to construct her Mind Map. For Maddison, the graphic organiser took less time and was less difficult to complete than it might have been without the template. The result was that Maddison had more time and her mind was free to attend to the final performance – extended writing.

Scaffold the use of graphic organisers

When students are new to using graphic organisers to help with writing tasks, they might also benefit from scaffolding. Use sentence stems or sentence-level practice tasks – like those in Hochman & Wexler's *The Writing Revolution* (2017) – to support your students in transforming non-linear representations into prose. Model to your students how to use the structure of a graphic organiser as a visual instruction plan. David demonstrated to Maddison how the superordinate branches of her Mind Map could be transformed into paragraphs.

Maddison's Mind Map template

Narwhal
Features
Males 10ft tusk
Inside-out tooth
Break through ice
Change colour as they get older
Facts
Food
Lives

Logan Fiorella & Richard Mayer

...sometimes students may need some guidance – such as being given a list of the main concepts (i.e., the nodes), a list of the relationships (i.e., the lines), or even a partially completed map.

Fiorella & Mayer, 2015

GRAPHIC ORGANISER TEMPLATES

Using templates can save you time and reduce the difficulty of constructing a graphic organiser. They can help students be more efficient tool users.

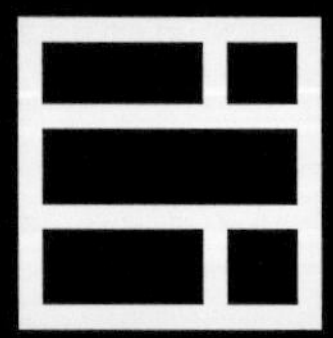

The arguments for and against template GOs

The argument against preformed GOs, according to David Hyerle (1996), is that they are no more than mindless activity sheets. Instead, he champions the use of *visual tools* that are constructed anew by teacher or student. Evidence, however, points in the other direction. Fiorella & Mayer's work (2015) shows both types are effective but that preformed GOs are more so. Less time is spent in learning how to construct them and more time devoted to the structural analysis of the text in mind.

Eric Lunzer

What is true is that analytic tasks are quite close to what well-trained readers do spontaneously when trying to come to terms with a difficult stretch of text.

Lunzer & Gardner, 1984

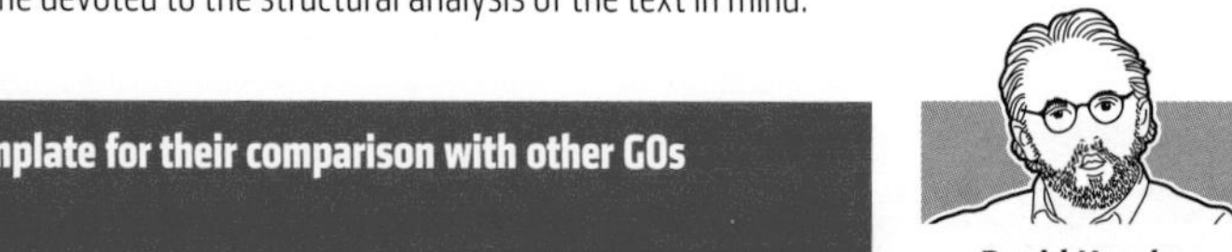

A GO template for their comparison with other GOs

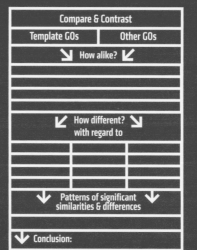

Compare & Contrast		
Template GOs		Other GOs
↘ How alike? ↙		
↙ How different? ↘ with regard to		
↓ Patterns of significant similarities & differences ↓		
↓ Conclusion:		

David Hyerle

Unfortunately, the worst-case scenario for the use of *graphic organisers* ... is when students repetitively use preformed organization charts as merely *fill-in* boxes on activity sheets.

Hyerle, 1996

Types of GO templates

Unsurprisingly, the types of preformed GOs mirror the types outlined on page 50. There are, though, more distinctions within each category. In Swartz & Parks' 500+ A4 pages of templates (1994), there are 16 different sorts, including: finding reasons and conclusions | generating possibilities | prediction | analogies.

The DARTS story

Lunzer & Gardner's 1980s DARTS project (*directed activity related to text*) grew out of studies on the effective use of reading. Diagrams and their tasks were based on three features: text-based lessons are part of the curriculum | the notion that there are text types | pupil discussion is critical to understanding.

Towards a synthesis

There has been much snootiness towards preformed GOs. Yet, when used as a resource that supports other strategies, such templates can be very time-efficient, in forcing students to expose and develop their thinking without devoting time to learning how to construct their own GO. Evidence supports this approach.

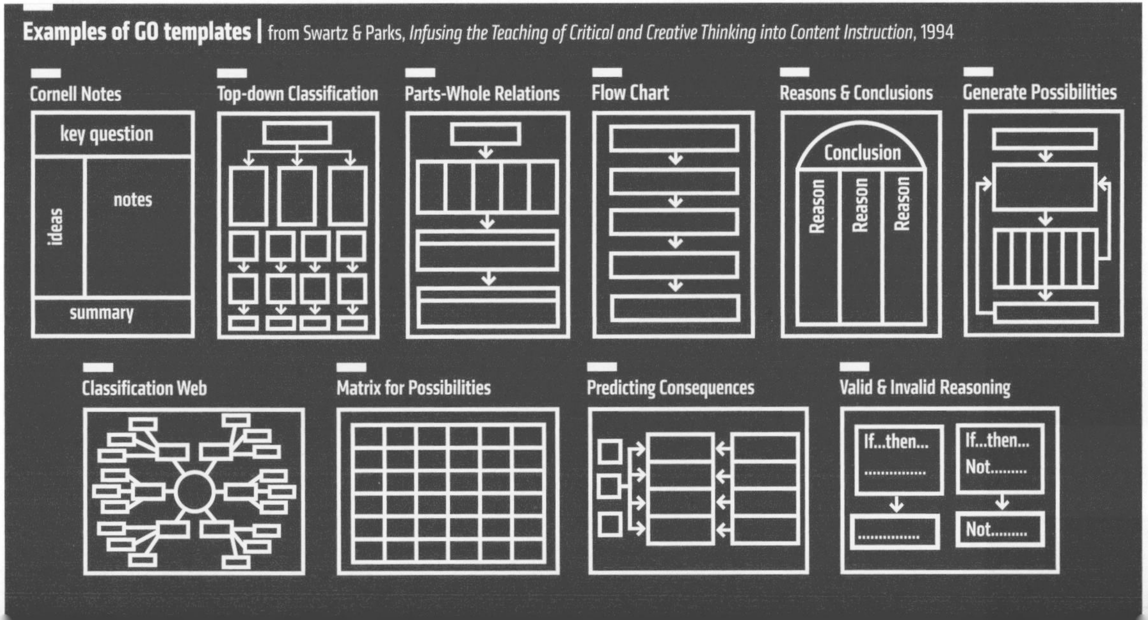

Examples of GO templates | from Swartz & Parks, *Infusing the Teaching of Critical and Creative Thinking into Content Instruction*, 1994

Cornell Notes
key question
ideas
notes
summary

Top-down Classification

Parts-Whole Relations

Flow Chart

Reasons & Conclusions
Conclusion
Reason
Reason
Reason

Generate Possibilities

Classification Web

Matrix for Possibilities

Predicting Consequences

Valid & Invalid Reasoning
If...then...
....
If...then...
Not.........
....
Not.........

Logan Fiorella

The mapping group [using graphic organiser templates] outperformed the control group on learning outcomes post tests, yielding a median effect size of d=1.07.

Fiorella & Mayer, 2015

REMOTE LEARNING

While learning remotely, provide your students with tools to aid their reading and writing.

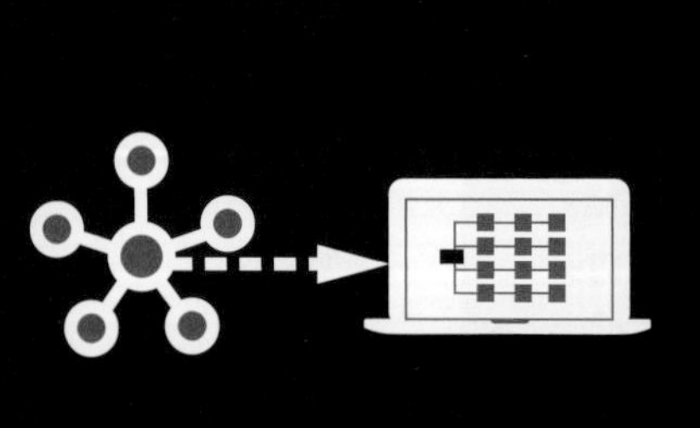

Tom Sherrington

Google Slides... Easy to see each student's writing and scan between them during the lesson. Easy to link to tasks, resources, create templates.

Sherrington, 2021

In Google Slides, create the graphic organiser you want your students to complete. Present each idea and concept by inserting individual text boxes. For the text box border, use a consistent colour and a solid line. To connect each text box, use the elbow connectors or arrows. For Concept Maps and Relations Diagrams, add a verb to each link. Type the verb on each line, making sure the text box border colour is transparent.

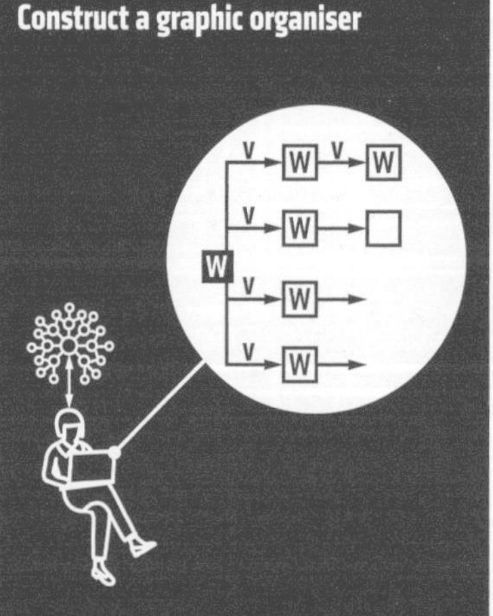

Duplicate the slide containing the completed graphic organiser. Hold down the shift key and select the text boxes you want your students to be able to arrange. Change the colour of the text to white. With the text boxes still highlighted, change their borders to dashed. Select *file* and download the slide as a PNG. Insert a new slide. Right-click anywhere on the new slide and select *change background*. Insert the PNG you have just saved to complete your graphic organiser template.

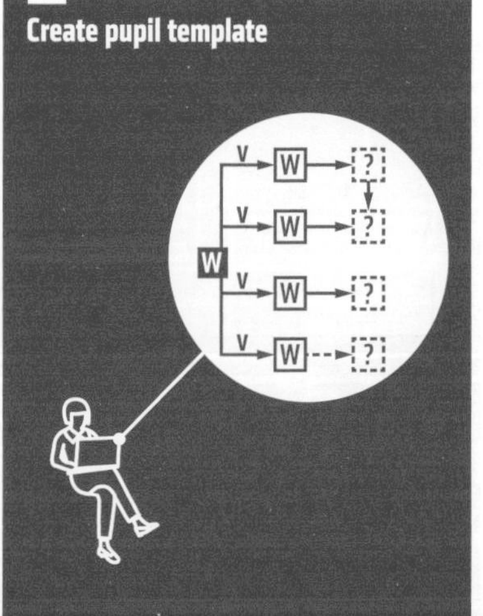

3

On the slide containing the completed graphic organiser, highlight every text box you formatted in step 2. Copy and paste these on to the template slide. Position, and randomly arrange, all the text boxes to the right-hand side of the slide. If students must read to complete their organiser, insert the passage of text on the left-hand side of the slide.

4

If the ideas and concepts presented in the graphic organiser would benefit from additional resources, insert hyperlinks. Highlight individual words and right-click. Select *link* and copy and paste the URL for any external website or file, saved in your Google Drive. If you want your students to complete questions or written tasks based on their graphic organiser, insert a new slide. Provide students with clear instructions and a text box(s) to write in.

5

Make a copy of the file you have created for future use. Delete the slides your students will not use. In Google Classroom, set an assignment and attach the student file. When prompted, select the option *make a copy for each student*. With the task assigned, the teacher can monitor students as they work. The teacher can give instant feedback or check for understanding by typing in the comments box.

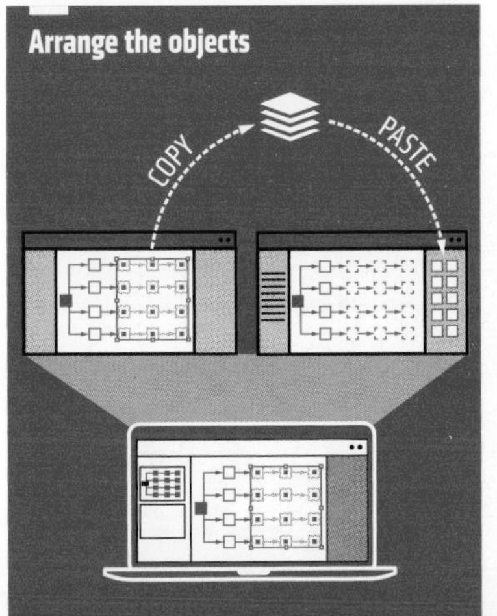

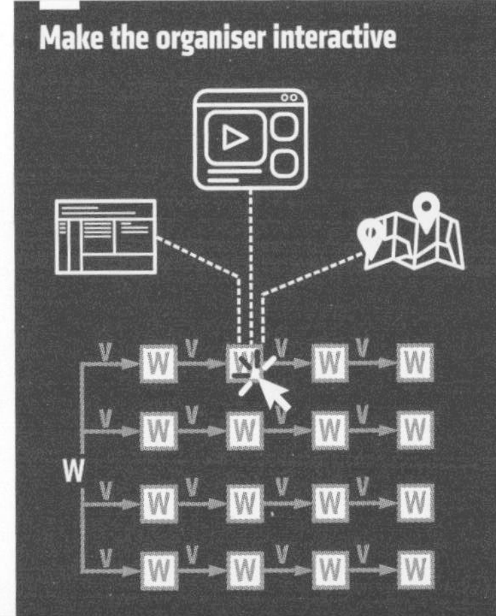

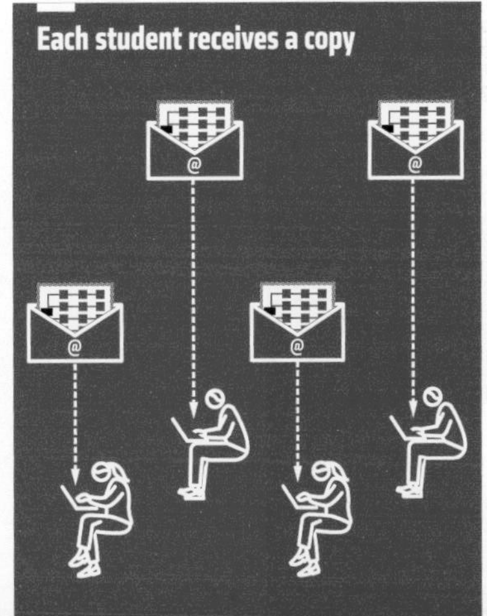

BEHAVIOUR NAVIGATION

When students feel upset or confused by a flurry of words, they are less likely to understand and commit to a plan to change behaviours.

Michael Grinder

When the content is volatile, the communicator wants to display the information visually – the third point.

Grinder, 2006

All conversations are personal. And addressing poor behaviour with a member of staff is particularly personal to the student. The more the student is not overwhelmed with their emotional reactions, the more focus they will have on the rational discussion and decisions to take. For that, the dynamics of three-point communication are especially effective, diminishing this emotional distraction.

Adopt three-point communication

1. The student looking forward
2. The teacher looking forward
3. The shared visual focus

The conversation is conducted via the *third point,* not directly to the student.

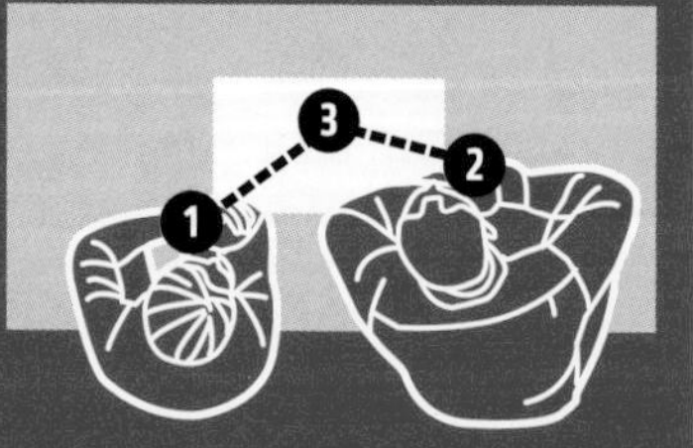

This may be the trickiest part. Instead of directly addressing – in granular fashion – what the student did that contravened rules, principles or values, ask them what they think was adrift in their behaviours. Continue along these lines until the student recognises and acknowledges the details of their behaviours under question. Note them down as below, in first part of the diagram.

3

In exactly the same way, ask the student to name and describe what the desirable behaviour looks like. The more detailed the descriptions from the student, the better. Note them down on the paper, or screen, at the opposite end, thereby creating a physical gap between the two. This gap will be immediately apparent to the student, and they will sense the direction of the remainder of the talk.

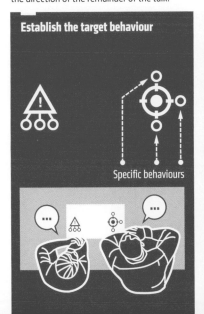

Establish the target behaviour

Specific behaviours

By now, the culmination and purpose of the talk and diagram become self-evident. Nonetheless, emphasise the gap between the two sets of behaviours and state the obvious — that the intention is to reduce this gap by creating a plan for its elimination. During this build-up over the stages, ensure you get agreement on the reality of the situation and building on it at each stage.

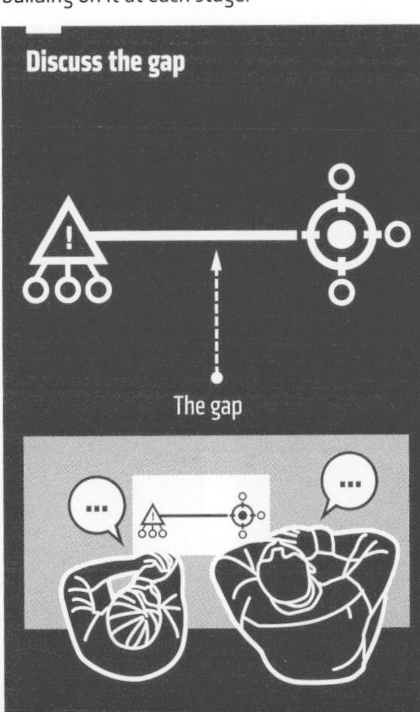

The resolution appears. Once more — and to the extent you feel is productive — request descriptions by the student of what might be intervening behaviours. Adopting a calm but relentless *broken-record* strategy is particularly effective. Once the solution is arrived at, date and sign it, as well as scheduling a monitoring date at which feedback will help measure the success of the plan's execution.

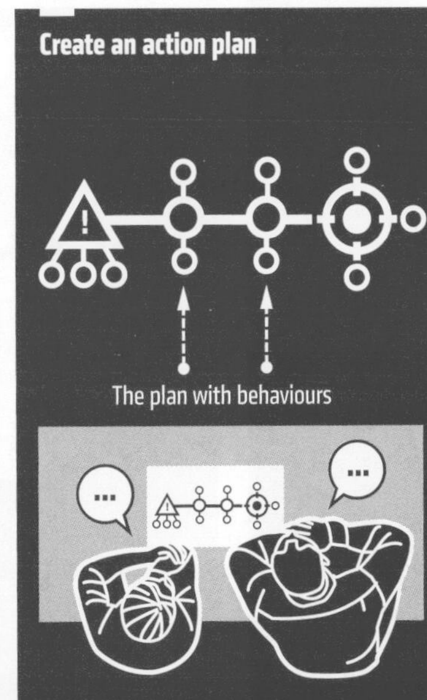

Pat Mirenda

Results indicated that the verbal contingency had no effect, whereas contingency mapping was related to immediate, dramatic, and sustained reductions in problem behavior and increases in alternative behavior.

Brown & Mirenda, 2006

HAND-DRAWN GRAPHIC ORGANISERS

Hand-drawn graphic organisers offer a direct connection between the ideas in your head and the tip of your pencil or pen.

Materials

In some cases, drawing a graphic organiser by hand can be quicker than the digital alternative. However, it would be remiss of us not to point out that it is still important to plan the organiser in advance and that you need to use the correct materials.

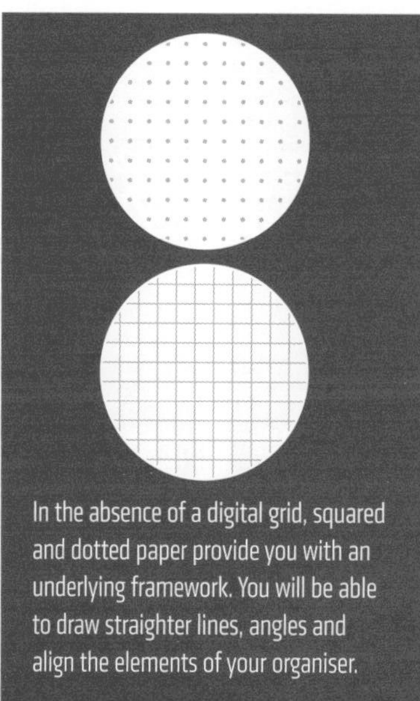

In the absence of a digital grid, squared and dotted paper provide you with an underlying framework. You will be able to draw straighter lines, angles and align the elements of your organiser.

Digital tools for drawing

When hand-drawing a graphic organiser, you will need to use a visualiser to display its construction. Alternatively, you might consider a graphic tablet. Digital tablet devices can be used, but we prefer a graphic tablet as they offer more friction than a digital screen. Friction gives you feedback.

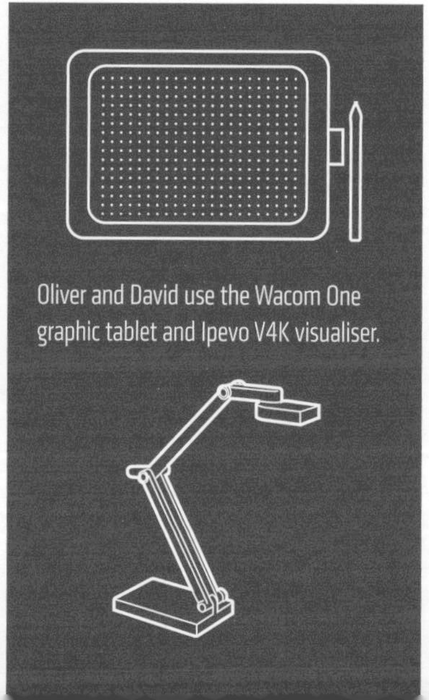

Oliver and David use the Wacom One graphic tablet and Ipevo V4K visualiser.

Pen craft: drawing

When drawing, fix your wrist and elbow. The movement of your arm should come from the shoulder. To draw a straight line, use dotted or squared paper and hold your breath as you are drawing it. Experiment with line thickness to highlight key parts of your organiser. Use a pen or pencil that is scratchy and gives you friction.

Pen craft: writing

When hand-drawing a graphic organiser, your handwriting must be legible. When using a visualiser, use the zoom-in and zoom-out regularly to ensure all your students can read your diagram. Refrain from using joined-up handwriting and write slowly. Use the extra time to narrate, emphasising keywords and concepts. Review your seating plan, making sure any students with visual impairments are closest to the whiteboard.

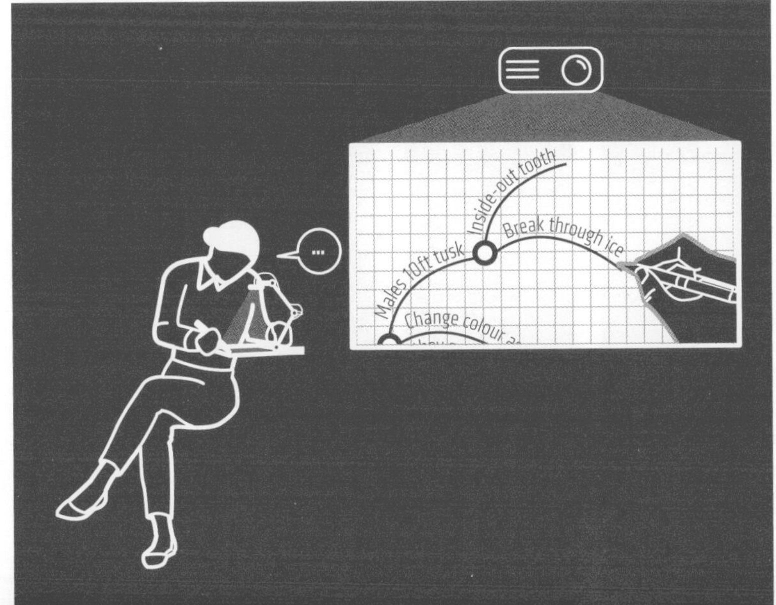

JARMAN SCRIPT

abcdefghijklmn
opqrstuvwxyz

ABCDEFGHIJKLMN
OPQRSTUVWXYZ

CAVIGLIOLI SCRIPT

abcdefghijklmn
opqrstuvwxyz

ABCDEFGHIJKLMN
OPQRSTUVWXYZ

Christopher Jarman

A Basic Modern Hand is the simplest form of the alphabet which can be written by hand without any extra loops, flourishes or conceits. It must be legible and economical.

Jarman, 1979

DIGITAL TIPS: PPT & GOOGLE SLIDES

Follow these recommendations to boost efficiency when constructing a graphic organiser in PowerPoint and Google Slides.

Robin Williams

Even when aligned elements are physically separated from each other, there is an invisible line that connects them, both in your eye and in your mind.

Williams, 2004

Insert guides

Gain neat alignment of all elements of your GO by inserting grids and guides.

Text box size

Adjusting the dimensions of a text box can be fiddly and cause inconsistencies. Follow these steps for precision and consistency.

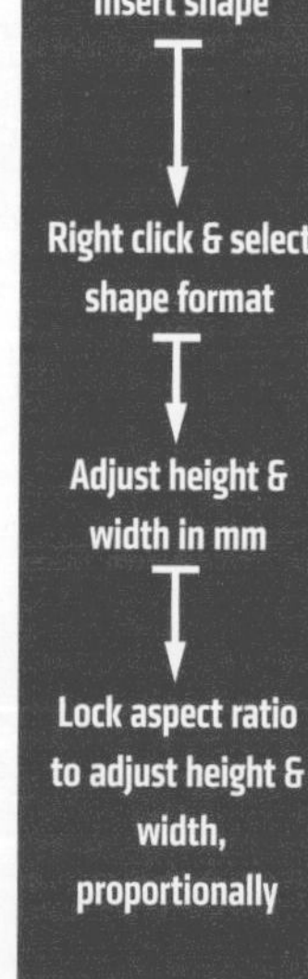

Insert shape
Right click & select shape format
Adjust height & width in mm
Lock aspect ratio to adjust height & width, proportionally

Duplicate text boxes

Save time by duplicating a text box after you have formatted it to your liking.

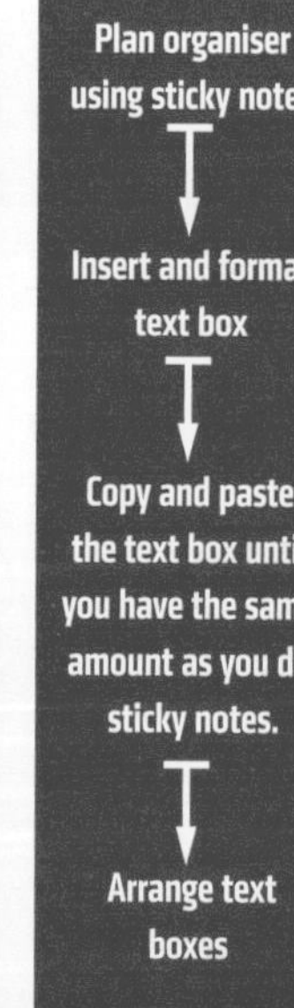

Straight lines and arrows every time

This simple step will give you perfectly straight lines horizontally, vertically and at 45°.

Hold the shift key on your keyboard as you draw your line or arrow

Connector points
Connector points save time connecting text boxes with lines or arrows. Elbow connectors are especially useful for complex organisers.

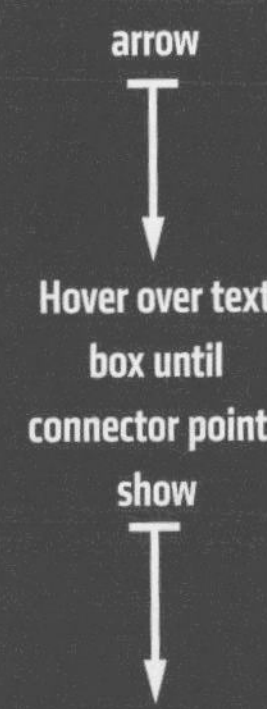

Insert line or arrow
Hover over text box until connector points show
Click and drag line or arrow to the connecting text box

Format arrow heads
Arrow heads that are too small might not be identifiable. Fix this by following these steps.

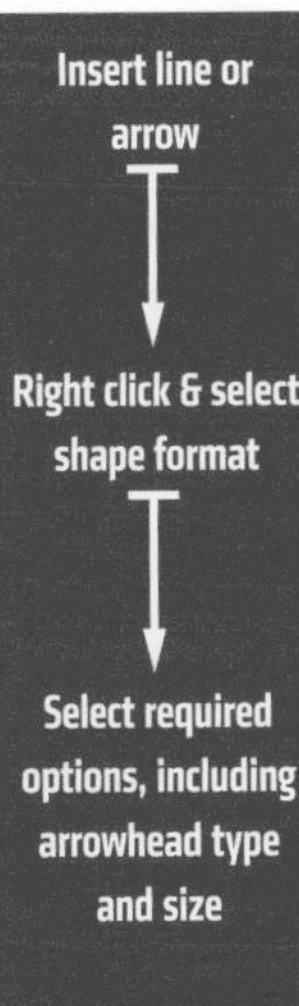

Insert line or arrow
Right click & select shape format
Select required options, including arrowhead type and size

Default line (PowerPoint only)
Setting a line as default dramatically speeds up the construction of a graphic organiser and ensures consistency.

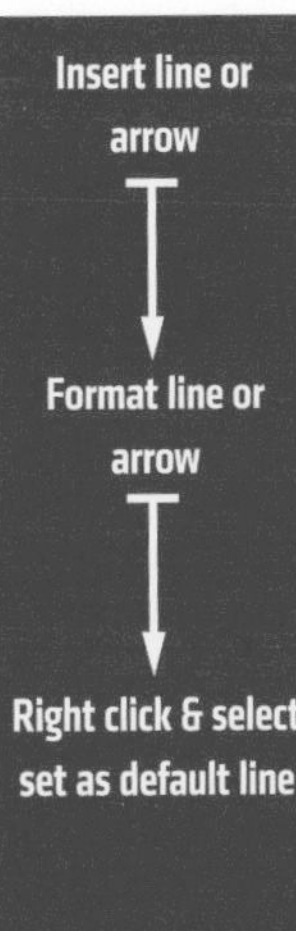

Insert line or arrow
Format line or arrow
Right click & select set as default line

Change text case with ease
Convert text case with ease and avoid troublesome spelling mistakes sometimes made when typing in uppercase.

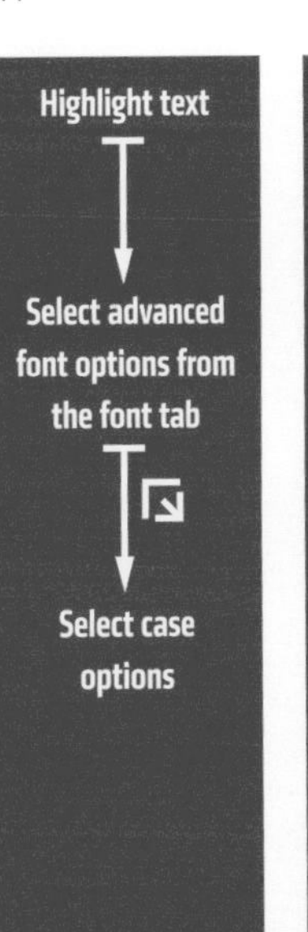

Highlight text
Select advanced font options from the font tab
Select case options

Create student templates
Templates save time when constructing a GO, helping those new to using them, especially when they are complex.

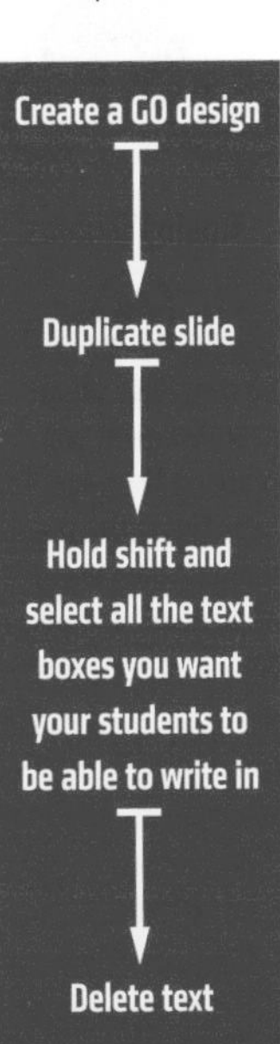

Create a GO design
Duplicate slide
Hold shift and select all the text boxes you want your students to be able to write in
Delete text

Dealing with overcrossing lines
It is always best to avoid crossing lines, but if you can't, minimise the problem by following these steps.

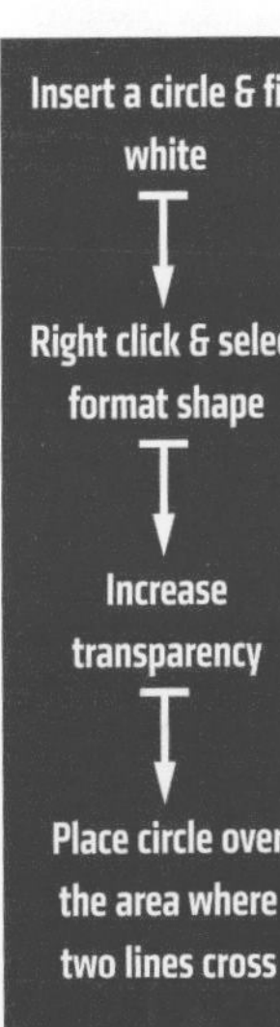

Insert a circle & fill white
Right click & select format shape
Increase transparency
Place circle over the area where two lines cross

Robin Williams

EA repetition of visual elements throughout the design unifies and strengthens a piece by tying together otherwise separate parts.

Williams, 2004

DIGITAL TIPS: KEYNOTE

Follow these recommendations to boost efficiency when constructing a graphic organiser in Apple Keynote.

Robin Williams

Be conscious about every element you place on the page. To keep the entire page unified, align every object with an edge of some other object.

Williams, 2004

Insert guides

Gain neat alignment of all elements of your GO by inserting grids and guides.

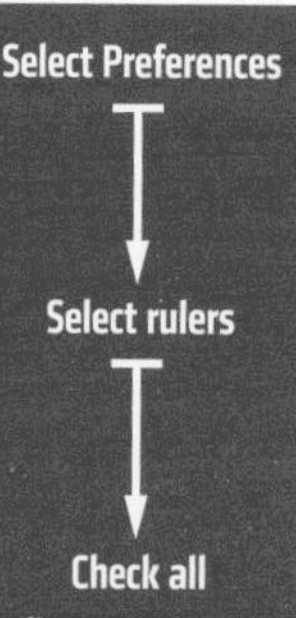

Text box size

Adjusting the dimensions of a text box can be fiddly and cause inconsistencies. Follow these steps for precision and consistency.

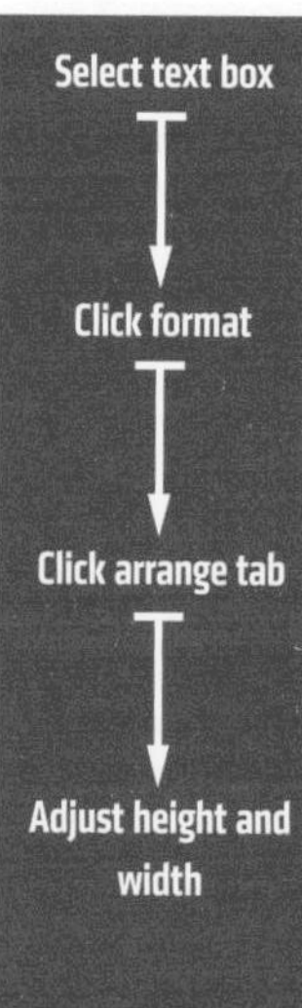

Duplicate text boxes

Save time by duplicating a text box after you have formatted it to your liking.

Straight lines and arrows every time

This simple step will give you perfectly straight lines horizontally, vertically and at 45°.

Hold the command key on your keyboard as you draw your line or arrow

Connector points
Connector points save time connecting text boxes with lines or arrows. Elbow connectors are especially useful for complex organisers.

Select connector line from shapes library
In style tab choose an end point to select an arrow head
↓
Click and drag the line from a text box to a connecting text box
↓
Double click on the green dot to switch between an elbow and curved connector

Format arrow heads
Arrow heads that are too small might not be identifiable. Fix this by following these steps.

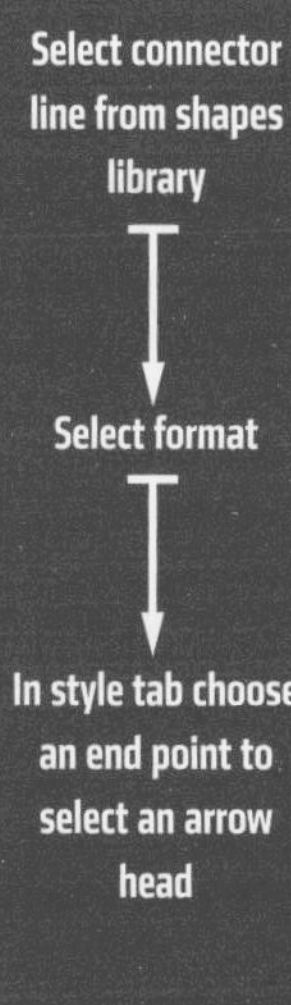

Easily align and distribute objects
Save time duplicating and arranging objects vertically, horizontally and evenly, by following these steps.

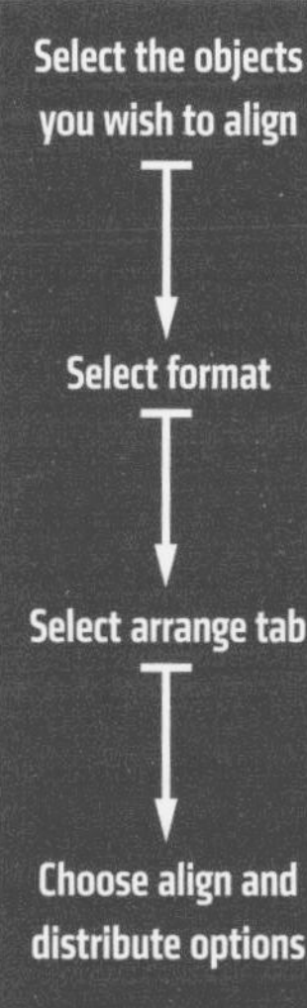

Select the objects you wish to align

Select arrange tab

Change text case with ease
Convert text case with ease and avoid troublesome spelling mistakes sometimes made when typing in uppercase.

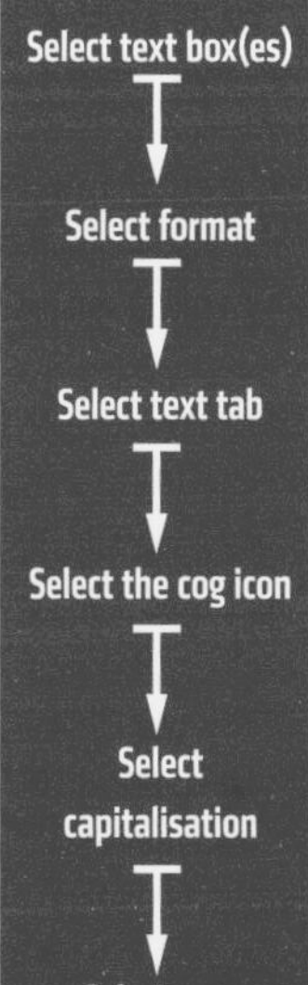

Select text box(es)

Select text tab
Select the cog icon
Select capitalisation

Create student templates
Templates save time when constructing a GO, helping those new to using them, especially when they are complex.

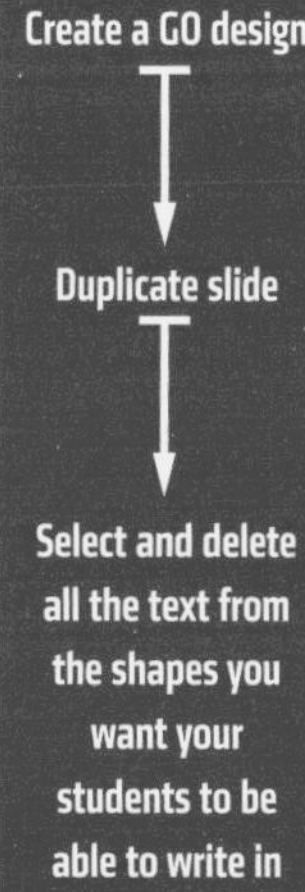

Dealing with overcrossing lines
It is always best to avoid crossing lines, but if you can't, minimise the problem by following these steps.

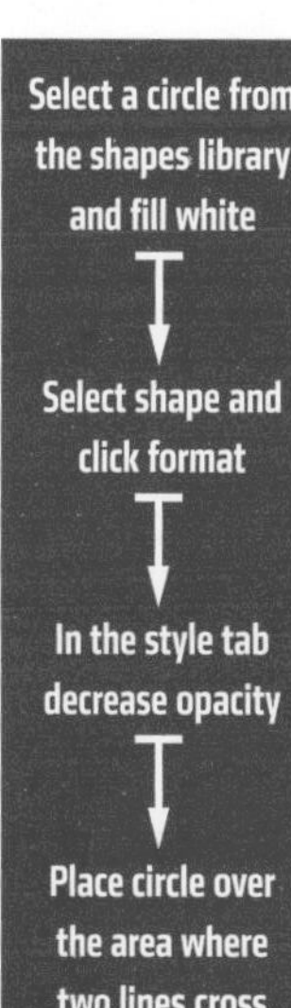

Select a circle from the shapes library and fill white
Select shape and click format
In the style tab decrease opacity
Place circle over the area where two lines cross

Robin Williams

If items are related to each other, group them into closer proximity.

Williams, 2004

DIGITAL GRAPHIC ORGANISERS

Digital organisation: Olly Lewis explains that technology affords us opportunities that would not otherwise be possible.

OLLY LEWIS
@Olewis_coaching
ollylewislearning.com

Elon Musk

You shouldn't do things differently just because they're different. They need to be better.

The argument for digital GOs

Instruction versus preparation is an enduring debate in education. Truth be told, we can have both, as there's merit at each parenthesis in sequences of learning. The view that a digital graphic organiser (DGO) is a crutch for teaching or learning is void of reason. The reasoning should surely be that a DGO supports teaching and learning through encouraging cognition and self-checking, enhancing and leveraging learning through the EXMF.

Organisers – a projection of schema – mitigate the limitations of working memory. The spatial metaphors afforded through technology offer a greater depth of functionality to leveraging more complex ideas through visual and visuospatial processes. Do you want two-dimensional functionality or the opportunity for several functions? Collaboration, editable, unlimited iterations, reformattable and accessible, time-saving, manipulatable, accessible, sharing, replication, dictation/audio recording and distribution are all aspects made easier by using technology. Thus, given these options, the digital GO arguably has more dexterity than its analogue counterpart.

Steve Jobs

It takes a lot of hard work to make something simple.

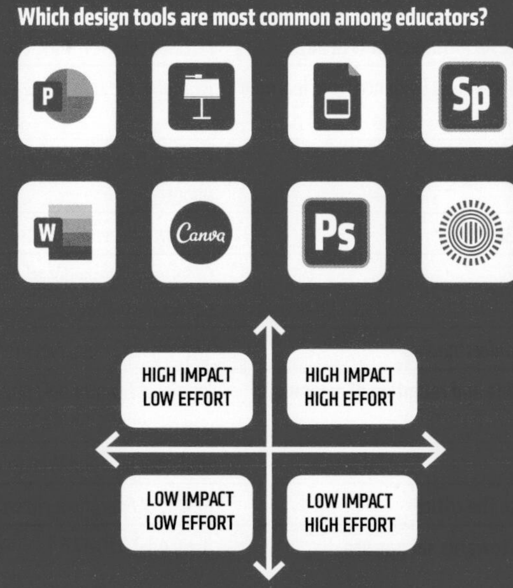

When deciding upon a digital application, Mark Anderson's (@ICTEvangelist) Impact-Effort Prioritisation Matrix helps us to ask the right questions when ascertaining the efficacy along with identifying the right balance of learning v cost. Questions to ask may include but are not exclusive to: what opportunity will this mode present regarding learning? At what cost does this come? Would learning be more coherent in a non-digital format? Is the juice worth the squeeze? Is this mode time-saving for the teacher and/or the student? How can the proposed mode enable more functionality?

Mark Anderson

> **Using technology as a gimmick devalues you as a teacher, devalues the technology and ultimately what you're doing in the classroom. Keep the depth of challenge.**
>
> Anderson, 2018

Advantages

Hyperlinks | QR codes | infinite copies | AR triggers | time-saving | collaboration | editability | voice recording | dictation | distribution | replication | AI | depth of opportunity | marginal gains.

Disadvantages

Screen time | cost | training | confidence | competence | infrastructure | battery life | connectivity.

T&L ideas for DGOs

- Have learners check their understanding by correctly editing/ reformatting the component parts of a premade DGO.
- Have learners narrate over an animated DGO.
- Have learners write questions for each link in a graphic organiser (these could be digitally added into the organiser itself).

Ahrens, S.	2017	*How to take smart notes*	zzzz.com
Al-Khwārizmī	2009	In Burton, D.M., *The history of mathematics: An introduction* (7th ed)	McGraw Hill, New York, US
Alibali, M.W. & Nathan, M.J.	2012	Embodiment in mathematics teaching and learning: Evidence from learners' and teachers' gestures	*Journal of the Learning Sciences*, 21:2, 247-286
Allen, D.	2015	*Mind like water*	Getting Things Done, www.gettingthingsdone.com/about
Anderson, J.R.	1990	*Cognitive psychology and its implications* (3rd ed)	Harvard University Press, Cambridge, US
Anderson, M.	2018	*So what? So that!*	GESS, www.gesseducation.com/gess-talks/articles/so-what-so-that
Anderson, S.P. & Fast, K.	2020	*Figure it out: Getting from information to understanding*	Two Waves Books, New York, US
Ausubel, D.P.	1960	The use of advance organizers in the learning and retention of meaningful verbal material	*Journal of Educational Psychology*, 51:5, 267-272
Ausubel, D.P.	1968	*Educational psychology: A cognitive view*	Holt, Rinehart and Winston, New York, US
Ausubel, D.P.	1978	In defense of advance organizers: a reply to the critics	*Review of Educational Research*, 48:2, 251-257
Axon, S., Speake, J. & Crawford, K.R.	2012	"At the next junction, turn left": Attitudes towards sat nav use	*Area*, 44:2, 170-177
Bellmund, J.L.S.	2020	Spatial and temporal reference frames anchor cognitive maps for memory	Talk hosted by Bottini Lab, 30 September 2020
Bellmund, J.L.S., Gärdenfors, P., Moser, E.I. & Doeller, C.F.	2018	Navigating cognition: Spatial codes for human thinking	*Science*, 362:6415
Blackwell, A.F. (ed)	2001	*Thinking with diagrams*	Kluwer Academic Publishers, London, UK
Bradford, P.	1990	Quoted in Wurman, R.S., *Information anxiety*	Pan, London, UK

Brown. K.E. & Mirenda, P.	**2006**	**Contingency mapping: use of a novel visual support strategy as an adjunct to functional equivalence training**	*Journal of Positive Behavior Interventions*, 8:3, 155-164
Busse. C., Kach, A.P. & Wagner, S.M.	**2016**	**Boundary conditions: what they are, how to explore them, why we need them, and when to consider them**	*Organizational Research Methods*, 20:4
Butcher, K.R.	**2014**	**The multimedia principle. In Mayer, R.E. (ed) *The Cambridge handbook of multimedia learning* (2nd ed, 174-205)**	Cambridge University Press, Cambridge, UK
Buzan, T.	**2012**	**Quoted in Van Vliet, V., *Tony Buzan***	ToolsHero, www.toolshero.com/toolsheroes/tony-buzan
Carter, R., Martin, J., Mayblin, B. & Munday, M .	**1984**	***Systems, management and change: A graphic guide***	Paul Chapman Publishing
Caviglioli, O.	**2019**	***Dual coding with teachers***	John Catt, Woodbridge, UK
Caviglioli, O. & Harris, I.	**2000**	***Mapwise: Accelerated learning through visible thinking***	Network Educational Press, Stafford, UK
Caviglioli, O., Harris, I. & Tindall, B.	**2002**	***Thinking skills and eye Q: Visual tools for raising intelligence***	Network Educational Press, Stafford, UK
Cepelewicz, J.	**2019**	**The brain maps out ideas and memories like spaces**	*Quanta*, www.quantamagazine.org/the-brain-maps-out-ideas-and-memories-like-spaces-20190114
Chen, P.	**2004**	**Peter Chen speaks out on paths to fame, the roots of the ER model in human language, the ER model in software engineering, the need for ER databases, and more**	*ACM SIGMOD Record*, 33:1, 110-118
Cheng, P.C., Lowe, R. & Scaife, M.	**2001**	**Cognitive science approaches to understanding diagrammatic representations. In Blackwell, A.F. (ed) *Thinking with diagrams* (79-94)**	Kluwer Academic Publishers, London, UK
Chevron, M-P.	**2014**	**A metacognitive tool: theoretical and operational analysis of skills exercised in structured concept maps**	*Perspectives in Science*, 2:1-4, 46-54

Chi, M.T.H., De Leeuw, N., Chiu, M-H. & Lavancher, C.	**1994**	**Eliciting self-explanations improves understanding**	*Cognitive Science*, 18:3, 439-477
Christodoulou, D.	**2017**	***Making good progress? The future of assessment for learning***	Oxford University Press, Oxford, UK
Clark, A.	**2008**	***Supersizing the mind: Embodiment, action, and cognitive extension***	Oxford University Press, Oxford, UK
Clark, R.C. & Lyons, C.	**2004**	***Graphics for learning***	Pfeiffer, San Francisco, US
Clarke, J.H.	**1990**	***Patterns of thinking: Integrating learning skills in content teaching***	Allyn & Bacon, Massachusetts, US
Clarke, J.H., Raths, J. & Gilbert, G.L.	**1989**	**Inductive towers: Letting students see how they think**	*Journal of Reading*, 33:2, 86-95
Claxton, G.	**2015**	***Intelligence in the flesh: Why your mind needs your body much more than it thinks***	Yale University Press, New Haven, US
Cooper, J.	**1979**	***Think and link: An advanced course in reading and writing skills***	Edward Arnold, London, UK
Corbett, P.	**2008**	***Story making and 3 stage methodology***	www.foundationyears.org.uk/files/2011/10/Story-Teling_Story-Making1.pdf
Covey, S.R.	**2013**	***The 7 habits of highly effective people* (25th anniversary edition)**	Simon & Schuster
Damasio, A.	**2007**	**Foreword to Blakeslee, S. & Blakeslee, M., *The body has a mind of its own***	Random House, New York
De Bono, E.	**1993**	***Water logic***	McQuaig Group, Toronto, Canada
Delrose, L.N.	**2011**	**Investigating the use of graphic organizers for writing**	*LSU Master's Theses*, https://digitalcommons.lsu.edu/gradschool_theses/2537
Donald, M.	**1991**	***Origins of the modern mind***	Harvard University Press, Cambridge, US
Education Endowment Foundation	**2018**	***Metacognition and self-regulation***	https://educationendowmentfoundation.org.uk/evidence-summaries/teaching-learning-toolkit/meta-cognition-and-self-regulation
Eysenck, M.W. (ed)	**1994**	***The Blackwell dictionary of cognitive psychology***	Blackwell Publishers, Massachusetts, US

Fiorella, L. & Mayer, R.E.	**2015**	***Learning as a generative activity***	Cambridge University Press, Cambridge, UK
Fisher, D. & Frey, N.	**2008**	***Better learning through structured teaching***	ASCD, Alexandria, US
Fonollosa, J., Neftci, E. & Rabinovich, M.	**2015**	**Learning of chunking sequences in cognition and behavior**	*PLoS Compututational Biology*, 11:11
Furst, E.	**2019**	**Meaning first**	*Efrat Furst* (blog), https://sites.google.com/view/efratfurst/meaning-first
Gantt, H.L.	**1919**	***Organizing for work***	Harcourt, Brace & Howe, New York, US
Gilbreth, F.B. & Gilbreth, L.M.	**1917**	***Applied motion study: A collection of papers on the efficient method to industrial preparedness***	Sturgis & Walton, New York, US
Gladwell, M.	**2018**	***Malcolm Gladwell explains where his ideas come from***	Open Culture, www.openculture.com/2018/04/malcolm-gladwell-explains-where-his-ideas-come-from.html
Gleick, J.	**1993**	***Genius: The life and science of Richard Feynman***	Vintage, New York, US
Goldin-Meadow, S.	**2003**	***Hearing gesture: How our hands help us think***	The Belknap Press, Cambridge, US
Goldin-Meadow, S.	**2014**	**How gesture works to change our minds**	*Trends in Neuroscience and Education*, 3:1, 4-6
Gray, D., Brown, S. & Macanufo, J.	**2010**	***Gamestorming: A playbook for innovators, rulebreakers, and changemakers***	O'Reilly, Cambridge, UK
Grinder, M.	**2006**	***Charisma: The art of relationships***	Michael Grinder & Associates, US
Harvard, B.	**2018**	***Maximizing the effectiveness of multiple-choice Qs***	The Effortful Educator (blog), https://theeffortfuleducator.com/2018/05/15/maximizing-the-effectiveness-of-multiple-choice-qs
Hattie, J.	**2009**	***Visible learning***	Routledge, Abingdon, UK
Hattie, J.	**2012**	***Visible learning for teachers***	Routledge, Abingdon, UK
Hawkins, J.	**2021**	***A thousand brains: A new theory of intelligence***	Basic Books, New York, US

Hochman, J. & Wexler, N.	**2017**	***The writing revolution***	Jossey-Bass, San Francisco, US
Hofstadter, D.	**2009**	***Analogy as the core of cognition***	Lecture at Stanford University, US, 11 September 2009, https://youtu.be/n8m7lFQ3njk
Hofstadter, D. & Sander, E.	**2013**	***Surfaces and essences***	Basic Books, New York, US
Holt, J.	**1967**	***How children learn***	Pitman Publishing, New York, US
Horton, P.B., McConney, A.A., Gallo, M., Woods, A.L., Senn, G.J. & Hamelin, D.	**1993**	**An investigation of the effectiveness of concept mapping as an instructional tool**	*Science Education*, 77:1, 95-111
Humphrey, A.S.	**2005**	**SWOT analysis for management consulting**	*SRI Newsletter* (Humphrey's analysis can be read here: https://rapidbi.com/history-of-the-swot-analysis)
Hyerle, D.	**1996**	***Visual tools for constructing knowledge***	ASCD, Alexandria, US
Ishikawa, K.		**Quote from Kaoru Ishikawa**	https://leansixsigmabelgium.com/wp-content/uploads/2014/11/Kaoru-Ishikawa-Quotes.jpg?ssi=1
Jairam, D., Kiewra, K.A., Kauffman, K.F. & Zhao, R.	**2012**	**How to study a matrix**	*Contemporary Educational Psychology*, 37:2, 128-135
Jarman, C.	**1979**	***The development of handwriting skills: A resource book for teachers***	Basil Blackwel
Jobs, S.	**2012**	**Quoted in Isaacson, W., How Steve Jobs' love of simplicity fueled a design revolution**	*Smithsonian Magazine*, www.smithsonianmag.com/arts-culture/how-steve-jobs-love-of-simplicity-fueled-a-design-revolution-23868877
Johnson, M.	**1987**	***The body in the mind***	University of Chicago Press, Chicago, US
Jones, F.H.	**2000**	***Tools for teaching***	Fredric H. Jones & Associates, Santa Cruz, US

Jones, F.H.	2009	Creating effective lessons the easy way with Dr Fred Jones (video)	https://youtu.be/MlnPwzg6TiQ
Jones, K.	2019	*Retrieval practice: Research and resources for every classroom*	John Catt, Woodbridge, UK
Kahneman, D.	2012	Quoted in Yong, E., Nobel laureate challenges psychologists to clean up their act	*Nature*, www.nature.com/articles/nature.2012.11535
Kelley, J.E. & Walker, M.R.	1959	Critical-path planning and scheduling	IRE-AIEE-ACM '59 (Eastern): Papers presented at the December 1-3, 1959, eastern joint IRE-AIEE-ACM computer conference
Kennedy, M.M.	2008	Teachers thinking about their practice. In Good, T. (ed) *21st century education: A reference handbook*	Sage
Kinchin, I.M.	2016	*Visualising powerful knowledge to develop the expert student*	Sense Publishers, Rotterdam, Netherlands
Kim, A-H., Vaughn, S., Wanzek, J. & Wei, S.	2004	Graphic organizers and their effects on the reading comprehension of students with LD: A synthesis of research	*Journal of Learning Disabilities*, 37:2, 105-118
Kirschner, P.A. & Hendrick, C.	2020	*How learning happens: Seminal works in educational psychology and what they mean in practice*	Routledge, Abingdon, UK
Kirschner, P.A., Neelen, M., Hoof, T. & Surma, T.	2021	*Let's get to work with productive learning strategies: Mapping*	https://3starlearningexperiences.wordpress.com/2021/04/06/lets-get-to-work-with-productive-learning-strategies-mapping/
Kirsh. D.	1995	The intelligent use of space	*Artificial Intelligence*, 73:1-2, 31-68
Knight, J.	2017	*The impact cycle: What instructional coaches should do to foster powerful improvements in teaching*	Corwin
Lakoff, G.	1987	*Women, fire, and dangerous things: What categories reveal about the mind*	University of Chicago Press, Chicago, US
Lakoff, G.	2013	What studying the brain tells us about arts education (video)	https://youtu.be/fpla16Bynzg
Lakoff, G.	2014	Mapping the brain's metaphor circuitry: Metaphorical thought in everyday reason	*Frontiers in Human Neuroscience*, 8:958

Lakoff, G. & Johnson, M.	1980	*Metaphors we live by*	University of Chicago Press, Chicago, US
Lakoff, G. & Johnson, M.	1999	*Philosophy in the flesh*	Basic Books, New York, US
Larkin, J.H. & Simon, H.A.	1987	Why a diagram is (sometimes) worth ten thousand words	*Cognitive Science*, 11:1, 65-99
Leontief, W.	1937	Interrelation of prices, output, savings, and investment: A study in empirical application of the economic theory of general interdependence	*The Review of Economic Statistics*, 19:3, 109-132
Lemov, D., Driggs, C. & Woolway, E.	2016	*Reading reconsidered*	Jossey-Bass, San Francisco, US
Levitin, D.	2014	*The organized mind: Thinking straight in the age of information overload*	Penguin, London, UK
Lewin, K.	1948	*Resolving social conflicts*	Harper, New York, UK
Lewin, K.	1951	*Field theory in social science: Selected theoretical papers*	Harper & Row, New York, US
Lo, M.L.	2012	*Variation theory and the improvement of teaching and learning*	Acta Universitatis Gothoburgensis, Sweden
Lunzer, E. & Gardner, K.	1984	*Learning from the written word*	Oliver & Boyd, Edinburgh, UK
Makel, M.C. & Plucker, J.A.	2014	Facts are more important than novelty: Replication in the education sciences	*Educational Researcher*, 43:6
Mandler, J.M. & Cánovas, C.P.	2014	On defining image schemas	*Language and Cognition*, 6, 510-532
Marzano, R.J., Pickering, D.J. & Pollock, J.E.	2001	*Classroom instruction that works*	ASCD, Alexandria, US
Mayer, R.E.	2004	Preface to Clark, R.C. & Lyons, C., *Graphics for learning*	Pfeiffer, San Francisco, US
Mayer, R.E.	2014	*The Cambridge handbook of multimedia learning* (2nd ed)	Cambridge University Press, Cambridge, UK
Mccrea, P.	2017	*Memorable teaching*	CreateSpace
McNeill, D.	1992	*Hand and mind: What gestures reveal about thought*	University of Chicago Press, Chicago, US
Michalko, M.	2006	*Thinkertoys: A handbook of creative thinking techniques*	Ten Speed Press, Berkeley, US

Michalko, M.	**2011**	***Twelve things you were not taught in school about creative thinking***	The Creativity Post, www.creativitypost.com/article/twelve_things_you_were_not_taught_in_school_about_creative_thinking
Mohan, B.A.	**1986**	***Language and content***	Addison-Wesley, Boston, UK
Moreira, M.M.	**2012**	***Freedom to teach and learn literature: The use of concept maps***	Palibrio, Bloomington, US
Moser, M-B.	**2021**	**May-Britt Moser – facts**	NobelPrize.org, www.nobelprize.org/prizes/medicine/2014/may-britt-moser/facts
Moyer, D.	**2010**	***The napkin sketch workbook***	Blurb Books
Musk, E.	**2016**	***Elon Musk's best quotes on business and innovation***	https://elonmusknews.org/blog/elon-musk-business-innovation-quotes
Myatt, M.	**2021**	***Getting the most from knowledge organisers***	Myatt & Co, https://myattandco.com/programs/collections-getting-the-most-from-knowledge-organisers
Nesbit, J.C. & Adesope, O.O.	**2006**	**Learning with concept and knowledge maps: a meta-analysis**	*Review of Educational Research*, 76:3, 413-448
Novak, J.D.	**1998**	***Learning, creating, and using knowledge***	Lawrence Erlbaum Associates, New Jersey, US
Novak, J.D. & Gowin, D.B.	**1984**	***Learning how to learn***	Cambridge University Press, Cambridge, UK
Novak, J.D. & Symington, D.J.	**1982**	**Concept mapping for curriculum development**	*VIER Bulletin*, 48, 3-11
O'Keefe, J.	**2021**	**John O'Keefe – facts**	NobelPrize.org, www.nobelprize.org/prizes/medicine/2014/okeefe/facts
Oloyede, O.	**2016**	**Monitoring participation of women in politics in Nigeria**	National Bureau of Statistics, Abuja, Nigeria

Paas, F. & Sweller, J.	**2012**	**An evolutionary upgrade of cognitive load theory: Using the human motor system and collaboration to support the learning of complex cognitive tasks**	*Educational Psychology Review*, 24, 27-45
Paas, F. & van Merriënboer, J.J.G.	**2020**	**Cognitive-load theory: methods to manage working memory load in the learning of complex tasks**	*Current Directions in Psychological Science*, 29:4, 394-398
Paivio, A.	**1990**	***Mental representations: A dual coding approach***	Oxford University Press, Oxford, UK
Pehrsson, R.S. & Denner, P.R.	**1989**	***Semantic organizers: A study strategy for special needs learners***	Aspen Publications, Maryland, US
Pehrsson, R.S. & Robinson, H.A.	**1985**	***The semantic organizer approach to writing and reading instruction***	Aspen Publications, Maryland, US
Petty, G.	**2006**	***Evidence-based teaching***	Nelson Thornes, Cheltenham, UK
Piaget, J.	**1952**	***The origins of intelligence in children***	International Universities Press, New York, US
Pinker, S.	**2005**	***So how does the mind work?***	Blackwell Publishing Ltd, https://stevenpinker.com/files/pinker/files/so_how_does_the_mind_work.pdf
Pinker, S.	**2014**	***The sense of style: The thinking person's guide to writing in the 21st century***	Allen Lane, London, UK
Poincaré, H.	**1902**	***Science and hypothesis* (*La science et l'hypothèse*)**	Dover Publications, New York, US
Reif, F.	**2008**	***Applying cognitive science to education***	MIT Press, Cambridge, US
Rico, G.	**1991**	**An article on Gabriele Rico, originally published by *The New York Times* (December 1991)**	
Rico, G.	**2000**	***Writing the natural way***	Penguin Putman, New York, US
Richards, E.G.	**1998**	***Mapping time: The calendar and history***	Oxford University Press, Oxford, UK
Rittle-Johnson, B. & Star, J.R.	**2011**	**The power of comparison in learning and instruction: Learning outcomes supported by different types of comparisons**	In Ross, B. & Mestre, J. (eds) *Psychology of learning and motivation: Cognition in education*, 55
Robinson, D.H. & Schraw, G.	**1994**	**Computational efficiency through visual argument: Do graphic organizers communicate relations in text too effectively?**	*Contemporary Educational Psychology*, 19:4, 399-415

Rosenshine, B.	2012	Principles of instruction: Research-based strategies that all teachers should know	*American Educator*, 36:1, 12-19
Rosch, E.	1974	Linguistic relativity	In Silverstein, A. (ed) *Human communication: Theoretical explorations*, Halstead, New York
Rosch, E.	1978	Principles of categorization. In Rosch, E. & Lloyd, B.B. (eds) *Cognition and categorization* (27-48)	Lawrence Erlbaum, New Jersey, US
Rosch, E.	1999	Interview with Professor Eleanor Rosch	www.presencing.org/aboutus/theory-u/leadership-interview/eleanor_rosch
Rummler, G.A. & Brache, A.P.	1990	*Improving performance: How to manage the white space on the organization chart*	Jossey-Bass, San Francisco, US
Russell, B.	1923	Vagueness. In Slater, J.G. (ed) *The collected papers of Bertrand Russell, volume 9: Essays on language, mind and matter 1919-1926* (1988, 145-154)	Unwin Hyman, London, UK
Shea, J.	2021	*Cognitive science v neuroscience: Retrieval at the start of a lesson or not?*	https://peerreviewededucationblog.com/2021/02/06/cognitive-science-v-neuroscience-retrieval-at-the-start-of-a-lesson-or-not
Sherrington, T.	2020	*Schema-building: A blend of experiences and retrieval modes make for deep learning*	Teacherhead (blog), https://teacherhead.com/2020/01/05/schema-building-a-blend-of-experiences-and-retrieval-modes-make-for-deep-learning
Sherrington. T.	2021	*Remote learning solutions: Crowd-sourced ideas for checking students' writing*	Teacherhead (blog), https://teacherhead.com/2021/01/10/remote-learning-solutions-crowd-sourced-ideas-for-checking-students-writing
Sherrington, T. & Caviglioli, O.	2020	*Teaching walkthrus*	John Catt, Woodbridge, UK
Shimojima, A.	2001	The graphic-linguistic distinction exploring alternatives	*Artificial Intelligence Review*, 15, 5-27

Slavin, R.	2018	*John Hattie is wrong*	Robert Slavin (blog), https://robertslavinsblog.wordpress.com/2018/06/21/john-hattie-is-wrong
Smith, C.	1826	Boroughbridge strip map in *Smith's new pocket companion of the roads of England and Wales*	www.bl.uk/collection-items/smiths-new-pocket-companion-of-the-roads-of-england-and-wales
Stachenfeld, K.	2019	Quoted in Cepelewicz, J., The brain maps out ideas and memories like spaces	*Quanta*, www.quantamagazine.org/the-brain-maps-out-ideas-and-memories-like-spaces-20190114
Stenning, K. & Lemon, O.	2001	Aligning logical and psychological perspectives on diagrammatic reasoning. In Blackwell, A.F. (ed) *Thinking with diagrams* (29-62)	Kluwer Academic Publishers, London, UK
St George, F. & St George, A.	1996	*Clear English: How to improve your style*	Bloomsbury Publishing, London, UK
Sutton, J.	2003	Porous memory and the cognitive life of things. In Tofts, D., Jonson, A. & Cavallaro, A. (eds) *Prefiguring cyberculture: An intellectual history*	MIT Press, Cambridge, US
Swartz, R.J. & Parks, S.	1994	*Infusing the teaching of critical and creative thinking into content instruction*	Routledge
Sweller, J., Ayres, P. & Kalyuga, S.	2011	*Cognitive load theory*	Springer, New York, US
Sweller, J., van Merriënboer, J.J.G. & Paas, F.	2019	Cognitive architecture and instructional design: 20 years later	*Educational Psychology Review*, 31, 261-292
Taba, H.	1962	*Curriculum development: Theory and practice*	Harcourt, Brace & World, New York, US
Tolman, E.C.	1948	Cognitive maps in rats and men	*Psychological Review*, 55:4, 189-208
Tversky, B.	2019	*Mind in motion: How action shapes thought*	Basic Books, New York, US
Tyson, C.	2014	Failure to replicate	*Inside Higher Ed*, www.insidehighered.com/news/2014/08/14/almost-no-education-research-replicated-new-article-shows

Van Merriënboer, J.J.G. & Kester, L.	**2014**	**The four-component instructional design model: Multimedia principles in environments for complex learning. In Mayer, R.E. (ed) *The Cambridge handbook of multimedia learning* (2nd ed, 104-148)**	Cambridge University Press, Cambridge, UK
Venn, J.	**1881**	***Symbolic logic***	Macmillan, London, UK
Walker, R.	**2018**	***Sentences and the web of knowledge***	Rosalind Walker (blog), https://rosalindwalker.wordpress.com/2018/10/17/sentences-and-the-web-of-knowledge
Waller, R.	**1981**	**Understanding network diagrams**	Paper presented at the annual conference of the American Educational Research Association, Los Angeles
Weinstein, Y. & Sumeracki, M.	**2018**	***Understanding how we learn: A visual guide***	Routledge, Abingdon, UK
Williams, R.	**2015**	***The non-designer's design book: Design and typographic principles for the visual novice* (fourth edition)**	Peachpit Press, Berkeley, US
Willingham. D.T.	**2009**	***Why don't students like school?***	Jossey-Bass, San Francisco, US
Wittgenstein, L.	**2001**	***Philosophical investigations* (50th anniversary edition of original published in 1953)**	Blackwell Publishers, London, UK
Wragg, E.C. & Brown, G.	**1993**	***Explaining***	Routledge, Abingdon, UK
Wright, A.	**2007**	***Glut: Mastering information through the ages***	Joseph Henry Press, Washington, US
Wright, A.	**2014**	***Cataloging the world: Paul Otlet and the birth of the information age***	Oxford University Press, Oxford, UK
Zwicky, F.	**1948**	**Morphological astronomy**	*The Observatory*, 68:845